How to Restore Your Collector Car

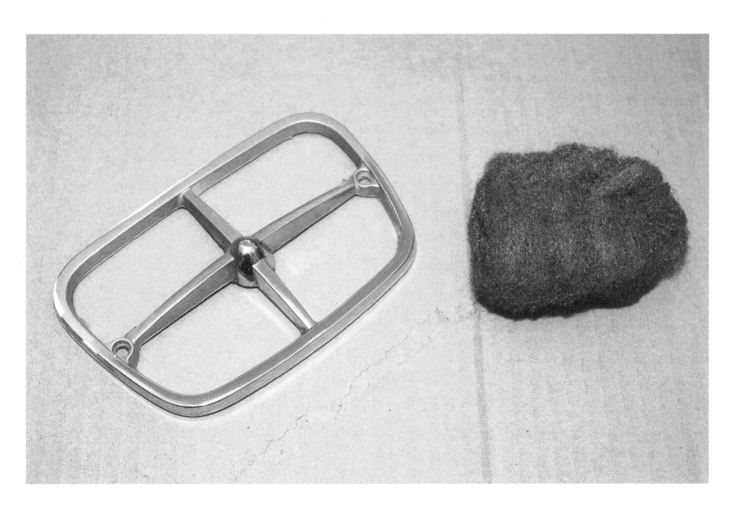

Tom Brownell and Jason Scott

motorbooks

This edition first published in 2009 by Motorbooks,
an imprint of Quarto Publishing Group USA Inc.,
400 First Avenue North, Suite 400, Minneapolis,
MN 55401 USA

Motorbooks titles are also available at discounts in
bulk quantity for industrial or sales-promotional use.
For details write to Special Sales Manager at
Quarto Publishing Group USA Inc., 400 First Avenue
North, Suite 400, Minneapolis, MN 55401 USA.

To find out more about our books, join us online at
www.motorbooks.com.

ISBN-13: 978-0-7603-3541-3

Editor: Jeffrey Zuehlke

Printed in the United States of America

On the cover: Few projects can offer the kind of
satisfaction gained by turning an old automotive relic
into a beautiful, road-going machine. *Jason Scott*

On the title page: Some restoration details require the
latest tools and equipment to get the job done right.
Other details require nothing more than a mix of steel
wool and elbow grease. *Jason Scott*

On the back cover: A proper restoration will often include
an engine rebuild. While most restorers will leave this job
to a professional, the more experienced and ambitious
types will do it themselves. This block has been mounted
to an engine stand so that the engine is at a comfortable
work height and can be rotated easily, and we're cleaning
the already machined block prior to rebuilding to make
sure no metal shavings remain in the engine.

Contents

Acknowledgments

In thanking the people who have been a part of this book, I need to begin by expressing gratitude for the many readers of the original 1983 book by this title who told me in letters, on the phone, and in person how much the book had helped them. Even when I was in the far-away country of Bulgaria, I was recognized by a collector endeavoring to restore his Jaguar with the help of my book. Without your encouragement, this new book would never have come about.

I owe a special debt of thanks to John Twist, founder and owner of University Motors, Ltd., for his very enjoyable Restoration Seminar and his "restore-one-part-at-a-time" approach, which I have carried into this book. Others whose willingness to answer questions and open their shops for photographs to make this book possible include Rich Jensen at Cruzin' Performance, Jerry and Scott Kohn at Corvette Central, Brent Ruby at Columbus Redi-Strip, and Scott Taylor of Scott's Body Shop. I deeply appreciate the support and encouragement of Erica at Hydro-E-Lectric, John at Metro Molded, and John Sloane at the Eastwood Company. Special thanks, too, to friends and teaching colleagues Vic Fowler, Phil Watson, and Newell Johnson for allowing me to photograph their cars.

To my wife, Joyce, thanks for putting up with "another book."

As with the first book, this book is dedicated to my father, Wayne J. Brownell, whose love for cars got all this started.

—Tom Brownell

Chapter 1
Why Restore a Collector Car?

A car is a complicated piece of machinery. Why would anybody want to take a time-ravaged car apart, replace all the worn and rusted pieces, rebuild the mechanicals, apply new paint and trim, and create a like-new vehicle? The investment in time and money isn't likely to yield big dividends. And even in like-new condition, we're probably talking about a vehicle that may be mechanically obsolete. So what's the motivation?

In simplest terms, restoring an old car or truck—an old vehicle of any sort—is about fulfillment. Maybe it's fulfillment of a dream, finally possessing that sports car, luxury car, or performance car that was out of reach when it was new. Maybe it's the fulfillment of a creative urge, to take something derelict and discarded and transform it into the jewel it once was. Or maybe the fulfillment comes from recapturing a slice of the past, giving memories a tangible see-and-touch expression. Fulfillment also comes by slowing life's pace, which is bound to happen both in the restoration process and in driving and enjoying an older vehicle. Physically as well as metaphysically, an old car puts us in the slow lane, where we see sights we otherwise would have rushed past and meet people we never would have passed

by without noticing. Restoring an old car offers the opportunity to experience life at a little deeper, more rewarding level—which really is what fulfillment is all about.

Restoring an old car is also about challenges, learning new skills, following not-so-pleasant jobs through to completion, and achieving the satisfaction of a finished product. The restoration process is about people, those who lend advice and give instruction, those who encourage, those who become new friends. And inevitably, the process of restoring an old car offers the opportunity for serendipity, the unexpected surprises that are one of life's mysteries—finding that searched-for missing part, a friend offering help at just the right moment, the answer to an obstacle suddenly appearing out of nowhere. There are easier ways to spend your time, but most aren't nearly as much fun—or rewarding.

For many, restoring an old car ushers in an entire change of lifestyle, not just more time spent "smelling the roses" and traveling in the "slow lane" or even making new friends, but a whole set of new activities revolving around owning and enjoying an old car. Typically, these activities arise from joining a club and include tours—sort of mini-vacations spent

Top on the list of reasons for restoring a collector car is the enjoyment you can have meeting and participating in activities with like-minded folks. Here, the Jaguar Club of North America is holding its annual meet on the grounds of Edsel Ford's mansion. Owning a collector car opens the door to a whole new set of pleasures.

with others of like-minded interest—and other car-related events that inevitably have a social focus. As one example, a restoration shop in my area sponsors annual "birthday parties" marking the business' anniversaries. Held in mid-January, not a very social month in the ice-frozen Upper Midwest where I live, several hundred customers, well wishers, and local old-car club members can be counted to show up, including families. The party is held out on the shop's service floor, giving everyone an opportunity to walk around and look over cars in various stages of their restoration makeovers—a reminder that our own cars will soon be emerging from their winter cocoons. An album of photos displayed by a local old-car club reminds us of the events and outings we've enjoyed, while slices of birthday cake munched on as we chat make for the relaxation in which new friendships are born.

Just as the car itself expands our world, an old car expands and enriches us. It's our transport to new experiences, fulfillment, and pleasures.

RESTORATION: A LEARN-AS-YOU-GO ADVENTURE

This book is designed to take you on a journey, a collector car journey. When you're finished, you will have preserved more than just a historic remnant; you will have visible proof of craftsmanship—a quality our society has nearly lost—on display in your garage. Before getting sidetracked by the end result, however, let's talk about where we begin.

Quite likely the starting point will be selecting and purchasing a collector car to restore. Although the term "old car" is frequently heard, "collector car" is a better descriptor. With cars, as with people, "old" is a relative term; it's said we're as old as we think ourselves to be: the age we'd be if we couldn't see ourselves in the mirror. Likewise with a collector car. There are bona fide collector vehicles less than 10 years old. While an owner of such a vehicle would feel foolish to say, "Let's go for a ride in my 'old' car," we're talking about vehicles that have already achieved preservation status. From there the age of collector vehicles retreats to the dawn of the motoring age. What's important is to select the collector vehicle that fits your interest, resources, and purpose.

There's More than One Way to Restore a Collector Car

If you're like most enthusiasts, as soon as you have your "new" old car at home in your garage, you'll be tempted to attack it, tools in hand. Repeatedly you'll be cautioned against taking this approach. A one- or two-day fit of disassembly can leave a car so scattered in pieces that 15 or even 20 years later there's a fender here, an engine there, a body rusting in outside storage, the title lost along with so many small parts and odds and ends that putting everything back together would daunt even a professional restorer.

Instead of wholesale disassembly, we'll proceed on a saner tact, a method loudly preached and wisely practiced by one of the nation's leading collector car restorers, John Twist, proprietor of University Motors Ltd., in Grand Rapids, Michigan. John Twist's approach: Take off one assembly at a time and rebuild it before proceeding to the next. "That way," says John, "if your boss suddenly promotes you to Istanbul, you can quickly put the car back together—maybe even load it in a container and take it with you." Otherwise, if you're looking at a shop full of pieces, who knows the car's ultimate fate?

Define Your Goal

Another reason not to start your restoration by taking the car completely apart: not all cars need to—or should—be reduced to their pieces. There are different types of restoration. For some, the goal will be to make the car "factory new," actually probably better than it came from the factory, but looking every bit as bright and shiny as it did sitting on the showroom floor. For others the goal may be "nearly new," still bright and shiny but not so perfect that it can't be driven. Other cars that have received loving preservation may need minimal restoration—some chrome renewed or a worn seat cushion replaced to look nearly factory fresh. These lovingly preserved original cars possess a quality restoration can't duplicate—a slight patina that comes with age and gives the car an heirloom look. If you're fortunate to find such a collector car, hopefully you'll preserve rather than restore it.

Research

To guide your decision on the restoration approach, you'll want to familiarize yourself thoroughly with the car's original appearance (so you can determine what's been changed and what you want the car to look like), its mechanical specifications, its strong and weak points, as well as its history (how many were made, and its role on the automotive stage). Learning about the car calls for research, which is done in a variety of ways: attending shows, looking at similar cars, and talking to owners; subscribing to collector car hobby magazines; joining clubs; and acquiring service manuals, sales brochures, as well as more recently written books describing the car.

Many first-time restorers begin by taking their car apart. "It's a recipe for disappointment," warns John Twist (above), owner of University Motors Ltd., a well-known MG restoration shop in Grand Rapids, Michigan. The wisest and best approach, Twist advises, is to restore your car one part at a time.

Technical seminars, often sponsored by clubs, are an effective way to learn restoration skills and techniques. Here, students receive instructions in how to restore a bright finish on aluminum parts by buffing and polishing. In the next step, they practice the process on the shop's buffing wheels.

Workshop, Equipment, and Skills

If you're a newcomer to restoring a collector car you'll need to locate a space for the project and equip the shop with the essential tools and supplies. Chapter 5 describes the space requirements of a car restoration project and talks about the shop needs. You'll also get a quick but important lesson on shop safety. Each of a collector car restoration project's many phases calls for new skills and sometimes specialized tools. One of the ways to learn the new skills is from DVDs and videotapes. Other ways include taking evening courses in useful skills like welding or engine overhaul at a technical high school or community college. Often clubs hold technical seminars at members' shops; you not only see the restoration process demonstrated, but also get to do some hands-on practice. These various learning methods, plus the old-fashioned approach of reading a service manual, are discussed as they apply to the various restoration steps.

The Dirty Work

Cleaning, degreasing, derusting, and paint stripping are necessary preparation steps before rebuilding or refinishing most older car parts. Several methods can be used to get parts clean and free of rust. We'll look at the options, which even include paint that "seals in" rust, making it possible to bypass the derusting step on some parts. Since cleaning, stripping, and derusting can be time consuming and tedious, there's also the option of hiring this work out. However, for finances and other reasons, having someone else do the "dirty work" for you is not always the best approach. Chapter 8 thoroughly describes each of the commonly used cleaning, stripping, and derusting methods—with some timesaving shortcuts.

Body and Paint

Metal repair—removing dents and rust—stands alongside major mechanical repair as most hobbyist restorers'

For most restorers, rust is the number one enemy. It's often hidden, as was the case here, and requires special tools and skill. Still, with training and practice, it's possible for the hobbyist to become highly competent in metal repair.

number one fear. "How am I going to fix this hideous-looking rust so that the repair is done right and doesn't show an amateur's touch?" Working with metal requires special tools and skills. For this reason, many hobbyists hire out metal repair to professionals, but it's possible to do highly competent, even craftsman-quality metal work yourself—and the investment in tools will be more than repaid by not writing big checks to the body shop. While becoming competent in the techniques of metal repair takes a fair amount of practice, Chapter 11 covers the steps in enough detail to get you started. Most important, you'll learn what not to do. Mistakes with metal can be expensive to fix.

Like metal work, painting is a high-skill process that's often hired out. However, doing the preparation steps can save lots of money and it's possible, through practice, to master the techniques for applying a professional-quality finish. Changes in technology, both paint products and application equipment, work for and against the hobbyist. Older, easier-to-apply paints are disappearing, but application technology is improving, making the modern paints easier to spray. Chapters 12 and 13 describe both

traditional and modern paint products and walk through the steps for their use.

Bright Trim

Nothing detracts from a collector vehicle's appearance more than pitted, dull, and rusted chrome plating and brightwork. In many cases, the brightwork is stainless steel and can easily be restored to a brilliant luster just by buffing and polishing—processes hobbyists can do themselves with a modest investment in tools and time. Renewing the gleam of chrome, on the other hand, takes a commercial plater's highly specialized equipment and expertise. But here, too, there are steps that hobbyists can do themselves, both to save money and to enjoy the satisfaction of renewing highly visible parts of the vehicle.

Beginning in the 1960s, manufacturers began to use plastic for many "chrome-plated" parts, especially interior trim pieces. Actually, the bright finish isn't chrome but an extremely thin coating of aluminum that, when new, shone with the brightness of chrome. Today these "plastic chrome" trim pieces, which often include instrument gauge panels, are likely to be dulled and may even have lost their bright coating. Since the trim piece's composition is plastic, not metal, the hobbyist may assume that the piece can't be restored and that a remanufactured or new replacement part has to be found. This isn't the case. Plastic chrome plating services can renew these trim items to like-new appearance if the plastic pieces themselves aren't badly damaged or deteriorated. Chapter 7 describes the processes for the plating of both brightmetal parts and plastic pieces, with tips and guidelines for receiving top-quality service at reasonable prices.

Interior Attention

Except in rare instances where a vehicle has received extremely good care and been driven few miles, the interior seat coverings, floor carpeting or mats, door coverings, headliner, or convertible top are likely to show wear and need to be replaced. One of the greatest boons to the car restoration hobby has been the appearance of upholstery kits, now available for a wide range of year and model cars and trucks. With a kit, hobbyists can be their own trimmers (the term for auto upholsterers) by installing seat, door panel, headliner, and carpet kits to make a vehicle look like new. Another advantage of kits is that most duplicate original materials in both color and weave pattern or design, something trimmers typically can't do. All the steps from removing old upholstery to purchasing and installing a complete interior kit are covered in Chapter 17.

Applying a high-quality finish requires skill and lots of practice, and modern paints are very expensive and highly toxic. Many restorers will leave this step to a professional. Shutterstock

Brakes

Regardless of how attractive a restored car may look, it's got to be drivable—and that means it also has to stop. The braking systems on older cars range, by design, from marginal to outright dangerous when they're measured against the instant stopping ability of modern ABS-equipped cars. To be safe in today's traffic an older vehicle's brakes have to work at peak efficiency, but a better approach may be to upgrade the braking system to more modern technology— something allowed in many restoration circles and strongly recommended for collector vehicles that will be enjoyed through tours and highway outings. Steps for rebuilding a collector car's brakes, and approaches to upgrading a vintage car's braking system so that it will perform to modern standards, are provided in Chapter 14.

Engine Compartment

What often sets an amateur's work apart from a professional restoration is the lack of attention to detail. Each chapter sets forth standards for a thoroughly professional finished product, but nowhere does detail attract notice as clearly as inside the engine compartment. Inevitably, you're going to open the hood and show off the vehicle's mechanical heart. This is something you'll want to do with pride and not embarrassment, hoping the boom box of a passing car will distract your audience so that you can quickly slam the hood back down.

Storage and Preservation

When you've completed your goal and the restoration project is finished, you'll want your work to last. How can you protect a restored car from aging? Proper storage is essential. Fortunately, modern products make it possible to seal a car as hermetically as if it were a museum piece— which for all practical purposes it is. Chapter 19 describes these products and explains their use. Important, too, is protecting your prized car from theft. Helpful tips are offered against this possibility.

Restoring an old car is, indeed, a learn-as-you-go adventure. It isn't necessary to know everything before you begin. Learning is more than a part of the process; it's one of the rewards—the satisfaction of mastering a challenge and developing new skills in the process, and then seeing the result of that skill emerge before your eyes. Of course, it doesn't hurt to hear admiring comments like, "You mean that *you* painted that car?!"

While it's possible that you picked up this book because the restoration candidate is sitting in your garage or backyard, it's also likely that the project car has yet to be found. In the next chapter we'll discuss cars that are promising restoration candidates, from both the standpoint of their styling and mechanical features, as well as their collector status (desirability and potential value), possible uniqueness, or performance and enjoyment characteristics.

You've joined a great hobby. Let's begin the journey.

Chapter 2
Restoration: What Does It Mean?

You've bought a collector car and you're going to "restore" it. Let's discuss for a few minutes what we're talking about. Besides cars, people also restore houses and furniture. What, exactly, does "restoring" something mean?

When we talk about restoring something, we usually think of bringing it back to its earlier—presumably original—condition. Yet there's some latitude in interpretation as to what this earlier condition is. For example, no one would literally restore a 300-year-old house to its original condition without electric lights, plumbing, and central heating (and likely air conditioning). With cars, original condition is generally interpreted as "factory new"—how the car looked as it sat on the dealer showroom, maybe even nicer, since mass-produced cars didn't get the attention as they moved down the assembly line that they receive at the caring hands of a restorer. But factory new isn't the only option. Some collectors would rather have a car that's been comfortably broken in. It's still new-looking, but not so factory fresh that it can't be driven on the highway for fear of getting a stone chip in the paint or dust on the suspension pieces. The goal in this case is to combine "like new" with the can-be-lived-in feeling of a

restored house. Then there's the example of the furniture restorers who take great care to preserve the patina that's come to the object through age. Some collector cars fit this category. They've been so lovingly preserved that it doesn't seem right to sand off that dull original finish or replace an interior whose only flaw is some sun-fading or age cracks in the leather. (The finish can be polished and the leather softened, even recolored if need be.) Restoration can have several destinations.

RESTORING TO "FACTORY NEW"

Restoring a collector car to its original condition can be a time-consuming and challenging process. It typically requires that the car be completely disassembled—down to the last nut and bolt. All mechanical assemblies are rebuilt, the chrome is replated, the body is stripped of its finish, all damage to the metal repaired, and every piece—chassis parts as well as body—brilliantly repainted. Also, the interior is stripped out and replaced with original-matching material. Literally, everything about the car is made new—using authentic parts and materials whenever possible. It's not a process for the faint-hearted. The search

Restoring a car to "factory new" means complete disassembly—down to the last nut and bolt—rebuilding all mechanical assemblies, replating the chrome, gutting the interior, and stripping the body of its finish. Literally everything about the car is made new. It's a time-consuming and expensive process, but the finished product will typically be better than when the car left the factory. Here, a completely disassembled body from a mid-1960s GM convertible is being media blasted to remove all paint and rust. Disassembly to this extent is required for media blasting, or the media will infiltrate instruments and any mechanical parts left on the car.

The terms "frame-off," "frame-up," or "ground-up" are sometimes used to describe a complete, factory-new restoration. Removing the body from the frame (on a body-frame construction car) allows the chassis to be completely disassembled and rebuilt as it would have been at the factory. Note that every chassis component has been stripped and repainted as new.

for an intake manifold, for example, with the correct casting stamping number to replace an incorrect part on the car can be maddening and expensive. Every detail requires minute inspection. In some arenas, such as Bloomington Gold, where competition for authenticity among Corvettes has been finely honed, restorers are even expected to duplicate assemblers' marks, which must appear in the correct locations on chassis members. For many collector car owners, restoration to this level goes a step, or more likely several steps, too far.

RESTORING TO "NEARLY NEW"

Somewhat less challenging, but still satisfying—especially if you desire to drive the vehicle—is restoring the car to a condition it may have been in when it was one or two years old. The factory smell is probably gone, and the finish may not be mirror perfect, but the car looks sharp and drives as new. With "nearly new" in mind, the disassembly process can be selective. If components prove sound, they can be cleaned and used as is. There's no need to fix what's not broken. Likewise, the chrome may be selectively replated. The result will never be a prize winner on the national show circuit, but the restoration may be good enough to take prizes at local or regional shows. While the effort and cost of restoration to this level should be less than that of "factory new," the car's value can be expected to be somewhat lower as well. The strongest incentive for restoration to "nearly new" is a car that can be driven and enjoyed.

A "PERIOD-CORRECT" RESTORATION

Some collectors and enthusiasts prefer to restore their car to a condition that it might have been in the day after it was originally brought home from the dealership, once it's had a few performance or appearance upgrades installed.

For 1950s cars, this might mean a set of "lakes pipes" or dual exhaust, or possibly a chrome engine dress-up kit or even a "Continental kit." Muscle cars were likely to receive a set of headers and maybe a set of aftermarket wheels, among other changes.

While some may think that such restorations are "the easy way out," in most respects, much of the car is factory correct. Only the handful of aftermarket parts would be different. A strict period-correct resto would use date-correct parts, which may be every bit as difficult to track down as factory parts—or more so.

One reason that some collectors prefer a "period-correct" restoration is that it gives them the flexibility to make improvements to the car that might make it more enjoyable to drive. In essence, a period-correct resto is the precursor to today's "resto-mod" approach. And many owners of period-correct cars point out, "We didn't like them stock when they were new, why would we want them that way now?"

RESTORING A VERY ORIGINAL CAR

They're far from common, but every now and then someone finds a car that's truly been treated like "one of the

Extremely well preserved original cars like this 1966 Ford Thunderbird may need very little restoration. This car's owner has decided that it's time for a fresh finish. Otherwise, the car is completely original.

Here's an example of how time and cost overruns occur. Early Chevrolet Camaros and Pontiac Firebirds, which are popular with collectors, had poor water management capabilities and insufficient factory rust-proofing in vulnerable areas, especially along the bottom of the windshield and the bottom of the fenders and quarter panels. This 1967 Camaro came from a dry climate and looked very rust-free, but removing the windshield revealed spongy metal along the entire length of the lower windshield brace and even an earlier repair that had been made with a section of aluminum downspout.

family." When I see a car that's been preserved with loving care, I usually do a double take, thinking I've taken a 30- or 40-year step back in time. A publisher of one of our collector car magazines owns just such a car. It's been in his family since new—and that was nearly 50 years ago. Despite its having served as family transportation for a half-dozen years and then as a college car for the family's two sons, and having sat stuffed away in a variety of garages for another 30 years or so, the car today looks like it's come out of a time vault. It has an aged patina (that distinctly mellow look), but at the same time an aura of originality that no freshly restored car can match. Cars like this should be tampered with as little as possible. An engine rebuild may be in order and a fender may need repair and repainting (taking care to match the adjacent finish), but basically it's a jewel to be polished and reverently enjoyed. Loving care is a condition that can't be re-created—though some have tried, only to discover that graceful aging is more difficult to duplicate than the look of factory new.

WHICH RESTORATION APPROACH TO TAKE?

When restoring a car to factory new, also called a frame-off or frame-up restoration, the project becomes as important as the end result. On average, a complete restoration to factory new will take 2,000 hours—that's 50 forty-hour weeks (a year of full-time labor), or four years of consistent 10-hour weeks, about the maximum a hobbyist can sustain and not jeopardize work, marriage, and other commitments. If the joy is in the process—offering a retreat

Restoring to "nearly new" is a selective process that repairs or rebuilds only those parts showing damage or wear. This type of restoration can save money and time, compared to a "factory new" restoration, but the car will look great and can be driven and enjoyed. Shutterstock

into a world of your own ordering, the satisfaction of learning new skills, and the pride of watching an item of beauty emerge from your labor—then the restoration will be self-sustaining, and you'll reap rejuvenation from your efforts. But if the purpose is only a show car at the other end, you're likely to give up before reaching the goal.

A frame-up, or factory-new, restoration has other demands besides time and perseverance. It's expensive. For a realistic cost projection you should multiply your original estimate—parts, tools, supplies, work like chrome plating and finish painting you're likely to hire out—by three. Completely dismantling a car also takes space, at least three times the space of a car that's fully intact. Unquestionably, a frame-up, factory-new restoration brings rewards, but it's not to be stumbled into.

Because "nearly new" doesn't require that everything be rebuilt, it's possible to take some shortcuts. For example, the body can be left in place on the frame and the chassis cleaned and refinished as well as possible in its assembled position. Or the engine compartment may be restored by working around the big hunk of iron in its midst. It's possible to produce a very high quality restoration under these conditions—and save lots of time in the process. But there's also the possibility that shortcuts may lead to difficulty or disappointment later on. For example, I left the cab attached to the frame while doing bodywork and mechanical restoration on a 1949 Studebaker pickup. The cargo box was removed along with front fenders and all forward sheet metal. When disassembly reached this point, it seemed simpler not to remove the cab. This proved to be a mistake. For one thing, the front cab mounts turned out to be rusted and had to be rebuilt, but their condition wasn't noticed until everything had been reassembled and the truck repainted. Bad call. The cab mounts should have been repaired before repainting. Simply stated, disassembly usually makes damage more visible.

I made another bad call with that Studebaker. One of the reasons for shortcuts (like the cab) was my time schedule.

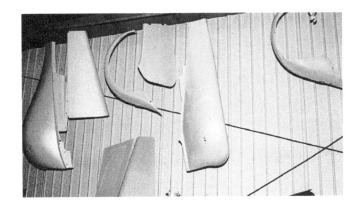

While you're restoring the car, you've got to find space for the parts. Here the solution is to hang the fenders from the shop's roof support.

I planned for less than a year (working at a recreational pace) to have the truck in "nearly new" condition so that I could drive and enjoy it. In point of fact, it took three years to make the truck roadworthy, much of that time spent correcting problems that would have been detected in an orderly disassembly/reassembly restoration process.

Aside from possible pitfalls (some of which are inevitable), the nearly new approach does have some benefits. The process is usually shorter, so there's not as great a likelihood of "running out of steam." It's also somewhat, but not significantly, less expensive. From the standpoint of driving the car, nearly new has the advantage that you're more likely to consider and make improvements or upgrades to ensure greater safety in today's often hazardous driving environment.

AUTHENTICITY VERSUS SAFETY

Most collector cars are mechanically obsolete. Although adequate for the highways they were designed to travel, their brakes, for example, may be downright dangerous. If the restoration goal isn't "factory new," then upgrading the brakes to a dual master cylinder, front disc braking system (possibly power boosted) offers a safety margin well worth considering.

While sure-acting, quick-stopping brakes are a first line of defense to avoid crashes, seat belts offer crucial protection to the car's occupants in the event of a crash. Prior to the mid-1960s, few cars were equipped with seat belts. (Ford installed seat belts, a padded dash, deep-dish steering wheel, and improved door locks on its cars in 1956 as standard equipment—but the public basically ignored these features and the manufacturer concluded that safety didn't pay.) If your collector car was built before seat belts were adopted, and you intend to drive the car, then seat belts should definitely be added.

COLLECTOR CAR HYBRIDS

Considering modern upgrades leads to what I call the hybrid approach. While adopting new brake technology may be a big step to some collector car purists, there's a bigger step in which all the technology—brakes, suspension, engine, drivetrain—is modern, but the body, trim, and interior (all that's visible about the car) are original. At least one company, Corvette Concepts of Sawyer, Michigan, has combined a modern chassis with an absolutely authentic (not a replica) 1957 Corvette body and interior. The result, which the company calls its Concept 1957 Corvette, is a classic collector design that has the mechanical attributes of a modern design. Building one of these new/old hybrids follows many of the same steps as a restoration of an original car (in fact, an original car may be the basis for the Concept 1957 Corvette hybrid), but the outcome could be a daily driver.

In recent years other hybrid products have appeared, only to disappear when their builders (typically small entrepreneurial shops) lost interest or encountered financial difficulty. One of the more notable was an MG TF roadster offered by Great Lakes Motor Cars. Like the Concept 1957 Corvette, the Great Lakes TF used authentic MG components (although a substitute fiberglass body was offered) in combination with a modern-engineered chassis. Because a small market niche exists for such new engineering/classic design automobiles, other examples are likely to emerge in the future.

Most collector cars are mechanically obsolete. If your restoration goal is to have a drivable car (known as a "driver"), you should consider upgrading the brakes with a dual master cylinder and a front disc/rotor system to ensure safety in today's traffic.

COMPARING THE RESTORATION APPROACHES

Each restoration approach has its benefits and drawbacks. The charts below are designed to help you select the restoration approach best suited to your reasons for restoring a collector car, the car's present and desired finished condition, and the likely commitment of time and money it will require.

Factory New

This is a "frame-up" (also called "frame-off") restoration in which every major component of the car is disassembled, all pieces are cleaned, stripped, repaired or replaced as needed, refinished, and re-assembled. The goal is to restore the car to exactly what it was like when it left the factory, or probably better. This level of restoration is required for serious show car competition and is the substance of a Number 1 condition car.

Pros

Complete disassembly and rebuilding means no overlooked repairs.

The process should give as much joy and satisfaction as the end result.

The end product will be beautiful.
Car will be brought to maximum-value condition.
After restoration, every detail will be absolutely authentic.

Cons

Complete disassembly requires lots of space and a very good system of organization.
On a leisurely 10 hours/week schedule, the typical frame-off restoration takes four years.
The restoration will be expensive.
The attention to detail won't be obvious to all but purists.
You probably won't drive the car.

Nearly New

Evaluation of the car's condition will determine to what extent it will be disassembled and rebuilt. Some components may be left as is. In most situations the car will be largely disassembled with most major components rebuilt, a new interior installed, much of the brightwork replated, and the exterior completely refinished. The end result should produce a solid Number 2 condition car that can be expected to take top awards in many local and regional shows.

Pros

Selective disassembly and rebuilding mean savings in time and money.

Restoration should not be as expensive as factory new.
Some deviations from authenticity may be taken for purposes of safety and drivability.
Restored car can be driven and enjoyed.

Cons

With selective disassembly, areas needing repair may be missed.
Car will not be brought to maximum value condition.
Deviations from authenticity may be objectional to purists.

With use comes the possibility of chips to the finish and other signs of wear.

Well-Preserved Original Restoration

Occasionally a collector car that's been extremely well maintained by its owners appears for sale. The car may have covered lots of miles, but it was always washed, waxed, stored in a dry garage, had the carpets vacuumed after nearly every outing, and still has the original spare in the trunk. Although a car like this could be seen as the ideal candidate for a factory-new restoration, aimed at producing a top contender for the highest levels of show car competition, an even stronger case can be made to preserve the car's originality, restoring or repairing only those components showing major wear or damage, and then to a degree keeping with the condition of the rest of the car. A very well maintained, selectively restored original should rank as a solid Number 2 condition car.

Pros

The car's well-preserved originality gives it a uniqueness no degree of restoration can duplicate.
Restoration time and expense will be kept to a minimum.

At many shows the car will compete in its own "original" category.

This car has always been driven and can continue to be enjoyed.

Cons

Some degree of wear will be evident, whether in slightly faded upholstery or age-checked paint.
Because of its condition, the car is likely to cost substantially more than the average restoration candidate.
Where an "original" category does not exist, the car may look somewhat worn compared to the fresh restorations parked alongside.
The car's original condition could produce some problems on the road.

Chapter 3
How to Select a Collector Car

Years ago when you went scouting for a collector car, which then were called simply "old cars," you had to shuffle along back roads, casting long looks through farmers' barnyards, peering around the backs of buildings, and scanning the edges of fields. All that has changed. Collector cars have come out into the open. Today, the chance of a desirable collector car turning up in a field, warehouse, or barn ranks only slightly higher than winning a jackpot lottery. And even should such a hideaway car be exhumed, chances are the owner, or the owner's estate, knows its value.

Collector cars abound, mainly because the automotive industry has entered its second century. In the first hundred years, lots of innovative, unusual, smartly styled, and outstandingly engineered cars were produced—and these are today's candidates for preservation and restoration. Of course, certain groups of cars, the "grand classics" of the 1930s and the early brass-era models, are almost entirely in collectors' hands. In these categories, very few unrestored cars exist, and when one emerges and is offered for sale, the price can seem a king's ransom. But in other categories, particularly cars built in the 1950s and later, there are lots of desirable examples to choose from, often at very modest prices.

Most people toying with the idea of owning an "old" car picture themselves with a car they wanted—but weren't able to own—when they first tasted independence. For some, it's a muscle car—that hairy-chested Pontiac GTO, 409 Chevrolet, Plymouth Road Runner, or Mach 1 Ford—feverishly admired, but an arm's length out of reach. For others it's an agile sports car, a racy MG, "bug-eyed" Sprite, storming Corvette, or curve-hugging Porsche. Still others picture a two-door coupe, pickup truck, station wagon, even a four-door sedan. With cars, our likes range to the distinctiveness of our personalities; let's zoom in for a closer view and look at some prime collector car categories.

Chevys, starting in 1955 when GM's entry model got its V-8, are hot with collectors. GM knocked out copies by the millions, so whether it is a 1958 Impala convertible, a 1967 Malibu Sport Coupe, or a 1972 Cheyenne pickup, good restoration candidates are still to be found. Likewise with Mustangs, though in both examples the really exotic models—like the Shelby Mustangs or the fuel-injected super performance "Bow Tie" cars—have been very thoroughly picked over.

British sports cars, also plentiful, particularly from the early 1960s on when import registrations began to register

Muscle cars, such as this 1968 Dodge Charger R/T, are always in high demand. Finding a good one and restoring it to its original condition can be a very satisfying—and potentially lucrative—project. Shutterstock

Convertibles are always popular with collectors. And as prices continue to rise for the top-rung classic cars, a new generation of collectors have turned their attention to less obvious choices, such as the Chevrolet Corvair. Shutterstock

in the hundreds of thousands, make enjoyable, easy-to-restore (if the body is sound) collectibles—as do the once-ubiquitous VW Beetles. While Volkswagen is relying on the popularity of the original Beetle to fuel sales of its New Beetle, a reverse stimulus also operates to fan collector interest (and raise prices) of the early models.

When picking out a collector car, don't overlook lots of lesser-noticed models, like Corvairs, which from 1965 on had well-engineered four-wheel independent suspension and European-inspired styling, and yet still battle their maligned image. Likewise, Studebakers—ridiculed for one model, the going-and-coming 1950 coupe, and praised for nearly all others—offer generally smart styling and snappy V-8 power, both cars and trucks.

In your collector car search, keep an eye out for neat one-offs, such as convertible conversions done by specialty shops, not the factory. These can be seen on Lincolns and Cadillacs of the late 1970s and early 1980s as well as other strictly coupe models like Pontiac's Fiero. Done right (careful inspection of the conversion work is in order), these one-offs make sure-fire conversation starters and are a joy to own. The same goes for pickup conversions, quite popular in the late 1970s on Lincolns and Cadillacs—the "image" Texas oil man's pickup.

Determining a Price Range

Once you've set your eye on a few choice models, you can check their affordability by looking in publications such as the *Old Cars Price Guide*, a quarterly, and the annual book-form listing *Collector Car Price Guide,* both available from Krause Publications (see Resources for publishers' addresses). The price guides typically show value according to conditions that range through categories from Number 1, representing absolutely pristine (this is typically a professionally restored, better-than-factory-new car), to Number 6, a junker, primarily a parts car. Determining which condition rating a car fits requires careful examination and a somewhat seasoned eye. If you're new to the collector car hobby, it's a good idea to take along someone well acquainted with the perils and pitfalls of used car buying when you go to select your prize. Lacking a friend to perform this service, you'll find a buyer's checklist at the end of this chapter.

The condition categories are subjective. Often you'll find a car that has some attributes of Number 3 (very good condition), such as operable mechanical components, but also Number 4 (good), in the way of a deteriorated interior. In these cases, you recalculate the value by averaging the Number 3 and Number 4 figures, then adjust up or down

LONG-DISTANCE BUYING ADVICE

With any ad—local or national, online or in-print—you really need to see and inspect the car. Sure, long-distance purchases have been done, but be forewarned: the disappointment ratio probably exceeds 50 percent. This doesn't mean that sellers set out to deceive buyers. It means that you can't really tell what the car is like from pictures. Too little detail can be seen, to say nothing of hidden flaws.

The obvious remedy is to inspect the car yourself. But if you can't physically inspect the car, due to distance, timing or whatever, you've got a couple of options. For one, you can spend a few dollars to have a professional appraiser give you his opinion. (Appraisers advertise their services in the publications listed in the Resources section of this book.) Or, if you've joined a club for the marque you're considering buying (a very good idea), contact a member in the car's vicinity and ask him/her to make an inspection on your behalf. Many enthusiasts will perform this service without charge. And these days, with cell phones as prevalent as they are, you can speak on the phone with your "proxies" and ask them what they're looking at, and direct them to check related aspects of the car, depending on what they tell you. I've even heard of some proxies taking pictures with their cell phone and sending it to the prospective buyer while he was inspecting the car!

If you elect to skip having someone inspect the car, then it's *caveat emptor*: buyer beware. I bought sight unseen once. I wasn't disappointed to the point of losing value, but the car wasn't what I expected, either. I decided it wasn't a keeper.

to fit the condition of the car. Even professional appraisers make these adjustments—all the time.

If the owner is asking more than the car's published value, you have two choices: (1) dicker and try to arrive at a compromise, or (2) ask yourself how badly you want the car and whether or not it has special features (like low mileage or a very unusual body style) that justify the owner's price. Otherwise, stick to your plan and move on. If the owner's price falls below the price guide value, it doesn't mean you're going to pocket a quick profit. In today's market, most collector cars will cost more than their sale value by the time they're restored. We're talking about a hobby here, a pastime, even a helpful therapy, not a get-rich-quick-scheme. The days of high-flying profits from ill-restored collector cars ended in a predictable speculative bust back around 1990.

Where to Buy

Potential collector vehicles seem to abound. Each week I enjoy reading the "Kenny's Klunkers" section of *Old Cars Weekly*, a weekly publication for the old car/restoration hobby where owners offer vehicles for prices below $700—the idea being to save them from being scrapped. Maybe I've been afflicted by a lifelong "Cinderella complex," but there's always something in the "Kenny's Klunkers" column that I want to restore.

Read the Classified Ads

So the cars are out there . . . but how do we find them? Clearly, one source is classified ads—in daily newspapers (typically under the "Classic/Antique Cars for Sale" heading), regional car swapper magazines (where you're also likely to see a picture of the car for sale), as well as "old car" hobby publications like *Hemmings Motor News*, *Old Cars Weekly*, and *Cars & Parts*. Local ads have the advantage that the car is close to home. The selection, however, is likely to be limited. Nonetheless, friends have found "jewels" in local ads. One spotted an A-400 Model A Ford, probably the rarest of its breed, advertised as a different, more common model. Another snapped up an Austin Healey Sprite, albeit too badly rusted to restore, but a great source of parts—including a weather-resistant fiberglass top. The national publications—*Hemmings*, *Old Cars*, *Cars & Parts*—offer a far broader range of vehicles, even such unusual items as the TC by Maserati convertible that often passes, unfortunately, due to styling similarities, as a much more common Chrysler LeBaron ragtop.

Online Boards and Auctions

With the advent of the World Wide Web has come a whole new way to shop for collector cars: virtually.

Online for-sale boards, like Craigslist.com, are great for both the seller and the buyer, because they're typically free. Sellers can post any vehicle they want, write as much of a description as they wish, and even post a handful of photos to give folks a good, initial look at the car, and it doesn't cost a cent, so almost anyone selling a car will post it on Craigslist, even if they don't expect to sell it from that listing.

Searching for cars on Craigslist doesn't cost anything, either, which makes it great for buyers, who can just sit at home and search or browse for the car or parts that they want. Another advantage of Craigslist is that when sellers post an ad, they have to assign it to a specific, geographically based Craigslist board; that makes it convenient for buyers, because you can easily limit your search to your own geographic area or the ones to which you're willing to travel.

Online auction giant eBay is another good site for buying and selling cars and parts online. Sellers do pay a nominal fee and a very small percentage of the sale price to eBay for the right to post their listing, but the site is a

As the most popular choice for most collectors, two-door models are becoming harder and harder to find. But high-quality four-door examples are often more readily available. Shutterstock

Many people pursue a restoration in order to own a car that they had always dreamt of having. No doubt this yearning accounts for the popularity of 1950s and 1960s sports cars, such as this Jaguar E-Type. Shutterstock

MG retained the classic roadster styling of the 1930s and 1940s with its T series sports cars through 1955. Relatively low cost and easy to restore, these cars, too, are popular with collectors. Shutterstock

highly active, worldwide marketplace with tens of thousands of buyers checking in daily to find their collector car or parts for it. The site has powerful search tools that make it a breeze for buyers to specify exactly what they're looking for, including a radius from their zip code, to keep the results geographically relevant.

Of course, a number of clubs, registries, and other collector car associations have classified sections of their Web sites, which can be a great way to find those rare items that might not do as well on eBay or Craigslist. However, some of the organizations do require membership in order to access the classifieds, so you might have a shell out a few bucks to troll through the ads.

Many collector car publications, including *Hemmings Motor News*, also have strong online classified sections, often because ads are run in both the print and online editions for one price.

Finally, most collector car dealers (or even regular new or used car dealers) post their inventory online on their Web site (and often on Craigslist and eBay, too), giving you yet more sites to search.

Speaking of searching … don't rely on sites like Google, Yahoo!, or Ask.com to find a collector car. While each of those sites should be included in your searching, it's important to understand that for technical reasons, not all online listings can be found by search engine "robots." For example, club listings that are locked behind a log-in are inaccessible, as are many others depending on how a particular site is designed. So, do your searches on the big search sites, but don't be disheartened if you don't find what you're looking for; it may still be out there, it just won't be quite as easy to find as you might have liked.

Visit the Auction Action

Auctions are another viable collector car sales arena. The most widely publicized are the big national events, such as the Barrett-Jackson auctions broadcast on Speed TV. If you've ever purchased at an auction, you know that the dynamics are much more complicated than just an object and a buyer. With lots of potential buyers, skilled auctioneers whip up a bidding frenzy that can inflate prices well above market value. Before selecting an auction as your buying arena, thoroughly familiarize yourself with the auction's rules. Better yet, observe a few auctions and see how they operate. As in any purchase, thoroughly inspect the car(s) ahead of time, carefully noting both their positive and negative attributes, and avoid the "passion of the moment." Here is one place it isn't necessary to win—unless you've mapped a win-at-all-costs course in advance.

Since pricing at auctions is dynamic—meaning the price is the winning bid, assuming that bid meets the seller's reserve—it's imperative to make a careful appraisal

WORTH SAVING . . . AT ALMOST ANY COST

Part of the natural life cycle of collector cars is that, eventually, even the most dilapidated car will reach a point at which it's worth restoring. It's simple math: if a "parts car" that costs $40,000 to restore can be sold for $60,000, that still equates to a tidy enough profit that it's a sound business proposition.

If restored correctly, there's nothing inherently wrong with such a car. In fact, it's not only a noble gesture to restore such a car (rather than crush it or part it out), but the restored car may actually be better than new, when completed.

of the car(s) for which you're considering bidding before you enter the auction arena. The price guides already mentioned are not only a good source of pricing/appraisal information, but the figures they cite are actually based on auction sales. Another excellent resource for anyone thinking of buying a collector car at an auction is a monthly publication called *Sports Car Market*. One of this publication's features is a critique of cars offered at major national and international auctions. Photos of the cars make it easy to identify the model being auctioned, but also give some indication of the car's condition from a visual standpoint. The critique describes the car's condition, lists the high bid, and notes whether or not the car sold for that figure—and more valuable, makes the kind of assessment that you'd hear from a very knowledgeable friend who'd witnessed the action. This is the kind of advice you might hear on a Jaguar XK-140 roadster: "Dark blue, black leather seats, chrome wire wheels; car had very straight panels, interior was excellent, and it appeared to run and drive very well as we watched it move around the auction area. A bargain if it ran as well as it looked."

Check Out Clubs

Clubs not only serve as clearinghouses for information, but they're also a great place to start when looking for a given make and model of collector car. Let's say that you've set your heart on owning a Chevrolet Camaro with the early 1967–1969 styling. At least two clubs serve this marque. By contacting the club you can get samples of their newsletters, which include cars-for-sale ads. By joining one or both of the clubs you can read about the features of the different years and models—helping to focus your target vehicle. If you attend any of the club's functions, you can meet other owners, who may be able to help find a suitable vehicle and are likely to become a very helpful information and support network once you begin your restoration project. Club addresses can be found in *Hemmings Vintage Auto Almanac* (a resource directory published annually) and the annual club issue of *Old Cars Weekly*, the hobby's weekly newspaper. As mentioned earlier, most clubs also have Web sites with classified sections and other excellent resources.

Shopping at the Corral

Probably the most exciting place to shop for a collector car is at the car corrals of swap meets. At the giant Hershey, Pennsylvania, collector car event, held in early October and sponsored by the Antique Automobile Club of America (AACA), the car corral is a car show all by itself. Practically every model of collector car is on display, from woody wagons to convertibles, sports cars, muscle cars, compacts, and sedans of early- to late-model vintage. Although they lack the carnival atmosphere of an auction, advantages of car corrals are that you get a chance to spend as much time as you want looking over the vehicle, including driving it within the limited confines of the car corral area, and you can dicker directly with the owner. Since the larger swap meets typically run several days, the same applies for the car corrals—so there's a chance to play a

In selecting cars from the 1960s, the iconic Pontiac GTO remains a popular choice. Shutterstock

When picking out a collector car, don't overlook lesser-noticed models like Corvairs and Studebakers, which offer novel styling and innovative engineering. Both makes are also represented by strong clubs. This is a Studebaker Hawk *Shutterstock*

waiting game with the owner, watching to see if the car's asking price comes down as the seller faces the likelihood of having to haul the car back home. Of course, there's also the possibility of losing the car to another buyer, especially if it is reasonably priced to begin with, is in good condition, and is a desirable model.

Many smaller, more localized shows also offer cars for sale—if not in a designated car corral area, then as part of the swap meet. Naturally, the selection will be smaller, but that doesn't exclude desirable cars. At regional swap meets in my area of the Midwest, I've seen very desirable cars and light-duty truck models offered at bargain prices. Unfortunately, I wasn't in a buying position at the time, or I could have made some opportune purchases. On one occasion, I'd just purchased a collector car a week before the swap meet where I found a car I'd much rather have had at about a third the price. I mention this experience as a caution. When selecting a collector car, don't be in a hurry. The right car is out there someplace. Be patient and you'll find it.

Inspecting a Collector Car

Let's assume you have found a car that piques your interest. Before handing the owner a check, you'll want to give the car a bumper-to-bumper inspection to make sure its value matches (or exceeds) the sale price. Where to start...? You're looking at a used—maybe well-used or used-and-abused are better descriptions—car so the inspections you'd make if you were buying secondhand transportation are a good place to begin. The first and biggest question: does the car run? Lots of cars of interest to collectors don't. Either they've sat so long that it's going to take a fair amount of tinkering—or some serious mechanical work—to get them going, or they've been partially disassembled and may even be lacking major mechanical components—like the engine. If the car can't be run, all sorts of other mechanical questions, like the condition of the brakes and steering, aren't going to have answers. You might as well assume the worst, and be pleasantly surprised if the transmission and other major mechanical components turn out to be sound. You just won't know the car's mechanical condition until you either get it running or start taking things apart.

You'll know lots more about the car you're buying if it runs, even if it runs lousy. If it will move, you can test the clutch and get a feel for the condition of the transmission, manual or automatic. You'll also have a measure of the brakes and steering. If you can take the car out on the highway, you can listen for clunking and grating sounds from other wear points such as the universal joints in the driveline and wheel bearings. Beyond the engine making "expensive-sounding" noises, you can at least partially gauge its condition by the oil pressure reading. Running cold, when first started, and at higher rpm, the engine

Today's exotic cars like the Dodge Viper, shown here, are sure to be tomorrow's collectibles. Shutterstock

If any mid-1950s car is more popular than a 1955 Chevy, it's a 1957 Chevy. More chrome, tasteful rear fender fins, and a hotter V-8 engine are the 1957 Chevy's attractions. Shutterstock

Later-model cars likely to gain collector status are those with a combination of advanced engineering, appealing styling, and low production. Possible candidates are the Alfa Romeo Spider Veloce sport convertible and the Peugeot 405 MI-16 touring sedan. Only low-mileage, prime-condition examples should be considered, as parts and service can be hard to come by. The Peugeot 405 MI-16 is shown here. When this car was introduced in 1988, it was awarded "Car of the Year" in Europe. Racing versions scored an unheard-of first- and second-place finish in the grueling Paris-Dakar Rally.

It doesn't take a lot of imagination to picture where this mid-1930s Packard convertible coupe has spent the last 30 years—likely in the back rows of a salvage yard. Definitely not a project for a beginning restorer. It might, however, make a usable parts car.

should nudge the needle on the oil pressure gauge past 30 psi, or at least the midpoint indicator on the gauge (assuming the instrument panel doesn't have just a red indicator light for oil pressure). Lower pressure under these conditions, or a needle pegged near zero running warm at idle, guarantees that an engine rebuild is in order. And be sure to pull the dipstick and look at the engine oil. If it's black as pitch, the engine hasn't seen attention in a long time. If the car has an automatic transmission, also pull this unit's dipstick. Healthy automatic transmission fluid is bright red; brownish transmission fluid with a burnt smell spells rebuild for this major mechanical component.

Keep in mind that the car's mechanical condition won't necessarily determine your yea or nay on its purchase. Components in operable condition may still be rebuilt, either to bring them into peak running condition or to upgrade them with new materials and technology. What you're looking to determine is as accurate a condition assessment as possible for the purpose of purchase price and restoration strategy.

Looking to buy a collector car? You'll find a huge assortment—nearly 2,000 cars—at the giant Hershey Car Show and Swap Meet car corral. Known simply as "Hershey," the event takes place in early October in Hershey, Pennsylvania, and represents the largest old-car gathering in the world. It's sponsored by the Antique Automobile Club of America. If the Mercedes 190 SL roadster shown here is in as sound condition as its appearance suggests, it could be a relatively easy restoration and could be counted on to appreciate in value.

"Kenny's Klunkers," a listing in the classified ad section of the Old Cars Weekly *newspaper, offers cars likely to be scrapped at prices under $700. Though a collector's initial investment in this pair of Willys Aero sedans might barely top $1,000, the cars' unit-body design could pose a substantial restoration challenge. The bottom line: price is not the only (or best) selection criterion.*

Having checked the mechanicals, what about the body? Are paint blisters visible over wheelwells or along lower body panels? Tiny bubbles in the paint indicate ugly rust underneath. Or maybe the rust is plainly visible—with holes in the fenders or body. Look carefully around the rear wheelwells inside the trunk; this is a prime rust-out area. What about the floors (or floorpan on unit-bodied cars)? Are these metal sections sound? On 1950s cars and light trucks before the manufacturers began using inner fender liners, look for signs of rust (those telltale bubbles or blisters) on the fender "eyebrows" above the headlights. Hopefully, you've remembered to bring the used car buyer's essential tool, a small magnet to easily check for body putty—a sign of repair work under the finish. The magnet trick is simple. Just run a small, flat magnet along the car's finish. You'll feel the magnet's attraction when steel is underneath. When this attraction is broken, the metal is covered by a layer of plastic filler. Very thin coats of filler under a high-quality finish are OK if they're backed by metal and used to smooth small blemishes. But thick

A friend and I were invited to view this Studebaker/Packard lineup at a club gathering. Careful inspection of a car's condition would be needed to make a purchase decision.

Swap meets can also be a source of candidates for restoration. Though weathered and worn, this Model T appears complete and includes some of the parts needed for restoration. That it runs is important in order to check the condition, not just of the engine, but also the transmission, steering, and brakes.

layers of filler hiding rust or dent damage mean you'll be looking at lots of time-consuming and potentially expensive bodywork.

Be sure to note the condition of the brightmetal trim. Dented brightmetal (windshield moldings and trim spears) can be straightened and polished, but dull, rusted, or pitted chrome plating (on the bumpers, grille, and taillight assemblies) will have to be commercially restored—an expensive process. Are all trim pieces on the car? Missing trim pieces are usually evidenced by small holes in the bodywork. Finding missing trim can sometimes be exasperating. If the car is a convertible, what's the condition of the top? Very likely this item will need to be replaced. If the top is missing, what is the condition of the bows? Is the top bow mechanism intact and operable? If the top appears to be in good condition, is the covering authentic

Online marketplaces like Craigslist.com, which has individual sites for each state and even many major cities, are great places to find your next collector car. Sellers can post detailed descriptions of the vehicles, and include several photos so that buyers get a feel for the car's condition.

in color and material? Prior to the 1950s, convertible tops were canvas. From the 1950s on, top fabric is vinyl, generally white or black, though sometimes color-shaded to match the vehicle. In the 1960s and early 1970s, convertible back windows were often a very thin tempered glass.

Looking inside, what's the mileage? Does the mileage appear accurate? In other words, if the odometer shows 57,000 miles, is this an actual 57,000 or 157,000? How do you tell? What do the owner's records show? Sometimes you'll find oil change markings (stickers on the doorposts) that indicate higher mileage (57,000 miles on the odometer, for example, and an oil change sticker reading 86,000 miles on the doorpost). Other signs of high mileage are worn brake and clutch pedal pads (the wear is typically on an outside edge where the driver slid his/her foot off the pedal), sag or "play" in the driver's door hinges, and extra wear or sagging cushions on the driver's seat.

What's the overall condition of the interior? Will the seat coverings need to be replaced? Does the fabric and pattern appear to be original? What is the condition of the carpeting or floor mats? How about the dash: are the instrument faces sharp and clear? Will the gauge facing need replating? Have extra holes been cut in the dash, maybe to install nonauthentic gauges or an aftermarket radio? If the car has a vinyl dash cover, is the cover cracked? Patch kits for dash coverings don't give a satisfactory "fix" and cover overlays aren't available for all vehicles. Replacing a cracked vinyl dash cover can be a serious undertaking. Are any interior pieces missing—for example, dash knobs, door handles, window cranks, clock, sun visors? Does the car have any damaged window glass, meaning not just cracks or chips, but deterioration (hazing) around the edges?

Be sure to look the car over as carefully underneath as you do on top. A friend owns a 1960s Ford convertible that looks super sharp from every angle other than a grease pit. I crawled underneath once because he'd popped

Auction sites like eBay are loaded with available collector cars. Good listings will have ample descriptions and numerous photos to give you a good idea of the vehicle's condition. But be careful of online scams—it's best to physically inspect the vehicle before buying. Or if it's too far away for you to see it yourself, have a friend or club member do it for you.

Early Beetles, like the 1960 model shown here, make a great entry into the collector car hobby. Restorable cars are still in relatively plentiful supply, parts are easily accessible, and the nostalgia value is high. When buying one of these cars, you're looking for authenticity. It's best to start by familiarizing yourself with the changes made in different years. That way you'll have a better sense of the extent to which the car you're looking at is still original.

Here's what the real Jeepster looks like. This sporty phaeton, made by Willys and sold between 1949 and 1951, is a popular collectible, supported by clubs and restoration parts sources. When searching for a special-interest collector vehicle like this, clubs are often one of the best sources.

a brake line and I had to pinch off the line and top up the master cylinder to get him home. "Ouch," was all I could think as I crawled underneath to reach the ruptured (and badly rusted) brake line. Its belly side told the car's history: parked for years in someone's field. At least the color of the entire frame, chassis members, and underbody panels were all one color—iron-oxide orange.

Other used-car inspection steps, such as jacking up the front end and "rocking" the front wheels to check for loose steering linkage and suspension fittings, are also in order. On front-drive cars, like the Oldsmobile Toronado, look

carefully for leaking (torn or ruptured) CV joint boots. Front suspension/driveline work is costly.

Up top again, open the hood and give the engine compartment a careful inspection. Is surface rust visible on the underside of the hood, inner fender panels, and firewall? If so, here's another indication that the vehicle has been stored outside (or in damp undercover storage—such as a dirt-floor shed). Has any attempt been made to keep the engine compartment clean, or is it a grease-sodden mess? Again, you're seeing signs of the car's prior care. Our younger son purchased a pickup truck from a fellow who

Mustangs from all the early styling series (1964–1966, 1967–1968, 1969–1970, 1971–1973) are great collectibles, especially convertibles. These cars were very prone to rust, so it's likely that any early Mustang you're looking at will have had some body repair in the vulnerable areas——fender lips, trunk, and the all-important body support structure underneath the doors. If possible, put that Mustang you're considering buying up on a lift and give it a careful inspection underneath. If everything is sound, you're in for lots of enjoyment. If the underside is spongy, you're looking at massive metal repair. Shutterstock

not only kept the finish and interior spotless, but who paid the same attention to the engine and undercarriage. Indeed, the truck looks and drives like new. A new truck for a used truck price—what a bargain!

Before finalizing a purchase decision, it's important to check two more important—indeed, in some cases critical—items. First, does the car have matching numbers? Although this term is often seen in ads, as in "car has matching numbers" or "numbers not matching," many collector car enthusiasts don't know what it means. In simplest terms, "matching numbers" means that the car carries the original engine, whose ID number matches the VIN (vehicle identification number) of the car; it should also have the original transmission and rear axle assembly. This matching numbers game can get a lot more complex, and does in highly competitive owner ranks, such as Corvettes and 1955–1957 Chevys. In these settings, it's not just the engine number that needs matching, but also the casting numbers on exhaust and intake manifolds; additionally, each part's date code must match the car's vintage. It takes immersion into the culture of these popularly collected

cars to know the full "matching number" scheme. Yet, very tangibly, the extent to which all the mechanical pieces tell the same story directly translates into value. A Corvette can be beautiful as a South Sea sunset, but if the numbers don't match, its value won't be much above a "driver."

The second critical area is like the first: Does the car's optional equipment, including a special trim package, match the data plate or accessory list—and in some cases the factory build sheet? Here's an example: it's fairly easy to gussy up a plain-Jane Pontiac Tempest or LeMans so that it looks like a much more valuable GTO muscle car. So, if what you bought is really a Tempest, but you paid a GTO price, you may enjoy the car, but it's not likely you'll recoup your investment. How do you tell whether or not the car's identity is true? Quite easily: GTOs and most other performance package cars are coded as such in their VIN plate and trim or data plate, which is often found on the firewall, doorpost, fender, or some accessible location. The trick is knowing, and deciphering (or "breaking down") the codes. Learning the coding is a simple matter of buying a reference book, such as the popular ID

Where possible, the best collector car investment is a no-rust, low-mileage original. A Ford Thunderbird makes a great collector car and may only need a fresh finish to make it show-worthy. Shutterstock

An ideal transport arrangement is with an enclosed trailer. Inside the enclosure, the vehicle is protected not only from weather elements, but also highway debris.

With Corvettes, the car's value is directly tied to such authenticity features as matching numbers, meaning that the engine and other mechanical components are authentic and original to the car. Shutterstock

Numbers books published by *Cars & Parts* magazine and available through booksellers such as Motorbooks. (See publishers listing in the Resources.)

In some instances—1967–1972 Chevy light-duty trucks are an example—an accessory list was pasted on the inside face of the glove box door at the factory. This list tells the optional equipment installed on the vehicle when it was built. A preserved or restored-to-original-condition pickup will have this list and equipment to match. Many Mopars featured a "fender tag" that was riveted to the driver's fender, under the hood—heavily optioned cars sometimes had two tags!

Another telltale item, the build (or broadcast) sheet, accompanied the vehicle as it traveled down the assembly line, telling the assemblers what equipment was to be installed on the vehicle. The assemblers tucked this sheet into an out-of-sight spot on the vehicle, as it neared the end of the line. Common locations are in the seat springs of the seatback or seat cushion, or in the trunk. When build sheets

are found and preserved, they tell a great deal of information, not only about the vehicle's equipment but also its date of assembly and assembly location.

Some cars can also be researched and documented through impartial third-party organizations, registries, or even the manufacturers themselves. PHS (formerly "Pontiac Historic Services") is one of the best known of these, for Pontiacs from the muscle car era. By sending the VIN of a Pontiac that you own or are thinking of buying, PHS will send you a copy of the original factory invoice for the supplied VIN, which lists which dealer ordered the vehicle, when, and with which options. PHS documentation is considered by most to be "absolute proof" that a Pontiac is what it's claimed to be, and, for some models like The Judge or an original Trans Am, PHS documentation (or original paperwork) may be the only way to prove a car's lineage, as those options were not coded into either the VIN or trim tag. Unfortunately, because PHS records are on microfiche, it takes several weeks to obtain the info packet, which

CHECKLIST: APPRAISING A COLLECTOR CAR

Rate each item on a scale of 1 to 5, using 5 as the maximum value.

EXTERIOR

1. Body _____

- Check for paint blisters (especially over wheelwells, along rocker panels, and on top of headlight "eyebrows") and other signs of rust.
- Sight along panels to inspect for waves or bulges, signs of poorly done body repair.
- Use a magnet to check for body filler, signs of damage or rust repair.
- On unit-bodied cars, small creases in the top or on the rear quarter panels can be a sign of earlier severe body damage.

2. Doors _____

- Look for paint blisters along the bottom edges indicating underlying rust.
- Do the doors sag when they are opened? Check the driver's door particularly. Sagging doors are a sign of worn hinges and an indication that you are looking at a high-mileage car.
- Check the condition of the weather seal around the doors and windows.

3. Hood and trunk _____

- Inspect the hood for ripples, dent damage, and for paint blisters along the leading edge where trapped moisture often causes rust.
- Check inside the trunk around wheel housings and the trunk floor for rustout. Moisture under the trunk mat is a sign of a leaking weather seal.
- Do the hood and trunk close and latch easily, showing proper alignment?

4. Top _____

- With convertibles, is the top made from original-type material? Vinyl tops appeared in the 1950s. Cars built prior to 1950 should have canvas tops.
- Does the convertible top have its original-style rear window? Many convertibles built from the mid-1960s to the 1970s had tempered-glass rear windows. Some convertibles built as late as the early 1950s had glass rear windows in metal frames.
- Inspect the top material for wear, deteriorated stitching, and discoloration.
- If the top covering is missing, check the condition of the bows. Are any pieces of the top mechanism missing?
- If the car has a power-operated convertible top, does the top mechanism work? Will the top raise and lower?
- Check metal tops for dents (note comment above about dents in tops of unit-bodied cars possibly indicating major structural damage).
- On cars with vinyl-covered metal tops, inspect the condition of the vinyl.
- Is the covering still tightly sealed and without rips or other damage?

5. Paint _____

- Where possible, compare the paint coding on the car's data plate with the color of the finish on the car. Is the car painted its original color?
- Check door jambs and inside the hood and trunk for indication that the car has been repainted and whether the repaint color matches the original.
- Inspect the condition of the paint. Does the finish show a high gloss, or is it dull with an orange-peel texture?
- Sighting along lower body panels, can you spot runs, drips, or sags in the paint—signs of an unprofessional finish?
- On fiberglass-bodied cars, does the finish show extreme cracking, a sign that repair work to the fiberglass is in order? On metal-bodied cars, paint cracking indicates a too-thick paint buildup (especially if the paint is a more brittle lacquer type), storage in widely fluctuating temperature conditions, and age.
  Note: If the car is in need of extensive metal repair, the condition of the finish is relatively unimportant since the car will need to be repainted.

6. Trim _____

- Inspect all chrome-plated trim pieces: bumpers, grille, headlight bezels, taillight housings, hood and trunk trim, etc.
- Is the chrome plating bright and lustrous or dull and worn so that the base metal or nickel plate shows through?
- Are plated diecast parts, such as taillight housings, badly pitted? Pitted diecast is difficult to repair.
- Is stainless-steel trim (typically used for body side moldings) dented or missing?
- Are grille insert pieces damaged or broken?

7. Glass _____

- Check for chipped, cracked, broken, or discolored glass. Discoloring first appears at the edges and spreads inward, and appears like a foggy haze.
- Does the glass have its factory markings, indicating originality?
- What is the condition of the glass weather seal? Is it dried out and cracked, not only creating an appearance blemish, but possibly allowing water to leak around the seal? Are there signs of water leakage either on the dash or package shelf behind the rear seat?

INTERIOR

1. Dash and instrument panel _____

- Are gauges original, intact, and working?
- Are accessory gauges such as a tachometer or "motorminder" included?
- Have nonoriginal gauges or an aftermarket radio been installed, sometimes by cutting extra holes in the dash that will need to be filled?
- Appraise the general condition of the instrument panel and dash. If the instrument panel is plated, what is the condition of the plating? Are all dash knobs in place? What is the condition of the plating on these items?
- If the dash has a vinyl cover, is the cover cracked?

2. The odometer's recorded mileage _____

- What's the car's recorded mileage? Does this mileage figure appear accurate, i.e., if the odometer shows 57,000 miles, is this an actual 57,000 or 157,000—or 257,000?
- What do the owner's records show? Do oil change records (perhaps from stickers on the doorposts) confirm the recorded mileage or point to a higher mileage (mileage shown on the oil change stickers is higher than the odometer reading).
- Other signs of high mileage are worn brake and clutch pedal pads, worn, sagging hinges on the driver's door hinges, or a well-worn driver's seat.

3. Upholstery _____

- Inspect the condition of the door panels, seat covering, and headliner.
- Do the interior coverings appear to be original? This is an important assessment, because even if the interior coverings are in good condition, but are not original, from a restoration point of view they will need to be replaced. So condition alone is not the criteria.

4. Floor coverings _____

- What is the condition of the floor covering? Are carpets worn, soiled, or torn? Is the carpeting or floor covering original color and pattern?
- Are step plates, often installed along the bottoms of door openings, deteriorated or missing? Typically these protective plates are made from aluminum, which will deteriorate in corrosive environments.
- If possible, inspect the condition of the metal flooring under the carpet or mats. Is the floor pan rusted?

5. Interior trim _____

- Are window moldings wood grained, chrome plated, or painted as original?
- Is the interior trim complete and authentic? Check for missing door handles, window cranks, etc. On cars with power windows and door locks, check to make sure these power accessories work.

ENGINE AND CHASSIS

1. Engine operation _____

- Does the engine run? If the engine won't run, you have no way of appraising not only its condition, but also that of most of the car's other mechanical components. In this case, you should assume the worst—that the car will need a complete mechanical rebuild, and be pleasantly surprised if this proves not to be the case.
- Does the engine make "expensive-sounding" noises (clunk-clunk knocking sounds from deep inside, the clackety-clacking of a loose or worn valve mechanism)?
- What is the engine's oil pressure? Just started and running under load, the oil pressure needle should be at least in the mid-range of the gauge. Warm and at idle, the needle should reside above the 0 point.
- Does the engine burn oil, indicated by blue smoke at the tailpipe?
- What is the condition of the engine oil? Black, tarry-looking oil indicates long intervals between oil changes and less-than-desired maintenance and care.

- Is the engine authentic to the car? Here you may have to locate the engine number and compare it to lists and decoding information available in source books listed in the Resources.

2. Engine compartment _____

- Evaluate the general condition of the engine compartment. Is the underhood area relatively clean (including the underside of the hood)?
- Are the engine and accessories painted authentic colors?
- Does the wiring appear to be original and in good condition or is the insulation frayed and lengths of obviously unoriginal wiring patched in?

3. Brakes and steering _____

- If the car can be driven, is it safe to take out on the highway?
- Do the brakes stop the car within a reasonable distance without pulling to either side, or making grating noises?
- Is the steering tight, meaning the car keeps in a straight line with minimal correction? Steering can also be checked with the car in static position by turning the steering wheel and having an assistant look to see how far the wheel can be turned without moving the wheels. This free movement is called "play," and anything more than a slight amount means some or all of the steering components need to be rebuilt.

4. Transmission operation _____

- If the car is equipped with a standard transmission and the engine runs, check the condition of the clutch.
- Does the clutch engage smoothly and fully disengage the transmission (do you hear grinding noises when shifting into low or reverse)?
- With an automatic, are the shift points smooth or does the transmission seem to slip, especially under acceleration?
- Check the automatic transmission fluid. The color should be bright red. If the fluid is a brownish color or has a burnt smell, the transmission has internal damage and will need to be overhauled.

5. Undercarriage _____

- Is the chassis clean and painted (unlikely on all but recently restored cars)?
- Do the engine, transmission, or rear axle appear to leak oil?
- On front-drive cars, like the Oldsmobile Toronado, look carefully for leaking (torn or ruptured) CV joint boots. Front suspension/driveline work is costly.

OVERALL

1. Authenticity _____

- Earlier inspections have looked at the originality of the paint, interior, and engine; now evaluate the car's overall authenticity.
- Consider accessories that are included with the car, such as special wheels, fancy wheel covers, and other dress-up items. Do these extras match the type and style of accessories originally offered on the car? Handsome as these items may be, if they're not authentic their presence may actually detract from the car's value.

2. Special features _____

- A higher-horsepower engine, fancier trim or interior (bucket seats and center console, for example), transmission type (manual four-speed or overdrive), a vinyl-covered roof or sliding sun roof, if authentic, add substantially to the car's overall value. Price guides may assign a premium of 10 to 30 percent to these features individually, or in combination. Adjust the value for special features the car may possess.

3. Desirability _____

- Now you're down to personal preference. What do you really like (or dislike) about the car? Maybe it's the color scheme (we're talking about the original color scheme as shown on the data plate coding, not what may currently be on the car). Or it could be the body style—that convertible or sports car you've always wanted.
- If the car resonates deeply in your being, add points commensurate with its appeal. If nothing connects, leave this category a zero.

Now total your points for all 20 categories. Compare the rating you have given the car to 100 points maximum. This detailed evaluation should be helpful in determining whether or not you want to buy the car and for establishing its value.

makes it difficult to incorporate into the process of making a timely decision. Of course, even with PHS or similar documentation—including original invoices, titles, and other paperwork—you still need to be skeptical. See the sidebar "Bogus Paperwork … and Cars" on page 38 for more info.

Armed with the results of a thorough inspection, you can proceed with the price negotiation process. The best advice here is to determine a fair price (a price guide is helpful, as is any knowledge you have about the actual sale price of comparable cars) and try to come to an agreement. Remember, there are always "X" factors, like other bidders, a special attraction you feel toward the car, a seller's reasons and motivation for selling, timing, the phase of the moon, who knows what else. What's important is that both you and the seller feel fairly treated.

Getting That New Purchase Home

You've located your collector prize, given it a thorough inspection, hopefully documented it, and negotiated the purchase. Now, how do you get that car—which may be a better candidate for an overhaul than a highway cruiser—home? Unless you've got your own car-hauling equipment (flatbed truck or tow vehicle and trailer), this step can be a dilemma. Let's look at some options.

The simplest and surest solution is to contract with a transport service specializing in hauling collector vehicles. You can find addresses and telephone numbers of the larger nationwide car transport services in a hobby publication like *Hemmings Motor News.* If you purchase a collector car at an auction, these transport companies are likely already on the scene, waiting to hire out their services.

Sometimes arrangements can be made with collector car dealers to have a car you've purchased from some other party picked up and transported to you on the return leg of a dealer's delivery. A Studebaker pickup I sold to a collector in Florida traveled to its new owner that way. The transporter, owned by a Florida collector car dealer, had a delivery to make in the Upper Midwest. After that drop-off, the driver proceeded to my address, loaded the Studebaker onto his flatbed truck, and headed home—and the return run probably paid for the whole trip.

A friend reports brokering the transport of a collector vehicle across country with an independent trucker. This was not without incident, since the trucker ran up some unexpected expenses en route (due to an ICC violation) and called, asking my friend to wire him money so that he could get his truck back on the road. Since the shipping fee was to be paid on the vehicle's safe delivery, you can imagine what ran through my friend's mind: "If I wire the

When hauling your collector car home on a flatbed trailer, make sure the vehicle is securely anchored down. Remove any parts that are likely to fall off, and stop periodically to check the vehicle's condition.

money, who's to say I'll ever see my car? But if I don't, I'm sure I won't see it." What seems to be the less expensive way sometimes isn't.

Another possibility: contact a friend with a trailering vehicle and offer an expense-paid vacation to haul home the newly purchased collector car. Some will find this an appealing adventure. If your hauling friend doesn't have a trailer, you may be able to rent a car-capacity trailer from U-Haul, Ryder, or another rental agency. However, be sure in advance that the tow vehicle is set up with the proper class hitch and is of adequate capacity for the load.

On some occasions, you may be able to drive the car home, though depending on the car's previous use and condition, the trip may not be uneventful. If you take this approach, arrange for someone to caravan with you—preferably in a vehicle that can provide a tow if the collector car breaks down. As further precautions, pack tools and at least the basics in spare parts, like an extra fan belt and radiator hoses, and maybe a spare fuel pump and various fluids. As you become familiar with your collector purchase, treat it tenderly and give yourself plenty of slack with other traffic. Remember, your goal is to make it home, not set a time and distance record.

With the car safely in your garage, your first impulse may be to tackle it with wrenches in both hands. Not so fast! Now is the time to plan a strategy, carefully and deliberately laying out the steps to the car's rejuvenation or restoration (not all cars need the same amount of work). It's a lot easier to take things apart than to put them back together, and if the taking apart process happens too much by impulse, you may cause yourself lots of extra work—to say nothing of the extra cost—and the energy, enthusiasm, and resources for the project may dissipate before the assembly steps ever occur.

Chapter 4
Research: Uncovering A Car's "Life Story"

I'm always impressed when an owner can tell me his car's life story, sometimes starting with the build sheet that accompanied the car down the assembly line, then the dealer invoice showing the car's sale to its original owner, and on through the former owners' registrations that trace the car to him. Knowing a car's genealogy and its factory pedigree brings a sense of kinship. It's not just an object. It has personality and history.

But a car's heritage is just one chapter of its story. There are also the events surrounding its design and production, which often reveal even more about the car's personality. Chevrolet's Corvette, for example, had its origins as a show car and has never strayed far from stardom. Then there's the car's popularity (was it literally one of a million or one of a thousand or one of only a hundred?), its reputation (including both its strengths and weaknesses), and the degree to which the car still reflects its factory pedigree. Unfortunately, cars carry only a thin outline of their life's stories with them. To flesh out the full story will send us sleuthing along a research trail.

Once started on, the research trail is likely to continue for as long as you own the car. The tidbits of detail that emerge in the restoration and ownership of a collector car can be amazing. I recently met a collector who has turned his garage into a veritable museum of information and memorabilia about his favorite cars—multiple Pontiac LeMans and Grand Prix—and he continues to learn about his cars and add novel items to his collection.

Although the research trail is more an odyssey than a straight line to a destination, it has a definite point of origin. For most people, research begins about the same time as taking ownership of a collector car does. A better point to begin is at the time when you contemplate buying a particular collectible. What you learn before buying may influence your decision and is sure to make you a smarter buyer. For example, knowing how Ford and Chevrolet built their unibody pony cars, the Mustang and Camaro, accomplishes two things: (1) it brings an awareness that rust in the support sections can mean serious repair to restore the structural integrity of the car, and (2)

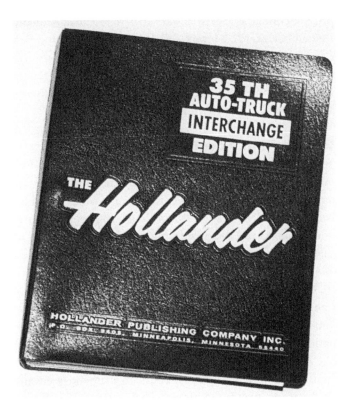

Extremely helpful in locating parts is a Hollander Interchange Manual. *Older editions of these automotive and truck parts reference books have been reprinted and are still available.*

it prepares you to look closely at the vulnerable support areas. Sure, you'll learn whether rust has compromised the car's structural integrity sooner or later—but it's much better to be aware of a problem like this before you buy the car rather than after.

HOW TO RESEARCH A COLLECTOR CAR

An abundance of information for most collector cars is easily accessible and conveniently packaged in the form of magazines, books, videotapes, and DVDs. Sales brochures, often available from literature vendors at the larger swap meets typically held in conjunction with car shows, provide a wealth of helpful information. In addition to showing outside details, they frequently offer views of the interior

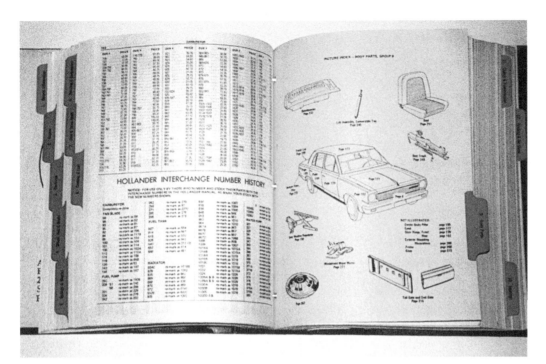

92 TIRE PRESS TABLE CODE	93 CONS. INFO. TABLE CODE	94 BUMPER HT. CODE	95	96 ENG. CERT	97	98	99	100	101	102	103	104	105	106
FAB		A	USAV8 2	PF012C677	11615	MDR258	65 21 OG	S	22 68 96 96	YEL9			GY W660	

Parts references in the Hollander Manual are grouped by application and are listed by make and model.

These three publications are at the core of the collector car hobby.

that may reveal desirable accessories (optional gauges or dress-up items like special upholstery patterns) as well as paint and trim schemes.

Along with sales brochures, there's a whole range of factory literature, including service manuals, dealer service bulletins, body repair manuals, parts and accessory lists, fact books for sales personnel, and in some cases even filmstrips, often comparing the car to competitor's products. (Since few people today have access to a film projector, the filmstrips can best be made viewable by having them converted to DVD.) Swap meets are a likely source for these and other factory literature pieces, as are literature dealers that advertise in collector car hobby publications. Or, if you're lucky, the video may have been converted and posted online at a service like YouTube.com or Google's video service.

Club publications round out the printed information resources. You'll find clubs catering to all major segments of the collector car hobby, from foreign cars to postwar special-interest models, to sports and muscle cars, to light-duty trucks, and beyond. In some cases clubs track a single styling series, like 1955–1957 Chevrolets or single-seat Thunderbirds. If your resources permit only a single research source, make it a club. Everyone owning a collector car should be tapped into a club catering to that particular make and model of car. Clubs are the collector car hobby's lifeline, providing not only interesting, useful, even essential information, but also monitoring legislation affecting owners of collector cars, their storage, and driving privileges, and even providing opportunities to develop enriching friendships.

I not only belong to clubs for collector vehicles I own, I've joined clubs for cars that are simply of interest to me—and what a wealth of information I've gained. During a Fiero fling, I learned to sort out the commuter scooters from the serious sports cars—indeed the Fiero came in both stripes, the latter already being a sought-after collectible.

The research sources described so far reveal mainly general features about the car. Before you undertake its restoration, you'll want to know specifically about your car. Much about a car's identity can be found on the data plate (locations are typically shown in the factory service manual), the encoded engine number, and (if you are fortunate enough to find it) the factory build sheet. Information

BOGUS PAPERWORK . . . AND CARS

When collector cars escalate in value, the potential for ne'er-do-well types to create fake cars escalates in lock-step. Sadly, it's often far easier to create a fake car and pass it off as the real McCoy than anyone would like to admit. There are generally only two things that are needed to create a convincing fake: a correct VIN and supporting paperwork.

A correct VIN can be pulled from a wrecked original, and transferred to the bogus car, either by riveting it in place of the bogus car's original VIN or by cutting out the section of the wrecked car's dash structure that contains the VIN, and grafting it into the clone. You should know that VIN tampering is a Federal offense that carries big-time jail terms if convicted – and fortunately, it's pretty easy to identify when (and therefore, by whom) the tampering was conducted.

Another way—far sneakier—for someone to create a convincing clone is to visit a car show, find a car that they want to clone, then simply record the VIN number and all the specifics about the car—possibly even by interviewing the owner and taking as many pictures as they want, with the owner's blessing. Then, once back home, they can create or order replacement VIN and trim plates with the original car's VIN and trim data (from the show) and attach them to their clone car. The scary part of such cars is that it's ridiculously easy for the criminal to further legitimize the car by registering it, since many states do not require a title, and there's no way for one state's motor vehicle bureau to know that the car may—or may not—be registered elsewhere! (And don't

forget that a lot of "trailer queen" show cars aren't registered, anyway.) Worse yet: if a potential buyer runs the VIN through a registry of service like PHS (formerly Pontiac Historic Services), the information will come back completely correct!

Unfortunately, there's no way for an impartial third-party (like the police or a court) to be completely sure which car is the legitimate one. Remember those questions that the criminal asked the owner of the original car? Well, the owner may have willingly given away the car's entire history, allowing the criminal to tell the same story, resulting in a "he said, she said" kind of standoff that can be extremely difficult for the legitimate owner to overcome.

Bogus paperwork is even easier to fake, thanks to modern computer scanners and laser printing equipment. It's trivially simple for a criminal to scan a factory invoice, add a couple desirable options, then print out a very convincing bogus version of the paperwork. The documents can then be aged to further the illusion.

Your best course of action is to be highly skeptical of any proof offered to you, and, when possible, do your own background checks. But still don't let your guard down then.

And if (or when) you own a collector car, don't let anyone see its VIN or trim/fender tags, and don't give out too much info when talking about the car. At shows, it's always a good idea to cover any VIN or trim plates (fender tags on Mopars) or stampings—at least the sequence number portion, which is the unique part. And make sure you keep your car registered, so that there's always a legal paper trail back to you.

---

encoded into the data plate varies, but typically includes the VIN, which is more than just a serial number. At a minimum, it tells the car's year, body style, engine type, and sequential production number.

The data plate also has coding for the original color (or color combination), interior trim scheme (upholstery type and color), original transmission type, rear axle ratio, engine type, and rated horsepower, and sometimes the carburetor configuration and engine compression ratio. Data plates are rich information sources.

Here's an example from a reader who wrote to me because of the "Questions & Answers" column that I write for *Old Cars News Weekly*:

"I bought a 1968 Ford fastback from an estate. It was a one-owner, garage-kept car with 110,000 miles on the 390-cid V-8 engine. There was no owner's manual in the car. It has the original spare and bias ply tires. What I want to know is whether my car is a Fairlane XL or a Galaxie XL. Is it a low-production car? The VIN is 8J60Y133891. The body number is 63C. The data plate lists Y for the color code and 4A for the

trim, 72 for the District number, 1 for the axle, and U for the transmission. The only things that are not original to the car are the jack and trunk liner. It has XL markings on the interior door trim and on both sides of the top plus the hood and trunk emblems."

Using the *Catalog of American Car ID Numbers 1960–1969* as my reference source, I responded as follows:

"Your car's body code 63C makes it a Galaxie 500 XL. The VIN tells that your car is a 1968 model, built in Los Angeles, is a Galaxie XL, and has the 390 V-8. The last 8 digits of the VIN are the car's production sequence number. Ford built 50,048 Galaxie 500 XL two-door fastback hardtops in 1968. Color code Y stands for Gold Metallic while the trim code 4A represents black vinyl. Your car's district code is Atlanta. The rear axle ratio is 2.75:1 and the transmission is Ford's C6 automatic."

See how much information is packed into the data plate? In my response I added the production total for this

These books are very helpful for restorers of Chevrolet products. They explain the coding on serial numbers and identify the application of engines and other mechanical components by their part numbers.

model, a figure best found in a reference source such as a book from the *Standard Catalog of American Cars* series (Krause Publications). Since the last six digits of the VIN represent a sequential production number, this number often leads to confusion with the total production number. In the example above, where Ford built 50,048 Galaxie 500 XL two-door fastback hardtops in 1968, the production sequence in the VIN (133891) is not—obviously— a number representing only Galaxie fastback hardtops. Rather it is a sequential number for all production at that assembly plant to date for the car's model year. However, if you have an indication of that plant's total production for the year, the sequential production number gives a pretty good indication of when (what month) the car was built.

As I mentioned in Chapter 3, there may be a registry or service like PHS for Pontiacs or Galen's Tag Service for Chrysler vehicles that can provide you with a packet of information about your specific vehicle, including a copy of the original factory invoice, listing all the options with which the vehicle was originally ordered.

Helpful engine coding information may also be stamped on the engine block. Here it may be possible to learn which assembly plant built the engine and the month and day it was built, as well as specifics about the engine itself: its displacement, horsepower, and likely transmission configurations. In cases in which the engine coding is not as detailed, you'll at least be able to tell the year the engine was built and the car into which it was installed. Again, you will need a reference book to help you locate

Factory ads and sales brochures give details about the vehicle's appearance when new, as well as special features.

and decipher the coding. For Chevrolet engines of the V-8 era, the most thorough reference source is a series of books titled *Chevrolet by the Numbers*, written by Alan L. Colvin and published by Robert Bentley Publishers (see Resources for publisher's address). The books in this series, which typically cover five-year spans, not only give the coding information for engine numbers, but also detail the casting numbers—which not only identify the engine type, but also its build date. Other casting numbers can be found on intake and exhaust manifolds, and in a "factory-new" restoration these should match with the engine casting. Colvin's Chevrolet engine reference books are equally thorough in helping restorers pair up all related engine parts.

Less detailed, but still helpful engine coding information for a variety of cars can be found in the *Standard*

SSION BELS	92 TIRE PRESS TABLE CODE	93 CONS. INFO. TABLE CODE	94 BUMPER HT. CODE	95	96 ENG. CERT	97	98	99	100	101	102	103	104	105
6	FAB		A	USAV8 2	PF012C677	11615	MDR258	65	21 OG	S	22 68	96 96	YEL9	GY W66

Some of the most helpful books to a restorer are factory assembly instruction manuals and shop manuals. Assembly manuals contain the detailed drawings used by the assembly line workers who originally put your car together, while service manuals were for mechanics to use to fix them. GM had separate chassis and body service manuals.

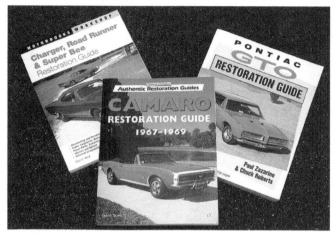

Restoration guides for your specific make, model, and year are a great complement to factory assembly and service manuals. Many are filled with restoration tips and techniques based on years of experience rebuilding the cars, which can often be very different from how the factory originally bolted cars together.

Catalog of American Cars series from Krause Publications and *The Serial Number Book for U.S. Cars 1900–1975* by Grace Brigham, published by Motorbooks. To see how these sources are used, let's say you own a 1964 Dodge Dart GT two-door hardtop. Mopar (Plymouth, Dodge, DeSoto, Chrysler) cars from the mid-1960s are popular collectibles because of their out-of-the-mainstream European-influenced styling, slimmer size, and sound engineering—including strong, long-life engines. Although Dodge offered its 1964 Dart with both V-8 and six-cylinder powerplants, the highly reliable Slant Six was the more popular engine choice. Let's assume the Dart we're talking about has the Slant Six, but since these engines were built in different sizes, you're not sure which engine is in the car. The Dart ID Number reference in the *Standard Catalog of American Cars 1946–1975* shows the engine code prefix, stamped on the right side of the block, to be V-17 for the 170-cid Slant Six and V-22 for the 225-cid engine. It'll take more sleuthing to crack the casting codes of this and other engines—that information sometimes can be found in reference books, including service manuals, and other times in technical articles appearing in club publications.

A question sure to come up in the restoration process is which other models, or even makes of cars or light-duty trucks, used the same or similar parts—body pieces as well as mechanical components. Knowing that a given part was used more broadly than on just your car greatly increases the likelihood of finding a replacement, whether it be used, new and unused (called New Old Stock, or NOS), or a faithful reproduction. First, though, you have

to know what other cars or trucks shared the same parts. This information is found in a *Hollander Interchange Manual*. Originally, the Hollander manuals were compiled to help auto salvage yards and independent repair shops determine applications for used parts. Because of their extreme usefulness to collector car and light truck restorers, however, Hollander manuals with parts interchange information reaching to the 1920s have been reprinted and are readily available.

I mention the Hollander books helping with parts for both cars and light-duty trucks because very typically the mechanical components of these vehicles interchanged. When my younger son needed a rear brake drum to replace a badly worn part on his 1970 Dodge truck, the Hollander manual told us that full-size Dodge car rear drums were the same. We easily located a car with the needed part in good condition in a nearby salvage yard—in those years Dodge built lots more cars than trucks.

Another example of the usefulness of the Hollander parts interchange books comes from the "Questions & Answers" column, where I received the following letter asking this:

"I have run ads two or three different times for a left side door to fit a 1969 Ford XL two-door hardtop. I have been offered a door from a 1970 XL convertible and one from a two-door hardtop. I have old crash repair books from when I was in business back in the 1960s, so I know they have different part numbers. I need confirmation from an interchange book to

SION 92	TIRE PRESS. TABLE CODE	93 CONS. INFO. TABLE CODE	94 BUMPER HT. CODE	95	96 ENG. CERT	97	98	99	100	101	102	103	104	105	10
6	FAB		A	USAV8 2	PF012C677	11615	MDR258	65 21 OG	S	22 68 96 96	YEL9			GY W660	

know whether either door will fit. The inside remote to open the door is completely different from 1969 to 1970. Could this hardware be switched with no hacking on the door or trim panels?

Checking the 35th edition of the *Hollander Auto-Truck Interchange Manual*, I was able to provide this response: "Ford's 1969 full-size models were all new for '69 and underwent only very minor changes, primarily limited to a different grille and taillight treatment, for 1970. Since the bodies didn't change, there should be no problem using a 1970 full-size Ford door on your 1969 XL. According to the *Hollander Interchange Manual*, doors from Ford's 1969 full-size two-door hardtop, fastback, and convertible are all the same. It looks like either door you've been offered should work. To make sure there's no mounting problems, and for appearance, you'll probably want to use hinges, door lock hardware, and interior panels from your '69, assuming you have these parts."

While we might expect to find interchangeable parts within a family of models, like the Dodge car/truck brake drum and Ford hardtop, convertible, and fastback door examples above, parts also interchange between different makes of cars. Here's a rather extreme example. In 1968 Buick offered its compact Special with an in-line six-cylinder engine coupled to a manual transmission. If you are familiar with Buicks, you're likely to suspect something a little odd. Buick built its reputation on silky smooth straight-eight engines. When Buick introduced a V-8 in 1953, the new engine's performance potential rocketed Buick to the Number 3 sales position by 1955. When a smaller, more fuel-efficient engine was needed for the company's compact line, Buick engineers designed an advanced aluminum V-8. After the aluminum engine developed cooling problems in the hands of consumers, a V-6 became the engine offering for Buick's compact models. (The aluminum V-8's cooling problems were easily correctable and this engine went on to enjoy long and distinguished service with Rover and Morgan in England.) So what was the source of the in-line six Buick offered in 1968? Chevrolet, of course—but then what's so odd about sharing engines within the corporate family? Nothing, really, but the transmission coupled to that engine is another story. It was supplied by Ford. Can you imagine

Left: *You'll also need good sources for parts and tools, too. Catalogs and Web sites for the Eastwood Company, Summit Racing Equipment, Sears' Craftsman tool line, and Northern Tool & Equipment not only have the right tools and supplies for the job, but they're also filled with ideas and information.* **Right:** *Finally, enthusiast publications like these can be great sources of information for your restoration. Technical articles often explain how to restore or rebuild various aspects of the cars, and the features show you how things should look. And, of course, the ads are helpful for finding parts and service suppliers. These days, there are specific publications for just about every make—there are even some for specific models, like Corvettes or Mustangs.*

SSION ELS	92 TIRE PRESS TABLE CODE	93 CONS. INFO TABLE CODE	94 BUMPER HT. CODE	95	96 ENG. CERT	97	98	99	100	101	102	103	104	105
6	FAB		A	USAV8 2	PF012C	677	11615	MDR258	65 21 OG	S	22 68 96 96		YEL9	GY W66

Researching a vehicle should start with its Vehicle Identification Number, or VIN, to authenticate the make, model/body style, and year, among other info. The restoration guide books can help you decode the info contained in your car's VIN, as can many sources online. But be careful not to give out your VIN number or to let strangers see it; treat it like your Social Security number to avoid cons and scams. This photo shows only part of this car's VIN.

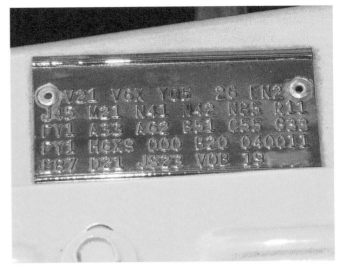

A trim or data tag, like this one attached to the inner fender of a Dodge Challenger, contains a wealth of information about your vehicle beyond what's known from the VIN, including its original color and original interior color and fabric. Chrysler vehicles even tell you the engine, transmission, and numerous other options. Again, for security reasons, don't let anyone who doesn't need to see your trim tag.

On many collector cars, engine assemblies were stamped at the factory to indicate which engine model it is (e.g., a Ram Air II vs. a Ram Air III). The "XS" seen here indicates this engine is some kind of GTO Ram Air engine, but to know which one, we need to dig further. The "312299" is the sequential engine ID number (similar to a VIN) that was assigned by the plant in which it was built.

the reaction if dyed-in-the-wool Buick owners had sensed that their cars were fitted with Ford transmissions! Now there's an interesting tidbit of information that, yes, you can pick up from a Hollander manual.

In researching parts sources we need to realize that sometimes the parts themselves tell the story. This is particularly true of bearings and bushings—which in many respects are "universal" items. Let's say you've disassembled a starter from a mid-1950s Studebaker and discover a worn armature bushing. Rather than seek out a Studebaker parts source, you can simply drive over to an auto parts store (not one of the "blister wrap" outlets, but a full-service store like NAPA or Car Quest) and ask the counter clerk for a bushing matching the ID and OD (inside and outside diameter) of the application. (In this case, the OD is taken from the bushing hole in the starter end plate and the ID from the armature shaft.) If the bushing matching these dimensions is a little longer than the hole in the end plate, the excess can be carefully trimmed off. The same approach applies to bearings, although here the width needs to match up as well. And there are other examples. Clutch plates sometimes interchange between completely dissimilar vehicles (the overall dimension of the clutch, number of splines, and diameter of the hole for the shaft serve as the basis of the match). Likewise with piston rings. A friend found he could use rings for a Chevy "Stovebolt" six as part of the rebuild kit for his Classic British Lagonda engine, the match-up measurements in this case being the cylinder bore size and piston groove dimensions from the Lagonda engine.

Unlocking a collector car's story becomes easy as you learn what resources to use. More often than not the most helpful tips come from fellow restorers. I asked a collector car owner who'd traced his car through six previous owners

ISSION LABELS	92 TIRE PRESS. TABLE CODE	93 CONS. INFO. TABLE CODE	94 BUMPER HT. CODE	95	96 ENG. CERT	97	98	99	100	101	102	103	104	105
6	FAB		A	USAV8 2	PF012C	677	11615	MDR258	65 21 OG	S	22	68 96 96	YEL9	GY W66

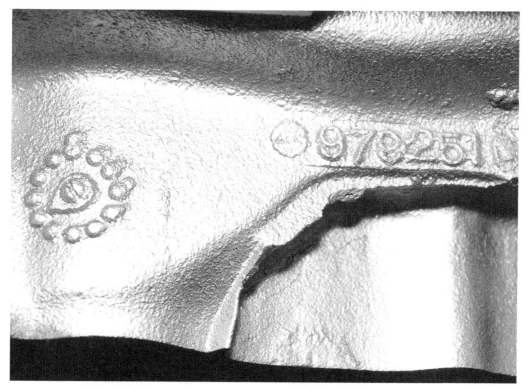

The same "XS" engine also features a casting number of 979251[?]—the last character is unreadable. Reference materials did not contain that number, but did have a similar number with an XS code, which suggests this is just a slightly newer revision of a 1968 GTO Ram Air II engine block, which is backed up by the Ram Air II-only (in 1968) four-bolt main bearing caps.

A variation of "matching numbers" is "date-code correct." As its name implies, the parts and assemblies have date codes that suggest they would have been available on the vehicle at the time the vehicle was built, even though they may not match the serial number of the vehicle to which they're fitted. In other words, they're the same as the parts that were installed originally, just not the very same parts that were originally installed. Again, using the XS engine block, we see that its date code is D247, which breaks down as being cast on April 24, 1967.

how he did it. I love a simple solution: he'd filled out a form at the Motor Vehicle Department and paid a search fee. The department's computer did the rest. Sometimes you'll hit a snag, he explained, when the car has been sold across state lines. Then you need to start the search over again at the Motor Vehicle Department in that state. Not critical information in most cases, but valuable perhaps if you've

been told your car was once owned by a celebrity, or for the same reasons some people like to trace their family tree.

Like going into an attic and discovering an old trunk packed full of someone's memories, museums and libraries contain treasure troves of information that may fill in details of your car's story that no individual is likely to know. I've tapped the phenomenal research archives of

43

SSION BELS	92 TIRE PRESS TABLE CODE	93 CONS. INFO. TABLE CODE	94 BUMPER HT. CODE	95		96 ENG. CERT	97	98	99	100	101	102	103	104	105
6	FAB		A	USAV8 2		PF012C677	11615	MDR258	65 21 OG	S	22 68 96 96	YEL9		GY W66

Other parts, like this cylinder head, also had various casting and stamped identification numbers. The 722 on this Pontiac head tells us that it's a rare, 1969 Ram Air IV head. Date codes are elsewhere and can be used to verify whether a certain head would have been installed on a particular vehicle.

Engines and rear axle assemblies also featured identification numbers and even paint markings that were assembly line "shorthand" to indicate which transmission went into which car. This side cover casting number indicates it was for a 1969 Muncie four-speed. The main case and bearing retainer likewise have casting numbers, while the main case is also stamped with the last six characters of the original vehicle's VIN.

the Henry Ford Museum in Dearborn, Michigan, for a variety of details not limited to the Ford Motor Company and its products. Significant collections of automotive sales and product literature, including original factory photographs, engineering drawings and specifications, corporate correspondence, production figures, and vast volumes of other information can be found at the Detroit Public Library, Detroit, Michigan; the National Automotive Collection in Reno, Nevada; and the Antique Automobile Club of America's National Headquarters library in Hershey, Pennsylvania, to name the more prominent sources. In some instances, corporations have made

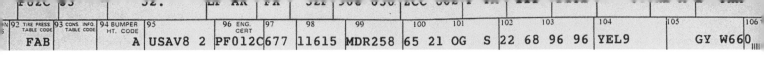

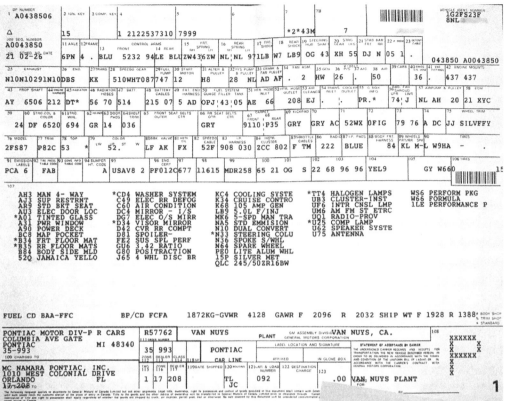

If you're lucky enough to find your car's broadcast sheet—which told assembly line workers which parts to install—or its original billing invoice, you can learn a ton about how your car was equipped at the factory. But again, don't let others see this document, because it contains sensitive information, such as the VIN, key codes, and other info that someone could use to perpetrate a crime.

their archives available to restorers and researchers, a prime example being Daimler Benz, whose characteristically thorough records on all its products reside at the Mercedes Benz Museum in Stuttgart, Germany. Corporate archives and literature collections from many other automotive manufacturers have been preserved by car museums and public libraries, as well as clubs, and in some instances the corporations themselves.

While learning your car's story is sure to fuel interest in its restoration, it's getting to be time to translate that interest into action. We'll start by getting the shop in order.

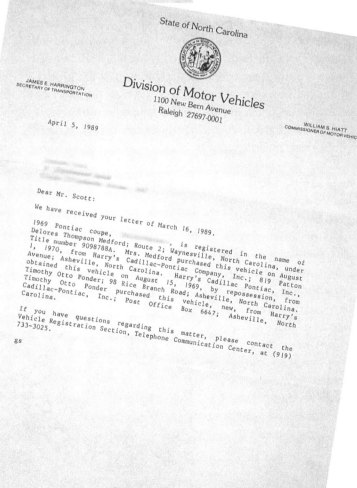

Title searches can tell you who the previous owners were and where they lived, which can enable you to contact them to get more info about your car than what you can learn simply from books or decoding its VIN or data tag info. If your car has been registered in multiple states, then you'll most likely need to contact each state's bureau of motor vehicles to have each perform a title search for you.

Chapter 5
Setting up Shop and Working Safely

Collector cars have been restored in driveways and carports, but realistically a restoration project requires indoor space—a two-car garage at a minimum. Even then, restoring a car in a residential neighborhood requires tolerant neighbors and zoning. The ideal restoration setting would be a shop, set up like a commercial repair facility, well lighted, insulated with a heating/cooling source for comfortable year-round working, a concrete floor, and plenty of storage and shelving space. Not many of us are likely to have the ideal facility, so let's explore some alternatives.

While it's possible to complete a frame-up restoration project in a residential two-car garage, neighbors protesting the noise of dents being hammered out of metal and zoning that may prohibit such activity present only the more obvious obstacles. Although the project may seem to only occupy one stall when the car is moved in, it will soon grow to fill both stalls and still you'll feel cramped for space. This means that for the duration of the project, which can be expected to take several years, the everyday cars will sit outside, joined by bikes, the lawn mower, yard tools, and whatever else currently enjoys indoor storage. Given these constraints, what are the options?

One solution is to team with a friend or relative who has a shop building, either for his own hobby use, farm, or business. A number of restorers have made arrangements of this sort, often pooling labor, tools, and talent in addition to shop space. One extremely energetic enthusiast tells me he and his partner turn out an average of one "factory-new" restoration a year, pooling their effort so that they work together Wednesday evenings—coinciding with their wives' night out—and individually other times during the week. Both have invested in tools, enabling them to equip the shop nearly as well as a professional restoration facility.

Another answer may be to rent space suitable for restoration work in a commercially zoned area. This has been my alternative to evicting the family cars from the garage. If space allows, another enthusiast may be invited to share the rent. I've heard of clubs renting or leasing buildings so that their members can share shop space. Also, some communities have "U-fix-it" centers where it's possible to rent a shop bay for the duration of a project. You probably wouldn't want to do the entire restoration in such a facility (the space rental costs could quickly get expensive), but such a center could provide relief from irate neighbors and

A huge shop, like this one, is an ideal environment to work in—it affords lots of room to move around while working on the car, and to maneuver parts and tools with minimal risk of damaging the car. And when you need to stop working on the car, you can leave things as is and pick right up where you left off when you return to the project—that's a huge help and saves tons of time during a restoration. Of course, few enthusiasts have such a facility at their disposal.

More common is a typical two-car garage, like this one. Though a bit cramped, and perhaps not quite as convenient, it can be more than adequate for your restoration project. Any workspace will do—even outdoors—but the bigger and better the workspace, the more conducive it will be to getting the project done quickly and conveniently.

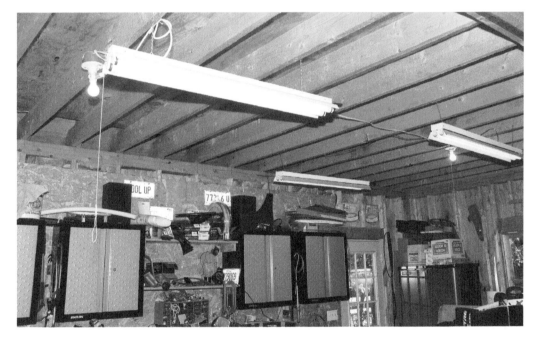

Proper lighting will make a . . . well . . . night and day difference in how your restoration projects turn out—and even how you approach them. A bright shop not only helps you see what you're doing better, but it's less dreary to work in, too, which has a measurable effect on your mental attitude throughout the project. Even these inexpensive fluorescent lights from a local construction supply store provide ample light to enable working late into the night.

zoning officials if you've decided to perform most of the restoration work in your garage.

For those contemplating restoring a collector car as a retirement activity, I'm told retirement communities have been set up on the car restoration theme, complete with leased space in a professional-quality shop building to interested residents. Here, too, there's an opportunity to share skills and labor as well as specialty tools on one another's projects, with separate storage and work space for each person's project.

A hobby/restoration shop is a common solution for many enthusiasts thinking of collecting cars as a long-term hobby. Beyond the obvious convenience, an advantage of owning your own shop is space to display car-related "automobilia"—posters, manufacturer or dealer signage, gas pumps, toy models, license plates—anything related to automobiles. Automobilia collections are the strongest value-appreciating area of the collector car hobby. A shop that affords space to display these items, which you're likely to pick up in the process of shopping for items related to

No matter what lighting you install in your shop, you'll also need some sort of work light. So-called "trouble" or "drop" lights should be avoided, because they pose a fire risk if gas were to splash on one, and you can get a nasty burn just by bumping one. Fluorescent or LED lights, like this rechargeable LED unit (which means no cord to tangle in the belts or fan!) are much handier and safer.

restoration, as well as room to work on the car and space to store parts, tools, and supplies, is every restorer's dream. The trick lies in making that goal a reality.

It's also worth mentioning "temporary" shelters that are available for relatively little money. Cover-It, Northern

Tool, and Portable Garage Depot are sources for temporary shelters that are akin to large tents with steel pole frames. They're available in a variety of sizes from single car storage shelters to ones large enough to accommodate a couple of semitrucks—with their trailers! Single car models can cost as little as $600–$700, though prices do climb to a few thousand for larger models. If set over a concrete slab, they can serve as an excellent storage and work shelter. And, if you live in a colder climate, using an inexpensive, torpedo-style, kerosene heater can often provide enough heat to make it reasonably comfortable to work in during moderate winter weather.

EQUIPPING THE SHOP

Whatever type of shop in which you're able to work, you'll need to equip it with a variety of tools and equipment that will be needed to remove parts, recondition them, and reassemble everything. Having the right tool for the job can make all the difference in the world between a job that progresses smoothly and quickly—or one that results in seemingly endless frustration and delays.

Basic Hand Tools

The most basic tools you'll need in whatever workspace you have are a good assortment of wrenches, ratchets, sockets, screwdrivers, pry bars, hammers, and others.

If you're setting up shop from scratch, you can often save money by purchasing a prepackaged tool set containing a variety of tools.

If you plan on working on your vehicle during the winter, you'll probably need some form of heat in your shop. The owner of this garage picked up a used but perfectly functional heater unit for next to nothing. Try to avoid heating systems that have an open flame (like many propane or K1 heaters), which might accidentally ignite gas fumes. And any heater should be kept off the ground and a safe distance from any combustible materials.

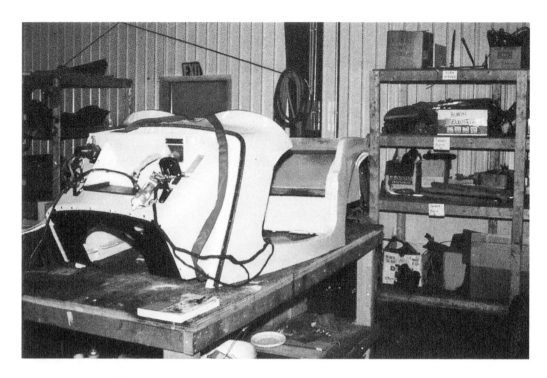

A sturdy workbench is the first priority for any shop. You can build the workbench yourself using 2×4 framing lumber and sheets of 4×8 plywood. John Twist, senior technician and proprietor of University Motors Ltd., a Grand Rapids, Michigan, restoration shop, has built his shop's workbenches to be rugged enough to support a car body.

Steel-constructed workbenches are ideal for welding and metal repair.

Sears' Craftsman tools are relatively inexpensive and conveniently available from local Sears stores or the store's Web site (www.sears.com). More importantly, they're generally held in high regard by automotive enthusiasts. One of the reasons folks like Craftsman hand tools is that they're backed by the best replacement guarantee in the business: if it breaks, you can return it to your local Sears store for a free replacement. The tools are generally excellent quality and very durable, but I've taken advantage of that guarantee on several occasions. It's a poor investment to buy tools that are not guaranteed; some are so poorly made they may not survive their first use.

Professional tools—such as those made by Mac and Snap-On—may not outlast a Craftsman piece, but they're likely to have better ergonomics and function better—they'll feel better in your hand and have a better fit on the part and provide more precise function. For example, a Snap-On ratchet has to turn only 5 degrees before engaging, as opposed to 15 or 30 degrees for the less expensive ratchets. The result is a better-performing, easier-to-use tool, which, for professionals at least, justifies the higher cost. The professional tool lines aren't sold in retail stores. Instead, they're sold by independent dealers directly to professional automotive service technicians right at their place of work, usually out of large vans. To buy from a Mac or Snap-On dealer, you can find their number in the phone book and arrange a visit to your address, call a local shop and find out when the dealer visits them so you can meet them there, or order from the company's Web site. Occasionally, you'll find these professional tools at a yard sale or listed on sites like eBay or Craigslist, or watch for shops that are going out of business and selling off their assets.

John Twist of the Grand Rapids, Michigan, MG restoration shop University Motors Ltd. has a maxim: "Never break a bolt." When buying your first wrench set, John advises, make it as light-duty as practicable. For a socket set, John suggests starting with ¼-inch or maximum of ⅜-inch drive. You can add the heavier duty ½-inch drive later when your hands have developed a "feel" for tightness. Larger ¾-

A LIST OF BASIC HAND TOOLS

A rather ordinary assortment of basic hand tools is usually sufficient to take things apart:

• **Wrenches (aka, "Spanners")**—Open- and box-end wrench sets (or combination wrenches, which feature one open end and the other boxed) are, perhaps, the most used tools in any mechanic's toolbox. These are needed to loosen bolts inaccessible to sockets or to hold the reverse side of bolts as they are loosened.

• **Socket sets**—¼- or ⅜-inch drive sockets and ratchets matching the measurement system used on the car being restored (metric, U.S. standard, etc.). You may also find that you need both shallow and "deep" sockets, as well as an assortment of 6-point and 12-point sockets. Six-point sockets are generally stronger and less prone to rounding a bolt head; however, 12-point heads are sometimes easier to work with. Elbows and extensions are common ratchet accessories to consider. And if you're working with air tools, you'll need sockets designed for such use (they usually feature heavier construction).

• **Adjustable wrenches**—Wheel bearings, rear axle, and other nuts may exceed socket and open- or box-end wrench sizes. Adjustable wrenches may allow you to work with larger fasteners that you occasionally encounter without the need to buy an expensive wrench. Note that adjustable wrenches are known for rounding fasteners, however, so they must be used with care.

• **Allen wrenches**—These are hexagonal-shaped rods that are inserted inside a fastener, as opposed to box-end wrenches that fit around a fastener. Allen wrenches are often used to tighten set screws on rocker arm locks, or on brake caliper retaining bolts.

Like sockets and wrenches, Allen wrenches need to match the car's measurement system: Standard U.S. or metric.

• **Screwdrivers**—Assorted screwdrivers, both Phillips and slotted, are commonly needed. The assortment should include long and short shanks, thin and thick blades. On many cars made since the mid-1980s, you may also need Torx drivers, which use a starlike recess in fasteners, or special Torx fasteners with a special tamper-proof stud in the middle of the recess.

• **Pliers**—Assorted pliers, including locking pliers (such as Vise-Grips) and tongue-and-groove pliers (such as Channel Lock) are handy for working with rounded-over bolts or other special situations.

• **Hacksaw**—A hacksaw and supply of fresh blades are useful for everything from restoring slots in screw heads to cutting rusted bolts. They're especially useful during the deconstruction phase of projects.

• **Metal files**—Files have multiple uses, from restoring the edges of rounded-over bolts to fitting parts and restoring stainless-steel trim.

• **Hammers**—Hammers and mallets always seem to have their uses for tapping parts into alignment or knocking them loose. A variety of sizes and styles are available for differing situations.

• **Alignment punches**—These are needed for all sorts of jobs, large and small.

• **Pry bars**—No, this doesn't mean large screwdrivers. Real pry bars are made to handle the forces you'll apply getting parts off or on . . . without bending or breaking, which could damage your car or injure you.

Of course, a shop is no good without tools, and when it comes to restoring a car, in addition to basic wrenches and sockets, you're likely to need specialized tools, like an air compressor, a hydraulic floor jack and sturdy jackstands, an engine hoist (which you can often rent) and even a creeper, among others.

MEASUREMENT UNITS

Wrenches and sockets are available in different measurement units, the most common of which are U.S. standard units, metric units, or British Standard Whitworth units.

If you're working on a European model, you'll likely need wrenches based on the metric system, often ranging from as small as 5 millimeters (mm) to 22 millimeters or larger. American vehicles made since about 1980 also typically use metric fasteners.

American cars and trucks made prior to about 1980 used fasteners based on the *inch* U.S. standard unit, requiring appropriately-sized wrenches, typically ranging from 5/16-inch through one inch. Note that some late 1970s through late 1980s American models may use a mixture of metric and U.S. standard fasteners, depending on when a specific component was designed.

Many British models made into the 1960s were equipped with fasteners based on a third system, the British Standard Whitworth. Whitworth wrench markings refer to the diameter of the bolt threads, not the distance across the flats of the bolt's head (to which both metric and American standard units refer). The Whitworth system is further complicated by the use of two different bolt head "standards" between bolts with BSW threads vs BSF (British Standard Fine) threads: BSF heads were originally one size smaller than BSW heads, until, during World War II, the head sizes were standardized on the BSF dimension.

If you've got a large enough (high enough) garage and plan to work on lots of cars in the future, you might want to consider installing either a two-post hydraulic lift, like this one, or perhaps a four-post model with ramps onto which you drive the car. Prices have come down considerably in the last few years, making them pretty affordable, and the four-post models can also be used to double your car storage abilities by putting two cars in one stall.

inch or 1-inch drive sockets aren't usually needed, unless you're working on big trucks or industrial equipment.

Other Essential Tools

Besides this assortment of hand tools, the basic tool set should also include an electric drill—preferably a heavier-duty model with a ¾-inch chuck and set of sharp drill bits. A small wire brush on a shaft that clamps into the drill chuck is very handy for cleaning small parts.

A hydraulic jack (preferably a rolling "floor" jack) to raise the car and a set of sturdy jack stands to support the car whenever its full weight is not resting fully on the tires should be considered critical for any shop, if only from a safety standpoint, but they're also very convenient.

For electrical work, you'll need a soldering gun, flux, and a roll of 50/50 solder.

A transparent face mask or safety goggles to wear while wire brushing or doing other activities that could send debris flying into your face or eyes, or when you're working with chemicals is also essential. Most find the full face mask offers better protection and is more comfortable to wear.

Other handy items include an assortment of clamps (recommended are clamps that are easily adjustable and can be applied with one hand) available from building supply stores; a rivet tool and supply of assorted rivets; a dental pic, for maneuvering or positioning tiny items; and a magnet on a long, retractable stem for retrieving dropped metal parts or tools.

Lighting

A dimly lit shop isn't very inviting and can actually be dangerous, because of the many cords and parts that can hide in the dark. Proper lighting makes every job easier, and it's absolutely essential for body and paint work.

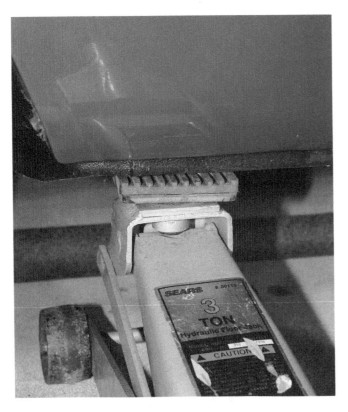

Of course, a good old-fashioned hydraulic floor jack is sufficient for nearly all jobs. Notice the rubber-covered saddle on this one, which prevents it from marring finished chassis components and minimizes the chance of the car slipping off it.

High-quality jackstands are essential items in every shop. You've heard the horror stories. **Never** *work under a car that's resting solely on a jack. And make sure your jackstands are rated for at least 50 percent higher than the weight you'll be resting on them, for a little safety margin.*

As with other tools, there are different lights for different situations.

A portable shop light can be easily positioned close to the work, to provide extra illumination where you need it most. The most common type of shop light—the "trouble light"—uses an incandescent bulb encaged in a protective wire shield with a hook on the top, to allow it to be hung near the work. Trouble lights have earned their name, and not for avoiding trouble—they cause trouble. Don't buy one. Instead, purchase a portable fluorescent shop light, which will not only give better illumination, but will avoid the "trouble" that can occur with a trouble light. The biggest risk of using a trouble light is gasoline dripping or spraying onto the light—which will instantly burst the bulb, igniting the gasoline. If the drip or spray has a supply source, you could see your whole car or shop or even yourself engulfed in flames—in an instant. This has happened. Another problem with inexpensive trouble lights is that the hook on the end of the shield never seems to align the bulb with the work. You take the time to hang the light properly near the work, then the light diabolically swings around so that the bulb shines fully in your face, with the

reflector on the back of the grid shielding the work. A fluorescent shop light avoids both these problems. Some are even battery powered, eliminating the cord, which can be inconvenient to work around or can get caught in moving parts, like a spinning fan, causing serious risk of injury or damage to your car.

For general illumination in your shop, you should seriously consider purchasing and installing fluorescent shop lights. Building supply shops like Home Depot and Lowe's often stock 48-inch, dual-lamp units at very inexpensive prices, making it feasible to buy enough to place them all around your ceiling. Gary Beineke, the creator of several 1971 Chrysler "wing cars" based on factory plans that were never put into production, equipped his two-car garage-sized shop with no less than 16 such light assemblies, and put them on several different switches, allowing him to vary how much lighting he has at the flip of a switch. He even has several units mounted vertically in the corners, which are especially helpful when doing bodywork.

The shop's brightness can be increased immeasurably by painting the walls, ceiling, and even the floor a light color, preferably white.

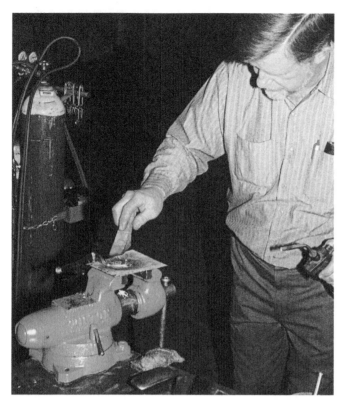

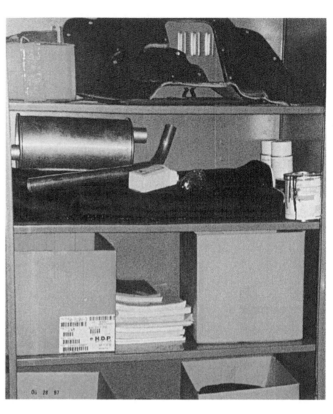

A rugged vise, like this trusty Wilton model, is an indispensable tool. If you spot a bench vise in a tool sale or auction with the Wilton name, be assured that this tool is nearly indestructible. Gregg Purvis, instructor for the University Motors Restoration Seminar, uses the Wilton vise for a leading demonstration.

You'll also need plenty of shelving to store spare and restored parts. Metal shelving like this can work great, but make sure it's sturdy enough to support whatever parts you elect to set upon its shelves.

Inexpensive wooden shelves can be constructed from scrap lumber. These were built to make use of the normally unused space under a steeply pitched roof. Old kitchen cabinets and counters are also excellent for storage (or as work surfaces) and can often be picked up for free when neighbors or friends are renovating their home.

Along with the basic tool kit you'll need specialty tools like this assortment of body hammers and dollies. The Eastwood Company

Workbench

Wood and steel benches are available for purchase from a variety of sources, like Sears or Northern Tool. Many have terrific features like numerous mounting points for vises or other tools, or adjustable legs. However, with some basic carpentry skills and tools, you can cost-effectively construct a workbench yourself using 2×4 or 2×6 framing lumber. By building the workbench yourself, you can customize the height of the legs to place the work surface at a comfortable working height for you—higher or lower, to match your stature—so that you won't be hunched over as you work at the bench. To make the bench sturdy, be sure to triangulate (i.e., add angled bracing to) the legs at both the end and long dimensions. And if you expect to need to move it, you can set it on casters—but make sure at least two casters are locking models, so that you can keep the workbench stationary when you don't want it to move.

To make the workbench durable and suitable for a variety of automotive-type work, cover it with sheet metal; a heating/air conditioning contractor should be able to direct you to a steel supply source, or look in your yellow pages. Sheet metal will allow you to weld on it without burning the wood, or you can rebuild a carburetor or spray parts cleaners without them soaking into the wood. The sheet metal can be held down with screws or machine bolts with the heads recessed into the metal so that parts can be moved around easily. For a really finished job, the ends can be capped with angle iron.

Vise

The workbench will need a rugged vise that's large enough to hold hefty mechanical parts like a driveshaft or control arm. As with other tool purchases, you should avoid no-name tools or those from discount marts, since such tools often break when stressed, potentially injuring you or damaging your car.

Sears sells sturdy vises. Another trusted name is Wilton. If you spot a bench vise in a tool sale (yard sale or auction) with the Wilton name, be assured that this tool is nearly indestructible.

Bench Grinder

The shop also needs a bench grinder, mounted either on the workbench or on a self-standing pedestal that can be securely bolted to the floor. The grinder will serve a variety of purposes—sharpening drill bits and chisels, deburing parts, even fitting small parts. If a wire wheel is mounted to one of the grinder's arbors, the tool can be used to clean bolt threads and remove paint and rust from other small items. My bench grinder is used daily for these sorts of purposes and is indispensable.

Shop Vacuum

For cleanup, you'll want a shop-duty vacuum cleaner. Again, Sears is a good source. If you're keeping a tight rein on the cash flow, you'll find a canister-style vacuum cleaner purchased for a few dollars at a yard sale will also do the job. I've kept a second-hand canister vacuum in my shop for years; they come with a greater assortment of attachments and work better for cleaning in small spaces than an industrial vacuum cleaner.

Specialty Tools

The basic tools described above will let you overhaul the majority of a car's subassemblies. However, there are a number of jobs—mechanical work, sheetmetal work,

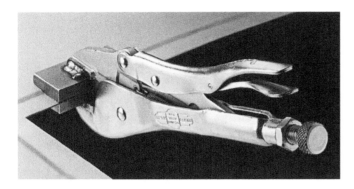

Other metalworking tools include flanging pliers, used to make patch panels for repairing body rust. The Eastwood Company

Power metal shears take the effort out of cutting out damaged metal and shaping repair pieces.

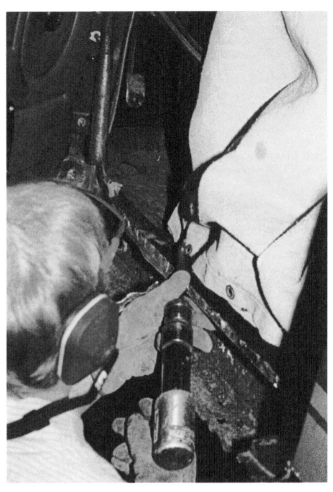

If body rust is extensive, you'll want to invest in an air chisel and an air compressor capable of powering this and other air-driven tools. Quality professional-grade tools from manufacturers like Snap-On give far superior service to discount tools from an off-shore source.

interior trim work, and paint refinishing—for which special tools are required to do the job correctly.

Torque Wrench—Top on the list is a torque wrench, used to tighten bolts to proper tension. Without a torque wrench, you'll be guessing at proper tightness, which means you're likely to overtighten or undertighten the bolt. Either condition creates problems. If you overtighten you risk breaking the bolt—something you'll wish you hadn't done if it's an exhaust manifold stud or a bolt in some other application that tightens into a casting where the broken portion can't be easily removed. If you undertighten, the assembly may work itself apart—as in the case of a wheel coming loose and causing the car to go out of control, or a connecting rod bolt that backs out, causing the rod to fail, destroying the engine. With a torque wrench, you have the satisfaction of knowing you're drawing bolts to their engineered tightness. Torque specifications for engine and chassis bolts—including wheel lugs—are typically listed in the service manual.

Taps and Dies—When a bolt does break, or you encounter a stud broken off in an earlier repair, the hole into which the bolt threads will need to be redrilled and the threads restored. The tools used to cut and restore threads consist of a set of taps and dies. Besides cutting and restoring threads, a tap and die set is also very useful for chasing (cleaning and sharpening) threads on bolts

Other useful tools include this specially designed bit for drilling out spot welds.
The Eastwood Company

or studs before reassembly. As with other tools, tap and die sets can range from inexpensive, poor-quality sets to high-priced, high-quality sets. Because of their lesser quality steel and poorly designed accessory pieces, the low-cost sets should be avoided. It's also worth noting that there are two types of taps: thread-cutting taps are for cutting new threads in a hole that previously had none, while thread-chasing taps are for freshening previously-tapped threads. The difference is that chasing taps remove less material, ensuring the remaining threads are strong enough to provide proper grip on a bolt's or stud's threads to hold the proper torque.

Other specialty tools you may find yourself needing at some point include: gear pullers and installers, piston ring compressors, tubing cutters and benders, electrical pliers, hog-ring pliers, door panel removal tools, micrometers, various gauges, and any of a number of tools for working on cylinder heads, and an assortment of bodywork tools for fixing dents and block sanding and other jobs.

The nice thing about specialty tools is that most don't need to be purchased until you're working in the area of the car where they're needed. With this in mind, special tools required for the restoration projects described in this book will be listed as they're called for in the applicable chapter. And remember that you might be able to rent items like coil spring compressors, ball joint removal and installation tools, and others from local auto parts stores or

tool rental companies. Or borrow them from friends who have already made the investment.

Larger Tool Investments

Depending on the work you need to perform on your collector car, you may find that you need to invest in some large and relatively expensive tools. While some are certainly optional, their use can greatly increase the speed with which a job can be performed, and they may have a significant impact on the quality of the job that you're undertaking. Of course, some jobs may be impossible without certain tools—like a welder for grafting in replacement sheetmetal patch panels.

Air Compressor—An air compressor with sufficient capacity to power air-driven tools, along with a sandblaster and paint spray gun, may be the collector car restorer's single largest tool investment. The limitations of working without an air compressor will be felt not only in time delays while you're waiting for jobs you could otherwise have done yourself, but also in money spent paying for services that could purchase this highly versatile tool. For all-around use, you'll need a unit powered by at least a 5 horsepower motor with a sustained air supply of 20 cfm. To power such a tool your shop will need to be wired for 220-volt service, which may require beefing up your shop's wiring. You'll find air compressors of the required capacity for sale everywhere, including many of the large discount building supply and home improvement marts. Campbell-Hausfeld and Ingersoll Rand are two trusted names of commercial-grade compressors. For less regular duty, Sears' Craftsman compressors may be adequate.

What you'll appreciate most is an air compressor's ability to turn large jobs into small ones—rust removal, for example. You can scrape and sand for hours and never really scour away all traces of rust. Or you can sandblast (or bead-blast) a corroded part and reduce it to bare metal in just a couple minutes. The same applies to painting. Without an air compressor and paint spray gun, your painting efforts are limited to aerosol cans or a brush. Although satisfactory for small parts, neither gives professional results on large surfaces. You'll find a similar advantage from being able to power air-driven tools, such as grinders, sanders, cutter tools, and wrenches. Not only does the work go faster, but also with greater accuracy. Another advantage is that air-driven tools typically cost less than their electric-powered counterparts.

And you'll appreciate having an air compressor in your shop in countless other ways, not necessarily related to restoring a collector car. It can be used to inflate bike tires, air mattresses, and inner tubes, and for other jobs. I even use mine to "dust off" the workbench.

Welding Equipment—Welding equipment—either gas or arc—presents a second large tool investment. In the metal repair chapter we'll discuss the advantages and disadvantages of the two major welding methods, flame and arc, and comment on which type of welding is easier for the amateur restorer to perform. But from the standpoint of usefulness, a gas-welding outfit is one of the handiest tools in the shop. Professional automotive technicians commonly refer to the welding torch as their "gas wrench"—meaning that the torch's heat is unmatched for loosening rust-frozen bolts. A torch's heat not only makes the job of removing stubborn bolts easier, but also helps prevent the bolt from breaking in the process of turning it loose—something you want to avoid happening. A welding torch can also be used to cut through damaged or corroded metal, a rusted-out exhaust system, for example, making quick work of what might otherwise be tedious disassembly tasks.

As a compromise, especially if you plan to purchase arc welding equipment for metal repair, lower-cost portable gas-welding outfits, which are commonly available, provide enough heating, cutting, and light-duty welding capacity to rank their purchase almost a must on the shop tool list.

Buffing Wheel—A buffing motor with assorted buffing and polishing wheels not only enables restoration of dull and damaged interior and exterior brightmetal trim prices, but may also be useful for refinishing magnesium or aluminum wheels and giving a gleaming sheen to brass and aluminum engine parts. Each of these larger investment tools takes some skill and practice to use, though the learning curve can be softened by instructional videotapes available from restoration tool suppliers such as the Eastwood Company.

The list of helpful and desirable tools could go on almost indefinitely—parts washers, sand blasters, engine hoists, engine stands, hydraulic presses, sheetmetal brakes, wheel dollies, or vehicle lifts. In some cases, you may need the tool's use only once, so does it make practical sense to buy an expensive tool for such limited use? Maybe. If restoring collector cars looks to be a long-term activity or if you do lots of tool swapping with friends who may help out with other items, you may be able to justify the expense.

Metal repair requires access to a welder. This stitch welder is easier and faster than conventional arc welding. The Eastwood Company

A portable MIG (Metal Inert Gas) welder like this Lincoln Electric model is relatively inexpensive and incredible handy. It can be used for body repair, frame repairs and reinforcement, and other tasks.

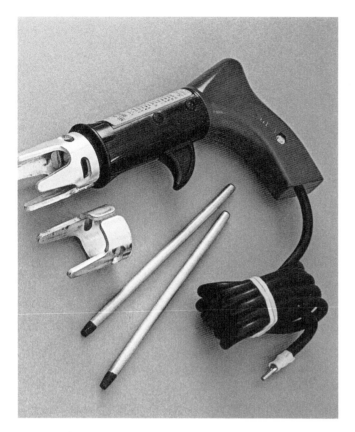

Duplicating factory welds often requires spot welding. This special gun allows spot welds to be made from only one side of the metal. The Eastwood Company

SUPPLIES

While setting up shop you'll also want to stock supplies used at various stages of the restoration process, including:

- Carburetor Cleaner—very useful as a solvent and cleaning agent
- Spray Penetrant (like WD-40)—for loosening hard-to-turn fasteners
- Masking Tape and Duct Tape—great for holding things in place during assembly
- Silicone Caulk—a multipurpose sealant, also useful for positioning and holding small parts and medallions
- Shop Rags or Shop Towels—for general cleanup
- Razor Blades—a great cutting tool
- Steel Wool—for cleaning and scouring
- An "old-fashioned" Oil Can with light oil or Automatic Transmission Fluid (ATF)—for lubrication and loosening stubborn fasteners
- Lithium Grease—for lubrication
- Construction Adhesive (like Liquid Nails)—various adhesion uses
- Upholstery Adhesive—for holding fabric in place
- Plastic Bags (garbage bags or dry cleaner bags)—for sealing and storing restored parts
- Clean-up Solvent (not gasoline)—biodegradable solvents are recommended for cleaning grease-soaked parts
- White Chalk—for temporary markings on upholstery or metal panels
- Fire Extinguishers—two minimum

WORKING SAFETY—MAKING SHOP SAFETY A STATE OF MIND

Safety is generally the last thing a hobbyist thinks about. Yet there's lots of potential for damage and injury working on a collector car. It's for precisely this reason that we need to make safety a top priority—and a conscious part of our activity.

Working safely begins with wearing proper clothing; leather boots or shoes rather than lightweight athletic shoes; full body covering (shop pants and shirt); safety glasses or a face mask; gloves (white canvas or latex) when appropriate; and a respirator when spray painting or working with toxic chemicals. Safety also means keeping the shop well lit. If you can't see what you're doing, you risk injury to yourself and damage to your project. Fluorescent shop lights are inexpensive and easy to install. Give yourself good lighting and even your mood will be brighter. Mental attitude plays a big part in safety. Let your shop be a place of relaxation, not a way to work out your frustrations. At the first mistake, take a break. Either walk away from the project or do something else. I enjoy listening to the radio and keep a chair and supply of car magazines in my shop for such diversion.

It's important to be especially mindful of the potential hazards of common shop chemicals. Gasoline, which shouldn't be used to clean parts—but often is—and of course is stored in the car's gas tank, packs enormous explosive power. All that's needed to unleash its explosive energy is a tiny spark. Further, gasoline's fumes, which may still exist in combustible quantity in a seemingly empty container, are more potentially explosive than the liquid itself. Then there are paints and painting products, many of which are highly toxic—to the point that they could kill you. (The painting chapters give a detailed description of which painting products are toxic and the safety precautions.)

Arc welding, if not observed through a welder's shielded glass, can burn the retinas of the eyes, causing blindness. (The risk of vision damage from an arc flash is often greater to bystanders who may have wandered into your shop—so be very careful not to arc weld in the presence of children.) Gas welding exposes the careless user to the danger of burns or worse calamities if any number of welding safety cautions are not observed. Power tools also carry a risk, though more to limbs than life. And, tragically, every so

High on the priority list of larger tool investments is a sandblaster. This tool makes quick work of cleaning rusty metal.

Safety is a state of mind and includes such measures as securely supporting the vehicle on rugged jack stands before working underneath.

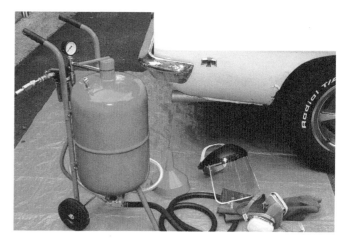

A portable media blaster lets you tackle larger jobs, like blasting all or part of a car's body, or its frame, or any object too large to fit in a blast cabinet. This reasonably priced Eastwood Company blaster also works with bicarbonate soda (a.k.a. baking soda) which is ideal for removing paint without damaging the underlying metal—or even glass, chrome, or plastic.

often we read of someone improperly jacking up a car and becoming severely injured when the support fails.

Safety is a state of mind—the attitude with which we approach our work. Most accidents could have been prevented if we had followed a few simple guidelines:

1. Quit when you feel frustration building. When everything seems to be going wrong, step back, consider the progress you've made, and take a break. Whatever obstacle you're trying to surmount will shrink in size with a fresh start.

2. Read and heed safety warnings on product labels and shop tools. Sure, the manufacturers put the labels on to avoid lawsuits, but nobody is going to sue if they're not injured or if nothing's broken.

3. Stay alert to safety. When you're working in your own shop, in familiar surroundings, it's easy to become casual—and careless. The idea that "I'll just leave the car on the jack instead of hunting for the jack stands" invites trouble.

HOW TO RAISE AND SUPPORT A CAR ON JACK STANDS

If you'll remember this simple line, "Jacks are for jacking, jack stands are for holding," you'll avoid the danger of a jack collapsing and the car falling on you while you're working underneath. It's a good idea to place a block of wood on top of the jack to even out the load—and never use a car's jack. One wonders just what a car's jack is good for, other than a boat anchor, but for shop use a stationary hydraulic jack, or better, a wheeled floor jack are the tools to use when elevating a car.

If the car needs to be raised more than a few inches off the floor, the correct procedure is to jack up the front, place jack stands under a secure location (behind the front cross-member, under the frame rails), then jack the rear of the car to the same height and support it with jack stands, then return to the front and repeat the process. If you jack the car too high in one motion, it may slip off the jack. As the car angles into the air, the jack has to move toward the car and the car toward the jack. Never jack up a car in gear! Leaving the car out of gear will allow it to roll in the direction of the jack. Also, if the car is in gear and the starter is accidentally engaged, the car will hop off the jack stands.

When the car is raised to the desired height and resting securely on jack stands, shake it to make sure it is steady on its supports. If the car gives any indication of falling, reposition the jack stands. Repeat this process until you are sure the car is stable and secure. If your shop has a sturdy overhead beam, slinging an anchoring chain under a sturdy support such as the front frame ends may give an extra measure of security before you crawl underneath.

Useful shop supplies include the items shown here. You'll find carburetor cleaner indispensable as a solvent and cleaning agent.

Special finish kits, such as this four-step painting set for reproducing a cadmium-plating look on brake system parts, are useful at many stages of the restoration process.

A SHOP SAFETY CHECKLIST

Use this list to establish safe working habits and monitor your safety awareness.

1. Avoid a messy shop. Clutter invites sloppy work habits; also, spilled grease and oil create fire hazards, especially in combination with power tools or a welding torch.

2. Keep parts and tools on shelves or in cabinets where they can be located easily and aren't lying about the floor inviting accidents.

3. Maintain sharp edges on cutting tools such as chisels and drill bits. The better the tools work, the less you'll have to.

4. Store any toxic chemicals in locked cabinets where they will be kept safely out of children's reach.

5. Always read tool and product health and safety warnings. Labels on chemical containers often list emergency antidotes such as washing the exposed area. When using chemicals that can be corrosive to exposed skin, such as phosphoric acid rust remover, keep a supply of water handy to rinse off any chemical that comes into contact with your skin.

6. Install a first-aid kit in your shop where it can be reached quickly.

7. If you are spray painting, install a ventilation system and wear a mask approved for the painting products you are using. Professional painters wear masks or suits ventilated to an outside air supply and paint in filtered spray booths that draw away toxic painting fumes.

8. Never work underneath a car that is raised off its tires unless it is securely supported by professional-grade jack stands.

9. Double up for safety. If you are working on an engine that is mounted in an engine stand, take the precaution of supporting the engine's weight with a chain or cable suspended from a sturdy overhead support.

10. Wear safety glasses and protective clothing when welding, grinding or cutting metal, sandblasting and similar activities, and when pouring toxic or corrosive chemicals that could splash against the skin or into the eyes.

11. Equip your shop with at least two fire extinguishers. Make sure the extinguishers can be easily reached and their location is clearly visible.

12. Use parts-cleaning fluid, preferably a biodegradable solution in a parts washer, for degreasing parts. Avoid cleaning parts in gasoline.

13. Be alert to the danger of shorts and sparks from old wiring. Disconnect and remove the battery before working on the car. Make sure your shop wiring will support the current load of your tools.

14. Develop the habit of anticipating the possible consequences of your actions. For example, never weld near a gas line or the car's gas tank. Remember that body panels may be backed with undercoating or upholstery. Welding on these panels could cause the car to catch on fire.

Chapter 6
Disassembly: Taking the Car Apart

I was enjoying the early May sunshine, doing errands around the house, when a friend called and said, "Let's take your car apart." I'd bought a Peugeot 405 MI-16, a sports sedan and a car in a category I consider late-model collectible. Peugeot pulled out of the U.S. market in 1991 and the MI-16, an upscale sports edition of the somewhat more common 405 model, had come to North America in very low numbers. My car had suffered a left front collision (the condition in which I bought it), so my friend was suggesting we remove the damaged parts to assess the extent of the repair, make a list of replacement items that would be needed, and get some momentum toward the car's restoration to "nearly new." It all sounded like a good idea—a pleasant afternoon of companionship and banter while we twisted wrenches and sized up the dimensions of the project. The second part was true; we did spend an enjoyable afternoon. However, as time would prove, a good idea it wasn't.

Several months later, when repairs to the front end—which turned out to be more extensive and required a much larger investment in replacement parts than I had anticipated—were completed, the car wouldn't run. (As a rule of thumb, any restoration project will cost three times the original estimate.) "Had to be running when it had the collision," my friend (who had sold me the car) sagely counseled. The car would start on just a couple of revolutions, but then the engine went ballistic, roaring off at ultrahigh idle and belching black smoke out the exhaust. Something was sure wrong and we hadn't tampered in any way with the engine. Unfortunately, as a later model, everything was computer controlled and we had no idea what had gone haywire inside the black box or even why. That answer came several months and nearly as many repair shops later, when the full-rich running problem was correctly traced to a scrambled or AWOL circuit in the ECU (electronic control unit—the computer that tells the engine what to do). But why had the computer "gone south?" As my friend said, the car had to be running to hit something. Turns out, the technician told us, moisture—that mortal enemy of electrical circuits—had gotten into the black box. But

Having been rebuilt and painted, this disc-brake caliper will be placed in a labeled box and set aside until needed.

the box sits way up under the hood. How could the ECU have gotten moisture sodden? Gulp! Must have been while the car sat waiting its turn in the body shop sans hood, one of the damaged parts my friend and I had removed on our sunny "havin' fun" afternoon.

I relate this story as a caution against the exuberance that often takes us over at the disassembly stage. Peter Egan, who writes a wonderfully entertaining monthly column for *Road & Track* magazine, relates going out to his garage one evening, mellow jazz playing on the CD, a few bottles of Guinness Stout in the workshop refrigerator, and in a fit of inspiration totally dismantling his MGB. When he stopped to consider the fruit of his evening's efforts, there lay the MG in piles of parts strewn about his garage. As Egan writes, after that moment there was no turning back. It was restoration with a vengeance or a trip to the salvage yard—nothing in between.

When your goal is a factory-new restoration, you're going to take the car completely apart, but not in a flurry of wrenches, chisels, and cutting torch. Instead the disassembly process needs to be slow and deliberate—so deliberate that you'll measure your progress in days, not hours. The pace is slow for three reasons: first, to document

A large tray is convenient for collecting all parts as they are removed. Later, the parts that will be reused can be cleaned and placed in labeled containers.

every disassembly step; second, to keep the disassembly from getting ahead of your enthusiasm and financial resources; and third, so as not to break anything.

DOCUMENTING HOW THE CAR CAME APART—SO YOU CAN PUT IT BACK TOGETHER

John Twist tells of a customer bringing his rare MGA Twin Cam engine in for rebuilding; it came in boxes and baskets. Not the kind of a project John likes to see, but this was an exception. Every part of the engine was meticulously labeled. "Shipping tags sprouted from every part," John related, "labeling every item, even down to which nuts held on the head." Now there's a model for disassembly. As the parts come off, tag them individually—or if you're less meticulous, sort and store each item in labeled boxes, such as "engine head bolts." You'll need lots of boxes, large and small, coffee cans, jars, and bottles. Collect the containers ahead of time. Also keep a log or journal. "Tuesday, removed engine. Disconnected throttle linkage (stored on middle shelf, garage south wall) . . . etc."

In addition to the notes, photographs taken at each major disassembly step are a great help when you're putting things back together. When the photos are developed, arrange them in an album, marking the disassembly processes they show and the sequence. You're going to be really proud of these photos when the car is finally restored and you'll probably mount a selected sampling on a poster to display with your car when you take it to shows—lots of collector cars tell their restoration story in this way.

High-resolution digital photographs—2 megapixels or larger—can be especially helpful because they can be magnified to show greater detail than may be visible in a standard photo print.

Similarly, if you have a camcorder, have a friend or relative make videotapes of the disassembly stages. You can watch the tapes for entertainment when you're in the slow going of some of the restoration steps, and they can be a lifeline when you're trying to piece things back together.

One more word of caution on disassembly: don't throw anything away until the project is completely finished—maybe not even then. You'll be amazed at the value some worn-out parts may have. Not all of today's replacement parts exactly match originals. If a reproduction fender or

Ziploc bags make handy storage for small items like screws and other fasteners. Be sure to label each bag with its contents.

Typically, in preparation for bodywork, the interior is gutted. With this Corvette, the disassembly is extensive, including even removing the instrument cluster.

hood won't fit, you can compare it to the damaged or rusted original. Perhaps the new part won't fit because the mounting holes are misdrilled or a flange is missing or in the wrong location. Once you know the problem, you can work out a fix. Otherwise, you're likely to think you've created the problem. Sometimes you may even wind up reusing a part you were sure you'd throw away. I did this once with a piece of headliner. I carelessly creased the piece for that location that came with a kit. Not wanting to buy another kit for just one piece, I sorted through the pieces I'd removed from the car and was able to cut a new section from one of the better preserved chunks of the original and finish the project.

KEEPING DISASSEMBLY IN PACE WITH YOUR FINANCES AND ENTHUSIASM

The flourish of disassembly (taking things apart is easy; restoring and putting them back together is the hard part) quickly leads to dismay and loss of interest. Where do I go from here? With a car completely apart, it's also easy to find yourself financially overcommitted. Before disassembling anything, you should project an estimate of what it will cost to restore the car to whichever condition level (the three restoration standards discussed in Chapter 2) you've targeted. The estimate can be made by pricing items that you know you'll need (like a new interior kit) from a supplier's catalog and getting rough price quotes for work like painting or an engine overhaul that you know you'll hire out. When you've arrived at what looks to be a realistic figure, multiply it by three. Now you have a fairly close approximation of the cost of restoring your car—not counting, of course, your own time.

Fortunately, you're not going to spend the entire cost figure in one amount. Assuming the restoration takes the average time period (four to five years), you can budget the cost over this period. But to do so, you'll need to plan your work and expenses accordingly.

The most practical restoration approach—which fits with any of the three condition goals for the finished

63

The engine is often removed for rebuilding while work proceeds on restoring the car's body.

product, factory new, nearly new, or original—is to restore each component as you take it off the car. With a frame-up factory-new restoration, you will seal and store each component as it is completed so that it will be ready when it's needed in the final assembly process. With a partial-disassembly nearly new or original restoration, the components can be placed back on the car when they're finished. This one-component-at-a-time approach helps you budget your restoration expenses and keeps up your enthusiasm for the project because you can always see finished work.

Disassembly and Restoration Sequence

The typical restoration sequence proceeds by the following steps:

1. Remove and send out chrome items for replating

This step begins the restoration process because replating chrome items can take several months, maybe even a half-year or more. Restoring a car is like cooking a meal. It's important that everything is done at the same time. Consequently, it makes sense to begin with items that are going to take the longest time to progress through the restoration process. Note that we're talking about chrome-plated items on the car (such as bumpers, diecast trim, parts of convertible top assemblies, and interior moldings on convertibles and station wagons), not brightmetal generally. Stainless-steel trim and "chrome-plated" plastic interior pieces can be removed and restored separately.

In some cases you may decide to buy new, rather than have old chrome parts replated. This is especially true of bumpers, where new replacement may be available at a fraction of the cost of straightening and replating the originals. If you make this decision, order the new chrome parts while you're having the others replated. This way all chrome-plated items will be on hand when you're ready for reassembly.

If you want to straighten and restore other trim pieces at this time (typically stainless steel, but possibly also nickel or brass), these parts will also be removed. The process for straightening and polishing brightmetal trim, as well as a complete description of the chrome-plating process, is presented in the plating and polishing chapters.

2. Gut the interior

Remove the seats, door and other interior panels, carpeting, and headliner. This step is in preparation for bodywork, but as each component comes out, the same "restore before removing the next item" philosophy prevails. This means that the seats should be disassembled, repaired, built back up, and recovered before taking out the carpeting or other things.

The reason for removing the interior items at this stage is to prepare the car for major bodywork (welding in a new floor or replacing body panels). With an original car, or restoration to nearly new, if the exterior only needs repainting—as opposed to major bodywork and repainting—the interior should be left as intact as possible and only the items needing to be restored should be removed and replaced.

Cutting out rust may leave the body structure looking like a skeleton, but where replacement panels are available, repairs proceed quite quickly.

DON'T BREAK THE BOLTS!
by Dirk van Rees

The most challenging feat in restoring my CJ2A Jeep was the water pump. The culprit? The most critical of four studs holding the water pump to the block had broken off flush with the block. Most likely it was sheared off when someone made an attempt to replace the pump. Years of use and weather had completely rusted the stud to the block. I drilled a hole and hammered in an extractor, which promptly broke when I tried to back out the stud.

Knowing what I know today, I would go straight to drilling out the stud and tapping the hole. The "easy-out" extractor is no solution, just an additional headache. It makes sense that if a hardened steel stud has broken off because the threads are locked, an extractor with a smaller diameter is also likely to break.

Nothing would drill out the hardened steel extractor. The manufacturer of the extractor even mailed a special bit to me at no cost. The procedure was to drill dry, no lubricants, using good pressure and high speed. I am a tenacious guy and able to get the most stubborn nuts in the most difficult places to reach, but this was impossible.

The trick was to heat the block surrounding the stud sufficiently so as not to cause too much of a temperature difference, which could crack the block. This was done with an oxyacetylene torch without oxygen—just gas, nice and easy. Once the surrounding area was hot, the welder hit the stud with a blast of oxygen gas mixture, which ignited the stud and extractor. Once the smoke settled I had a rough hole I could drill out, tap, and insert a helical thread into to get to the original thread size—and fortunately, no cracks.

Interior components like the seats that have been rebuilt and recovered should be sealed in plastic bags and stored for installation back in the car at a later date. Where interior items are worn and need to be replaced, interior kits (where available) should be purchased at this time. With convertibles, this includes a new top. Otherwise, the worn items should be taken to a trimmer specializing in upholstery work on collector vehicles so that new items can be made. Replacement interior coverings should be stored flat until reassembly in the car. Details about renewing the car's interior are found in the interior chapter.

3. Remove and overhaul the engine, gearbox, suspension, and wiring

This step typically interrupts work on the interior and bodywork/refinishing. On a frame-up or factory-new restoration, all mechanical components will typically be removed, disassembled, and rebuilt. Again, keeping with our one-component-at-a-time philosophy, we'll focus our attention on one mechanical assembly at a time (though the engine and transmission are often removed as a unit).

If you decide to send the engine out to be rebuilt (as opposed to rebuilding it yourself) or while waiting for machine work to be done, you can rebuild the carburetor, generator, and other engine accessories—sealing and storing each as it's finished. Likewise, you can rebuild other driveline and suspension parts, including the rear end, springs, and other assemblies. If, as is the case on some cars, the entire front suspension removes as a unit (by unbolting a front cross member or axle assembly), all components in that unit can be cleaned, rebuilt, and repainted for reassembly in one series of steps.

With a frame-up or factory-new restoration, mechanical work may proceed apace with bodywork. In other

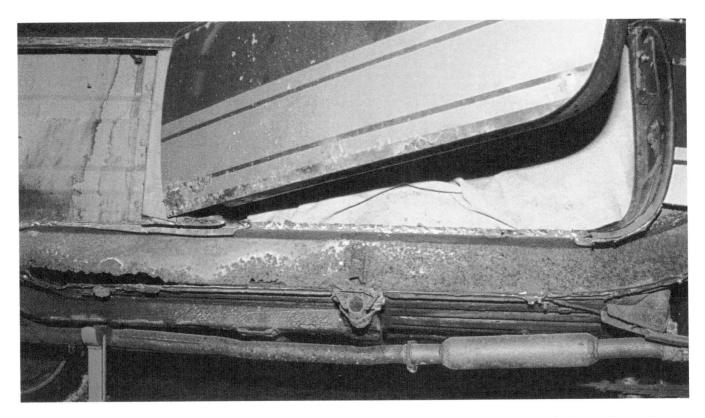

On unit-bodied cars, such as this MGB roadster, the doors are kept in place while structural repair is completed. Without the doors, the body would sag and buckle in the middle.

settings where the car is not going to be completely rebuilt, mechanical work should precede bodywork. It's important to get the car running before investing in expensive body repair.

On cars of 1950s vintage and earlier with cloth-insulated wiring harnesses, the insulation has probably deteriorated, necessitating that the wiring harness be replaced. Likewise, with a factory-new restoration, the wiring harness will probably be replaced, both for appearance and functional purposes. On cars with plastic-insulated wiring, where the restoration goal is either nearly new condition or preservation of a highly original car, the connectors may be cleaned, or corroded ones replaced, and the wiring left otherwise undisturbed—but only if the insulation is intact and the harness is in good condition with all circuits operating. Directions for inspecting and replacing a wiring harness and for troubleshooting faulty circuits are given in the wiring chapter.

4. Perform all necessary bodywork

In situations of major rust repair and panel replacement, the body is left mounted to the frame until all metal repair is completed. This ensures that the body retains its structural integrity. On unit-bodied cars, the doors are kept in place until structural repair is completed—the doors serving the function of the frame to help prevent the body from buckling in the center and causing critical measurements to be lost. Bodywork may also entail cutting out and redoing earlier repairs, straightening dents, and filling extraneous holes drilled in body panels to mount nonfactory accessories such as lights, mirrors, or radio antennas. If any of these accessories will be replaced on the car later, the holes can be redrilled. It's easier to redrill a hole than to have to fill a hole after the car has been finish painted.

If panels such as fenders are removed, they are straightened, any rust damage is repaired, and the old finish is stripped off or prepared for priming, then the panel is coated with a rust-proof primer before being carefully stored or remounted on the car.

5. Prepare the body for finish painting

Depending on whether the car is being kept as original as possible and on the condition of the existing finish, all layers of paint and primer may be stripped off to expose bare metal (or fiberglass). This process can be accomplished chemically or mechanically—either way being relatively tedious and time consuming, and therefore something you'll probably do yourself rather than hiring it out. If you've invested in an air compressor and spray painting gun, you're also likely to prep and prime the body—though you may leave finish painting for a professional. There are two reasons for having the finish paint professionally applied: A top-quality finish takes skill and special equipment, and the painting products can be highly toxic.

All mechanical work is completed prior to finish painting so as not to mar or damage the paint. However, this mechanical assembly/painting process may proceed in stages, with underbody/underhood/interior surfaces being primed and finish painted, then the body remounted on the chassis, which presumably has all mechanical assemblies in place, then the wiring installed. Now the body may be painted and window glass refitted.

6. Remount trim and exterior accessories

The car is gathering a completed look. Remounting the bumpers, trim, and other exterior items like headlights and mirrors goes fast and hastens the car's finished appearance. Now you see why chrome items are sent out early for replating and the reason for restoring each item as it's removed from the car. If you reach this stage only to remember that the bumpers are still lying dented and rusted in a corner of the shop and that the brightmetal trim still needs to be straightened and polished, you're in for a big disappointment. How much better to pull these restored items from inventory and put them on the car. Indeed, the end is in sight.

7. Replace the interior

We've reached the final step. However, we're going to have to be extremely careful. It's very easy to mar the finish when installing the door and interior panels, laying the carpeting, replacing the seats, and fitting the headliner. Use plenty of protective cloths (old sheets and blankets) and work very carefully. The consensus is that it's easier to install the interior without damaging the finish than it is to apply the finish without damaging the interior. If you haven't already done so, you'll also glue new weather seal in place around the door openings and trunk.

Finally, the long, patience-stretching, time-consuming, financially demanding process is over. Like a mother with her baby, a gardener with his/her harvest, or an author with his/her book, you're admiring the finished product.

How to Take the Car Apart

Despite the cautions against impetuous disassembly, the process of restoration requires that we take things apart. How do we know the right way? Do we just proceed by intuition: loosen a bolt here, pry a little there, try to make the parts come loose? If intuition is our approach, we're sure to do more damage as we take things apart.

A better approach is to know the right way to get the pieces to come apart. Window crank handles, for example, are typically held in place by little "C" clips that are easily popped off (and popped back on again) with a window crank handle removal tool. Body assembly manuals,

All bodywork is typically completed before mechanical reassembly. However, the painting process may proceed in stages, with the underbody, underhood, and interior being primed and finish painted, then the mechanical components installed, with exterior finish painting occurring later.

On a partial restoration, as is under way on the car in the foreground, the body may be left on the frame and major mechanical assemblies, such as the engine, rebuilt while still on the car.

provided to dealerships by manufacturers and available today through automotive literature vendors, show the steps for removing window crank handles and the tool to use. Likewise, shop manuals detail mechanical disassembly steps—both in the right sequence and specifying the correct tools. The problem with disassembling components of a collector car using body or shop manuals as a guide is that age often causes things to come apart very differently (and with more difficulty) than they did when new. Here tricks and tips passed down by experienced restorers can be of great help. Often these tricks are published in technical articles in club magazines and can be learned in restoration clinics and classes such as the technical seminars offered by University Motors Ltd. (see Appendix for a description of the University Motors Restoration Seminar).

John Twist at University Motors has a simple, sure-fire trick for removing steering wheels, as an example. He removes the horn button and loosens the nut holding the wheel to the steering shaft until the top of the nut turns past the end of the shaft. Then he sits in the driver's seat and grasps the outer rim of the steering wheel firmly with both hands at 180 degree positions on the rim. A helper places a hammer squarely over the nut and with another, larger hammer raps the first with a sharp blow. As the hammer strikes, John gives a hard jerk on the steering wheel. If the wheel doesn't come loose the first time, the process is repeated. Usually, a couple of such coordinated shocks

pop the steering wheel loose. The other alternative, trying to remove the wheel with a puller, is sure to damage or destroy the plastic at the base of the hub.

Storing Parts after They've Been Removed

As parts are removed from the car they need to be labeled and stored so that they won't be damaged and can be easily located. Small items like nuts and bolts should be placed in labeled containers. Large-mouth jars with lids are ideal because the jars can be sealed to keep the parts from spilling out and being lost. Plastic containers are recommended over glass, which will break if dropped. Even as you're contemplating a restoration project, it is a good time to collect a variety of containers that can be used to collect and store parts. Besides jars, cardboard boxes are needed to hold larger items. The extrathick cardboard boxes from liquor stores are useful for holding smaller assemblies like carburetors, headlight and taillight assemblies, or trim items. The boxes should also be labeled with the items they contain. A roll of wide masking tape and a felt marker are ideal for labeling. Parts should be stored on shelves or a storage loft so that they're not underfoot.

Following the procedure recommended in this book, each assembly should be restored as it is removed from the car. For example, let's say that we begin by removing the bumpers and chrome-plated trim so that these items can be sent out for replating. The bumpers attach by brackets and are removed most easily by unbolting the brackets where they attach to the car. The brackets can be removed more easily with the bumpers lying on the shop floor. So now you have the bumpers ready to pack and ship to the plater, and you have the brackets and bolts. Before packing away the brackets, they should be stripped of paint and rust, metal prepped to prevent rerusting, primed, and finish painted. The bolts are similarly cleaned and painted if that's how they looked at the factory, or set aside for plating. When the brackets are finished being painted, they can be wrapped in pairs and placed in durable plastic bags, which are then wrapped and securely sealed with duct tape, labeled, boxed with the other similarly wrapped and labeled bracket sets, and stored until needed. This piece-by-piece restoration, sorting, and storage procedure may seem more time consuming, but it is actually the most efficient way to go. It will prevent parts from being lost—with consequent lost time and frustration—and possibly cost—to locate or purchase replacements.

When the windshield and rear window glass are removed, they should both be stored standing up. Even though glass appears solid, it is actually liquid. (Tests have shown this by straddling a wire with a weight attached to each end over the top of a vertically positioned sheet of glass. Over time, the wire will cut through the glass.) Lying curved glass flat risks distorting it.

The interior is reinstalled as one of the last steps. At this stage, great care has to be taken to avoid marring the new finish.

Fabric items, like headliner or seat coverings that will be reused, also require proper storage. These items should lie flat and not be folded. Folds may show as creases when the fabric is reinstalled. Likewise, new fabric pieces, such as seat coverings or a convertible top, should be unpacked as soon as they are received and stored flat. Otherwise the folds from shipping may be difficult to remove. Avoid storing fabric in direct sunlight, which can cause fading, or in places where rodents may decide to use your car's seat coverings for a nest.

If at all possible, avoid outside storage for any part of the car, including body and chassis. Decay will set in more quickly than you think. Parking your restoration project outside on damp ground for just one season—maybe while the engine is out and being rebuilt—can cause a coating of mildew to develop on the interior, rust scale to form on the underbody surface, and brake cylinders or calipers to seize—not a pretty picture. If you lack inside storage, look into renting space or find some other solution.

Maintaining Your Interest in the Project While the Car's in Pieces

Keeping interest in a long-term restoration project can be a challenge. You'll save yourself much frustration during restoration if you can focus your interest on the project—making your time in the shop a solace, relaxation, change of pace from your everyday life—and not on getting the car finished for this occasion or that event. Of course people are going to ask you about your progress: "Aren't you ever going to finish that car?" If you've been taking the restore-each-assembly-as-it-comes-off approach, you can always point out what you've accomplished. "See, the seats are all done. Here are the new chrome bumpers. Look at this beautiful carburetor and intake manifold, all ready to sit back on the engine (as soon as that's finished)." Of course, restoring a car for the sake of the project also has its downside. You may never want to finish. Here, though, there's an easy antidote. Just buy another project.

If, on the other hand, you find yourself partway through the restoration and have an incurable itch to drive the car, you've got two options. Put the restored pieces back on the car and drive it for a while. You can always come back to the project later. Or, if you're too far along in the disassembly process or don't want to disrupt your restoration, buy another collector car as a "driver." You can sell the driver when the restoration is finished, or maybe it becomes your next project car. Once bitten by the collector car bug, new projects have a way of inviting themselves into your shop—and life.

Chapter 7
Restoring the Car's Brightmetal Trim

If you're following the approach of restoring each item or assembly as it is removed from the car, the first pieces you'll take off are the items with brightmetal plating—most likely the headlights, taillights, the grille, bumpers, emblems, hood ornaments, as well as the trim spears, rocker panel moldings, and other brightmetal trim parts. These you'll sort into two categories (or piles), parts that need to be replated and parts that can be restored to a bright luster by polishing and buffing.

Parts that may require replating are likely to be the steel trim pieces like bumpers and diecast trim including taillight housings, emblems, hood ornaments, possibly some of the grille pieces. Diecast is a manmade metal, light in weight and porous. While steel bumpers will show their need of replating by a dull and possibly rusted finish, diecast deteriorates by blistering and pitting, usually with a white powder residue forming inside the blisters and pits.

The other pile, items needing polishing, will usually include stainless-steel trim pieces or aluminum, and, on vintage cars, brass items. Sometimes you may have well-preserved chrome-plated items that need only some light polishing to restore their luster. These items would also go in the polishing and buffing pile.

Parts needing replating will be sent to a professional service, so we'll turn our attention to the plating pile first. To obtain desired results, the chrome-plating process can take several months, perhaps a half-year or more, so we're advised to get this process started early in the restoration. If we store the plated parts, waiting to have the items replated later when we're about to reassemble the car, there's the possibility that some of the pieces may be lost or be in too poor condition for quality plating. The delay of locating replacement or better quality parts, plus the lengthy time frame of the plating process, may significantly delay finishing and enjoying the car.

The first step is to inspect the parts and make some decisions. The chrome-plating process is expensive. The best way (and about the only way) to control or reduce costs is to send only good quality items out for plating. So what do you do about chrome-plated items with lots of

Until relatively recently, most cars were equipped with a variety of brightmetal trim pieces, like these around the windshield and along the roof drip rail of a Pontiac Firebird. Missing, damaged, blistered, or scratched trim is unsightly and detracts from an otherwise outstanding restoration.

rust, dents, tears, and pock marks (in the case of diecast trim)? Basically, you've got three options:

1. Shop the reproduction parts catalogs for replacement brightmetal trim.

2. Repair the poorer quality trim parts from your car yourself before sending them to the plater.

3. Locate better-condition replacement parts.

Let's look more closely at these options. Where new trim parts are available, they will almost always be cheaper than having original parts rechromed. Reason: they're manufactured and plated in assembly-line fashion, often in countries not having as stringent environmental controls as the United States. (The plating process uses toxic chemicals, which have high-cost safety stipulations for their use and disposal.) Unfortunately, in some cases, along with being cheaper, the reproduction trim parts (typically grille pieces, nameplates, and bumpers) may also be of lesser quality than original items. Poorer quality original trim pieces often can be repaired, and we'll look at how to do so shortly. If better quality original parts are available at reasonable prices, this may be the best approach—from the standpoint of both quality and cost.

LOCATING A CHROME-PLATING SERVICE

Assuming some of the brightmetal trim is ready for plating, the next step is to locate and contact a plating service qualified (and willing) to renew the parts. Plating services fall into two categories: commercial and restoration. A commercial plating service (typically found via an Internet search or by looking in the Yellow Pages telephone directory of larger metropolitan areas) specializes in production plating work for anything from costume jewelry to office furniture. You'll probably use a commercial plater's services for replating chassis and body fasteners, but it's unlikely that you'll have much success persuading a commercial plater to take on your car's exterior trim pieces—nor should you want to. The problems are these: the plater doesn't want unhappy customers and knows that the production process is unlikely to produce a high-quality chrome finish on a highly visible trim piece—so the likely response to your request is "No!" But you also need to be aware that the commercial plater's inventory tracking process may be somewhat inadequate, opening the possibility that some of your parts may be lost in the plating process—a very disturbing experience for you! For exterior trim parts, the service to contact is a restoration plater, advertising in a collector car hobby or wooden boat magazine—or better—recommended by other restorers.

Chrome plating is often described as being like a thin coating of clear lacquer applied over a raw part. The clear lacquer coating hides none of the part's imperfections. The same is true of a bright chrome finish. For the chrome finish to have the deep bluish luster associated with rich, quality chrome plating, and to hide imperfections that may exist on the part, the plater has to take the parts through a three-step copper, nickel, chrome process. The reason

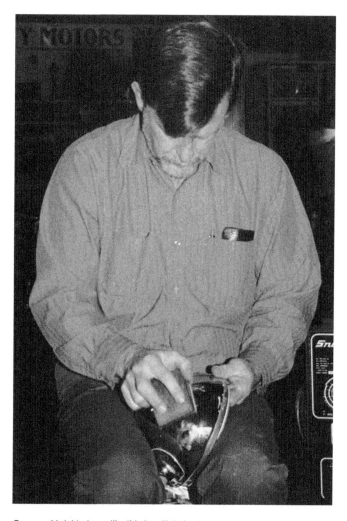

Damaged bright pieces like this headlight bucket can be straightened with a small-headed trim hammer, then smoothed with sandpaper. Dents are worked out by tapping around the dented area in a spiral motion, starting at the outer edge of the dent and working toward the center.

for sending parts to a restoration plater is that a commercial plater may not apply the three plating layers. This can seriously undermine the quality of the finished product since without the underlying copper layer, the chrome plating won't make a good bond with the metal and may peel off like tin foil in a few months. In fact, this is exactly what happened to chrome plating on U.S. cars produced between 1951 and 1953. With copper in short supply due to the Korean War, manufacturers skipped the copper layer, and the chrome lasted less than a year on cars driven where salt was used to melt ice on highways. The nickel layer gives the chrome its deep, bluish body, so skipping any part of the preparation process seriously affects the final result. In talking with the plater, make sure your parts will receive the full three-step copper, nickel, chrome plating process.

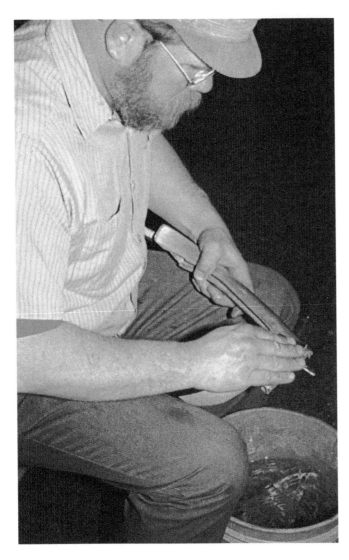

Notice the wet-sanding technique is used in polishing this windshield stanchion. With wet-sanding, the sandpaper is periodically dipped in water, both for lubrication and to clean the grit.

HOW THE PLATING PROCESS WORKS

Also crucial is the effort the plater expends preparing the parts for plating. New plating can't be laid over old, so first the parts have to be stripped to bare metal, using reverse electrolysis to remove the plating layers and an acid bath to eliminate rust. If rust has attacked the metal, leaving the surface pocked with pits, the part will be aggressively buffed to smooth the finish by abrading away some of the metal. Now the part will be placed in the copper plating tank—where it may sit for anywhere from 20 minutes to 4 hours. The copper layer serves three functions: it provides a base for the nickel layer; it enhances the luster of the nickel (and consequently the chrome) plating; and because copper is soft, it can be buffed to fill imperfections in the base metal. A badly pitted bumper, grille, or trim piece may require several passes through the copper plating/buffing cycle before the finish is smooth enough for nickel and chrome layers. A commercial plater won't expend this effort, which is why a restoration plater's services are required for all but production work—meaning any plating that appears on fasteners and chassis pieces.

Once a smooth finish is obtained, the parts progress to the nickel-plating tanks, where the layer responsible for the penetrating bluish tint of quality chrome plating is laid down. Nickel plating takes about 20 minutes. The parts are then rinsed and pass to the chrome tank for the final step. Chrome plating requires only a few minutes (the chrome layer is the thinnest—but also very hard and durable if the preceding steps are done correctly). When parts emerge from the chrome tank they are covered with a glistening butter-colored film. The shiny chrome finish appears after the final rinse.

When you receive the gleaming parts back from the restoration plater, they're likely to be individually wrapped, accompanied by a packing list. Be sure to check the parts received against the list (or, lacking a packing list, against your shipping record). Note any missing items and follow up promptly with the plater to make sure nothing gets lost. Then reassemble any disassembled items and box and label the assemblies. Finally, store these items in a dry location so they'll be preserved in the condition they were received in until they're needed for the car.

BALANCING QUALITY AND PRICE

Many restoration platers offer various quality options—with different price scales. At the top is 10-point, or "show" chrome, what we see at a concours on elegantly prepared cars. If we're budget-conscious, but also recognize the importance of gleaming chrome to the impression our collector car is going to make, we may rationalize, "I'll save some money buying reproduction bumpers and trim, so I can have the grille and taillights plated in show chrome." Although this may sound logical, mixing the quality of the chrome work on a collector car is a mistake. The reproduction bumpers, though free of dents and pits, won't have the deep, penetrating brightness of show chrome. So, if nearby parts have been plated to the higher standard, items with the lesser quality chrome will look shabby in contrast. Better to keep things consistent.

If you're doing a frame-up or factory-new restoration and all brightwork will be rechromed, opt for show-chrome quality, if possible. On a nearly new restoration, where a mixture of original and reproduction trim will be used—and where some original parts may be rejuvenated

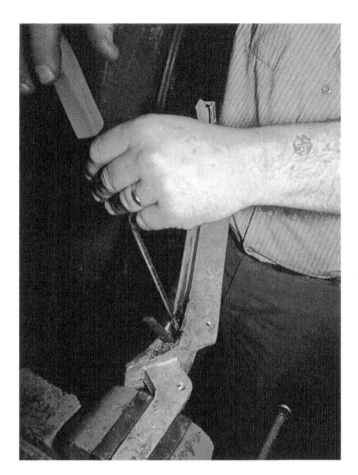

Whether the trim pieces are metal parts being replated or aluminum or stainless parts being polished, it's necessary to remove all extraneous hardware from the brightmetal item.

Round parts such as this SU carburetor suction chamber can be polished by placing them in the chuck of a lathe and working the metal with increasingly fine grit sandpaper.

by polishing—show chrome is probably a mistake for the reasons above. Instead, ask the restoration plater for a quality that more closely matches the plating standard of the reproduction or original parts. The same applies to restored brightwork on an original car where factory standards were substantially below show chrome.

Platers will tell you that the most important factor in price—even beyond the standard of the plating—is the quality of the parts. Rusted or damaged parts that have to be restored by metal craftsmen and then repeatedly copper plated and buffed to fill pits and traces of repair are going to wear a very expensive price tag. High-quality parts (the ideal being NOS) that need only be stripped of their original chrome and taken through the three-step plating process have the highest assurance of satisfaction and the lowest relative price. So when you contact the plater, be sure to give an accurate description of the parts. You may be guided to try to locate better items.

When the plater receives your parts, the shop will send you an inventory list of the parts along with a written estimate and time frame for the work. Be sure to keep the inventory list and estimate. If anything you sent isn't returned, you don't want the shop claiming they never received it—sending you on a search for what may be an impossible-to-find item. (It's important to check the plater's reputation for keeping track of inventory before contracting with them for your plating business.) Some platers are extremely punctual on time schedules, while many aren't. That's why it's important to get the plating process under way early in the restoration.

SAVE MONEY BY DOING PREP WORK YOURSELF

Like many steps in a collector car's restoration (engine overhaul and finish painting being two examples), it's possible to save money on the plating process by doing some of the preparation work yourself. One preparation step you can and should always do is disassemble the items as much as possible before sending them to the plater. For example, with headlights that have attached mounting brackets,

Door handles are another good example of a difficult-to-restore item. Note the scratches and "blistering" on this handle. Fortunately, many such parts are available in reproduction form, with a flawless finish.

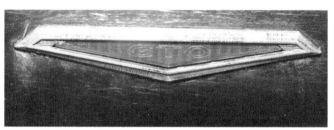

These simulated fender vents are made of diecast metal, which can be difficult—but not impossible—to restore, because the metal is so delicate.

This GTO's marker lamp lens is in good shape, but the plastic trim around it—with its chromelike plating—needs careful attention to be saved. In this case, reproductions are available, but not all plastic parts are available in reproduction form, so you may need to locate a plastic chrome plater in Hemmings or by searching on the Internet.

drill out the rivets holding the brackets before sending the headlights for plating. New plating won't adhere to joints between parts. You may ask, "How can I replace the rivets?" You won't. Instead, you'll use stainless-steel carriage bolts with a dab of silicone sealer around the head to seal out water, and LokTite on the threads to prevent the bolts from loosening.

If some of the chrome items are damaged (with dents or tears) and better quality replacements aren't available, you can have a commercial plater strip off the old plating and then work out the dents and weld cracks or tears as described below.

It's sometimes also possible to work though an intermediary who does the buffing and brokers the plating through commercial platers. I have used such a service and found the quality to be as good as a restoration plater and the cost somewhere between what I would expect to pay a commercial and restoration plater. Buffing is a high-skill but low-tech process, so this intermediary will likely have a commercial grade buffing stand in his home workshop where he will prepare the parts for plating, after they have had the original chrome and other plating layers stripped off. He'll then consign the parts to a commercial plater with instructions only to apply a copper layer to a specified

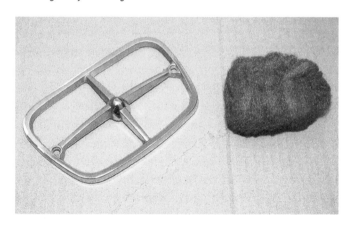

This diecast parking/turn-signal lamp bezel looked pretty grungy, but a few minutes with some steel wool cleaned it up to respectable condition.

depth. He'll then pick up the parts, buff the copper as necessary to fill pits and other surface imperfections, and send them back again for plating—either a copper buildup for another round of buffing, or the three-step copper, nickel, chrome process. As might be expected, using an intermediary significantly expands the time to work the

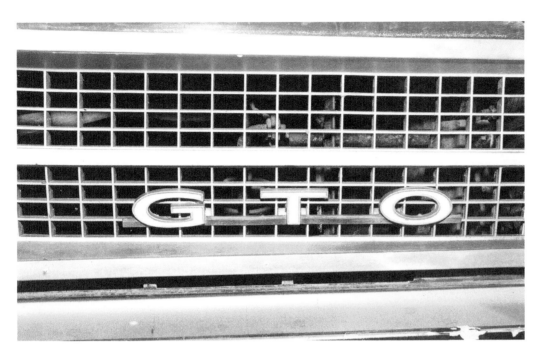

Here we see a plastic grille section and a plastic, plated, and painted emblem. Because of the brittleness of original plastic—more than 40 years old, in this case—restoration may be extremely difficult. Emblems of this sort are secured with speed nuts on small studs that protrude from the back of the emblem; unfortunately, removing the speed nuts often destroys the studs and possibly the entire emblem.

parts through the plating process. Typically, individuals performing this service don't advertise—generally they're doing the service to generate part-time income—so you'll hear about them through other restorers or shops.

REPAIRING DAMAGED CHROME TRIM

Using a small-headed trim hammer, work out dents by tapping around the dented area in a spiral motion, starting at the outer edge of the dent and working in toward the center. The typically thin metal of chrome-plated parts, like headlight buckets, will bulge and stretch easily, so tap lightly, holding a finger against the back (depression) side of the dent to sense the force of the tapping and to feel the metal return to the correct contour. As you're working out the dent, run a sanding block with 360 or finer grit sandpaper across the repair area to check for high and low spots.

If your car is equipped with bumper guards, you'll probably find dents to be directly in front of a heavy mounting plate and therefore inaccessible from behind. To repair the metal, you'll have to cut the mounting plate with a die grinder, repair the dent, then MIG weld the plate back in place.

Welding repairs can be filled and smoothed by careful brazing. Solder can be used to fill small pinholes, and a special lead-free solder available from Caswell Electroplating (see Resources) can be used for filling surface imperfections. However, since solder is softer than the adjoining metal, there's a danger it may be melted or torn out by the buffing process. This is a reason for doing your own buffing, as described shortly. Special products are also available from

A close-up of this Firebird's bumper shows that the chrome is pitted and scratched and just plain worn off in places. Fortunately, the metal is solid and not dented or damaged, so replating it should be fairly easy . . . once you locate a chrome plater. Because of the hazardous chemicals, there are relatively few chrome platers in the country, so don't be surprised if you have to ship your parts off to be rechromed.

Caswell Electroplating to restore and prepare broken and pitted pot metal pieces for plating. Deteriorated diecast trim pieces are among the most difficult, expensive items to repair and restore. However, given enough patience and persistence, and products designed for use with diecast trim, renewal of these sometimes one-of-a-kind trim items is possible.

Buffing wheels can be used to give luster to a wide variety of parts, including aluminum castings such as this blower chamber. The Eastwood Company

RESTORING STAINLESS STEEL OR ALUMINUM TRIM

Much of a car's brightmetal trim is stainless steel—and in more recent years, aluminum. This trim doesn't need to be replated, but it has probably lost its original luster and may be dented or scratched as well. While you can send this trim to a service that specializes in restoring automotive brightwork, you can also do this work yourself at considerable savings. You'll need an electric motor, a set of buffing wheels, and an assortment of polishing grits and buffing compounds. The expense to set up a buffing station can be minimal if you have an extra electric motor on hand. If you decide to buy the motor as well as the buffing and polishing products, you'll still be money ahead—and enjoy the satisfaction that comes from turning a battered part into a piece of gleaming metal that looks like it just came from the factory.

The first step is to work out any dents or gouges in the metal using a hardwood dowel, bolt, or small trim hammer (following the dent removal method used with chrome-plated parts above). When the surface feels and looks flat, rub a fine file across the area you've been working. Be careful not to cut deeply into the metal. You're using the file to check for high and low spots, which become visible where the file cuts into or passes over the metal. When the file shows the surface to be essentially smooth, you'll remove the deeper file scratches and hammer marks by sanding.

BUFFING WHEEL AND COMPOUND SELECTION CHART

Materials	Steel, Iron, Stainless, or Other Hard Materials	Soft Metals, Brass, Copper, Aluminum, Diecast, Zinc	Chrome, Nickel, Plate	Solid and Plated, Gold, Silver	Plastics
Step 1—Rough Compound Buff	Emery Sisal	Tripoli Spiral/Ventilated	N/A	N/A	Plastic Loose/String
Step 2—Intermediate Compound Buff	Stainless Spiral/Ventilated	N/A	Stainless* Spiral	N/A	N/A
Step 3—Final Compound Buff	White Rouge Loose Section	White Rouge Loose Section	White Rouge Loose Section	Jewelers Rouge Canton Flannel	Plastic Canton Flannel String

NOTE: Condition of the workplace dictates the steps necessary. Some places may only require final finishing (Step 3). Refer to our Expanded Wheel, Greaseless Compounds, and Abrasive Rolls for more aggressive action.
*Use caution to prevent buffing through plating.

Buffing wheel and compound selection chart. The Eastwood Company

ELECTROPLATING ON THE STOVE TOP

I've been inside commercial plating shops and seen the elaborate equipment used to electroplate metal parts. What a surprise, then, when I spotted an ad in the color section of *Hemmings Motor News* for a company selling do-it-yourself plating kits you could use at home on the stove top. Curiosity got the best of me and I decided I had to give the kit a try. A few days later the UPS man trotted up our front porch steps with a box about the size of a coffee carafe. The shipping label told me my Caswell electroplating kit had arrived.

For the trial run I'd cleaned up a pair of window pulls from our century-old Victorian house, a decorative eagle from my junk box, and a Ford toolkit wrench. In preparation for plating, I wire-brushed the window pulls to strip off several coatings of paint and packed the wrench in Rusteco, a derusting chemical that's not only biodegradable but supposedly drinkable (I haven't done the latter test). The eagle went into the plating solution as is.

It took me awhile to figure out the mixing proportions for the plating bath. The instructions called for 6 percent of one chemical and 20 percent of the other by volume. My nonmathematical mind kept trying to convert 6 and 20 percent measures into something simple like teaspoons and tablespoons. Finally, I reasoned that 6 percent of 100 percent is just a tad over 1/20th, so that's how I mixed the solution, using my wife's quarter-cup measuring cup. Adding slightly over half a quarter-cup of chemical A (6 percent) to two quarter-cups of chemical B (20 percent) and 7½ quarter-cups of distilled water (74 percent). It worked.

The directions call for heating the mixture to 80 degrees F. and maintaining that temperature for 5 to 15 minutes. I decided against using my wife's meat thermometer (reasoning that I'd nickel plate the thermometer's metal probe), and I couldn't find a glass thermometer (other than the units in our medicine cabinet), so I gauged the solution's temperature by placing the flat of my hand against the glass beaker holding the plating solution.

Fifteen minutes didn't produce much of a result, so I let the solution work (bubbles gurgling up from the metal) for about 45 minutes. If I approached the mouth of the plating beaker I could detect some odor, but the smell dissipated as I stepped away. Nor did my wife detect any offensive odor when she entered her kitchen, which is probably the most important test.

A kitchen range is all that's needed for the Caswell plating process. The plating chemicals are mixed by volume in a beaker that is largely filled with distilled water, then heated to 100 degrees Fahrenheit. A slightly pungent odor is emitted when the plating solution begins to work.

As the instructions advise, the plating finish matches the surface of the part before plating, dull on rough- or brush-finish parts, bright on polished parts. I considered the process a success. The window pulls have an attractive antique look and the wrench has a protective nickel coating on the section I plated. The kit appears ideal for myriad small items. I've saved the solution, which the instructions say can be reused, the possible penalty being longer plating times. When I'm finished, the kit has a supply of ammonia, which neutralizes the solution so it can be disposed of safely.

Besides the liter-sized nickel plating kit I tested, Caswell Plating supplies larger-capacity kits with tank sizes up to 16 gallons and a range of plating solutions besides nickel, including copper, zinc, even gold. For information, contact Caswell Electroplating, 4336 Route 31, Palmyra, New York 14522-9719, 313-597-5140, or www. caswellplating.com.

This can be done by hand, starting with 220-grit wet/dry sandpaper and a wooden or rubber block and progressing to finer grits. If you're working with any quantity of trim, you'll find hand-sanding the metal to remove scratches and hammer marks to be slow and very time consuming. An expander wheel mounted on an electric motor with various grit sanding belts makes the work proceed at almost a production pace. With an expander wheel, each time you change sanding belts, change the approach to the part at a right angle from the previous sanding.

Once the scratches are removed, the part can be polished to a high gloss. The preferred polishing/buffing setup is a double arbor motor with a coarse wheel installed on one end of the shaft and a softer wheel on the other. This way it is not necessary to change wheels between buffing steps. Beginning with a rough wheel and coarse grit (a Sisal wheel for fast, aggressive cutting and a coarse emery grit), the part should be buffed in small sections until all areas have been worked. Be careful not to hold the part in one spot, because the aggressive grit and harsh wheel can

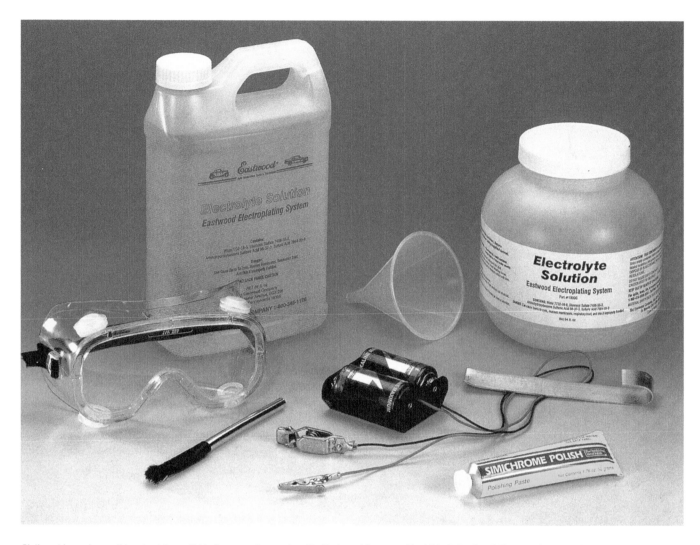

Plating at home is possible using kits available from suppliers such as the Eastwood Company. The kit includes the plating container and all necessary chemicals—even the electrical source. The Eastwood Company

distort the part's contours or cut holes in the metal. After the part has been coarse buffed, a softer spiral wheel is used with a milder grit. This intermediate buff is followed by finish buffing using a soft loose-section wheel and a coloring compound to bring the metal to high luster.

Those new to the buffing/polishing process typically apply too much grit to the wheel and forget to clean the wheel before going to a milder grit. Putting too much compound on the wheel is not only wasteful, but the extra compound also clogs the wheel, hindering the buffing action. Black streaks on the work piece are signs of too much compound. These streaks can be cleaned off with a soft cloth soaked in solvent. The easiest way to make sure that none of the harsher compound remains on the wheel as you move to a milder grit is to use a different wheel for each buffing step. Lacking this, you can remove leftover compound from the buffing wheel with a tool called a

rake. One other important caution: never take your eyes off the part while buffing.

Plastic parts like taillight and parking light lenses can also be restored by buffing. Typically, original plastic lenses will have a dull look caused by tiny scratches. If you use a soft spiral wheel and special plastic buffing compound, followed by a finish buff with a flannel wheel, the scratches can be removed, giving the plastic a shiny new look. When buffing plastic, take special care not to remove part numbers or other detail features.

Besides brightening and restoring trim and plastic items, polishing and buffing can also be used to produce a chromelike finish on aluminum parts like alternator housings and intake manifolds. These parts did not come from the factory with a shiny finish, so buffing is not to be done as part of restoration. However, shiny engine compartments appeal to street rodders and others. Hand-held grinders can be used to polish small recesses on these parts that can't be reached by the expander wheel.

Aluminum or brass items that have been polished to a gleaming finish need to be protected from tarnishing and oxidation by a light coating of clear lacquer. An aerosol spray can makes a convenient applicator.

For those who would like to see the polishing/buffing process demonstrated before trying it themselves, a video titled "The Art of Buffing" is available from the Eastwood Company.

PLASTIC "CHROME" PLATING

In the 1960s, American automakers discovered the versatility of plastics. Ford's hot-selling Mustang used stamped vinyl to simulate a hand-sewn leather dash cover. Pontiac used plastic for the nose piece and bumper on its pace-setting GTO. Door panels that formerly had been made of fabric-covered cardboard were increasingly replaced with more durable plastics. Even interior trim pieces, brightly chrome-plated, were now being made of plastic.

Gregg Purvis demonstrates the Eastwood plating kit with an assortment of small fixtures.

Now that 1960s cars and light trucks are considered collectibles and have fallen into the caring hands of restorers, the widespread use of plastic material on these cars is both a blessing and a curse. The material doesn't corrode like steel or decay like fabric, but vinyl dashboards do crack and the chrome-plated trim pieces lose their shine. R-ecovering dashboards basically requires laying on a new piece of vinyl—not easy, but not impossible either—so the big question to many restorers is what to do about the ratty-looking chrome-plated plastic trim.

Call a plating service listed in the telephone yellow pages about replating a plastic dashboard from, say, a 1967 GTO, and you'll get the response: "Plate plastic? I can't put that stuff in my tanks." So what do you do?

For starters, don't spray the plated plastic trim items with "chrome" paint. The stuff inside the spray paint can is plain old aluminum paint and won't, under any circumstances, produce the shiny chrome finish you see on the paint can's cap. The problem with using chrome paint to try to restore plated plastic trim parts isn't just that you'll be disgusted with the results—there'll also be the problem of getting the paint back off the plastic when you decide to have the piece professionally restored.

The answer to restoring plastic chrome-plated trim items, typically dash panels, armrests, and transmission tunnel covers, is simple. Just send the parts to a plastic chrome-plating service. Yes, there are businesses that specialize in plating plastic, and there are even a few that cater exclusively to the car restorer.

The reason electroplaters won't rechrome plastic is that the bright finish on these trim pieces isn't chrome. The chrome-appearing finish is actually produced by a microscopically thin layer of aluminum applied through a process called vacuum metalizing. One of the reasons manufacturers switched from metal to plastic trim is that the vacuum metalizing process does not use the toxic and environmentally damaging chemicals required with electroplating. Actually, the vacuum metalizing process is extremely simple—although you can't duplicate it in your garage because of the expensive equipment required.

The vacuum metalizing process works like this: the parts to be plated are mounted on racks, which are placed in a drumlike container. The drum is sealed and its atmosphere pumped out, forming a vacuum. Now a dozen or so tiny slivers of aluminum, which are attached to a tungsten filament located in the center of the chamber, are heated to 1,200 degrees, at which point they disintegrate and millions of aluminum atoms go floating about the drum. The thin coating of aluminum that accumulates on the trim

The popularity of 1960s vehicles with collectors has created a need to restore the plastic chrome-plated parts, most noticeably instrument panels and dash facings.

ANSWERS TO COMMON PLASTIC PLATING QUESTIONS

How do I tell if the plating is chrome or vacuum metalizing?

Although chrome is applied primarily to metal and vacuum metalizing to plastic, processes have been developed to metal plate plastic. If you plan to have the part replated, you can determine whether the brightmetal finish is actual chrome or a microscopic coating of aluminum by rubbing the plated-appearing finish with 4 ought (0000) steel wool. A vacuum metalized finish will scour off. Chrome won't be touched. Knowing the type of plating will help direct you to the appropriate service, one electroplating plastic or one doing vacuum metalizing.

How do I remove chrome plating?

If you want to have chrome-plated parts restored by vacuum metalizing (it's typically a less-expensive process), you can strip off the chrome plate by soaking the parts in muriatic acid for anywhere from three days to three weeks. When the chrome is removed you can send the parts for vacuum metalizing.

How do I repair damaged plastic?

You can fix broken plastic parts with epoxy glue.

How do I mask vacuum-metalized parts for painting?

Don't use masking tape. It will lift the plating. You can mask areas not to be painted with Post-It Notes (the adhesive is gummy enough that it won't life the finish). You can also mask the vacuum metalized finish with Vaseline. To be able to see where you have applied the Vaseline, mix in some food coloring. An artist's brush works well to spread the Vaseline. When it comes time to remove the masking lubricant, use a soft cloth dipped in diluted solvent.

How do I remove woodgrain appliqué?

Some plastic-plated dashboards had wood appliqué covering the areas surrounding the gauges. This appliqué needs to be removed before sending the parts for vacuum metalizing. It will be replaced as part of the refinishing/ restoration process. To remove the appliqué, place a putty knife under a corner and begin to lift the wood grain covering. If the appliqué doesn't pull loose easily, place the part in a food freezer for a few hours. The cold will make the glue brittle and the appliqque will peel off easily.

pieces creates a brilliantly shiny finish that looks identical to chrome.

Besides eliminating chemicals in the plating process, vacuum metalizing differs in another significant way from electroplating. One reason for the popularity of chrome-plating metal parts is the hardness and durability of the chrome. Henry Ford replaced chrome extensively with stainless steel on his 1930–1931 Model As, and when these cars could be found stashed behind farmers' barns, the discoverers were often amazed at the condition of the "chrome." Stainless steel doesn't rust under normal conditions, but it sure does scratch. Aluminum is even softer and disfigures more easily yet. In contrast, chrome is tough and takes a lot of abuse without showing it.

When the plated plastic parts come out of the vacuum metalizing chamber, their shiny finish is so delicate that it could be wiped off with the stroke of a finger. Obviously, you can't put parts with that delicate a finish on your car. So what do you do? Actually, you don't do anything. The plater sprays a coating of clear urethane on the parts and the invisible paint layer protects the chrome finish underneath.

So don't try to polish vacuum metalized parts with a chrome cleaner or other chemicals. You'll cut through the clear urethane, and in a flash you'll have wiped off the atom-thick plating. Ford didn't think to protect the vacuum metalized speedometer cage on its 1957 automobiles—the first application of this technology in the auto industry—and in a short time the plating had been rubbed off, exposing the bare plastic.

Vacuum metalizing can be applied to any material. This means that hobbyists can have plated metal parts restored

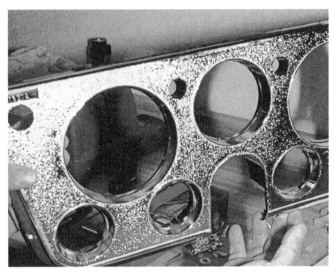

These "before" and "after" photos show how effectively replating can make a plastic part look like new. The instrument panel in the "before" photo is a good sample of the condition of plastic parts received for replating. Note where the plated finish has worn off the part exposing the bare plastic. Although this part appears ready for the discard pile, it is actually a good candidate for replating because there is no damage to the plastic.

by the vacuum metalizing process, too. And that's good news, because unlike electroplating, vacuum metalizing can be applied over filler. Gel-coated fiberglass parts also take well to vacuum metalizing.

Shops that restore plated plastic parts using the vacuum metalizing process can be found through ads in collector car hobby magazines (and the Resources listing in this book). The plater probably has a price list for vacuum metalizing the more standard parts, such as dash bezels. For other items you can typically get a plating estimate. If the parts have any painted surfaces (plastic dash bezels typically do), you should note what areas are painted. A good way to record exactly what is painted is to take color photographs of the parts. In some cases, the plating service may offer to repaint the part for a small additional cost. If this is the case, have the plating service do the repainting. You'll save a tedious masking job as well as the painting hassle.

Now you can carefully package the parts and send them off for renewal. Expect the process to take four to six weeks. When the parts come back from the plating service, you'll be amazed with the results. Formerly dull, shabby-looking trim pieces will be gleaming with the bright new metal coating. If any areas of the parts were painted, this step needs to be done before replacing the parts on the car. Plastic chrome platers warn not to use masking tape (which may lift the metalized finish) but instead recommend covering areas that aren't to be painted with Micro Mask, a water-soluble product that is spread on with a paintbrush. For best results, use a modeler's airbrush to spray paint the part.

After the paint has dried and the masking is removed, the part is ready to be reinstalled on the car, assuming all interior painting and upholstery work are completed. Sometimes plastic-plated parts will be components of a larger assembly, like the instrument panel facing, in which case some reassembly is required first. Usually, this just means reversing the disassembly steps, but sometimes more restoration work is required, such as placing new number decals on the instruments, repainting gauge needles, and the like. When reinstalling the plastic trim parts on the car, be careful not to force or crack the plastic. When the job is finished, the new plastic chrome trim will give your car's interior the sparkle it had when it left the factory.

Chapter 8
Cleaning, Stripping, and Derusting

As you take parts off the car, you're going to encounter dirt, grime, and rust. So the first step toward restoration is going to be cleaning off the dirt and grime and removing the rust. Often you'll encounter layers of paint that also need to be removed. Cleaning off dirt and grime with a putty knife, scrub brush, and solvent is a slow, exasperating process. Likewise, trying to remove rust by sanding or wire brushing is also tedious and not very effective. In this chapter we'll look at ways to expedite the cleaning, stripping, and derusting processes as much as possible, so that your time can be concentrated on the more fulfilling tasks of rebuilding and restoring the car.

CLEANING—VARIOUS METHODS

If we're going to remove caked-on grease, dirt, and road grime more easily than scraping off the buildup, we've got to use chemicals to loosen the grime, allowing it to be washed off the parts. Depending on equipment available, there are several approaches. Dirt- and grime-encrusted parts can be cleaned fairly effectively using a commercially available degreasing agent like GUNK (available from auto parts stores or the auto supplies section of discount marts) and a garden hose. Just follow the instructions on the product label. The chemical works best at warm temperatures (a warm, sunny day). This job is more efficient with a collection of parts rather than a single item, since the instructions require time for the chemical to work. Thick grime and grease will likely require additional scraping or brushing, but the GUNK (or comparable product) is quite effective by itself (along with a strong rinse) with lighter coatings. In some cases, the degreaser may also strip off paint.

POWER WASHING

If you have a portable power washer, the degreaser's action can be made more effective by the stronger wash blast. On some power washers, a detergent can be mixed with the wash blast, also increasing the cleaning effectiveness. Lacking this tool, parts needing cleaning can be taken to a coin-operated car wash (a do-it-yourself, not a drive-

Lacking a power washer, you can take parts needing cleaning to a coin-operated car wash and clean them using either the engine cleaning or detergent cycles.

through wash) and cleaned using either the engine cleaning or detergent cycles. A car wash is also very effective for cleaning engine compartments. It's impossible to keep the spray off the engine's electrical system, so be prepared for drying off the distributor, spark plugs, and coil wires to get the car started after its bath. Take care not to spray water into a carburetor/fuel injection intake or air cleaner. Be sure to bring a supply of clean rags or shop towels to dry off the electrical components after washing.

To help keep the electrical system as dry as possible while cleaning and degreasing the engine compartment at a coin-op car wash, leave the engine running. As more and more water splashes around the engine compartment, the engine will eventually die. When the job is finished, you'll need to remove the distributor cap and wipe the cap dry, inside and out. After you've gotten the engine started and have driven the car home, remove the distributor cap again. You'll find that additional moisture has collected inside the cap since it was cleaned at the car wash. If you neglect this second dry-off step, you'll find the engine won't run the next time you're ready to start the car.

Products like Simple Green are effective for cleaning light to moderate dirt and grease from a car. We've also used oven cleaner successfully—just like in your oven, allow it time to eat away at the grease before trying to remove it. Such products are generally only to be used prior to a restoration, as they may damage the finish on restored parts.

A parts washer tank—even a small one—can be a great tool for cleaning dirt and grime from parts like valve covers, timing covers, oil pans, and numerous smaller suspension components.

It won't work in every shop, but if you've got a hot water supply, investing a few dollars in a second-hand dishwasher (yup, the kitchen appliance) will get you a great cleaning device for small parts. Warning: don't try to run a batch of car parts through the household dishwasher on the sly.

The ultimate power washing tool, and a more expensive tool investment than many hobbyist restorers are likely to make, is a steam cleaner. Only a cold water supply is needed; the heating unit, which is part of the device, is usually fueled by kerosene or heating oil. When using a steam cleaner, it's important to take precautions to avoid scalding yourself with the steam, which sprays out under high pressure. The steam's blast literally melts away thick coatings of grease and grime, leaving engine blocks, transmission housings, rear axle assemblies, any mechanical part large or small looking factory fresh in a matter of minutes. Since this isn't a tool you'll use often—unless your car collector friends find out you've got it—you may want to inquire about a steam cleaner's availability from tool rental shops. An afternoon's rental session should enable you to clean

Paint can be stripped off large surfaces like the door skin shown here using chemical paint stripper. The chemical will soften and lift the paint from the surface, but won't remove it. With stubborn coatings you may have to strip the paint one layer at a time, scraping off each coating with a putty knife. After all the paint is removed, you'll typically need to clean the surface with a dual-action (DA) sander.

an engine compartment and the car's entire undercarriage (frame and drivetrain). Raising and supporting first one side of the car then the other on jack stands will enable you to clean the chassis components. Thorough cleaning like this prior to disassembly not only makes the parts-removal process easier, but also a lot less messy.

CLEANING WITH STRONG DETERGENTS

Rather than using a high-pressure spray to wash off grease and grime, parts can be soaked in a strong detergent bath made with a commercial cleaning product like Trisodium Phosphate (TSP), sold in hardware stores; just follow the mixing proportions listed on the product label. A plastic pail can be used as a practical-sized container for the detergent bath. Drop parts needing cleaning into the pail, and then cover it. Small parts can be submerged in a colander for easy retrieval. Larger parts can be fished out of the bath using a large cooking spoon or ladle. Thick grease and grime coatings may take several hours to loosen.

Like most detergents, TSP works best in warm water and warm ambient temperatures, so filling the pail with hot tap water and preparing the bath on a warm, sunny day will yield faster, more effective results. Chemicals of any sort, even if only harsh detergents, should not be used where they might attract notice and investigation by children and pets. Be sure to wear rubber gloves and full clothing, plus a face mask, when preparing, placing items in, or retrieving them from the concentrated detergent bath.

CLEANING WITH CAUSTIC CHEMICALS

Rather than washing off grease and grime with detergents, you can also use caustic chemicals to dissolve or eat the grimy buildup. Like the TSP bath, a cleaning/degreasing solution using caustic (alkaline) chemicals can be brewed up in a metal or plastic pail. Warning: when using caustic chemicals, wear rubber gloves and full clothing to avoid skin contact; wear a full face mask to prevent the chemical solution from splashing into your eyes; and avoid prolonged breathing of any chemical fumes. Also, never use caustic chemicals in the vicinity of children or pets.

Caustic soda, or lye, which is the active ingredient in Drano, Liquid Plumr, and similar household products for opening clogged drains, makes a highly effective cleaning and degreasing agent. As the instructions on the product label note, the chemical works best when warm. If a metal container is used and placed over a small camping stove, the chemical can be warmed near the boiling point, increasing its caustic action—both on parts and skin. Be very careful if using hot lye as a degreasing agent.

After several heavily coated parts have been degreased using the caustic chemical process, a layer of grease will collect on the solution's surface. Adding detergent helps dissolve the grease, but the grease can be removed more effectively by periodically skimming off the grease film. Otherwise, parts will get a thin grease coating as they are pulled from the bath. Even a slight grease coating prevents effective derusting and raises havoc with painting. Parts that are contaminated with a grease film should be washed with detergent before derusting and painting.

After parts are removed from the caustic solution they must be washed thoroughly. A garden hose works well to rinse off the slimy alkaline film. Thorough cleaning is important. Any alkaline film left on the part's surface gives the metal poor wetting or paint-bonding properties, and any chemical remaining in seams may eventually leach out, lifting the paint. However, washing presents another problem: cleaned metal is prone to rapid rusting. To protect against rusting and provide the wetting necessary for painting, cleaned parts can be wiped with an acid-etch solution (typically containing dilute phosphoric acid) available from auto parts stores selling refinishing products. An alternative product, Rusteco, described in this chapter's section on derusting, also protects against rust and provides excellent wetting for paint adhesion.

As the caustic chemical solution is used, it will gradually lose its strength. This does not occur rapidly. I have cleaned parts in a lye tub over a period of several days before noticing an appreciable loss in degreasing potency.

The easiest way to clean off grease, paint, and even rust is to have a metal laundry do the work for you. Redi Strip, whose Columbus, Ohio, operation is shown here, is the leader in commercial chemical stripping.

When this does occur, the solution can be restored to full strength by adding more chemical. However, the caustic chemical degreasing bath will eventually become contaminated with sludge and have to be disposed of by placing or transferring the solution to a sealed container that can be taken to an appropriate toxic chemical dump.

CLEANING BY USING PETROLEUM SOLVENTS

Although shade tree mechanics have made do for years cleaning parts in basins or pails, the most efficient way to degrease parts using a petroleum solvent is with a parts washer. Relatively inexpensive parts washers consisting of a sturdily supported work-height basin, storage sump for the solvent, pump, and spray nozzle for washing the parts are available from several restoration tool suppliers. Gasoline should never be used as a cleaning/degreasing solvent. Petroleum-based cleaning solvents are available through most auto parts stores. Better than petroleum-based solvents, however, are water-soluble biodegradable degreasing solvents, which can be purchased from the same supplier as the parts washer. The water-soluble biodegradable solvents have the advantage that the spent chemical does not

need to be disposed of in a toxic waste dump—which is the proper disposal facility for petroleum-based solvents.

DISSOLVING GREASE USING SAFE, ENVIRONMENTALLY FRIENDLY GREASEMASTER

While all the previously described cleaning products will remove the heavy buildups of grease and grime typically found on older car parts, none is completely harmless to the environment, and all pose a health hazard to some degree if prolonged contact occurs with exposed skin, or if the chemicals splash into the eyes or are ingested. Grease-Master, in contrast, is safe, nontoxic, and biodegradable. Because it is formulated largely from the waste of organically grown plants, GreaseMaster is benign, has an almost neutral pH, and can legally be disposed of in wastewater or used as a plant fertilizer.

Unlike detergents that emulsify, or solvents that dissolve grease, GreaseMaster lifts the buildup, leaving no oily film on the surface of the part. The cleaned surface can simply be rinsed and painted. The product works extremely well with a power washer or can be used as a bath. A pint-size container will yield 50 gallons of cleaning solution,

Immersing an entire car body removes coatings from every surface, internal as well as external. Along with the application of a rustproofing primer to external surfaces, a rust-prevention coating also needs to be sprayed into interior cavities like rocker panels. The difficulty of reaching some of these internal surfaces is the major deterrent (along with cost) of the commercial stripping process.

which can be reused by allowing the sediment to settle and the oils periodically skimmed off the top. If used with a power washer, a bed of hay under the wash area will collect oil and grease, leaving the runoff so clean that the familiar oil film rainbow effect can't be seen on the water's surface.

For extremely thick coatings, a GreaseMaster gel is available that can be used to pretreat the coating. After they have soaked for several hours, the thickly grease-encrusted parts can be power washed to peel off the buildup. This relatively new product is seeing widespread use by professional restoration shops as well as industry acceptance.

Another option that we've used in the past was spray oven cleaner. It's designed to cut baked-on grease, which makes it very similar to grease on drivetrain, chassis, or suspension parts that have been exposed to considerable heat (such as from the exhaust system). After spraying on a thick coat of oven cleaner, let it sit—just as you would to clean a non-self-cleaning oven—then use either a pressure washer or, preferably, a steam cleaner to hose everything off. A high-pressure car wash spray may also be suitable for removing the grime.

A product's safety, both to the user and others (children or animals) who might have contact, as well as to the

environment, should be a major concern to the collector car restorer. It only takes a few minutes to set up some kind of barrier to trap the oil, grease, and gas that you wash off the car—not to mention the harsh cleaning chemicals. If you're doing your cleaning on a paved or concrete surface, you can surround the car with old bath towels, which will act just like a boom, allowing much of the water to pass through, but preventing the crud and many of the chemicals.

GreaseMaster and many other detergents and solvents are now available in environmentally friendly versions that pose virtually no risk to your family, your pets or the environment, yet still provide exceptional cleaning properties.

STRIPPING OFF PAINT

If the car hasn't been repainted and the original finish is sound (the paint isn't checked and shows no signs of flaking or peeling), then the finish can be sanded and primed and prepped for a new finish coating. If, however, the finish is several layers thick or is badly blistered (blisters or bubbles in the paint indicate underlying rust or moisture or chemicals leaching onto the surface of the metal through improper body repairs), the old paint should be removed so that all damage to body panels can be noted

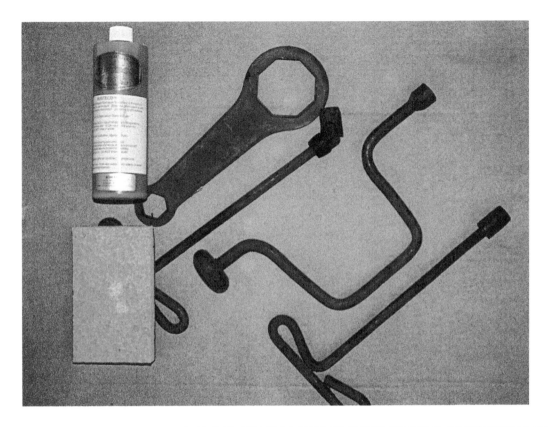

Ecoclean promotes its GreaseMaster degreasing and Rusteco derusting products as safe to use and environmentally harmless. The instructions on the Rusteco container call for abrading the rust with a scouring pad to help the chemical reach the metal.

PROTECTING CLEANED PARTS

There is a benefit to greasy, oily parts: the grease and oil protect them from rust. Unfortunately, it also makes them attract dirt and dust, so they end up looking dingy and gross.

This is important to remember, because once you clean your parts—by whatever method you use—you need to protect them so that they don't rust, corrode, or otherwise become contaminated.

Metal parts can often be sprayed with a zinc coating, or just a clear paint, but you need to be careful of the paint's sheen. A high-gloss clear will result in an incorrect-looking finish. The Eastwood Company offers low- and medium-gloss (satin) finish clears that can preserve the part without tipping anyone off that it's been painted.

Another option for parts that no longer have the original, "new metal" look is to spray them with a paint that approximates the original finish. Again, The Eastwood Company sells a variety of paints for just such uses.

Lastly, there are special processes to which parts can be treated that not only restores their original finish—like black oxide for hood latch components, or tin-zinc electroplating—but provides vital protection against rust and corrosion. Some parts that have been treated to these processes may still need to have a clear finish applied (with the correct sheen) to preserve the restored finish.

Don't forget that many new replacement parts—especially engine, suspension, or brake components—will quickly rust if not cleaned first (to remove any oils or grease from the manufacturing process) then protected.

After you remove the old grease, dirt, and maybe even the painted finish, you need to think about how to protect the cleaned part from becoming rusty or otherwise tarnished. The Eastwood Company has a variety of protective finishes that can be applied—either temporarily or permanently—depending on the material and the desired finish. These are three of the company's popular finishes: Spray gray, which gives a natural as-cast finish; Aluma-Blast for an aluminum-like finish; and Detail Gray for machined metal parts. It's wise to apply a clear finish atop these, as added protection.

Rusteco is available both as a liquid and a gel. To remove a coating of surface rust, I immersed this wrench from a Ford toolkit in liquid Rusteco for about 24 hours. Since the chemical does not attack the metal (it dissolves the rust), I did not need to be concerned about leaving the part too long in the derusting bath.

and repaired and an entirely new finish applied. Paint is typically removed through a combination of chemical and mechanical processes.

Paint will be removed from small parts that are chemically cleaned using the caustic chemical bath described above. A strong detergent solution of TSP, also described above, will often remove paint as well, though not as rapidly or thoroughly as a caustic chemical solution.

CHEMICAL STRIPPING

Paint can be stripped from larger surfaces, including body panels, using a chemical paint stripper (available from auto parts stores selling refinishing supplies). The paint stripper will soften and lift the paint from the surface, but won't remove it, so the process often takes on several more steps. Following the directions on the paint stripper product label, as the paint begins to bubble and lift, it is scraped off the surface using a putty knife. Not all the paint comes off this way—sometimes you may encounter very stubborn coatings that seem almost impervious to the chemical stripper. If the stripper allows most of the paint to be scraped off, whatever traces of primer or finish coat remain can be sanded (a dual-action sander, a tool

In situations where it's neither convenient nor possible to physically or chemically remove rust, corrosion can be stabilized and rendered inert using a rust converter chemical, available from a number of sources.

described in the painting chapter, works well for this) or scoured off using a wire brush mounted in the chuck of a portable electric drill.

When using a chemical paint stripper, it's important to perform the following procedures:

1. Thoroughly remove all paint from the area you're stripping. Any residue will show up under a finish coat.

2. Clean off all traces of stripper. Any chemical left on the area you're stripping or on adjoining surfaces will interfere with the priming and finish painting process. Be especially sure to clean all paint stripper out of body seams and crevices.

3. Clean and prep the surface for primer coating. Prime bare metal to prevent rusting.

HAVING A COMMERCIAL STRIPPER DO THE WORK

An alternative to tediously stripping off paint by hand is to have major panels like the doors, trunk, and hood—or even the entire car—chemically stripped by a commercial stripper. The commercial leader in chemical stripping is the Redi Strip Company, which serves collector car restorers through franchise locations primarily in the East and Upper Midwest. Because parts of the car body would have to be trucked or trailered to the Redi Strip location, the practicality of this option is limited to those living in proximity to cities where Redi Strip or some of its competitors operate. (Collector car hobby publications, like *Hemmings Motor News*, carry ads that list Redi Strip

Rust is often abraded out of the windshield channel using a sanding disk, wire brush, and die grinder.

Here, a bodyman is grinding light rust from the inside bottom edge of a door skin.

As an alternative to chemical stripping, the factory finish is often removed by sanding.

thoroughly cleaned, down to bare metal. (Using a reverse electrolysis process, the Redi Strip franchises can also remove rust.) Since any damage to the metal is now evident, this is an ideal time to do metal repair. However, the bare metal is also highly prone to rust. For temporary rust prevention, the Redi Strip franchise can put cleaned parts through a phosphate dip at extra cost. If the parts are stored indoors in a dry environment, the phosphate coating should prevent rusting while any damage to the metal is being repaired. But for longer-term rust prevention, both the interior and exterior surfaces need to be coated with a rustproofing sealer. On hoods, doors, and trunk lids, an effective way to coat inside surfaces is to pour a rust-inhibiting paint through the holes in the stiffening panel on the backside of these parts, then rock the part back and forth, swishing the paint around until it covers all of the inside surface. Interior surfaces of fully enclosed panels like door pillars can be rustproofed using wax-based coatings available from commercial services like Ziebart.

If commercial chemical stripping has a downside (apart from the limited number of locations), it's cost. Commercial strippers will usually give a cost estimate over the phone, but to do so they need a detailed description of the parts. Their rates are calculated on a time-in-the-tanks and labor basis, so batches of small parts can often be stripped for the same price as individual items. The process is not inexpensive and the limited number of locations, and consequent shipping/hauling costs, are likely to be the major deterrents to the commercial cleaning, stripping, and derusting service.

STRIPPING PAINT WITH ABRASIVE MEDIA

Paint and other coatings can be quickly and effectively stripped off parts by blasting with some type of abrasive media—sand being the most common. Abrasive blasting should not be used to strip paint from large, flat sheet-metal panels, as the blast's force can stretch and distort the metal. A thorough description of the media blasting process follows in Chapter 9.

DERUSTING THROUGH VARIOUS PROCESSES

Even cars that have spent their life in the dry Southwest are likely to have some rust—even if it's only a light coating of surface rust where the paint has weathered off. Collector cars from other regions, especially where salt is used to melt the snow from highways, may be riddled with rust. Rust holes in metal will have to be repaired, but even surface rust has to be removed or neutralized; otherwise the rust

franchise locations and phone numbers; for chemical stripping services in other locations, consult the telephone yellow pages of larger cities in your geographic region.)

Having a commercial stripper tackle the dirty work of cleaning off caked-on grease and mud, layers of paint, and gobs of body filler saves time, but metal laundering isn't a drive-through process. Parts that are candidates for the stripper's bath have to be disassembled as completely as possible. Immersion in the stripper's vats will remove rust proofing, seam caulking, and body filler—virtually all applied fillings—but it won't clean covered surfaces. In preparation for stripping a car body, the interior must be gutted (seats, upholstery, carpeting, dash instruments, etc.), and the glass, weather seal, all exterior trim, doors, hood and deck lids, and everything else must be removed down to the bare body.

When the parts emerge from the stripper's tanks, all surfaces of the metal, including hidden interior areas, are

will continue to fester, eating away at the metal, eventually loosening any filler and lifting the paint.

Two processes can be used to remove rust. One attacks the rust mechanically, the other chemically. The simplest mechanical method for attacking rust is to scour the metal with a wire brush. This may look effective, but it isn't. Even though all traces of rust scale and telltale orange coloring may be removed, leaving what appears to be shiny, bright metal, microscopic traces of rust likely still remain in pits where they're able to grow and attack the metal.

Scouring or scraping rust off metal is more effective if combined with a chemical rust-removal process. Rust can be attacked and neutralized chemically either with an acid solution or an organic antioxidant. Both types of chemicals are used in similar ways, but the method by which they attack the rust, their chemical properties, precautions associated with their use, and their ultimate disposal differ greatly.

Acid Derusting

Since acid will attack metal, a plastic or hard rubber container must be used to hold the acid bath. Plastic garbage cans with snap-on lids work well, since acid derusting solutions have a distinct garlic-and-onions odor. Acid will not penetrate paint or grease, so parts must be thoroughly stripped before entering the derusting bath.

While many acids are effective derusting agents, phosphoric acid, sold by auto parts stores carrying refinishing supplies and restoration suppliers, such as the Eastwood Company, is a readily available and effective rust-removing chemical. Diluted with water to the recommended working strength, the acid solution is relatively harmless, but you should wear full clothing, rubber gloves, and a face shield to protect skin and eyes. If any acid does splash onto exposed skin, it should be washed off immediately with water.

Although larger, more deeply corroded parts may need to soak for several hours, possibly as long as several days in the dilute phosphoric acid solution, thin metal parts should be checked every few minutes because the acid attacks the metal as soon as it finishes eating rust. Springs and tempered steel parts like wheel spindles should not be derusted by acid pickling (as the acid bath is called) because the process causes a reaction called hydrogen embrittlement that weakens the metal. Nonferrous parts (aluminum, brass, copper) should not be placed in the acid bath, either. These metals will be quickly eaten by the acid. Components containing springs or nonferrous parts should be completely disassembled before derusting in the acid bath.

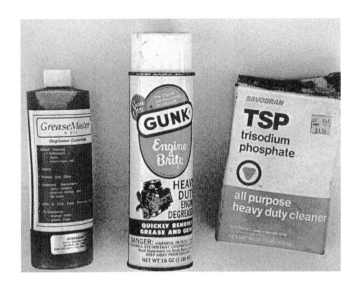

Here are three of the most useful products for cleaning grease-coated parts. GreaseMaster, left, is a commercial product available only from its distributor, Ecoclean. GUNK is widely available in auto parts stores and discount marts. Cleaning products containing TSP are available from hardware stores.

When all traces of rust are gone, the parts can be removed from the acid bath. The metal will be coated with a yellowing-gray film. This residue will retard rerusting, but the parts should be painted for lasting protection. Over time, a grayish sludge will accumulate at the bottom of the derusting solution. The chemical's working life will be prolonged if you dispose of this residue. The easiest way to do so is to slowly pour the acid from one container to another, taking care not to agitate the sediment. After most of the acid has been transferred, pour the sludge into a plastic container (like a milk jug) that can be disposed of in a safe manner.

Organic Derusting

Unlike acids, which remove rust by eating the metal, Rusteco (a companion product to GreaseMaster, described in the section above on cleaning) works by chemically removing the oxygen from the oxidation—in effect, deoxidizing the metallic oxide. After Rusteco has done its work, what you'll see is a surface coating of blackened, powdered metal. This powder coating is easily removed by wiping, brushing, or pressure washing.

Because it is composed primarily of organically grown plants, Rusteco has nothing in its makeup that is hazardous to the environment or the user. Further, the product works with any metal, not just iron or steel, also removing oxidation from aluminum or copper. Because it attacks only rust, the chemical does not do further damage to the parts. Of importance when derusting wheels or suspension

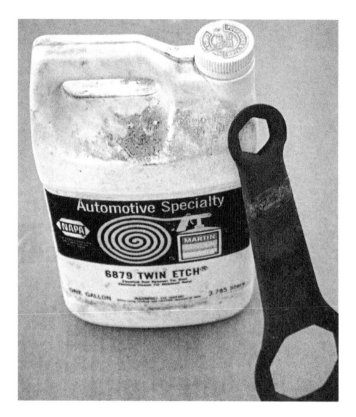

Dilute phosphoric acid, available under a variety of names from auto parts stores selling automotive painting products, is an effective derusting agent for small items.

pieces, Rusteco will not cause hydrogen embrittlement—a condition associated with acid derusting that can dangerously weaken stress-prone metal.

Available either as a liquid or gel, Rusteco can be used as a dipping bath or a gel coating, which can be wiped on large parts. (The distributor recommends first spraying on a mist coating and covering the gel with thin plastic sheets to keep the chemical moist and active.) Cleaned derusted parts are ready for painting, though a Rusteco mist spray will provide a temporary protective coating against rerusting as long as the metal is stored in dry conditions.

Additional benefits—Rusteco works great to loosen rust-frozen bolts; it's better than penetrating oil because it dissolves the rust that is binding the bolt. Also, unlike acids, Rusteco does not affect paint. It has additionally

been used to derust instrument gauges without damaging the gauge's painted face. And think about this: washing the powder film left on the metal after the Rusteco treatment onto the lawn or garden gives the plants a shot of safe, liquid fertilizer.

Both Rusteco and its companion product GreaseMaster fit their manufacturer's slogan well: "Providing Environmentally Safe Solutions for the Twenty-First Century." See Resources for supplier information.

Stabilizing, Sealing in Rust

Where it's not convenient or possible to physically or chemically remove rust, the corrosion can be stabilized or rendered inert and sealed in using a variety of rust-containment products. These products work on two principles: (1) that active rust can be converted to an inactive coating and (2) that a hard paint layer sealing off the underlying metal will stop further corrosion. While not a total solution to the corrosion problem, these products are effective at arresting rust and may be effective for the period of time you are likely to use and enjoy the car. The permanent solution to the problem of rust is always to remove and replace the rusted metal or eliminate the rust.

Among the more popular rust sealer/stabilizers are POR-15 (the initials in the product name literally mean paint over rust) and Corroless. While both products have their merits, POR-15 is subject to deterioration by ultraviolet light (and is therefore best used on chassis parts or covered with a finish paint). As a preparation step, all loose rust should be scraped off and the remaining rust coating scoured to clean metal as effectively as possible. Essentially a paint, the rust sealer/stabilizer is then brushed or sprayed onto the metal in a thick coating. POR-15 has the additional disadvantage that any product remaining in the can is likely to harden unless carefully sealed. Corroless can be reused.

With the possible exception of Ecoclean, each of the derusting methods described above has limitations either in application or effectiveness. The next chapter presents the most widely used and effective derusting method—abrasive blasting, also highly effective in removing paint.

Chapter 9
Abrasive Blasting

What used to be generically called sandblasting is now called abrasive blasting or, more often, "media blasting." The process hasn't changed, but a wider variety of media than just sand is used to prevent damage to the items being cleaned. For softer metals like aluminum or brass, or engine blocks where sand dust could block vital internal passages, and for some plastics, glass beads are an excellent blast media. Walnut shells, too, are used when a softer abrasive material is needed.

A more recent addition to the blaster's arsenal is bicarbonate of soda—more commonly known as "baking soda"—which is a highly flexible media that can be used for everything from body panels to aluminum engine parts to engine blocks. Soda blasting also happens to be very forgiving, in that it won't harm glass, plastic, or brightmetal trim if you accidentally blast those items. (Prolonged exposure to the media stream could cause damage—especially to soft plastic, so you should still be cautious.) Baking soda even leaves a minute, powdery residue on metal parts that helps protect them from rust or corrosion for several days after cleaning; however, this residue should be cleaned off prior to applying any kind of finish to the part, to ensure proper adhesion. You also need to be aware that because of the ultrafine sizes of bicarbonate of soda particles, you need special mixing valves and nozzles to blast with it.

For more aggressive blasting, silicone carbide cuts through even heavy rust. And for general-purpose rust and paint removal, beach sand remains a low-cost, readily available blast medium.

Whether it's a car frame or a wire wheel, abrasive blasting will quickly strip off solid coatings and leave the metal shiny new. The process is simple and so widely applicable to a collector car restoration project that investment in at least hobbyist-level equipment is almost a must.

COMPARING TYPES OF ABRASIVE BLASTING EQUIPMENT

Basically, there are two types of abrasive blasting equipment: siphon fed and pressure fed. Both are powered by an air compressor. The siphon type is cheaper, but also less effective because it uses the compressed air to suck the sand or other media into the blast stream. The siphon blaster's lower price relates to its simple design—essentially

a container to hold the medium, a hose for the air supply and another for the medium, and a nozzle to which both hoses attach. In principle, a siphon blaster works much like a carburetor. At an orifice in the nozzle, air from the compressed air line rushes past a port or vent connected to the hose from the medium supply. A vacuum created by the orifice sucks the medium into the air stream, where it is then forced through the nozzle opening and onto the part. Siphon blasters are effective for small parts like door hinges or a seat frame. On larger items like wheels, you may lose patience before getting the job done.

A pressure-fed blaster, shown here, uses the air supply more efficiently, allowing longer blasting periods and making this type of blaster more effective on larger parts.

The pace of the blasting is directly related to the capacity of the compressed air source. This convertible body required an industrial capacity compressor to provide a continuous air supply.

Pressure-fed blasters use the air supply to pressurize the container holding the medium, which is then forced out a hose and through the blast nozzle onto the part. Since the compressed air is pushing the medium, the air supply is used more efficiently, allowing longer blasting periods and giving the medium more force, thereby making this type of blaster more effective on larger parts. It's the need for a container strong enough to be pressurized that raises this type of blaster's cost.

Besides the equipment, two factors critical to abrasive blasting's success are an adequate air supply and dry media. Smaller nozzles and shut-off valves allow lower capacity portable air compressors to power hobby-size blasters, but at the penalty of slower operation. Fast, efficient operation requires a larger air supply than what's available from most portable compressors. One possible solution is to couple two portable compressors in tandem using a "T" coupling. Collector car restorers sometimes pool equipment for larger jobs like abrasive blasting a car frame. The other solution is to use a highly versatile and very useful industrial capacity stationary compressor, perhaps after business hours at a service facility, or by purchasing this equipment yourself.

AVOIDING THE MOISTURE PROBLEM

For abrasive blasting to be successful, it's essential that the media be dry. Otherwise, the media may plug the hose or clog the nozzle, quickly turning the blasting session into a very frustrating experience.

Moisture can contaminate the blast media from two sources. One is the air compressor. When the compressor is operated in high-humidity conditions moisture in the air is drawn into the compressor tank where it can condense, forming a pool of water on the bottom of the tank. For this reason, it's a good idea to periodically remove the pipe thread plug on the bottom of the compressor tank and allow accumulated water to drain from the tank. Water in the compressor tank not only can be drawn into the air stream, but also will breed rust, eventually rotting out the tank. Because of the prevalence of moisture, either from ambient humidity or water in the tank, an air compressor used for media blasting should have a moisture filter in the air line, typically between the outlet from the compressor and the air hose. This moisture filter or separator is drained periodically to remove accumulated water.

Moisture originating with the air compressor is also controlled by using metal piping, rather than relying on rubber hose to carry the compressed air from its source to the blasting equipment. Metal pipe has two advantages over rubber hose. First, it typically has a larger diameter, causing less restriction, and second, the colder pipe will cause moisture to condense, drying the air. If the pipe is fitted with drain valves, accumulated water can be drained off periodically, again helping prevent moisture contamination. With a metal piping system, shorter lengths of air compressor hose are needed, reducing constriction.

An alternative to metal piping is PVC pipe, which offers many of the same benefits as metal, but without the possibility of rust forming in the lines, which could clog your tools, or worse, damage the parts you're working on.

Because of the possibility of contaminants in the pipes or hoses, I actually run two filters on my compressor: one at the compressor, before the air enters any hard metal or PVC pipes, and a second at the exit points, where I connect air hoses. In addition, I periodically use my air nozzle to allow any contaminants in my hoses to be blown out.

The second source of moisture contamination is the medium itself. Sand attracts moisture if stored in high-humidity conditions or if gathered from a wet setting like a beach. Baking soda is also especially prone to absorbing moisture and clogging. Moist or wet sand has to be dried by spreading out a thin layer on a tarp or plastic sheeting exposed to bright sun. When the sand is powdery dry, it is ready for use. Other media may also attract moisture, though not as seriously as sand.

PREPARING PARTS FOR ABRASIVE BLASTING

Using media ranging in abrasiveness from soft to sharp allows you to strip and clean brass, aluminum, steel, and even fiberglass parts using the abrasive blasting process. However, it is very important to disassemble component parts, remove body panels, and disassemble chassis pieces as much as possible before blasting. A collector car enthusiast in our area allowed a body shop to abrasive-blast the body of his MGA roadster to remove the old finish using sand. The shop did only minimal disassembly, removing windshield, seats, and other interior panels. The engine was left in the car, presumably covered. Still, after blasting, sand was everywhere—behind the instrument glass, inside the heater, brake master cylinder, engine generator and starter, even the engine itself. This enthusiast spent as much having the sand removed as he did having the car painted. Not a financially rewarding deal.

While media such as poly abrasive or walnut shells work well for removing paint and produce as much dust as sand, the residue and overspray from abrasive blasting are not easily contained. Nor is there any effective method

Abrasive blasting works best on parts that have been completely disassembled, either in preparation for metal repair or rebuilding. Mike Cavey

When using abrasive blasting to strip and clean sheet metal, be careful with flat panels. A stretch of flat metal can very quickly become distorted under the high-pressure blast. Sheet metal with curves and crowns, as seen here, can typically be abrasive-blasted without damage or distortion.

Removing old paint coatings allows any stress cracks and other damage to the fiberglass to be repaired and the body prepared for painting.

for sealing out the blast media. Blast a sealed differential or a transmission and the inside will still be full of sand. If mechanical parts are being abrasive-blasted, plan to completely disassemble and rebuild them before use on a car. If a gas tank is abrasive-blasted, know that there'll be dust and media inside and that you'll replace many, many fuel filters before the tank is finally clean.

The abrasive blasting process works best on parts that have been completely disassembled, either in preparation

for metal repair or rebuilding. If you're looking at abrasive blasting as a quick and easy way to strip paint from body sheet metal (actually, it is the original quick and dirty way) and the body hasn't been completely gutted and removed from the chassis, then use a chemical or mechanical paint-removing process described in the preceding chapter.

DOING ABRASIVE BLASTING

The abrasive blasting process is noisy, and with most media, especially sand, it is dirty. Cabinets designed to contain the media and associated dust and debris allow the process to be done inside. This is very helpful when the location of your shop, perhaps in a residential neighborhood, won't allow you to do abrasive blasting outside. The cabinets allow abrasive blasting to be done year-round and have the additional advantages of enabling easy recycling of the media and are especially convenient for cleaning small parts. Naturally, the size of the cabinet determines what size parts will fit inside. In capacity, abrasive-blast cabinets range from bench-top units for blasting small parts to industrial capacity models that will hold parts as large as a fender. For larger components, such as a car frame, the blasting has to be done outside.

Using a blast cabinet to contain the parts and media frees you from wearing a hood, face mask, or other protective clothing. Working outside, however, you must wear the abrasive blaster's protective hood with face shield, respirator, and full protective clothing. Hoods equipped to deliver a fresh air supply (through a breathing hose supplied by an air pump) help ensure that fine media particles aren't inhaled into the lungs. This type of hood can also be worn for spray painting—the two applications making it, perhaps, a desirable purchase. Heavy leather gloves, such as those welders wear; leather work shoes; a long-sleeved shirt; and work pants complete the abrasive blasting outfit. Even if you are doing the blasting on a hot day, you should not expose bare skin to the abrasive blast.

The air compressor must be located outside the blast area, since dust particles could clog the compressor's filters and ruin the motor bearings. Regardless of the precautions you may take to seal off pant legs or shirt sleeves, media dust and debris from the parts being blasted will sift through your clothing. When the activity is finished, you'll be filthy and ready for a shower. Be sure to shake out the clothing you wore, maybe even soak the items down with a hose, before placing them in a clothes washer. The amount of dust that penetrates your clothes is a convincing sign of the importance of wearing a professional-grade respirator or drawing breathing air from a fresh air supply.

Fiberglass bodies, as on Corvettes, can be stripped using softer media like glass beads.

Proper abrasive blasting garb includes the full hood and heavy gloves shown here. The Eastwood Company

BLAST MEDIA SELECTION CHART

Blasting Media	Removal of carbon, rust, and paint	Paint removal with no rust	Paint preparation	Transmission and engine cleaning	Brazing and welding preparation	Glass etching (frosting)
Glass Bead	Good	Good	Good	Good	Better	Good
Aluminum Oxide	Best		Best	Good	Better	
Silicon Carbide	Better		Better		Best	Best
Walnut Shells		Better		Best		
Poly Abrasive		Best		Better		
Bicarbonate Soda	Good	Better	Better	Better		

Abrasive Media should be selected to match the blasting project.

Here's an aluminum intake manifold being blasted by bicarbonate soda. Note the clean, original surface exposed just ahead of the carb mounting surface and how the "baking soda" didn't harm fine details like the Winter's Foundry snowflake casting. It took only about a minute to clean the entire intake to like-new condition—even the brass plugs and fittings looked new.

Actually operating the abrasive blaster is as simple as the machine itself. First, the unit is attached to a source of compressed air. The canister (on siphon blasters) or tank (on pressurized blasters) is then filled with media matched to the items being blasted. For soft metals, such as brass and aluminum, glass beads are used to remove coatings without damaging the metal's surface. For fast abrasion on heavy rust, media like steel grit or aluminum oxide may be used. Most readily available and general purpose is beach sand, available from lumber yards and mass merchandiser garden shops. With a siphon blaster, the pickup hose is often simply inserted into the media (sand) supply—saving the effort of filling the canister. Pressurized blasters have a mixing valve at the bottom of the tank, which, along with the lid that seals the tank, has to be closed. Now, assuming proper protective clothing is worn, the blasting can begin.

To use a siphon blaster, simply point the nozzle at the work piece and press the trigger. You may experience a delayed action while the air stream sucks up the sand. With a pressurized blaster, first open the nozzle shutoff (if the unit is so equipped), then in a gradual motion open the mixing valve. Aim the nozzle so that the medium strikes the work piece at about a 45-degree angle. Paint and rust will spray off the metal much like dirt being hosed off. When the sand (media) mound is consumed or the tank drained, close the nozzle and shut off the air supply. On

A siphon blaster is a much simpler device than a pressurized blaster, consisting only of a siphon gun and a container to hold the medium. However, it is not as effective as a pressurized blaster for cleaning heavy rust scale or larger parts.

pressure-fed blasters you'll also close the mixing valve. When the dust settles, you can take off your hood and refill the blaster. To allow the media to be reused, a two- or three-sided pen is often constructed as a backdrop to the blasting area. This pen has two advantages: it helps control the dust and it collects the media, which can often be swept up and recycled.

When using abrasive blasting to strip and clean sheet metal, be very careful with flat panels. A long stretch of flat metal can easily and quickly become stretched and distorted under the high-pressure abrasive blast, requiring a skilled metal craftsman to repair the damage, or more likely a replacement part. If the body panels on your car consist largely of flat expanses, you may want to test the abrasive blast's effect on a scrap part using a softer medium and lower air pressure setting. Sheet metal with curves or creases, like a trunk lid or fender crown, can typically be abrasive blasted without damage. Nonetheless, always use care and caution when directing an abrasive blast at thin sheet metal. Make several light passes over the area rather than attempting to clean all coating and rust in one heavy pass. Never blast sheet metal with chrome, plastic, or glass attached.

Sometimes it's desirable to abrasive-blast only a small area—a rust blister on a door or fender, for example. In these situations the tool to use is a spot blaster. A soft rubber cup over the nozzle contains the media and focuses the blast on the spot needing cleaning. If the rust blister or other blemish needing cleaning is larger than the diameter of the rubber cup, the spot blaster can be slowly walked

across the part's surface. As long as the lip of the cup is kept pressed firmly against the work surface, only minimal dust escapes. Paint and rust are stripped to bare metal in seconds. The spot blaster is a very useful tool when doing partial restoration or repair.

After blasting, the metal needs to be treated to prevent rusting. Left untreated, the bare metal will quickly acquire an orange coating—a telltale sign of rust. Applying a wash coating of dilute phosphoric acid (available at auto parts stores selling refinishing products) or Rusteco (the organic antioxidant described in Chapter 8) will protect against rapid rusting. Any necessary straightening, welding, or filling should be done in bare metal. Otherwise, the metal should be primed and painted without delay.

After blasting parts, you'll likely want to dust them off using dry compressed air, then apply something to protect the fresh, clean finish. Products like Eastwood's Diamond Clear are great for protecting bare metal surfaces.

Even if the metal looks new, some restorers like to apply a few coats of Eastwood's metal detailing paints, Spray Gray, Detail Gray, and Aluma-Blast for a long-lasting, like-new finish.

Chapter 10
Metal Repair

After stripping body metal clean of paint and rust, you can see the metal's true condition more accurately. Layers of paint may have covered earlier body repairs, and dents may have been masked by plastic body filler. If the metal has been abrasive blasted or dipped in a chemical stripping/derusting bath, most likely any filler that was on the metal panel is now gone. If the finish was removed using a chemical stripper or sanding (or combination stripper and sanding), filler may still be obscuring the panel's true condition. In this case, the filler should be removed using either a sander or grinder. Any rust damage should now be visible as holes, ranging from pinpoints to gaping openings in the metal. Likewise, dents and distortions should be equally visible. It's time for assessing the extent of the damage and developing a strategy for repair.

DEVISING A METAL REPAIR STRATEGY

We'll begin by honestly assessing the damage. If we're fortunate enough to have a car that has spent most of its life in a dry climate, the metal may need only some minor dent repair, and perhaps only a few extraneous holes filled (for awkwardly placed radio antennas, accessory lights, or souvenir badges). However, if the car is from a moist climate—or worse, the Rust Belt—metal damage may be extensive. Entire panels (fenders and the floor) may need to be replaced. Possibly the entire body looks like its best use would be recycling stock for a steel mill.

If entire panels need to be replaced, the best possible solution is reproduction panels from a restoration supplier specializing in that make and model vehicle; an alternative answer is better-condition originals. If you contacted parts

Where entire panels need to be replaced, it may be possible to purchase new reproductions from a restoration supplier. Be forewarned, however, that the quality of these reproduction panels varies greatly. The metal is likely to be thinner than original stock and the shape may also vary from original. This rear quarter panel on a 1967 Camaro required extensive rework by a skilled metal technician to approach the original fit.

Where an entire panel isn't needed, damaged metal can often be replaced with a patch panel. These smaller pieces are many times more widely available and easier to install than a larger panel assembly.

sources for catalogs and joined a club supporting your vehicle during the research step, you're now well equipped to determine the availability of reproduction body parts. For many popular collector cars—early Mustangs and Camaros are examples—reproduction panels for virtually all external sheet metal, including floor panels, are available from restoration suppliers. Two words of caution, however: (1) reproduction sheetmetal pieces are not always an exact match for originals (it's important to check the quality and reputation of the supplier), and (2) reproduction body parts are sometimes molded fiberglass rather than steel—this is especially true of fenders and hoods. That's not to say fiberglass body parts can't be used (after all, they won't rust), but unless you're restoring a Corvette they're not going to feel, sound, or look exactly like original.

Where reproduction panels aren't available, you're going to have to work out a solution from other alternatives. These include the following options: Option 1, repair what's already on the car. Where this is the only option

(typically, because the car is rare or unique), the result is likely to be time consuming, to require considerable skill, and to be expensive. Option 2, find a replacement original. Sometimes it's possible to locate an NOS fender, hood, or other large body panel salvaged from dealer inventory. Leftover factory parts are clearly the most desirable option and also likely to be expensive. An alternative is a used but good-condition replacement panel. Sometimes these can come from a parts car of a more common body style. One restorer of a letter-series Chrysler 300 convertible tells of using the rust-free floor from a more plentiful two-door hardtop to replace the completely rusted-out floor in his convertible. Option 3, fabricate a replacement. This may work for flat floor panels but isn't viable for fenders or compound curved body panels, unless you're a consummate metal craftsman with such Old World tools as an English wheel.

Maybe the rust isn't widespread throughout the whole panel; maybe the rust and dent damage is localized so that

A WORD OF CAUTION

One important word of caution when repairing damaged metal: don't remove the doors until all other metal repair is completed. The doors establish critical body dimensions that can be lost if structural metal is cut out and replaced with the doors removed. Likewise, on cars with separate body/frame construction, if possible leave the body mounted to the frame while repairing or replacing structural sections of the body, like floors and rocker panels. The frame serves as a jig to preserve proper body alignment, something essential if the hood, doors, and trunk, as well as the fenders, are to fit properly and for the car's overall appearance when the body repairs are finished. On unit-bodied cars, the frame structure is integral, and the doors will be used to keep the body from sagging or collapsing in the center.

ONE SIDE AT A TIME

Another important guideline: work on only one side of the car at a time. Remember, the goal is to not get the car so far apart that it can't be put together fairly quickly if need be. Repairing metal damage one side at a time has another advantage. You can elevate the side of the car you're working on, tipping it at an angle and supporting the raised side solidly on jack stands, to make the work more visible and easier to reach. Caution: once the side of the car you'll be working on first is raised and supported on jack stands, grab hold of a fender, bumper, or door handle and rock the car to make sure it is securely supported. You don't want the car to move or tumble off a jack stand while you're pounding away with a hammer and chisel trying to loosen a section of metal. If the shop has exposed overhead trusses or beams, you may want to double the safety by slinging a chain fall or using a length of heavy chain or rope to secure the car from above.

When reproduction panels aren't available, you're going to have to fabricate. To repair the bottom door lip, this restorer has rolled two lengths of steel using a heating/air conditioning contractor's metal brake. The panel had to be made in two pieces, welded together, due to the limitations of the brake.

it can be cut out and replaced or covered with a patch. Panels contoured to match common rust-out sections of fenders and doors, as well as susceptible body areas like floors or rear wheelwells, are available from restoration suppliers for a wide range of popular collector vehicles. When damage can be repaired with a patch panel, you have two advantages: the patch panel will be cheaper than buying a new fender, door, or other large replacement panel, and you'll be keeping as much of the car's body sheet metal as original as possible.

Where a needed patch panel isn't available from a restoration supplier, an NOS item can sometimes be found (in the 1950s and earlier, when cars were built of more substantial metal, patch panels were commonly used by auto body shops to repair minor metal damage). When searching for NOS parts, a *Hollanders* manual, described in the research chapter, is very helpful since the same repair panel may fit several different cars. As an example, when my father restored his 1941 Series 61 Cadillac convertible, he found that rocker panels from a 1940 Buick sedan (cut slightly shorter to match the convertible's two-door body) made a perfect replacement.

When neither reproduction nor NOS repair panels are available, suitable patch sections can often be cut from used body parts that may have damage in other areas. Again, these can sometimes come for cars of different make and body type than the restoration recipient. The final option is to make the patch from a piece of sheet metal. This is

Rust can strike anywhere. This GTO's roof has been exposed to the elements for countless years, and as a result, its paint has dried and peeled away, exposing the metal beneath. Most of this is still surface rust, which can be removed with a grinder, but some areas will be too thin and will need to be patched ... or the entire roof skin may need to be replaced. Fortunately, for many popular collector cars, aftermarket replacement panels are available from a number of sources, which now allow you to essentially rebuild a car with all new sheet metal. But be warned that not all reproduction panels will fit spot-on, and may require some "adjustments" to fit properly, so always test-fit and adjust them prior to painting.

what a metal craftsman would do. Tools for contouring patch sections are available from the Eastwood Company.

Cutting away Damaged Metal

After assessing the extent of rust damage and determining a repair strategy (whether to replace entire panels, use repair panels, or a combination), the next step is to cut away damaged metal. Severely rusted panels may seem the easiest to remove, but this is not the case, since rust dulls cutting tools much more quickly than clean metal. Several methods can be used to cut away damaged metal.

1. Hammer and chisel. By far the slowest, most time consuming, most labor-intensive, and frustrating, but requiring only common hand tools, a hammer and chisel get the job done—barely. If you're forced to this Stone Age method, keep the chisel sharp (using your bench grinder), make the hammer a hefty one, and wear gloves and a face shield.

2. Metal nibbler. You won't have much success cutting body sheet metal with hardware store variety metal shears

(intended for cutting soft metals like aluminum). However, a metal nibbler (available from restoration tool suppliers like the Eastwood Company) slices through steel as thick as 16 gauge fairly easily. Be sure to order the extra blade sets.

3. Cutoff grinder. Here's a tool that'll slice through body sheet metal as easily as if it were paper. Grinders can be electric or air powered. The air-powered tools are cheaper, but require at least a 3-horsepower air compressor with a minimum tank capacity of 30 gallons. Be sure to wear a face shield and heavy gloves.

4. Air chisel. Buy a quality tool, keep a sharp chisel, and you'll slice through sheet metal quicker than you can say, "Hey, this is fun!" Remember, rust will dull the chisel a lot faster than clean metal, so make your cut away from the rust.

5. Air nibbler. A similar tool to Number 3, but faster since it uses compressed air for power, and not the muscles in your hands and forearms. The Eastwood Company

One way to remove old metal is with an air chisel.

markets a power nibbler that mounts to the chuck of an electric drill. It isn't as efficient as the air nibbler, but will certainly be easier to use than a hand tool.

6. Oxyacetylene torch. Absolutely the fastest way to cut through anything, an oxyacetylene torch is the ultimate tool for slicing away damaged sheet metal as easily as opening a pop-top soda can. But let's not forget the torch's limitations (other than its possible absence from our tool kit). You don't want to use a torch to cut metal that's backed by upholstery or undercoating. You can't use a torch in the vicinity of gas lines or the fuel tank. You shouldn't apply the torch's heat to a large, flat section of body panel.

7. Plasma cutter. A plasma cutter is akin to a welder, in that it creates a plasma arc that literally melts through metal, usually up to ¼-inch thick. Like a welder, you need to be careful not to warp panels, but plasma cutters usually

allow you to pass through panels quickly enough that the heat does not saturate into a panel, causing warpage.

At the factory, the body was assembled by spot welding panels to each other. These spot welds are quite easily recognizable, even under layers of paints, as small fingertip-size circles aligned in seams, such as doorjambs, where panel sections join. Although it's possible to remove panels by cutting along the edge of a seam, it's better to remove the panel with the seam lip intact, and to do so requires cutting the spot welds. It seems a simple process, especially where the spot welds are visible; however, the metal at the spot weld is very hard, requiring special cutters. These spot weld cutters, as the tool is called, are available from professional tool suppliers like Snap-On or restoration suppliers like the Eastwood Company. A professional tool with a hardened cutter tip can be used for several hundred cuts without resharpening. Attempting to remove spot welds with a drill using a carbon steel bit has two problems. First, even a good quality bit will dull quickly, either requiring lots of resharpening or lots of bits. Second, you don't want to drill a hole entirely through the spot weld. Rather, the intent is to drill out the spot weld in only the top layer of metal. Often a seam or joint will have several layers of metal. Ideally, welds should be cut through one layer at a time, allowing the panels to be removed in the reverse sequence from which they were installed. This can be a tedious, time-consuming process and here you'll find that badly rusted cars come apart much more easily than cars where the metal is in better condition. However, severe rust is much harder to repair because once you've removed all the damaged metal, there's nothing left for the new pieces to join.

When all the spot welds holding a panel in place have been drilled out, the panel can sometimes simply be removed, leaving the pieces it was joined to intact. Other times seams elsewhere on the panel will have to be cut apart. If spot welds in underlying metal have been left intact, the new panel can be made to look factory-installed by rewelding at the spot locations.

Attaching New Metal

In some cases a replacement panel, like a fender, is simply bolted on. This, needless to say, is the easiest repair method. However, in many cases, if the outer panel (typically a fender) has rust damage, the inner structure that the panel bolts to is also likely to be rotted and require patching. In nearly all cases, the new metal is going to be joined by welding. Since several welding processes can be used, we'll compare the options. Believe it or not, for a number of applications, including replacing the outer panels

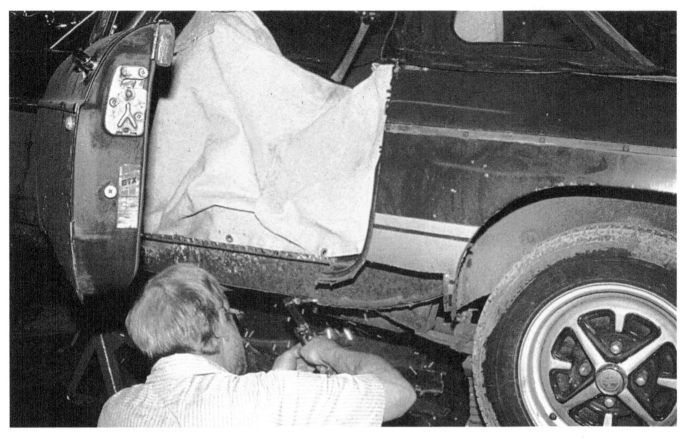

Another way to cut through anything is with an oxyacetylene torch. But don't overlook the torch's limitations. You don't want to cut metal that's backed by upholstery or undercoating with a torch, and you can't use a torch in the vicinity of gas lines or the fuel tank. And the heat of the torch could distort the metal you're cutting or the surrounding metal.

Many bodymen prefer to use an air-powered cutting wheel to remove damaged metal. It's fast and cheap, and because it cuts quickly, it allows you to progress at a pace that doesn't heat-soak the metal, thus minimizing warpage and distortion of remaining metal.

The welding technique used most commonly for sheetmetal repair is MIG welding. The advantages are localized heat, which lowers the risk of metal distortion. The process is easy to learn.

Regardless of the welding technique, you've got to figure some way to clamp the panels tightly together. These plug binders, available from the Eastwood Company, provide nearly 20 pounds of holding power each. They are inserted into ¼-inch holes drilled at intervals along the seam. When the panel is welded into place, the plug binders are removed and the holes filled, either by gas or MIG welding.

(called "skins") on doors, the new metal can be glued in place. Gluing is replacing welding in new car assembly, and the same high-strength metal-to-metal glues used by new car manufacturers are also available to hobbyists.

Gas Welding

Gas welding with an oxyacetylene torch is the most versatile method for joining replacement or patch panels as well as filling small holes and assisting in working out dents. This is the method most likely to be used by professional restorers—and the only method used by metal craftsmen. Gas welding has several advantages to the hobbyist restorer, as well as some drawbacks.

Advantages If a welding torch has been purchased to help with disassembly, the tool investment has already been made.

At least a moderate level of skill with gas welding can be achieved with a short period of training and practice.

A gas welding outfit has other uses in body repair besides joining metal, including shrinking stretched metal, brazing, and soldering.

Disadvantages Gas welding applies intense heat to the metal and can cause thin sheet metal to contort so severely that a metal craftsman's skills may be needed to repair the damage.

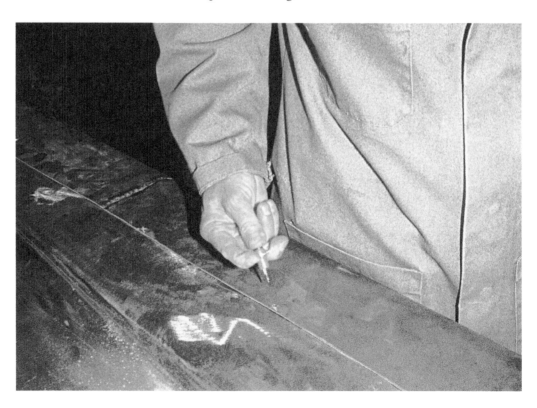

Another clamping method is with special welding clamps that are a variation on the familiar Vise-Grips. These special welding clamps are available from auto parts stores selling body repair supplies and from the Eastwood Company.

Although relatively little practice is needed to create a basic weld, mastery of this form of welding is an art that one could spend years perfecting.

Arc Welding

Arc welding uses electric current to heat the metal at the point of contact to a molten state. In its basic form, arc welding is better suited to heavier metal like repairing a frame or chassis pieces than joining body metal. However, several variations of the arc welding process apply to body repair. These include:

MIG welding, which uses wire for the electrode and gas instead of flux (or flux core wire) to shield the weld.

TIG welding, which is similar to MIG in operation but applicable to a wider range of metals and has the capability of higher quality welds.

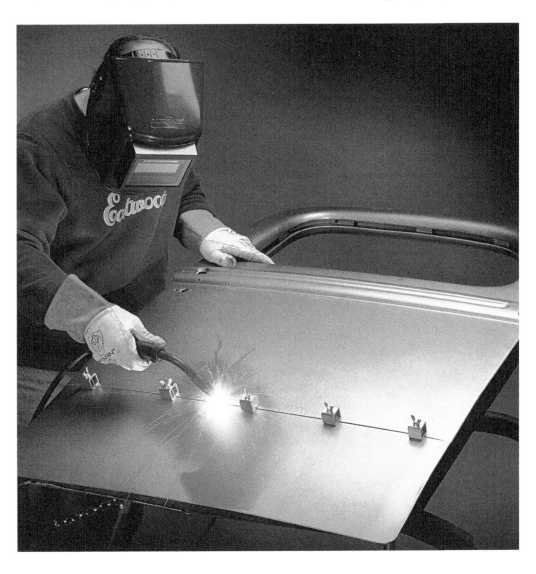

Once the panels are clamped tightly together, the seam can be joined using a MIG, as shown here, or by gas welding. The Eastwood Company

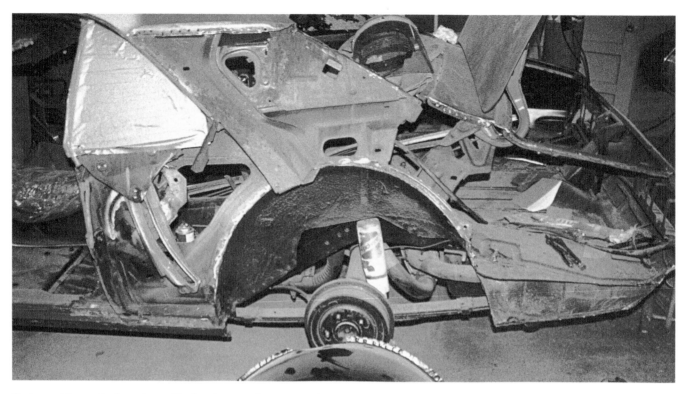

Rust around the rear fender arches and trunk well may require that the entire rear quarter section of the car be cut away and replaced. The extent of repair may seem extreme, but it is sometimes easier to replace entire sections of the car (when new parts are available) than to patch just the rusted sections.

If the body hasn't been chemically dipped or sandblasted, surface rust is likely on inner panel surfaces. The rust can be neutralized by sanding off loose scale and treating the metal with a rust neutralizer product or a coating of a paint-over-rust (POR) product that seals in the surface oxidation.

LEARNING TO WELD

Although it's possible to teach yourself either gas or arc welding by using the manual with the welding equipment and watching instructional videotapes or DVDs, you'll be sure to learn proper safety habits and become a more proficient welder if you enroll in an adult education class in welding offered at an area technical high school or community college.

Safety precautions are not the kind of information most people pay a lot of attention to when they're trying to teach themselves a skill. In a welding class you will learn that ultraviolet rays from an arc flash can cause retina damage; consequently, you will be told that you must use a helmet specially designed to shield your eyes whenever you are arc welding. You will also be instructed to develop the habit of warning bystanders when you are about to strike an arc. Since a child's curious eyes are drawn to the welding action, you must be very careful not to weld when children are around.

Welding requires protective clothing similar to that worn during sandblasting. Heavy leather gloves, work clothes, leather shoes, welding goggles (for gas welding) or a helmet (for arc welding), and a cap will protect your eyes and keep sparks and hot metal from burning your hair or skin.

When you are working with equipment that produces several-thousand-degree temperatures, you have to think of the possible consequences of seemingly harmless habits. Carrying a butane lighter in your pants or jacket pocket, for example, invites disaster. If a spark from the welding operation were to ignite a butane canister, the tiny lighter could explode with deadly force.

Some other good safety tips include:

• making sure you are not standing on damp ground when arc welding

• never putting oil on regulators, hoses, torches, or fittings of a gas welding outfit

Besides the benefit of thorough instruction, welding classes often give students the opportunity to practice newly learned skills on projects they choose. If you decide to learn welding in order to repair rust damage to your car, a welding class may be an ideal opportunity to get acquainted with different types of welding equipment before purchasing your own.

Practice welding on scrap metal you have lying around the shop before you touch your car. These beads (if you can call some of them "beads") were made with a MIG welder. It's sometimes good to lay down a practice bead before doing real welding work if it's been awhile since you've welded or if it's a particularly cold day, to make sure the welder's settings are correct.

Spot welding, which duplicates the welding process used at the factory to assemble the car body.

Stitch welding, which uses a thin electrode to imitate the MIG process without the cost of a MIG welding outfit.

Advantages

Using a MIG or TIG welder, a hobbyist restorer can weld a professional-looking seam with a minimum of training and practice.

The localized heat of arc welding in its various forms minimizes panel distortion.

Spot welding duplicates the factory method of joining major body assemblies.

Because of limited heat buildup, MIG welding is ideal for filling unwanted holes in body panels.

Disadvantages

Arc welding creates very hard welds that are much more difficult to work on than softer gas welds.

Types of arc welding suited to sheet metal (namely MIG and TIG) require expensive equipment; lower cost alternatives (stitch and spot welding) have limited application.

Arc welding equipment lacks the versatility of use of gas welding.

Brazing and Gluing

Brazing joins various metals using a variety of filler metal alloys, including brass (copper and zinc), silver, aluminum, nickel, and chromium. Brazing has the advantage of requiring lower heat than welding, and is therefore less likely to distort or melt the metal being worked. Its disadvantage is that a filler joint is not as strong as a weld, and

Rust on this inner trunk well panel will need to be neutralized or sealed before the outer panel skin is replaced. Otherwise, this inner section will rust through, allowing moisture to seep behind the new panel and undo the repair.

A new quarter panel quickly finishes this side of the car.

the brazing flux is likely to leach out of the joint and blister the paint. Still, brazing may be the only repair option on aluminum and diecast (pot metal) parts. An oxyacetylene or Mapp torch is used to melt the brazing rod.

Gluing as a method for attaching repair panels may sound preposterous, but it works. Not only does gluing work, it's increasingly used in the assembly of new cars. A prime instance of where gluing can replace welding is in

attaching a repair panel when replacing door skins. Only recently have manufacturers treated the insides of doors with rustproof coatings. Left uncoated at the factory and exposed to moisture through rainwater dripping past the window seal, outer door panels often show rust damage along the lower edges. For cars that have become popular with restorers, including early Mustangs and Camaros, replacement outer door skins are available from restoration suppliers. Tack welding has been the common method for attaching new door skins. Gluing is much easier and just as effective.

The problem with any type of welding is heat distortion of the metal. Gluing does not use heat, and therefore causes no distortion. Glues for attaching metal body panels are available from suppliers of automotive paint and body-repair products. You'll want to use a glue that works over paint. After removing the old door skin, the inner door stamping should be cleaned and derusted by sandblasting or a chemical process. The window and door lock mechanisms should be removed, cleaned, and lubricated. The cleaned and stripped inner door panel can now be painted with a rust-resistant coating such as a zinc primer; likewise the door skin. When the paint dries, the window and door lock mechanisms are installed. Now you're ready to attach the new door skins.

A thick bead of glue (approximately ¼ inch or more in diameter) is then laid along the entire length of the flange on the inner door stamping to which the door skin attaches. The door skin is aligned over the flange, and the overlay, which serves as a crimping tab to hold the door skin in place, is hammered back against the flange using a body hammer and dolly. In some cases a couple of tack welds may be needed for support bracing in the window area, but otherwise the glue, in combination with crimping the door skin over the inner door flange, is as effective as welding to secure the new panel. A couple of added benefits besides the absence of metal-distorting heat: the glue acts as a seam sealer, preventing moisture from ever penetrating the crimping seam. Unlike welding, glue doesn't disturb the paint, so the rust-resistant coating is still completely intact.

Should anyone wonder whether or not gluing works, auto body repair professionals say that the glue bond is so strong that they have to use air chisels to separate glued panels—the same as they would for welded metal.

Welding Repair and Replacement Panels

Whether you're making a patch repair or installing a replacement panel, the first step is to decide which type of seam to use where the new and existing panels meet. Many professional restorers and metal craftsmen use a butt joint. Here, the edges of the two panels are cut so they align exactly and then the panels are welded together along the seam using a minimum of filler rod.

Easier, because the seam does not have to be as precise, is a lap joint. Here a flange is crimped or rolled along the edges of the patch or repair panel, then the new panel is

Rust-out along the bottom of the windshield opening may look impossible to repair, but cutting back the damaged metal reveals a support structure sound enough to hold the repair panel.

fitted into place, with the flange fitting underneath the existing metal, and the two metal sections are clamped or spot welded together. With a lap joint, the panels should be welded both on the outside where the existing metal butts against the flange crease and on the inside where the edge of the flange lies against the body metal. If the inside of the flange is not filled, either by welding or with seam sealer, moisture can seep into the gap between the flange and body panel, eventually rusting away the repair. Note that on a lap joint, gluing, described above, can often be used in conjunction with spot welding—which is done to hold the panel in place.

Simply overlapping the panels and welding along the edge of the new metal is the easiest—but also the most unprofessional—approach to fitting a patch or replacement panel. Since overlapping raises the height of the metal, and the panel's contour along the seam will be further distorted when the overlap is covered with filler, this approach is suitable only in hidden repair areas like replacing or patching sections of the body or trunk floor.

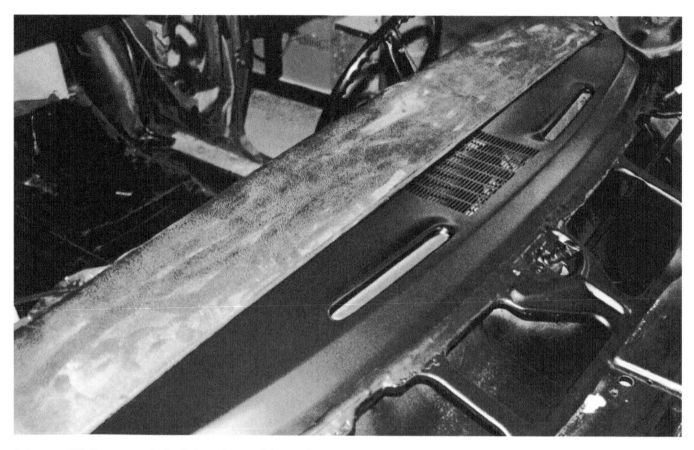

In the case of this Camaro, reproduction dash panels are available to replace the metal that is commonly rusted in this area.

Believe it or not, for many applications, including replacing door skins, the new metal can be attached by gluing. A special metal adhesive is used that forms as strong a bond as the metal itself.

To see how patch and replacement panels are installed, let's work through the process. In our example we'll be fitting a patch panel, but the procedure applies as well to repair panels.

When using a gas welder, a technique called hammer welding is often done to make a seam that requires very little, if any, filler. With this technique, as you finish each half-inch of weld, set the torch down and quickly hammer and dolly the weld before it has a chance to cool. Gas welds are much softer than arc welds and can be worked in this way. With arc welding, or gas welding without the hammer technique, the weld bead will have to be ground down to prepare the surface for filling and primer painting. In either case, very little filler should be required and you will have a permanent repair.

Filling Holes

It's the rare collector car that hasn't had holes drilled someplace in the body for mounting accessory items like a radio antenna and spotlight or any variety of auto parts store dress-up items. If the accessories were not factory installed, they'll probably be removed, likewise the dress-up trinkets, leaving holes that should be filled during the

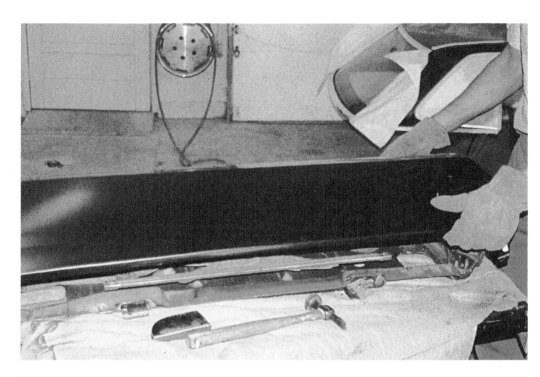

Now the door skin is fitted in place.

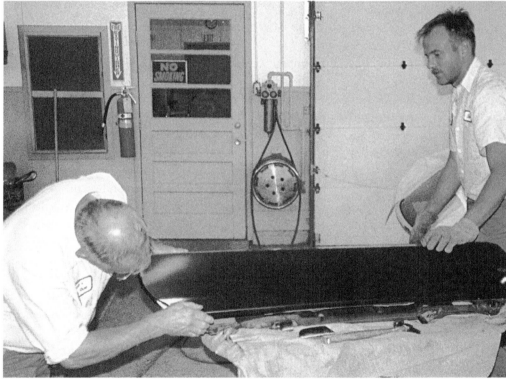

Usually fitting the door skin is a two-person job.

body restoration process. On convertibles, if the fastener locations for a new convertible top and top boot may be different from those on the car, the fasteners should be removed and their holes filled.

Small holes, such as those from a screw or bolt, can be filled by welding or brazing. If gas welding equipment is used, then the hole is best filled by brazing because of the lower heat. Using a MIG welder to fill small holes is easier and better suited to the job. With larger holes, such as the mounting hole for a spotlight, a plug will need to be cut and welded into the hole using the techniques described above for welding in a patch. Plastic filler should never be used to plug holes, however small the hole may be. Filler is water-porous and any moisture reaching the hole from

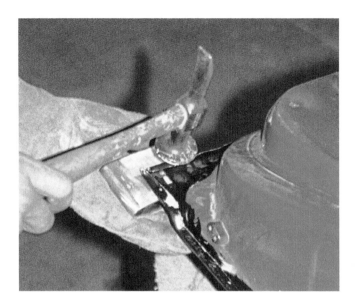

Next, the edges of the skin are crimped into place using a body hammer and dolly.

To finish the job, the skin gets a couple of tack welds at the corners.

the underside will penetrate the filler and eventually blister and lift the paint. Besides, the filler is likely to work loose, again damaging the finish.

It's possible to become overzealous in filling holes. Certainly holes along the sides of the body for trim clips or those on the hood and trunk lid for emblems should not be filled. However, if you're sure the hole isn't factory stamped or drilled (stamped holes, such as those for trim clips, are typically elongated), fill it. It's always easier to redrill a hole that's been filled than to try to fill a hole after the car has been finish painted.

Shrinking Stretched Metal

Whenever you work with metal, welding in patches or repairing dents, you risk stretching the metal. This stretching can occur in two ways. If you're bumping out a dent, it's possible to stretch and weaken the metal, causing an oil can effect (a condition resembling the in/out popping effect one experiences when using an old-style oil can). This condition occurs when dent work thins out the metal so that it loses its rigidity. There's no trick to tell if the metal has weakened enough for the oil can to occur. Just press against the panel. If a section of the panel pops back with the ease that might cave in a soda pop can, the metal has been stretched and lost its strength. When the metal is left in this weakened state, it flexes as you drive down the highway, and someone pressing against the panel can easily dent the weakened section. Although you will be able to press the dent back out easily if you can reach the back side of the panel, the flexing

metal will cause the paint and any filler to fleck or pop off, requiring more repair.

Metal stretching can also occur when heat is applied to the metal. The most likely occurrence is when you are welding in a patch panel. If the panel heats up too much, the metal may suddenly bulge. Or as you finish the area that you've been welding, you may discover a high spot that can't be flattened into the surrounding metal.

In either situation, where the metal has stretched and lost its strength, causing an oil can effect, or where heat has stretched the metal, causing a bulge, the solution is to metal-shrink the problem area. This shrinking process can best be compared to putting little knots in the metal. Where the metal is weak, the knots provide strength to restore the lost rigidity. Where the metal has bulged, the knots shrink the bulge.

Metal shrinking isn't an exotic art practiced only by skilled craftsmen. It is very easy to do. The most important ingredient in metal shrinking is speed, so you will want to have the supplies and equipment you will need laid out before you start. For equipment, you will need an acetylene torch with a welding tip, a torch lighter, goggles, a body hammer and dolly, and a small bucket of water and a damp rag. You begin by lighting the acetylene torch and adjusting the flame to the same neutral cone that you would use for welding. Next, you heat with the torch a spot about the size

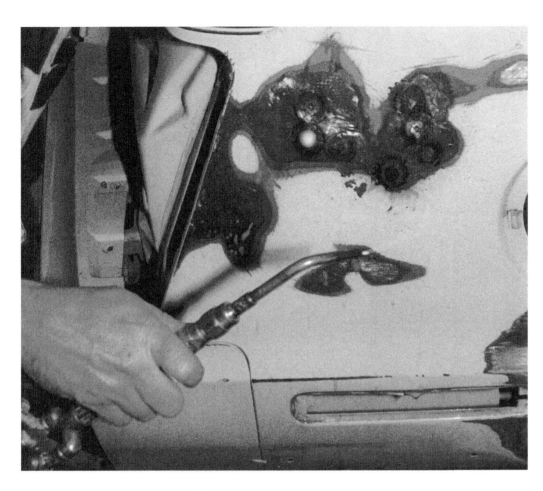

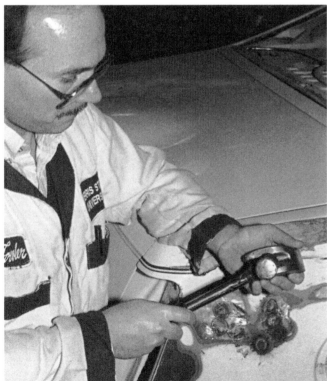

Next, you'll work the metal around the spot with a hammer and a dolly.

of a dime in the flexible area or bulge until the spot glows red. This accomplished, you'll work the metal around the heat spot with the hammer and dolly. The hammer needs to strike the metal at an angle directed toward drawing the metal into the heat spot. Although any smooth-faced body hammer can be used, special hammers with serrated surfaces that grab and pull the metal are made especially for heat shrinking. When the spot turns black, quench the heat with a damp rag. This combination of drawing the metal into the heat spot, followed by rapid cooling, tightens and shrinks the metal.

To strengthen a panel where the metal has been stretched so that it oil cans, several heat shrinks may be necessary. You can tell if the metal's strength has returned by pressing lightly against the stretched area. If the metal still pushes in, more heat shrinks are needed. If you are flattening a bulge, you will check to see if the surrounding metal has absorbed the high spot by placing a flat edge (the side of a body file works well) against the distorted area. If the straight edge contacts the panel along its length (except, of course, on curved surfaces), then the bulge has been removed. If some of the bulge remains, a few more heat shrinks may be needed.

METAL REPAIR

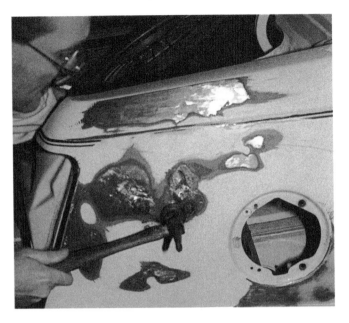

The hammer needs to pull the metal toward the heat spot.

1. Hold the patch over the damaged area and scribe along the perimeters of the patch.
2. Cut out the rusty/damaged section.
3. If you plan to make an overlap joint, make the cut ¼ to ½ inch inside the scribed area.

   If you plan to make a butt joint, match the cut to the size of the patch.

   Note: Sometimes it's desirable to cut the patch to more closely match the damaged section. The idea here is to limit as much as possible the length of the weld.
4. If an overlap joint is used, crimp the edge of the patch so that it will fit underneath the overlap. The crimp or flange can be made with a hand crimper, pneumatic crimper, or rolling crimper.

   If a butt joint is used, make sure the cutout exactly matches the size of the patch. The gap should be no larger than the thickness of the filler rod.
5. Grind paint and surface rust away from the weld area to a distance of 6 to 8 inches.
6. Before welding, spray a rust-preventative coating under the original panel and on the back side of the patch. The Eastwood Company's Cold Galvanizing Compound works well.
7. Secure the patch using clamps or tack welds, then go along the seam welding ½-inch sections at a time, alternating from one side of the patch to another to reduce warpage. You can fill in the skips in the weld as the metal cools. If you are using gas welding, a heat sink putty or metal rags should be placed around the weld area to help prevent metal warpage.

Because heat shrinking crystallizes metal, it's not possible to work the repair area completely smooth with a body hammer and dolly alone, a process called metal finishing. In most cases, some filler will be needed.

It's best to practice metal shrinking before trying it on your collector car. For a practice panel you can use a damaged fender from a body shop. To prepare the practice area, grind off the paint on a section a foot or so square. To create the oil can effect, just slap the section back and forth a few times with the heel of your hand until it collapses on thumb pressure. A bulge is easily created by heating the metal. The first heat shrink should be placed in the middle

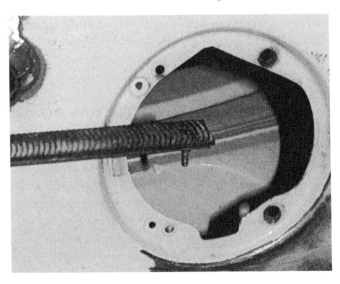

As the bulge begins to shrink, you can check the contour of the panel with the flat edge of a body file.

of the stretched area or bulge. Several small shrinks (about dime size) are better than a large shrink. Don't put the shrinks so close that they touch each other.

Heat shrinking is really no more difficult or complicated than simple acetylene welding or metal bumping (it uses both skills) and is a necessary metal-working technique for anyone doing auto body repair work.

Cold Shrinking

If you don't have a torch and need to shrink the metal on a body panel, either because hammer and dolly work has created an oil can effect, or to remove a bulge from earlier panel repair, you can cold shrink the metal. This is done with a ball-peen hammer and grooved dolly. What you are doing is putting a pinch in the metal. If you can't buy a grooved dolly, you can file or grind a groove into a flat dolly. Cold shrinking leaves a pinch that needs to be covered with filler but is otherwise as effective for shrinking a stretched area or flattening a bulge as heat shrinking.

Chapter 11
Smoothing Dents and Repairing Metal

Rust isn't the only form of metal damage restorers contend with. Dents are common in cars that have seen active service before being set aside for restoration. Straightening small dents, the kind that occur commonly in parking lots, takes more patience than special skill. Repairing collision damage, on the other hand, involves many of the same skills used to rout rust. The techniques of dent repair aren't especially complicated, and the best way to learn is by doing.

To straighten dents you'll need a few basic body tools. These consist of at least one body hammer (a special hammer with a large, flat head) and one or two dollies (hand-held metal blocks used to back the hammer blows). Hammers and dollies come in a variety of sizes and shapes for straightening flat areas, reshaping contours, and working in confined spaces. Sources of auto body repair tools include the Eastwood Company, auto supply stores, and professional tool manufacturers like Snap-On. In addition to body hammers and dollies, you may find a dent puller very useful in straightening body damage that can't

be reached from behind. Other useful auto body tools include assorted metal files and pry bars. Often, you can make pry bars yourself using shop scrap.

Straightening a Dent

The first step is to find a way to get access to the back side of the dent. Dents in fenders can often be reached from inside the wheelwells (sometimes an inner fender or liner may need to be removed) after removing the wheel to gain enough space to swing the body hammer. Rear fender dents are often accessible from inside the trunk, and on some cars and light trucks the fenders can be unbolted and removed for repair. Dents in door panels can sometimes be reached by removing the upholstery. Typically, the reinforcing panel will block access to the dent with a hammer, but it is usually possible to insert a pry bar through a hole in the reinforcing panel to push out the dent. (If a door has collision damage, and a new skin is available, reskinning is usually easier than repair.) Removing the car's interior gives access to dents in side panels or the roof.

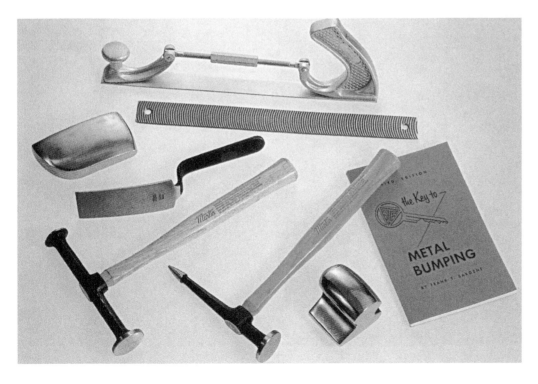

To straighten dents you'll need an assortment of body hammers, dollies, and a metal file. The Eastwood Company

To straighten a dent, work from the outer edges, always pounding against a dolly. Working toward the dent, gradually smooth the metal. If you start by banging away at the center of the dent, you stand a good chance of stretching the metal. (Note discussion of metal stretching in the previous chapter.) As you work across the dent, continuously feel the metal for smoothness with your fingers and the palm of your hand. Smaller ripples and bulges can also be worked out by gently pounding the body hammer against the dolly. To check progress, run a file across the dent. The file will graze high spots and leave the metal untouched in low areas.

Dents that are located where both sides can't be worked by a hammer and dolly, such as those on hoods and trunk lids of cars from the 1950s and newer, can often be straightened with a pry bar. Tire irons can sometimes be used for this purpose, as can sections of pipe that have been flattened on one end, or a leaf from a spring. Inner reinforcing panels on hoods, trunk lids, and doors have openings through which the pry bar can be inserted, and it can hopefully reach the dent. By swinging or pivoting, the bar can be used like a hammer to tap the dent against a dolly, always working from the edge of the dent toward the center. Special pry bars with curved ends can be made to straighten hood lips and fender flanges.

Dents that can't be reached with a pry bar can be straightened with a dent puller. This tool has a sheet-metal screw attached to a metal rod. A hole is drilled in the dent,

The high and low spots of a dented area are easily revealed by wrapping the sandpaper around a straight edge, such as a paint-stirring stick.

Even new panels may need filling to smooth surface irregularities. Here, a fresh door skin is being lightly sanded to show high and low spots.

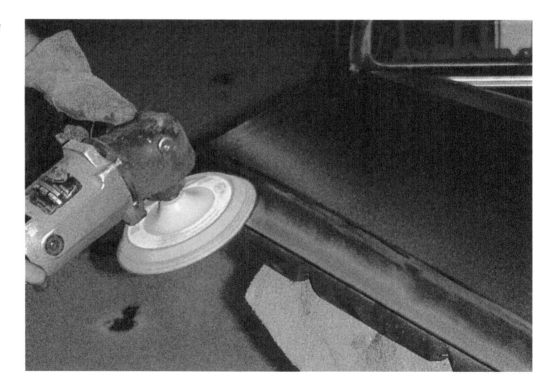

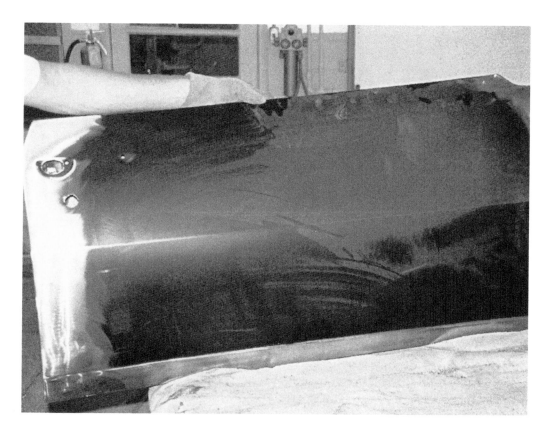

then the puller is screwed into the hole. With the puller firmly attached to the metal, a weight that slides on the rod is slapped sharply back against the handle. The impact of the weight hitting the handle snaps the puller, forcing out the dent. Usually a series of holes have to be drilled and the puller has to be exerted against each one to smooth the dent. After the dent has been smoothed as much as possible, the holes are filled with a touch of welding rod.

Filling Minor Surface Irregularities

While skilled bodymen are often able to smooth dents without resorting to filler, for hobbyists who are still learning body repair, some filler is usually needed. Prior to the 1950s, body solder or lead was exclusively used as a filler. Then, with the advent of synthetic materials, plastic body filler came into common use.

Plastic filler's ease of application has given it a reputation for misuse, and you'll hear owners of restored cars boasting that only lead was used in metal repair. The truth is, in its heyday, lead was as misused in many of the same ways as plastic filler is today.

The misuse of any filler comes from heaping on filler to cover, rather than smooth, minor surface irregularities along a welding seam or dent repair. However, lead did have one advantage over plastic filler: When a bodyman decided to shortcut rust repair by globbing lead over a

For very minor irregularities, finishing putty can be used. This filler product is mixed and applied the same as body filler.

The putty dries quickly and can be smoothed by light sanding.

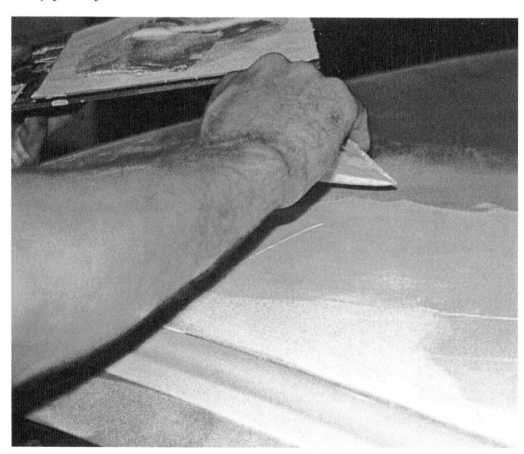

Where filler is used, a thin coat is spread over an area that extends out from the dent. Most of the filler will be removed by sanding.

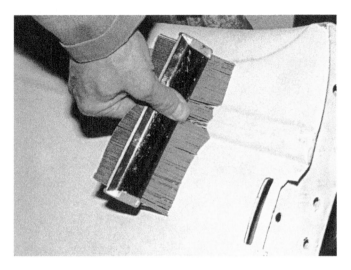

This tool, with its flexible feelers, can be used to make sure a contour that has had metalwork and filler conforms to the original shape.

rust-perforated panel (instead of cutting out the rotted metal and welding in a patch), the lead would seal the repair against moisture seepage. If plastic filler is similarly globbed onto metal that's been ventilated by rust, the repair will be short-lived, because, unlike lead, plastic filler is porous and allows moisture to seep through, blistering the paint and eventually lifting the filler.

When repairs are done right, either product is suitable—and acceptable. Since plastic filler is universally accepted by today's auto body repair industry and requires fewer specialized tools and no special skill, we'll work with it first.

Sanding removes most of the filler, leaving only a skim coating to ensure a perfectly smooth surface.

Using Plastic Filler

In order for the filler to stick, all paint and primer has to be removed from the repair area and the metal has to be clean. Since the filler will be spread over an area larger than the repair, paint should be sanded or abrasive-blasted in a radius of a foot or more from the repair area. Although filler is not applied just to the repair, it is spread in a very thin skim coating, blending the repair into the surrounding metal.

As previously stated, plastic filler is extremely easy to use. The secrets to success are purchasing fresh filler and following the mixing instructions on the can. Plastic filler is available from auto supply stores and the automotive departments of discount marts. Filler products are sold by auto supply stores carrying automotive paints and supplies,

Seams between body panels were often smoothed at the factory by leading. When a panel section is replaced, this seam should again be filled by leading.

where the stock tends to be fresher and higher quality, are recommended.

Plastic filler must be mixed with hardener before it can be used, and use only the quantity needed for the job at hand. Before scooping filler out of a freshly opened can, stir the contents to a smooth consistency. For a mixing palate you can use a section of cardboard, plywood, or other flat, smooth-surface object. The hardener is supplied in a tube and is typically colored red or blue. Add drops of hardener to the filler following the mixing proportions listed on the label. Now stir the hardener into the filler until the hardener is evenly spread throughout the mixture. As the hardener is mixed into it, the filler will change color. A consistent color indicates a smooth mix.

Apply the filler as soon as it is mixed. Plastic applicators of various widths are available from the store where you purchased the filler. Spread the filler in thin skim coats across the repair area, letting the coating blend into the metal as you move away from the repair. Once mixed with hardener, the filler dries quickly, so you have to work rapidly, spreading the filler in smooth strokes across the repair. As soon as the filler begins to set, leave it alone. Trying to work the filler as it hardens may damage what you've just applied. Depending on temperature and humidity, the filler will harden in about 15 minutes, when it can be grated or sanded smooth and another light coating applied, if needed, to fill any remaining imperfections.

For professional results, two special tools are required: a grating file (available from automotive departments of discount marts and auto supply stores) and a board sander (available from auto supply stores selling auto body repair supplies or specialty tool suppliers like The Eastwood Company). A grating file is an inexpensive tool that looks like a kitchen cheese grater with handles. A board sander is, as the name implies, a board of varying length with clips attached to hold a strip of sandpaper, and a handle for holding and movement. The grater will quickly slice through the filler, removing high spots and bringing the filler into contour with the repair area. Since the grating file leaves a rough surface, the board sander is needed to smooth the filler for priming and to finish contouring the repair. Where filler is applied over a curved area, a flexible board sander should be used. This tool's bendable backing allows the sandpaper to follow the panel's curved contour. As the filler is sanded, it creates lots of dust, so wear a respirator along with a face shield.

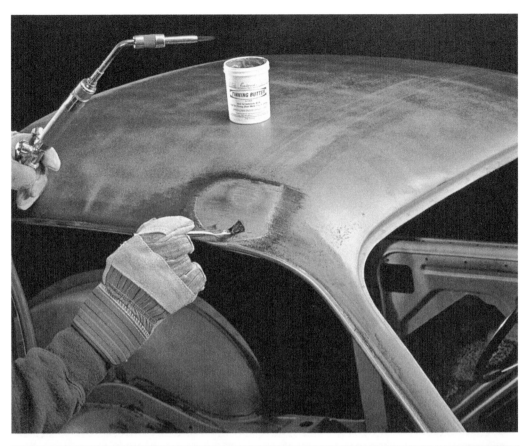

In order for the solder to stick, the body metal first has to be coated with flux, then tinned. All leading products shown in this sequence are available from the Eastwood Company. The Eastwood Company

Next, the repair area is heated sufficiently so that the solder can be puddled over the metal. The Eastwood Company

The wooden paddle used to smooth the solder is dipped frequently in a tub of tallow. The Eastwood Company

Tallow allows the paddle to slide easily over the solder and keeps the wood from burning. The Eastwood Company

Typically, the first grating/sanding sequence leaves low spots needing more filler. However, only a small amount of filler needs to be mixed and spread, and only in spots needing additional buildup. When the fill-in spots have dried, they are grated and sanded smooth with the overall repair. This process may need to be repeated several times until the filler is completely smooth and conforming to the repair area's original contours. When the repair is finished, more than 90 percent of the filler will have been grated and sanded off the car and will be lying in piles of white powder on the shop floor. This is as it should be. Filler, whether plastic or lead, has one purpose: to fill minor imperfections remaining from dent or metal repair. And remember, plastic filler is water-porous; it must always be applied over a metal or fiberglass backing and should never be used to plug holes.

Filling Metal Repairs with Lead

Using body solder (more commonly referred to as lead) as filler for body repair looks like child's play when you watch an experienced craftsman at work, and with the proper tools and supplies, the skill really isn't difficult to learn. However, because lead is toxic, additional precautions are required that the hobbyist may be inclined to overlook. First, use hand tools—a body file and sanding block rather than a power grinder or sander—to smooth the lead. Power tools create too much toxic dust. Avoid inhaling or ingesting the metal by wearing a respirator capable of filtering out lead dust and take simple but often overlooked precautions, like keeping coffee and snacks out of the work area. Ample ventilation is also important. The amount of lead dust a hobbyist might expose him/herself to in a restoration project is quite minimal; nonetheless, lead is a recognized health hazard and warrants reasonable precautions.

Body solder is a mixture of tin and lead. The particular alloy—that is, the proportions of tin and lead the solder contains—varies according to the job. Two factors determine which alloy is best suited to bodywork. First, the alloy should contain a high enough percentage of tin to make a strong bond with the base metal. Second, in order to spread the filler in a thin layer, the alloy has to stay pliable over a broad heat range. An alloy with high lead content turns from a solid to a liquid state so abruptly that it may run off the metal before it can be spread. Alloys used most commonly for body soldering contain either 20 percent tin and 80 percent lead (20/80) or 30 percent tin and 70 percent lead (30/70). Of the two, 30/70 gives better adhesion and greater flex, and since it is a softer alloy, it is easier to work. Another advantage: 30/70 alloy (often called plumber's solder) melts at 490 degrees Fahrenheit, as opposed to 530 degrees Fahrenheit for 20/80 solder. The lower melting temperature reduces the risk of metal warpage to the repair area. If you buy body solder from a restoration supplier, the sticks will be 30/70 alloy. If you buy solder from another source, look for the alloy stamping on the sticks.

Preparation steps for smoothing a repair for lead are the same as for plastic filler. All paint needs to be removed from the area where the filler will be applied and the metal must be free of rust and wiped clean of dust with a painting preparation solvent. While metal craftsmen can apply body solder to vertical or horizontal surfaces with equal ease, beginners should limit themselves to horizontal surfaces. If you are filling a repair located on the side of a fender or a door, you should probably take the part off the car (assuming it's removable) and place it on sawhorses so that the work surface is lying horizontally.

Unlike plastic filler, body solder won't adhere to bare steel. In order for the solder to make a good bond, the metal has to be coated with flux, then tinned. Specialty suppliers selling body solder kits for collector car restorers provide a tinning butter that contains flux, tin, and enough lead to make a good bonding base for the body solder. This preparation product is brushed on the metal and heated so that it melts and coats the repair area.

Heat is a critical factor throughout the leading process. The metal has to be heated enough to melt the solder, but not overheated, which can cause the panel to warp and distort. A welding torch is not necessary for body soldering. A propane torch, used to sweat solder into plumbing joints, will work as well, and depending on your skill, a propane soldering torch may be easier to use. If you are using a welding torch, install a large tip and adjust the flame so that it spreads out in a soft, yellowing cone. (The Eastwood Company sells a special soldering tip that allows a soft flame using acetylene alone.)

As long as the solder sticks to the metal and is paddled reasonably smooth, your leading experience has been a success.

Shaping the Solder

With a vixen file (also called an English file), shape the filler by working from the edges of the repair area toward the center. Old-time metal craftsmen used to wet the file with turpentine to keep from grating the soft metal and rub wax into the file teeth to keep the solder from sticking. As with plastic filler, the objective is to have as little lead covering the repair as possible. It's likely, therefore, that most of the solder will end up as shavings on the floor. Since body solder is expensive, it may be desirable to collect shavings on a scrap of clean cardboard and save them in a "mush tin" for the next leading job. If a steel container is used, the filings can be melted with a torch, scooped out with a paddle, and spread directly onto the repair area.

After the filler is filed to the contour of the repair area, it needs to be sanded smooth. Be sure to wear a respirator and avoid wiping your face with your shirtsleeves or glove while working with lead. You don't want to inhale or ingest this toxic substance. When the filler has been filed and sanded smooth, wipe the entire area with ammonia or a solution of sodium bicarbonate to neutralize any traces of flux that may still be on the metal. Then the area can be treated with a metal preparation solution to etch the metal for painting. Properly applied, body solder delivers the two important qualities restorers look for in a filler: invisibility and endurance.

For those wishing to watch the leading process before trying the technique themselves, a video showing body solder used in a collector car's restoration is available from the Eastwood Company.

Chapter 12
Applying the Primer Coatings

When body panels or other metal parts have been stripped by abrasive blasting or a chemical process, or damaged panels have been replaced or repaired through the filler step, a primer coating needs to be applied to keep the metal from rusting and to provide a base covering for the finish paint. Primer coatings are also applied over an existing finish to provide a bonding layer for the new finish. Among their many purposes, primer coatings can provide a strong antirust barrier and serve as a filler for slight surface imperfections.

Since primer coatings are required on nearly all metal parts during various stages of restoration, the hobbyist restorer will benefit from learning the uses of different types of primer and invest in the equipment to be able to apply the primer coatings in his/her own shop. We'll talk first about the types of coatings and then look at how

primer is applied. By doing the primer painting yourself, you'll easily pay back your equipment investment, and if you're able to deliver the car to the finish painter with all the primer preparation work done, you'll save the equipment investment many times over.

TYPES OF PRIMER

For years the basic rule in automotive painting has been to make sure the primer and finish paint are compatible. Traditionally, this meant that lacquer primer was used with a lacquer finish and enamel primer with an enamel finish, although an enamel top coat could be sprayed over a lacquer base. If the reverse was attempted, the more aggressive solvents used with lacquer paints would eat into the enamel base, lifting or wrinkling the primer layer, often requiring the surface to be stripped to bare

After the body has been stripped by abrasive blasting or a chemical process and damaged panels have been replaced or repaired, a primer coating needs to be applied to keep the metal from rusting and to provide a base coating for the finish paint.

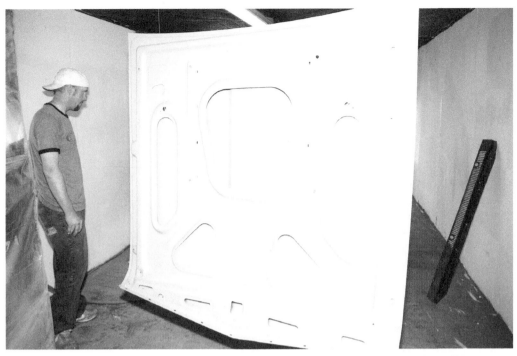

Existing finish coats that will be primed and repainted must first be cleaned with a painting preparation solvent to remove all traces of wax, grease, and other coatings.

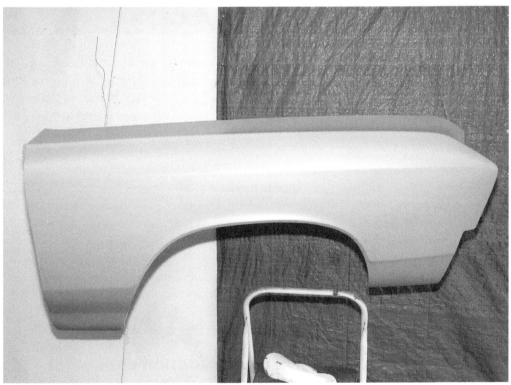

By suspending the part from wires, the painter can gain easy access to the backside of the removed panels, allowing even areas that would normally not be accessible to be primed.

metal and the painting process repeated from a fresh start. Today, compatibility between the primer base and the finish coatings means that all painting products must be selected from the same "system"—a term automotive paint manufacturers use to emphasize the interaction that has been formulated into modern primers and finish paints. Each product within a paint system has a specific function and must be applied in a set sequence. When this system regimen is followed, the base primer coating bonds strongly with the bare metal or existing finish, also creating a corrosion barrier. Additional coatings of primer-surfacer ensure a smooth preparation for the final finish, while a primer-sealer coating caps the primer base, providing a bonding layer for the final finish.

Often, panels that can be removed are best removed for sanding and priming, as was done with this hood. This ensures that all surfaces—including those that would be covered by hinges or where the panels mount—are properly prepared and primed.

Most modern painting products are two-part, meaning that both the primer coatings and finish paints require a catalyst (the second part) to harden. Two-part paints also use solvents to achieve a sufficiently diluted consistency for spraying. Although many two-part automotive paints contain potentially harmful isocyanates (chemicals that pose a severe health hazard), others are isocyanate-free and can be sprayed by the hobbyist without serious health risk. Whether or not the product label warns of isocyanates, the hobbyist-restorer needs to read and follow health and safety precautions, including wearing a professional-grade respirator whenever applying any painting product (products containing isocyanates require a respirator fitted to a full face mask or a breathing hood and external air supply) and spraying only in a well-ventilated area.

Although older lacquer and enamel paints and primers are still available in some areas, modern system paints are vastly superior, to the extent that the hobbyist concerned about the longevity of his/her restoration project will ignore the traditional products. Among their superior attributes, modern paints bond chemically, creating a highly durable finish. Older-type paints bonded mechanically (the primer coat gripping to microscopic crevices in the metal that had been etched into the surface with acid or an existing finish that had been roughened by sanding). System paints are also far less labor-intensive. For example,

today's primer-sealer coatings are nonsanding, thus eliminating this time-consuming preparation step for the final finish. Significant for collector cars that spend entire seasons in storage, two-part paints are formulated for very little shrinkage. With lacquer paints, especially, shrinkage could visibly distort the finish in a relatively short period of time. Given the extensive preparation work and expense of a quality finish, one doesn't want to repeat the painting process for a long, long time. For long-term durability and superior appearance, as well as ease of application, modern system paints are the hands-down choice.

Yet despite their advantages, modern paints have not altogether replaced traditional lacquer and enamel primers and finish paints, so traditional products will also be discussed, along with paint-over-rust products that greatly expand upon paint's traditional uses.

TYPES OF APPLICATION EQUIPMENT

For primer coating small chassis parts, the simplest, most convenient applicator is probably an aerosol can. Automotive primers in aerosol cans are available from auto parts stores as well as the automotive departments of discount marts. Naturally, the aerosol products have limitations—on body panels they're not suitable as a base for finish coating and they're typically not used to cover large surface areas. Another chassis primer coating, which is also simple to apply, is the POR product that goes on with a brush.

TRADITIONAL PAINTING VS. MODERN TWO-PART SYSTEM

Traditional Painting	Modern Two-Part System
Lacquer or enamel primer	Etch primer (for bonding with a base metal finish) or paint-over-rust (POR) product (to seal in surface rust)
Lacquer or enamel primer-surfacer	Zinc phosphate or zinc chromate primer (to create a corrosion barrier)
Lacquer or enamel finish	High build primer, sprayed either undiluted or diluted with solvent (to fill minor surface imperfections)
	Primer-surfacer (to cap the primer layers and provide a smooth surface for the finish coating)
	Sealer (to seal the primer preparation and provide a bonding layer for the finish coats)
	Base coat/clear coat final finish

For all other primer applications, spray-painting equipment is required, meaning you'll need an air supply and a painting gun. Conventional spray painting uses compressed air to diffuse a mixture of paint and solvent and then blast this mixture against the surface being painted. The force of the air diffusing and blasting the paint (as much as 60–65 psi) causes a substantial volume of both paint and solvent to rebound from the painting surface, where it then forms a cloud around the painter before either being sucked out of the painting area by a fan or swirling around and eventually condensing on surrounding objects. The high air pressure of conventional spray painting makes it a messy process, which if not done in a filtered spray booth leaves paint dust throughout the shop.

Because of environmental concerns with the quantity of painting solvents being released into the atmosphere by conventional spray painting (as well as the economic concern over the large quantity of wasted product), a high-volume low-pressure (HVLP) spray-painting technology has been developed. If anything, HVLP is easier for the hobbyist restorer to master than conventional spray painting, and the significant reduction of overspray and

The old finish is prepared for priming by a process called wet sanding. Here, the sandpaper is periodically dipped in water during the sanding process. (Note the 5-gallon bucket nearby.) The water serves as a lubricant and prolongs the life of the sandpaper.

On a repair, only the damaged areas will be sanded and primed for repainting.

resulting painting dust means that the shop may not need to be partitioned for painting to occur.

Just as system paints have replaced traditional painting products so, too, HVLP is replacing conventional paint spraying with professionals and should also be the choice for hobbyists.

HIGH-VOLUME LOW-PRESSURE PAINT SPRAYING

The cost of professional-quality HVLP paint-spraying equipment is about the same as comparable quality conventional equipment. Likewise, entry-level or hobbyist grade equipment is also comparably priced. With equipment cost not being a factor, the differences in the two systems are (1) a substantial reduction in product waste, which not only saves costs (today's painting products are very expensive), but also means that your shop isn't filled with painting overspray, (2) a turbine air supply eliminating the risk of oil and moisture contaminating the paint job, and (3) preheated air for quicker drying and less chance of runs.

Another advantage of HVLP, if your shop is wired only for 115-volt current, as is supplied to normal household outlets, is that you won't have to hire an electrician to rewire your shop for the HVLP turbine. It simply plugs into any nearby outlet. Air compressors capable of keeping up with the air supply needs of a conventional spray gun, on the other hand, require 240-volt current.

The spray gun used with HVLP is specially designed for this type of spray painting. Typically, the gun is made of a molded plastic composition for better heat insulation than metal guns and is designed to atomize the paint at low pressure. The HVLP paint gun works only with its companion turbine. For automotive paints, a turbine supplying 60–80 cfm of air is required. If HVLP paint spraying has any disadvantage, it's the single-use nature of the equipment. Unlike an air compressor, which can power tools and has a multitude of shop uses, an HVLP turbine is used only for painting. For those wishing to avoid investing in single-purpose tools, HVLP paint guns are available that work with a conventional air compressor capable of

delivering 10–12 cfm of airflow at 90 psi. Since these guns blend two very different paint-spraying systems, some compromises can be expected. An oil filter and moisture separator need to be installed in the air line to prevent contamination of the painting product, and the air isn't preheated, so the drying cycle will be like conventional paint spraying. These mixed-technology HVLP paint guns perform satisfactorily for applying primer coatings, but are not recommended for finish paints.

CONVENTIONAL HIGH-PRESSURE PAINT SPRAYING

An air compressor capable of powering air-driven tools or for media blasting will have sufficient capacity for spray painting. For spray painting, the air compressor must be equipped with an air regulator (used to set the pressure of the air delivered to the spray gun) and an air filter that will both prevent any moisture from entering the air line and

On this Studebaker Hawk, rust-prone areas along the fender edges have been repaired and primed in preparation for repainting.

filter out any rust or debris from the air tank. A ⅜-inch ID hose is recommended over the ¼-inch hose often supplied with portable air compressors. You'll want to install quick-disconnect connectors between the air hose and spray gun, and matching connectors on the blow gun and any air-powered tools. The quick-disconnects allow easy interchange between tools.

Sometimes you can buy the compressor and spray painting gun as a package. While the spray gun supplied in this arrangement may be adequate for applying primer coatings, it probably will not be suitable for finish coatings. Inexpensive (under $100) spray guns are available that appear identical to the higher cost professional models, but are seriously inadequate in performance. In selecting a spray gun, choose a quality name and examine its features.

For both HVLP and conventional spraying, a professional-grade painter's respirator is essential. Warning: Never spray paint wearing only a fabric dust mask. The highly toxic two-part primer or finish paints containing isocyanates require a special respirator and full face mask or a painter's hood connected to a fresh air supply. Two additional health/safety measures: Keep painting supplies in a locked cabinet, and install an exhaust fan to help ventilate the spray area. (A squirrel cage blower from a hot air furnace adapts well to this purpose; furnace filters over air inlets help prevent dust and airborne matter from being drawn into the painting area.)

Preparing the Surface

Although one would think the starting points for the primer sequence would be either bare metal or an existing finish, today it's also possible to prime and paint over rust. While this is generally not advisable, there may be no practical alternative when the car is not being completely disassembled. In this case, one of the paint-over-rust products (POR-15 and Corroless being the most popular) can be brushed or sprayed over rust that has been scraped or sanded to remove all loose scale. These paint-over-rust products work by sealing in the corrosion and stopping the process of oxidation (which we call rust). Since the

The prime coat is thoroughly sanded to remove all surface imperfections.

132

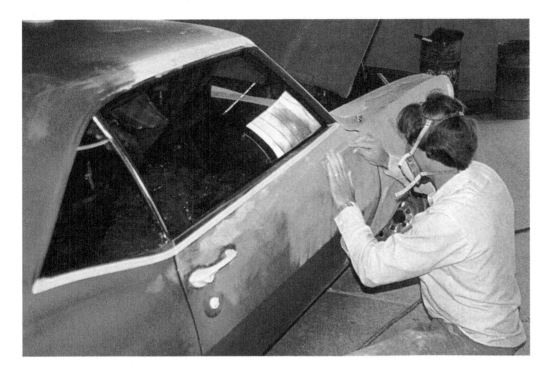

paint-over-rust products are compatible with both two-part and traditional primers, either type of coating can be built up on this base.

For bare metal, the surface is wiped with a wax and grease remover then with a conditioner product (sold under various names such as Twin Etch, Chem Grip, and Metal Prep) consisting of diluted acid. The conditioner removes any light rust and etches (microscopically roughens) the metal's surface.

An existing finish requires several preparation steps. First, all areas being repainted (which typically include the door openings, underside of the trunk lid, possibly the firewall, and underside of the hood, in addition to plainly visible surfaces) are washed thoroughly with detergent and warm water, rinsed, and allowed to dry. Next, the finish is cleaned thoroughly with wax remover to eliminate all wax residue, but especially traces of silicone wax, which severely affects paint adhesion and flow. The wax remover is wiped off with absorbent towels until the towels no longer pick up traces of wax. Then the old paint is roughened by sanding. To avoid creating sand scratch marks that may show in the new finish, sanding should be done with 360-grit or finer automotive wet/dry sandpaper. Any deep scratches or blisters in the old finish should be sanded down to bare metal. If the blister has formed because of rust, the metal needs to be sandblasted (a spot sandblaster is the ideal tool) or cleaned with a grinder or wire brush (a rotary brush held in a drill chuck works well). However, only sandblasting ensures that the rust has been completely eliminated. With

grinding or wire brushing, tiny traces of rust are likely to be hidden in rust pits within the metal's surface. To remove this hidden rust, the metal should be treated with a derusting chemical described in Chapter 8. When an area of the old finish has been cut down to raw metal, the surrounding paint needs to be sanded so that it tapers smoothly to the bare steel. This process is called feather-edging.

Preparation steps for refinishing fiberglass-bodied cars differ somewhat from those with steel bodies. Fiberglass won't be pocked with parking lot dings or rust, but it is prone to cracking. A finish that is marred by crisscross check marks indicates aged, road-weary fiberglass underneath. Painting over these hairline cracks won't make them go away. The new finish will only highlight the cracks. Most commonly the cracking originates in the fiberglass substrate, which means that the old finish must be stripped off using paint remover. Then the tiny cracks can be filled with two-part finishing filler. This product has a thinner consistency than the filler that's used with metal repair, allowing it to spread easily in a smooth, thin layer. When the filler dries, it is block sanded (meaning the sandpaper is held in a sanding block rather than simply being rubbed across the surface by hand) for a smooth finish. The success of this process is best measured by sighting across the surface in a good light, preferably sunshine.

How to Apply Primer Coatings

Traditionally, painters often mixed old-style lacquer and enamel paints and primers with their respective thinners

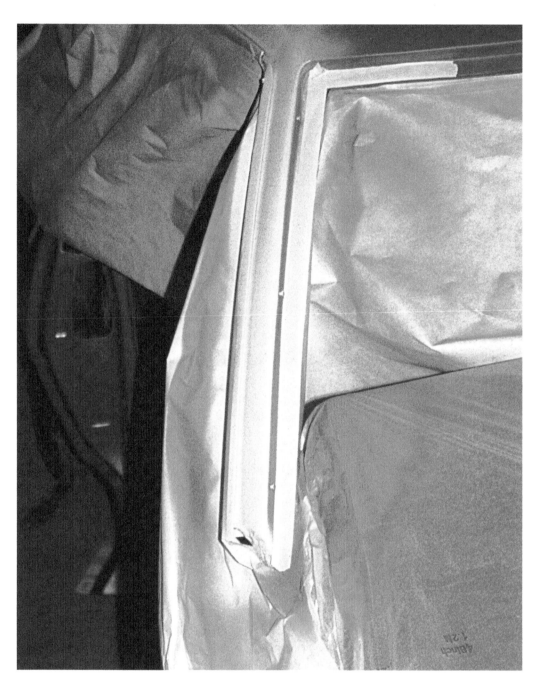

Applying a light coating of contrasting color primer and then sanding also helps reveal surface imperfections needing more attention.

and reducers the way a cook adds ingredients to a familiar recipe—largely by "feel." This inaccurate approach won't work with modern two-part paints and primers. With the new systems products, it's essential to read not just the product labels, but also information sheets that the manufacturer has provided to describe the product's use. Not only is it necessary to mix exact quantities of paint, catalyst, and reducer, it's also essential to observe the time intervals during which the product can be worked and recoated. Two-part paints and primers lock together chemically, providing each new layer is applied during the allowable time window. When the window closes, the bond

between layers won't occur. With some products, the bond can be reactivated by spraying another coating of the same product. In other cases, the finish may need to be sanded and another base coating applied. The instruction sheets tell what conditions apply. These will vary among the different products within a manufacturer's painting system.

Each primer product's specific mixing/reduction formula is printed on the label or available in an information sheet that needs to be strictly adhered to in preparing the product for spraying. The hobbyist can measure out the quantities of the mixing formula with a high degree of precision using a common measuring beaker (from either the housewares

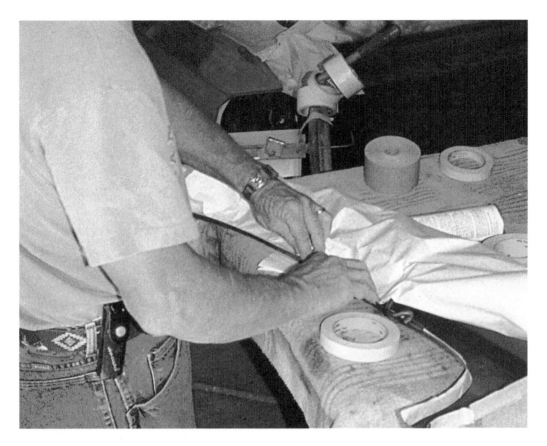

When the priming stage is completed, any areas not receiving a fresh finish coating need to be masked. Here, the restorer masks the inside surface of the car's fender skirts. Only the visible outside surface will be repainted.

Primed and masked (below and opposite), with the grille, bumpers, lights, and most trim parts removed, this Camaro awaits its turn in the painting booth.

department of a discount mart or a photographic supply store) and containers to hold the mix (wide-mouth plastic jars work well). It's important that the mix be thoroughly stirred and poured into the spray gun cup through a strainer (available at automotive paint supply stores).

Let's assume we're priming bare metal. The first coating is likely to be a zinc primer, which contains a moisture barrier to seal the metal from rusting. Old-style lacquer and enamel primers were water-porous, meaning that a bare metal part that had been primed and put away in storage would likely be speckled with rust when it was retrieved for use. Zinc primer has a curing time interval during which the next coating (a high-build primer or primer-surfacer) needs to be applied for the chemical bonding to occur. However, zinc primer is one of the products where this bonding opportunity, or window, can be reactivated by applying another layer of the same product. Consequently, bare metal can be coated with zinc primer and put in storage.

Along with the mixing ratio and curing time, the product label and information sheet list temperature and humidity range in which the manufacturer recommends the primer be sprayed. Moderate temperature (75–80 degrees Fahrenheit) with low humidity are the optimum conditions. The spray gun is held at a distance of 8 to 10 inches from the painting surface and moved parallel to that surface (not swept across the surface in an arc) with each pass overlapping the previous pass by about one-third.

If a thicker buildup is desired, the primer can be recoated as soon as the first coating flash dries, meaning the surface is sticky enough to hold a new coating. Applying the coatings too thick or too fast will cause runs. In a primer coating, runs and other surface blemishes can be sanded out, but fixing mistakes can be time consuming and it's better to spray a smooth primer layer.

After the first primer coating has dried, you're likely to see pits and scratches in the surface that need to be filled. Since primer has a dull finish, a strong light (sunlight is optimum) is often needed to see surface flaws. Filling pits, scratches, and other surface imperfections is typically done by spraying on a coating of high-build primer. For a thick coating, this product may be able to be sprayed without reducing. After the high-build primer coating has set up, it is block sanded wet using automotive sandpaper that has a special backing that does not disintegrate in water. For block sanding, a rubber block that conforms to surface contours is used. The sandpaper is dipped periodically in a conveniently located bucket of water, which both cleans the sandpaper and lubricates the sanding process for a smoother finish.

Since minor imperfections are very difficult to see under the primer's dull finish, painters commonly spray a light guide coat of a contrasting color primer. Lightly sanding this guide coat with 400- or 600-grit sandpaper quickly reveals high and low spots as well as pits, scratches, and other blemishes. If these blemishes are deep, they can be most easily filled with a thin epoxy glaze coat, which can be either brushed on or applied with a plastic squeegee. The older type lacquer-based glazing putty (which was squeezed out of a tube) should be avoided. This product will shrink under the finish coating, creating more problems than it cures. Several layers of high-build primer, with guide coats and more block sanding, may be needed to eliminate all the blemishes.

The primer preparation is now ready for a coating of primer surfacer. Following the system regimen, the primer surfacer may produce a finish so smooth that sanding isn't needed. If light sanding is needed, a 600-grit or finer 1,200- or 1,500-microgrit sandpaper should be used. The primer-surfacer coating is the base for the color finish. Any imperfections in this base will be reflected (and magnified) in the finish. The secret to a brilliant finish is perfect preparation. Any flaws in the primer surfacer should

be filled and sanded, and another light primer-surfacer coating applied before the final sealer coating caps the primer preparation.

Sealer has several purposes and can be used over traditional primers as well as system products. With traditional painting products, sealer prevents solvents in the finish paint from swelling sand scratch marks or penetrating the primer layer and lifting an original base coat. Sealer also helps prevent pigments from bleeding out of a base layer. While sealer is typically clear, sometimes a small amount of finish paint is mixed with the sealer to create a color base.

Before applying the seal coating, be sure to note the manufacturer's time window for finish painting, which may be just a few days. If you're applying the primer coatings and are planning to have a professional painter spray the color finish, careful timing and coordination may be needed to make sure the car is delivered to the painter and finish painted before the window of opportunity expires.

A car's finish will never be better than its primer preparation. Because application of the primer coatings requires more patience than finesse, it's a step the hobbyist restorer can take not only to help ensure a desired quality of finish, but also to save money in one of the single most expensive items in a car's restoration—the cost of the final finish.

Chapter 13
Applying the Finish Coat

Although it seems unthinkable in this high-technology age where manufacturers spend millions and auto body repair shops spend hundreds of thousands of dollars on the equipment required to apply automotive finishes, at the dawn of the automotive age, cars were painted with a brush. In fact, it was this brush-painting technique that most seriously threatened Henry Ford's assembly line idea. With the moving assembly line, cars could be put together at a rate approaching one a minute, but painting—the end of the pipeline—could take as much as a day. Ford's solution: paint every car black (the quickest drying color then available). Naturally, Henry Ford also switched from brush painting to spray painting to speed up the application process.

For years, spray painting was a relatively simple art that even handymen with access to a spray gun and compressor could do with reasonable success. A car collector friend still enjoys driving a Model T roadster he and a college

Unusual finishes like the crackle coating on this heater unit can be duplicated using special paints available from restoration suppliers. Mike Cavey

Mechanical parts can be painted to the look of freshly stamped steel using detail paints from the Eastwood Company.

138

Interior areas like this inner door panel are finish painted before the body exterior.

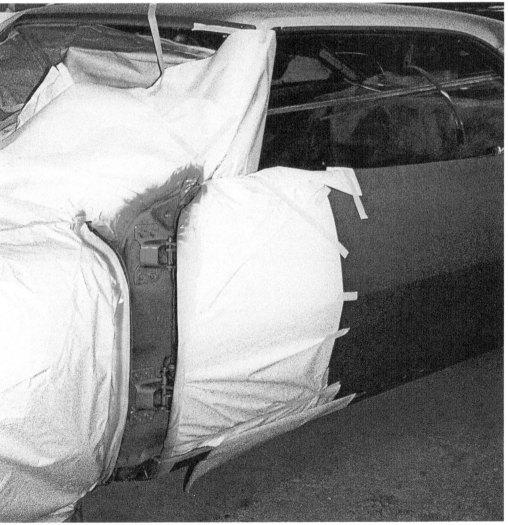

The cowl section and hinges should be finish painted before the front fenders are installed.

When an inner surface like the underside of a hood is finish painted, the color is brought out around the grille opening and other panel mating surfaces (as seen on this Studebaker) to ensure a complete coating.

pal painted one afternoon in the driveway to his parents' house. He tells how they'd just finished applying the final lacquer coating when a car came careening into the driveway, throwing up a cloud of dust. Naturally, some of the dust settled into the still-drying paint and today that Model T looks—you guessed it—like it was painted in someone's driveway on a dusty afternoon.

Applying a deep gloss finish paint is more than good timing; it's an art. While the finish paint choices used to be lacquer or enamel—lacquer being easier to apply due to its fast drying characteristics and enamel a tougher, longer lasting, but typically lower gloss finish—today automotive finish suppliers talk about their paint systems. This means a complementary range of products extending from the initial primer layer through several primer-surfacer coatings to a sealer and culminating in a catalyzed two-step base coat/clear coat finish. The new systems yield a deep luster that surpasses even the most fastidiously applied lacquer finish for depth and shine and provide a durability that far exceeds yesterday's enamel. However, the catalyzed paints in this new generation are highly toxic, to the degree that they should be avoided by the hobbyist whose attitude toward safety can best be described as casual. This book's recommendation, strongly supported by the paint manufacturers, is that you have a professional apply your collector car's finish paint. Though a professionally

supplied finish will be one of the single largest restoration expenses, the cost can be justified in lasting quality and—not insignificantly—your having avoided exposure to toxic painting chemicals.

Even though you have a professional apply the car's finish, chances are you'll still be finish painting many of the car's parts, especially the chassis and mechanical pieces and assemblies. In many cases you'll spray on the finish using an aerosol can with products like the Eastwood Company's Golden Cad (a painting kit imitating the factory cadmium plating on brake parts) or Chassis Black (a duplicate for the factory's chassis paint). If you've invested in paint-spraying equipment for the priming steps, you may want to final finish larger chassis items with that equipment instead of aerosol cans. Less toxic finish paints than the catalyzed urethane products still exist, and this chapter will discuss their use and application. If you want to escape the use of toxic chemicals altogether, then it's possible to finish coat many of the car's smaller parts using environmentally friendly powder coating. While powder coating used to be a professionals-only product (due to the high cost of the application and baking equipment), The Eastwood Company's low-cost HotCoat system easily makes powder coating a do-it-yourself process for the hobbyist restorer. In this chapter we'll look at the finish painting options you can realistically—and safely—do yourself.

It appears that the door on this Camaro has been painted with green primer, but in reality this is a base coat awaiting the clear finish. Because the base coat in a base/clear system has a very dull finish, it is difficult to tell if the color is a correct match until the clear coat has been applied.

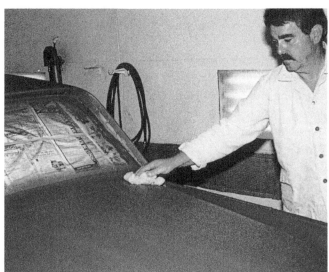

To make sure the surface is completely free of dust, as a final preparation step, the car is wiped down with a tack rag.

What Were the Car's Original Colors?

This is the first question most restorers ask when they begin thinking about finish painting their cars. Usually there's some evidence of the major body color, which may still show in the door openings, inside the trunk, or under the hood. If you stripped off the paint, you saw the original color as you worked down through the layers. But a

To make sure no dust remains in seams or crevices, the car is dusted off with an air nozzle.

141

No modern automotive painting product should be sprayed without wearing, at a minimum, a professional grade painting mask.

visual sense of the factory color alone isn't enough; you want to know the color's name, what other colors may have been part of the car's original paint scheme, and how they can be duplicated in a modern paint. If you've done the research steps described in Chapter 4, you know that your car's original color scheme is coded on the data plate. Using a decoding source such as the American Car ID Number books published by *Cars & Parts* magazine, you can find out the original color names. Unfortunately, knowing the names of the colors doesn't guarantee that an automotive paint supplier can mix you a color match in a modern paint.

Paint needs to be mixed in precise proportions. A kitchen mixing beaker serves this purpose. The paint is also filtered as it is poured into the spray cup.

As paint manufacturers developed synthetic and then urethane paints, they converted the mixing formulas for paints likely to be in demand, and of course preserved the mixing formulas for current colors. This means a restorer of a modern collectible like a Pontiac Fiero would have no difficulty finding a color match, just knowing the finish color's name. For colors used perhaps in the last 20 years, this is the case. But what if your collector car is a 1960s Pontiac Tempest and the paint code on the date plate translates to Cordovan? Can you walk into an auto parts store selling painting products and walk out with a properly formulated color match in synthetic enamel? Not too likely. So what do you do?

Where a mixing formula isn't available, the easiest way to duplicate an original color is to locate a color chip. This chip isn't a chunk of paint from the car, but rather a color sample from a paint supplier's book dating to the era of your car. If you've located an auto parts store selling painting products that has been in business for several decades, chances are the owners still have these old color chip books somewhere in their inventory and will look up the chip for you. Otherwise, old color chip samples are available from literature dealers and at swap meets.

With the color chip you'll find both the paint's name and a color code number. With this paint code, a paint supplier can find out what color matches for which mixing formula are available (either by punching in the paint code on a store computer linked to the manufacturer's data base or calling the number in to a zone office). The computer listing will also helpfully tell whether the match is perfect or off by a certain tint (deeper brown, for example). What's needed for this search is the paint manufacturer's color chip, not a color photo from an ad or sales brochure, which won't have the paint code and is likely to be misleading—even inaccurate—due to color shifts in the printing reproduction process.

In situations where the mixing formula isn't available from the paint supplier, other options are to check for a paint source with a supplier selling restoration parts for your collector car and to ask fellow car club members with similar cars painted your desired color where they got their paint. Either source may be able to direct you to a mixing formula or a matching modern paint.

Should I Stay with the Original Type of Paint?

Many restorers believe that a restored car will lose its authentic look unless it's finish painted with the original type of paint. Should you use the original type of paint?

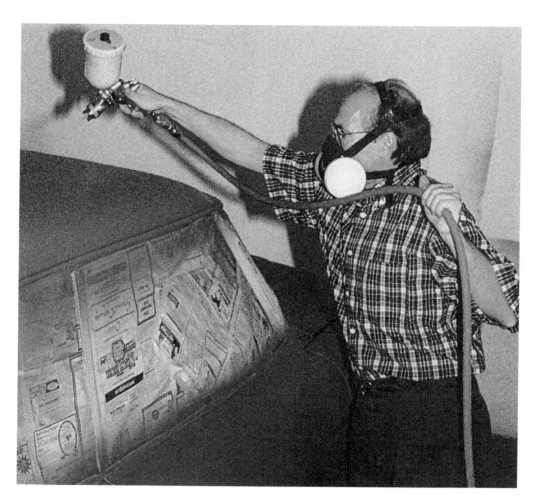

The almost universal answer is no. While it may be possible to locate an original-type nitrocellulose lacquer to finish paint a 1930s vintage car (duller looking but more durable alkyd enamel began to be used in the 1940s) and tediously apply the multiple layers of paint—sanding between layers—for an extremely high gloss, the thick paint will be highly brittle and porous. Not qualities that lead to long life. Unless the car is stored where temperature and humidity can be carefully regulated, the finish will begin to crack and chip within a short time, a condition not easily repaired. The only answer will be to strip off the finish and repaint the car, which is obviously time consuming and very expensive.

In nearly all cases, the paint to use, both for high gloss and durability, is a modern two-part (paint and catalyst) base coat/clear coat finish system in which the base coat provides the color and the clear coat gives the color depth and gloss. Not only will a correctly applied base coat/clear coat finish match the gloss of old-style lacquer and surpass the durability of enamel, the clear coat serves a double function of also protecting the finish from corrosive airborne chemicals and harmful sunlight.

The downside of finish painting a collector car with a modern two-part catalyzed painting product is that you're not going to apply this paint yourself—at least you shouldn't unless you have access to a professional painter's spray booth and a ventilated painting hood. Catalyzed paints require these health/safety devices because their vapors contain extremely toxic isocyanates, which, if inhaled in toxic quantity, can induce a condition known medically as ARDS, short for Acute Respiratory Distress Syndrome, which manifests the same symptoms and possible outcome as a heart attack. More than one hobbyist thinking that modern catalyzed painting products can be sprayed wearing a dust mask or paper filter respirator has collapsed in his shop and been rushed to a hospital emergency room. Catalyzed paints are not for hobbyist use; if you want a truly spectacular finish, and value your health, this is a job you'll hire out to a professional.

At What Point During A Restoration Should Finish Painting Occur?

You've completed the bodywork, and chances are some of the mechanical work is under way with the engine out

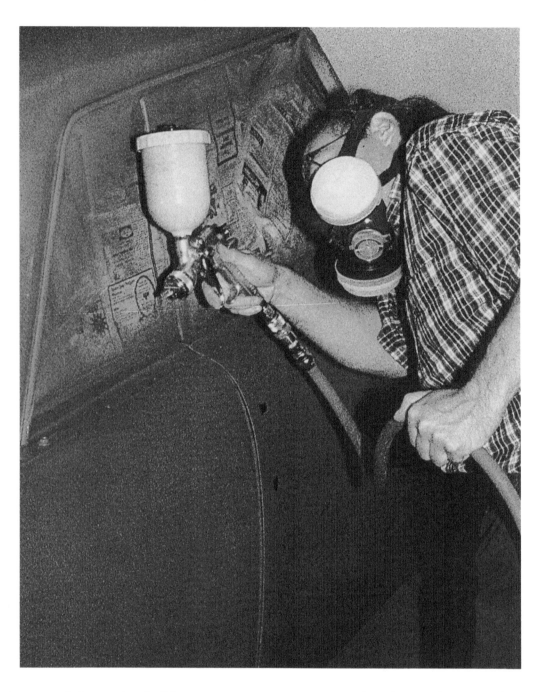

The painter needs to pay attention to detail, so as not to miss edges around window moldings and wheel openings.

APPLYING THE FINISH COAT

of the car for overhaul and progress being made rebuilding the brakes (as described in the next chapter). Is this the time for finish painting? Should you wait until all the mechanical work is finished? Or should the new upholstery and interior be installed first?

In order to detail the engine compartment, finish painting should be done while the engine is out of the car. You'll need a rolling chassis, though, to get the car into and out of the paint shop, so it's best that suspension, driveline, and brake work be completed. Professional restorers all agree on the painting and upholstery sequence. Have the car finish painted before installing

new carpet, recovering and replacing the seats, door panels and headliner or convertible top. It's too difficult to mask off the interior to make sure the overspray and paint dust don't soil or ruin new upholstery. It's easier to be careful not to scratch or mar the paint while replacing the interior on a finish-painted car.

Aside from these guidelines, the timing of the finish painting may be controlled by the hardening period of the sealer coat (if a catalyzed sealer was applied at the end of the priming/preparation sequence). Sealer is meant to be finish painted within a certain period of time—and if not, the sealer may continue to harden, making it an unsuitable

144

base for a finish coating. If sealer is used, check the manufacturer's recommendations for the acceptable time lapse before finish painting.

After the car returns from the painting shop, your goal will seem a lot closer and you'll be eager to begin replacing bumpers, trim, emblems, and other items and accessories removed from the car in preparation for painting.

FINISH PAINTING YOU CAN SAFELY DO YOURSELF

Assuming you've limited your do-it-yourself finish painting to applying the color coating to chassis members, mechanical assemblies, and accessory items, you have the option of three application methods: (1) specialty coatings sprayed from aerosol cans; (2) conventional or HVLP spray painting using less-toxic synthetic enamel, and (3) environmentally friendly, low-health-hazard powder coating. Each method has its particular applications, so ideally you'll use all three.

Specialty paints formulated to match the fresh casting look on engine components such as alternators, the yellow cadmium plating on carburetors, and the silver cadmium plating on a variety of chassis fasteners, mounting brackets,

TIPS FOR REPLACING EMBLEMS AND TRIM

With emblems, rather than trying to refit the fasteners, place a dab of silicone sealer on a couple of tabs as you push the emblems in place. The silicone will hold the emblems securely, yet allow them to be removed easily if needed.

As an alternative, place small rubber O-rings on the tabs instead of the metal fasteners. The O-rings will secure the emblems and are easily removed.

Place fiber washers under snap fasteners (used with convertible tops, top boots, and tonneau covers) to prevent the fastener from cracking the paint when it is tightened down.

Put a dab of clear silicone sealant on holes in the body before replacing trim pieces. The silicone prevents water seepage and rust.

pulleys, and clamps are available primarily from the Eastwood Company and packaged in easy-to-apply aerosol cans. A collection of these paints makes it easy to complete the restoration of a variety of mechanical and accessory items without having to wait for parts to come back from a plating shop or setting up the spray gun and mixing

Having a partner help hold the air hose lets the painter concentrate on his work.

The fresh paint needs to harden before the masking is removed. Rushing this step can damage the finish.

a batch of paint for what can be accomplished with the aerosol spray in a few minutes. While the aerosol coatings are not meant for large items like a frame (although little-noticed chassis parts can be painted using aerosol cans), they're ideal for small mechanical and accessory items, like the car's jack.

Conventional or HVLP spray painting using synthetic enamel or nonisocyanate two-part paints enables the hobbyist/restorer to finish coat wheels, the frame, and suspension members. Unlike primers where humidity and temperature variations don't cause troublesome color shifts or loss of gloss, finish paints need to be sprayed within the recommended temperature range and reduced with solvents matching the ambient temperature and humidity conditions. The paint supplier can recommend the solvent best suited for the painting conditions: slower drying for warmer temperatures or faster drying for colder temperatures (though not below 65 degrees Fahrenheit).

The spraying technique for finish paints is the same as primers, but more critical. Keep the spray gun facing parallel to the work surface for the entire pass and overlap the previous sweep by about one-third. Move the gun slowly enough to build up a sufficiently wet coating for rich gloss, but beware of too much buildup, which can cause runs.

Spray painting can also be used to clear coat raw metal parts such as brake lines that weren't painted at the factory.

The clear paint's invisible coating won't show and will prevent brake and fuel lines, fasteners, and other items that were neither plated nor painted at the factory from developing an unsightly patina of rust. Preparation steps consist of simply polishing the bare metal with steel wool and wiping down the surface with a painting preparation solvent. For small parts, clear coatings are also available in aerosol cans.

DO-IT-YOURSELF POWDER COATING

Solvent-free powder coating has to be the most significant development in automotive finishes since the spray gun. Not only does powder coating have widespread application in car restoration, it has become the easiest do-it-yourself painting technique since the brush. Early powder coat systems were professional-use only, requiring expensive application equipment and large (and highly expensive) baking ovens. Hobbyists used (and continue to use) these professional powder coat services primarily for coating large chassis members like frames and suspension pieces, as well as smaller mechanical and decorative parts.

The breakthrough in do-it-yourself powder coating came in early 1998, when the Eastwood Company developed its HotCoat powder coating system, consisting of an application gun and 115-volt AC household current power unit, selling for $150, which is comparable to a good quality spray-painting gun. In developing its do-it-yourself powder coating system, the Eastwood Company initially had concern over hobbyist access to a baking oven, until the obvious solution dawned: a discarded but still functioning kitchen oven. (An oven used to prepare food and located inside the household should not be used to bake powder coated parts.) Eastwood reasons that the hobbyist can either install a second-hand oven in his shop or work out a sharing arrangement with a fellow restorer. The other requirement, a source of compressed air, can be supplied by a light-duty air compressor, or even a portable compressed air-storage tank of the type used to pump up tires. The result, for a relatively low-cost investment, is that the hobbyist now has a painting system that doesn't require complicated mixing formulas with solvents, catalysts, and hardeners; exposure to toxic chemicals; the potential of environmental damage; costly construction like a ventilated painting area; or a high level of skill. The HotCoat powder coating system's only limiting capacity is the size of the used kitchen oven. Yet when you think of it, what items suitable for powder coating other than a frame, driveshaft, differential, and steering column don't fit inside a normal oven? Not a lot.

The beauty of powder coating isn't just the freedom from mixing formulas and solvents. The baked-on finish is virtually guaranteed to be free of runs. And the finish is tough. Drop a powder coated part on the floor and the finish won't chip, meaning powder coated chassis and suspension parts won't be flecked with chips if the path to the eating establishment chosen for the car club's annual banquet is a crushed stone drive. Best of all, Eastwood's HotCoat powder coating gun requires about as much finesse as hitting the target with a shot of Old Spice.

Although powder coating can be a one-step finish applied over bare metal, the coating can also be used over filler and primer if these products can withstand the baking temperatures of up to 500 degrees Fahrenheit. The recommended filler is Evercoat Metal-2-Metal and the primer Corroless Rust Stabilizer, a product that offers the advantage of added corrosion protection. Bare metal parts need to be wiped or washed with a metal prep solution to make sure the surface is clean of grease, oil contamination (including fingerprints), or dirt and shop dust. After the parts are clean, you need to wear vinyl gloves to avoid recontaminating the metal with body oil. Unlike paint that is sprayed, powder coating wraps around corners, so it's important to mask any surfaces you don't want coated using a special high-temperature tape. Before spraying on the powder, it's also a good idea to check how the part will fit in the oven. In most cases you won't want to lay the part on the oven rack (the rack may wipe off the powder) so your options are to suspend the part by wires or use high-temperature plugs to support the part on a metal tray. (Both the special wire and plugs are available from

When the paint has hardened, the finish can be buffed to a mirror gloss.

Small parts such as the headlight rims and air vent doors are painted separately.

Eastwood.) Some parts may require ingenuity to figure out the best baking arrangement. Another concern is that baking can release contaminants that have seeped into porous metal parts like diecast pieces, or aluminum and iron castings. Contaminants boiled out of the metal in the baking process will show up as pits in the powder coat. Unlike with plating, where these bubble marks are always potential (because immersion in the plating solution introduces new contaminants into the metal), with powder coating, cast parts can be prebaked to purify the metal.

Applying the powder coating is the fun part of the process. If you're acquainted with spraying liquid paints, you're going to be surprised. The powder doesn't spray out in a ferocious blast like conventional spray painting; it doesn't even waft out like HVLP painting. Instead it puffs out like a child blowing the seed head of a dandelion. Because the part being powder coated is electrostatically charged, the powder drifts only in one direction: onto the part. Also unlike liquid painting, where the spray gun has to be held steady, the powder gun should be shaken

Solvent-free powder coating has to be the most significant development in automotive finishes since the spray gun. Not only does powder coating have widespread application in car restoration, it is the easiest do-it-yourself painting technique since the brush. With the HotCoat powder coating system shown here, hobbyist restorers can coat smaller chassis and engine parts with a tough finish that is impervious to gasoline, even brake fluid, and won't easily chip. The Eastwood Company

Here's the finished Camaro we've been seeing in earlier metal repair and priming photos. Replicating the racing stripes is an art best left to professionals.

slightly (a technique that takes a little practice) to help ensure the powder reaches all desired surfaces and doesn't clog in the gun.

When the part is thoroughly coated (if you miss a spot you can come back to it; if the powder seems to lie too thick, you can blow it off and recoat), you're ready to place the part in the oven. The powder coating needs to bake or cure for about 15 minutes. The first couple of times you do this you'll want to watch what happens. As the powder heats, it begins to melt, flowing out into a smooth, glossy coating that looks identical to paint. In fact, powder coating has all the attributes of paint without the hassles. If you desire to improve smoothness or luster, the cured powder coating can be microsanded (using 1,000- to 1,500-grit sandpaper) and compounded, or buffed using white rouge and a loose section buffing wheel.

Cleanup is a simple matter of blowing any powder residue out of the gun with an air nozzle. No solvents are needed for the cleanup process! If a box or tarp was laid on the floor space where the powder was applied, any powder collected in this way can be strained through a paint filter and recycled.

One of the complaints about early powder coating was the limited color selection. Powder colors still are not available to match the array of liquid paints, but color choices are increasing. Of course, if chassis parts are the main object of powder coating, the color selection need be no broader than that of Henry Ford's Model T. For other frequently powder-coated parts like wheels (powder is the ideal coating for wire wheels that were originally painted) the available color selections fit at least generic (aluminum, black, silver, red) applications. For engine parts like valve covers, all major manufacturer engine colors are available. With powder coatings' growing popularity, the color range is constantly increasing.

Whether you decide to powder coat parts yourself (the simplicity of the process, relatively low cost, and absence of toxic catalysts and environmentally hazardous solvents all say you should) or have professionals do the work, you'll find the coating is superior to what you'll get with liquid paints in nearly all respects, color choice and oven size being the limiters. Once you've tried powder coating with the Eastwood system, you'll be hooked—so much that you'll find yourself looking for stuff to powder coat just for fun.

Chapter 14
Inspecting and Overhauling Car Brakes

In the restoration process, overhaul of the car's mechanical systems typically occurs in conjunction with bodywork and painting. Since mechanical work, metal repair, and painting each call for a different mental focus, equipment, and skills, often the various restoration aspects are interspersed—mechanical work for a period of time, then bodywork, then more mechanical, back to bodywork, painting, and so on.

There's no key as to which mechanical system should be rebuilt first. On a frame-up restoration, usually the steering and suspension are the first systems overhauled for the simple reason that they're the first pieces hung back on the frame. But the engine might be sent away for overhaul while the frame is being sandblasted and individual components like the carburetor, generator, and starter, or the transmission and rear end might be rebuilt as a change of pace from bodywork. Whatever the sequence, eventually you'll come to the brakes—which are far and away a car's most important mechanical system, since whatever goes needs to stop—and quick, reliable stopping is not a given on older cars.

No matter how roadworthy and mechanically sound a collector car appears to be, the braking system should always be inspected and nearly always overhauled and rebuilt. Brake systems on older cars need attention for several reasons, the most important being the fact that hydraulic fluid attracts moisture, which attacks the system from the inside out, often rendering a hydraulic braking system in much worse condition internally than it appears to be from external examination. On cars built prior to 1967, failure of any single part can cause failure of the entire system (in other words no brakes); the four-wheel drum braking systems used on American cars prior to about the mid-1960s are marginal at best. If you want to be safe—and not sorry—the car's brakes will receive the same thorough attention regardless of whether you're doing a factory-new frame-up restoration in which all mechanical assemblies are disassembled, inspected, and repaired, a nearly new restoration that focuses only on

For the process of inspecting or overhauling the brakes, the vehicle must be securely supported on jack stands.

those items needing overhaul, or an original preservation where obvious wear dictates both the cosmetic and mechanical repair.

On drum brake cars, the condition of the brakes can be inspected by removing the brake drums. The condition of this brake set is essentially normal. The shoes do not show excessive wear and fluid is not leaking from the wheel cylinder (located in the 12 o'clock position on the backing plate).

To understand why the braking system needs our attention, let's follow the action from the point when we press the brake pedal until the car slows to a stop. As the foot pedal is depressed, it presses a plunger in the master cylinder (mounted under the floorboard on cars and light trucks through about 1955 and on the firewall of later models). The plunger compresses a small amount of hydraulic fluid, sending a pulse of pressure through the brake lines to the four wheels. Here, the pressure expands the fluid in the wheel cylinders, forcing the brake shoes (or calipers on disc-brake-equipped cars) against the brake drums (or rotors with disc brakes), slowing the vehicle.

That is what is supposed to happen. Now let's look at what can go wrong on a worn and out-of-repair brake system. First, the bushings that allow the brake pedal to rotate freely on its shaft may have worn so that the pedal binds when pressed, requiring extra foot and leg pressure. Next, corrosion from moisture trapped in the hydraulic fluid may have rusted the inside liner of the master cylinder, allowing fluid to leak past the plunger, thereby reducing pressure to the lines. This problem becomes increasingly acute as the car is driven because each time the brake pedal is pressed, some of the brake fluid that leaks past the plunger seeps through the master cylinder seals. Now, as the

fluid pulse travels through the brake lines, a corroded line may spring a leak, causing the pressure in the lines to drop to nothing—and whoops, no brakes! Assuming the lines hold and the pressure pulse reaches the wheel cylinders or disc brake calipers, corrosion inside the wheel cylinder or disc caliper can jam the piston, preventing braking action or creating fluid leakage, or both. If the piston responds to the fluid pulse, worn linings or pads, grooved or out-of-round brake drums or rotors may further reduce braking efficiency. When a combination of problems occur, as is likely, you'll be hanging onto the steering wheel white-knuckled, pressing on the brake pedal for all you're worth, and praying for the car to stop.

INSPECTING THE CAR'S HYDRAULIC BRAKING SYSTEM

Although the most serious deterioration of a hydraulic braking system will be internal, typically caused by a combination of wear and corrosion, an external inspection can give you some clues to the system's overall condition. Note: an external inspection is especially important to determine whether a collector car you are considering purchasing (or maybe have just purchased) is safe to drive. The first step in this inspection is to locate the master cylinder. When

A great upgrade that's usually easy for drum brake cars is to install finned drums in place of nonfinned drums. The fins greatly improve cooling, which helps prevent the shoes from overheating and glazing over. Some companies offer oversize drums (like those that were often part of towing packages) and even iron-lined aluminum drums, which further resist heat buildup.

you've found the master cylinder, remove the filler cap or plug and check both the fluid level and the color of the hydraulic brake fluid. The fluid should be at or near a full mark on the master cylinder. Fresh fluid will be clear and transparent like water but with the consistency of light oil. Fluid that's brownish in color, has a thick consistency, and shows traces of water indicates (1) a brake system that has had very little maintenance and (2) severe internal corrosion. Next, inspect the condition of the brake lines (typically you'll find this tubing routed inside the frame

channels on the driver side of the car) for corrosion and signs of leaking. At the front wheels, fluid passes from the steel lines to the wheel cylinders through rubber hoses. Turning the wheels away from the car (first one side then the other) should make it possible to look into the wheel wells to inspect the condition of these hoses. If the rubber appears dried out and is badly cracked, the brakes have received little maintenance. Cracked hoses can leak or rupture and are a disaster waiting to happen.

On disc-brake-equipped cars, the condition of the discs can often be seen through slots in the wheels (after the wheel covers are removed). Corroded discs indicate either long storage in high humidity or frozen calipers. Grooved discs signal badly worn pads (another sign of poor maintenance) and deteriorated braking action.

While an external inspection gives indications, internal inspection is needed to find out the braking system's true condition. With both drum and disc brakes this inspection starts by removing the wheels. Caution: whenever the wheels are removed, be sure to support the car on jack stands. On cars equipped with disc brakes (most U.S. cars built since about the mid-1960s have discs at the front wheels and drums at the rear), removing the front wheels exposes both the disc and caliper to easy inspection. Although you still can't appraise the caliper's internal condition, you can get a measure of how much wear has occurred to the pads. For a clearer picture of pad wear, you'll need to remove the caliper, which will also show the condition of the seals around the piston and possibly the condition of the piston (if the pads are badly worn a sizable portion of the piston may be showing). Note: Replacing pads and other steps involved in overhauling disc brakes are described later in this chapter.

Braided steel flex lines are another excellent upgrade over the stock rubber hoses. The braided lines don't balloon under pressure, so you get a better pedal feel and improved transfer of pedal pressure to the caliper pistons or wheel cylinders.

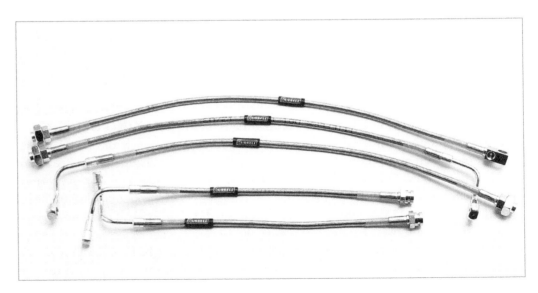

If you do improve the efficiency of your rear brakes, you may need to install an adjustable proportioning valve in the rear brake circuit to decrease line pressure and prevent the rear brakes from locking up prematurely.

With drum brakes, you'll need to remove the brake drums, which requires loosening the brake adjuster (check the service manual for this procedure). Often the adjuster will be rust-frozen (a condition that's not talked about in the manual). With luck, the brake shoes will be worn enough so that the drum can be removed. If not, you've got a problem. You can try squirting penetrating oil onto the adjusting wheel through the opening in the backing plate, or you may have to heat the adjuster with a torch.

Front brake drums come off by loosening the spindle nut. This done, the brake drum should slide toward you. If the drum seems stuck on the brake shoes, grab the edges of the drum to work it back and forth, over the shoes. If the shoes have worn a lip around the outer edge of the brake sweep area, the drum may begin to loosen and then lock against the shoes. Sometimes you can work the shoes over this lip. If not, you'll need to retract the shoes some more with the adjuster.

As the front drums pull loose, the large washers that sit behind the spindle nut and outer wheel bearing typically slide off the spindle. These parts should be picked off the spindle and placed in a container for safe keeping before they fall onto the shop floor. It is important not to mix bearings from one wheel to another, a situation avoided by placing containers at each wheel to hold parts as they come off.

Due to differences in rear axle designs, the rear wheel drums on some cars remove more easily than others. But again, the first step is to back off the brake shoes with the adjuster. On most cars since the mid-1950s, the rear drums are held in place by the wheels, which in turn are secured by the lug nuts. With the wheels removed, you should be able to pull off the drums. Sometimes the drums are rusted to the axle flange; spraying penetrating oil around the outline of the flange, then rapping the drum a couple of times

Whether the brakes are being rebuilt as part of an overhaul or a complete restoration, all new hardware should be used. Old springs and clips used to secure the brake shoes lack the strength of new parts and can fail.

Few people think of changing brake fluid, but it should be done regularly—at least every two or three years. Use only DOT 3 or DOT 4 fluid on the street, not silicone-based DOT 5 fluid, which can't absorb any moisture and eats brake system seals, and thereby compromises the safety of your braking system.

of thick linings, smooth drums, and clean parts. If so, you can be pleasantly surprised. But even if the brakes appear to be in good condition, some maintenance/overhaul steps are still in order, and you may want to consider upgrading the braking system for safety.

SAFETY UPGRADES

Prior to 1967, all U.S. cars routed the brake fluid from the master cylinder to the wheel cylinders through a single supply line. Rupture of that line or loss of fluid at any of the wheels or the master cylinder caused a loss of braking action on the whole system. As a friend of mine had happen to him, you might press on the brake pedal, have a rusted line pop a leak, and klunk, the brake pedal would drop right to the floor with absolutely no response from the brakes. Luckily, my friend's car lost its brakes in a parking lot. Think about the same event on a steep downgrade. For 1967, the federal government mandated a split system in which the front and rear brakes each had a separate fluid supply. This system can also fail, but it's not as likely as the older, single line.

One upgrade strongly recommended if your collector car was built prior to 1967 is converting to the split hydraulic system. This safety upgrade requires only replacing the single master cylinder with a later dual master cylinder, adding a proportioning valve if the front brakes are also being converted to disc-type, and rerouting the brake lines to the front wheels. For cars built shortly prior to the government's split-system mandate, the upgrade is generally simple—just substitute parts that are newer than the car by a year or two. On other, typically older, cars, the conversion is more complex, sometimes requiring relocating the master cylinder from an under-the-floor location to the firewall.

The second upgrade, often done in conjunction with the first, is converting at least the front wheels to disc brakes. Drum brakes have an inherent design flaw that makes drum-equipped cars unsafe in today's densely packed, frantic-paced traffic: When the brakes are applied, the friction lining on the shoes presses against the drums. Heat builds up and is absorbed by the metal (typically cast iron) drums. As the metal heats, it expands. Now the shoes need to push farther for the linings to make contact, creating more heat, more expansion, and so on. In addition, though heat is transferred from the shoes to the drum, much heat remains in the shoes, causing them to literally melt and glaze over on the surface, which in turn causes the friction efficiency to fall off and the brakes to feel spongy, like you're pressing the brake pedal into marshmallows. If the

around the flange area (on the flat surface beside the lugs) with a heavy hammer usually loosens rust's grip. On cars built prior to the mid-1950s, it's common for the brake drums to be taper-fit to the rear axle and held in place by a nut threaded on the end of the axle. Removing this style of rear brake drum requires a special puller.

With the drums removed, what you're likely to see are worn linings (a wafer-thin layer of friction material over the metal brake shoes), scored drums (deep scratches in the drum lining's contact surface), a great deal of dusty material (residue from the worn linings), coating on the backing plates, brake shoes, and other internal surfaces, and possibly dark sediment (a mixture of leaking brake fluid and lining dust) around the wheel cylinder. It's possible that you may also see other signs of damage such as broken springs and hardware, even cracked linings.

Possibly, especially if the car has seen good care and regular maintenance, you'll see a very different condition

Brake drums, suspension members, and all other parts associated with the brake overhaul should be cleaned and painted.

heat buildup is severe enough (as might occur on a long mountainous downgrade or on a racetrack), the brakes can give way (fade out) altogether. In the era of drum brakes on racing cars, it was common for drivers to hurl their cars around winding road courses with no brakes whatsoever after the first few laps—a real test of the drivers' mettle.

Disc brake upgrade kits are available for a wide range of drum-brake-equipped collector cars. This chapter describes one such upgrade using off-the-shelf parts. You're not likely to make these upgrades to a trophy restoration, where authenticity is important and the car is seldom driven on the highway, but they're strongly recommended for a collector car that you expect to drive in highway traffic. If the driver ahead of you in an ABS, power disc-brake-equipped new car decides to stop, it's going to happen right now! With a 40-year-old drum-brake-equipped car, no matter how well maintained the brake system, even assuming you hit the brake pedal the instant you see brake lights flicker ahead of you, stopping your car is going to be a slow-motion version of what's happening ahead. Along with the screech of rubber sliding on the pavement, you're likely to hear the sledge-hammer sound of crashing metal.

Overhauling Drum Brakes

Brake parts for most collector cars are in relatively good supply. A complete brake system rebuild will require the following:
- Brake shoes
- Brake shoe hardware kit (clips, springs, etc.)
- Flex hoses (two front, one rear)
- Wheel cylinder rebuild kits; possibly new or rebuilt wheel cylinders
- Brake lines (lifetime stainless-steel lines are available for many cars)
- Master cylinder rebuild kit; likely a new or rebuilt master cylinder
- Resurfaced or replacement brake drums

Two low-cost specialty tools (available from auto parts stores) significantly ease the brake system overhaul process:
- Brake spring pliers (this tool lets you remove and install brake shoe return springs with the flick of a wrist, rather than playing tug of war)
- Parking brake helper (to remove and install the parking brake cable)

On most cars and light-duty trucks since the mid-to-late 1950s, the wheel spindle that attaches to the brake backing plate on drum brake vehicles, or the dust shield and caliper assembly on disc brake vehicles, is connected to the front suspension A-arms by ball joints. Typically, the ball joints and other suspension pieces are inspected for wear and replaced as part of the brake overhaul process.

Referring to your shop manual, you'll disassemble the brake mechanism starting at a front wheel (with drum brakes, the front wheel setup is typically simpler than the rear because it lacks the parking brake mechanism).

Here's a tip. Redo the brakes on one side of the vehicle at a time. That way you can look at the other side for a guide to fitting all the parts back together correctly.

After you undo the retaining springs and clips and remove the shoes, the wheel cylinders come off with two

bolts reached from the rear side of the backing plate. In the front, the brake line connection to the wheel cylinder is through the rubber flex hose. If this hose is hardened and cracked (typical on an aging collector car) it can simply be cut. At the rear, the brake tubing connects directly to the wheel cylinder. If the fitting has become rust-frozen to the wheel cylinder, the line will also have to be cut.

After removing the backing plates, you will see the whole brake assembly in pieces in front of you. The next step is to clean the backing plates (using the techniques and processes described in Chapter 8) and prepare them for refinishing. Then you can clean and inspect the drums.

Front brake drums ride on two bearings. The outer bearing came off when you removed the drum. The inner bearing, located at the rear of the drum's center opening, is held in place by a seal and is still in the drum. These inner bearings can be removed using a special wheel bearing puller (a hook-shaped tool that looks like a tiny crowbar) or by tapping on the perimeter of the inner race with a long punch inserted through the hub. But there's a speedier method commonly used by mechanics who are paid by how quickly they complete their work: To remove the inner wheel bearing, replace the nut and washer on the spindle, then slip the brake drum over the nut so that the hub rests on the spindle. Now pull the drum toward you in a sharp, downward tug. This will snap the bearing cage against the spindle washer, popping the bearing free nearly every time.

The drums need to be inspected for cracks, warpage, and adequate metal on the lining sweep walls. If the drum has cracked from excess heat buildup, the crack will usually show on the lining sweep area. (The Eastwood Company sells a special dye to detect nearly invisible hairline cracks. This is great also for checking used parts purchased at swap meets or salvage yards.) Warpage is checked by laying the drums, face down, on a flat surface. Drum wall thickness should not be less than 20 percent of original. Maximum brake drum ID measurements are often listed in the reference section of the service manual. The ID dimension is most accurately taken with a special brake gauge, available from the Eastwood Company and specialty tool suppliers. The drums may need to be turned on a brake lathe to make sure the lining contact area is smooth and in a true circle, so the measurement should show enough thickness to offset the metal that will be lost. Cracks, warping, or thin walls call for replacement drums.

Brake drums that pass these tests can be prepared for painting by sandblasting or treating the surface with a deoxidizer like Rusteco. Acid should not be used on brake drums, because it can make the metal brittle.

On disc-brake-equipped cars, inspection and replacement of worn parts is a simpler process than with drum brakes. Removing the wheel puts all parts into open visibility and allows easy access.

Wheel cylinders leak fluid or become gummed due to moisture in the hydraulic fluid. Standard brake fluid, which the Department of Transportation designates as DOT 3, attracts moisture like a sponge. For this reason, service manuals call for flushing and replacing the brake fluid every year or so. In real life, this is seldom done and the result is moisture-laden brake fluid sloshing through a car's brake system. Corrosion eventually eats the system from the inside. Chances are you'll see this damage when you peel back the seals, pop the pistons, and hold the wheel cylinder casting up to the light to inspect the condition of the cylinder bore.

Typically, the inside of the brake cylinders will be scarred with pits. If the pits are no deeper than small scratches, a smooth bore can be restored by honing with a grinding stone. This isn't something you would do at home, but would be done by an automotive machine shop—a service sometimes available through auto parts stores. If pits have scarred the metal, you'll either purchase new cylinders or have the old ones relined. The same procedure applies to the master cylinder.

If the wheel cylinders and master cylinder show signs of internal corrosion, it follows that the brake lines are also rusting from the inside out (as well as from the outside in). While the manufacturer used regular steel tubing, restorers often opt for stainless steel—which is sold in correct prebent lengths for a wide range of collector cars by a variety of suppliers, and carries a lifetime guarantee.

Having the wheel cylinders and master cylinder relined has advantages over just replacing the old parts with new ones. First, relining is generally less expensive than buying new parts. Second, brake rebuild services, like White Post Restorations in Virginia, reline the cylinder bores with rust-proof stainless steel, ending the corrosion problem forever.

One word of caution. When rebuilding any brake system component, never use a petroleum-based lubricant on internal parts. Wheel cylinder rebuild kits will typically contain small vials of special lubricant to be used for this purpose. If not, special brake system lubricant can be purchased at an auto parts store, or the parts can be lubricated with brake fluid.

In some cases, the relined cylinders will be returned completely rebuilt, ready to install. In others, you may have to rebuild the cylinders using a kit that includes new rubber boots and springs, but typically requires that you reuse the original piston(s). When the original wheel or master cylinder pistons are reused, they are first polished with 0000 steel wool and carefully wiped clean. The cylinder bore is also wiped clean with a lint-free cloth, then coated with the special lubricant. The spring is inserted into the cylinder before the pistons (two for wheel cylinders, one for the master cylinder). The pistons are lubricated and pressed against the spring so that the dust boot(s) can be slipped over the end(s) of the cylinder. A few drops of the special lubricant will help the dust boots slide over the end of the housing.

Once the caliper has been removed, the rotors are removed for resurfacing or replacement.

On wheel cylinders, new bleeder screws are available from most auto supply stores.

With all the parts in hand (new or rebuilt wheel cylinders, brake shoes, spring/hardware kits, and flex hoses), the brakes are assembled following the steps in the service manual (the reverse of disassembly). However, service manuals frequently omit two important steps. (1) Within a brake assembly, often there is a front brake shoe and a back shoe (forward facing and rear facing) with the difference being which part of the metal shoe is covered by lining. If you are overhauling the brakes one side at a time, you can look at the brake shoes on the other side of the car to see which shoe should face forward. Otherwise you'll need to look carefully at the illustrations in the service manual. (2) After replacing the brake drum, the shoes should be adjusted until they wedge against the drum, then loosened until the drum turns without rubbing on the shoes. This procedure seats the shoes for even contact when the brakes are applied.

Whenever internal corrosion necessitates replacing or relining the wheel cylinders and master cylinder, the brake lines should also be replaced. As mentioned earlier, in a restoration stainless-steel lines are recommended over regular steel lines for two reasons: (1) stainless-steel lines will be unaffected by moisture entering the brake system, and (2) stainless-steel lines won't corrode externally, preserving the car's freshly restored look. Plain steel lines can be clear coated to preserve the fresh steel's shiny new look, but inside they'll still be subject to corrosion.

While it's possible to bend and fit new lines from precut and flared lengths of brake-line tube available at auto parts stores, a better approach is to use correct length lines bent to the original shape from restoration suppliers. These exact-fit brake lines not only help maintain the car's original appearance, but they're also easier to install, which is important for making sure there are no fluid leaks in the system.

For safety, it's desirable to upgrade the master cylinder to a dual reservoir unit for a split braking system. If this upgrade is contemplated, then dramatically improving the car's braking response by converting the front brakes to discs should also be considered. These upgrades are often available in kit form and can sometimes be done using manufacturer's parts, as described in the next section.

Upgrading to Disc Brakes

No matter how defensively you drive, drum brakes really aren't safe in today's traffic. This relegates original drum-brake-equipped collector cars either to parades or touring in the company of other collector vehicles. For those planning to enjoy driving their collector car, replacing the drum brakes at the front wheels with modern-style discs is a safety must. (Converting only the front brakes to disc-type provides the needed safety margin, since on front-engined cars more than 60 percent of the braking action occurs at the front wheels.)

Disc brakes first appeared on aircraft and were adopted successfully to automobiles in the early 1950s by Chrysler and Crosley. At the time, however, neither owners nor mechanics were familiar with disc brake maintenance, leading the pioneering manufacturers to revert to drum brakes. Discs reappeared on performance cars in the 1960s due to the inability of manufacturers to design fade-resistant drum brakes. Today, disc brakes are standard equipment on virtually all vehicles.

A drum-brake-equipped collector car can be converted to front disc brakes through three approaches: (1) by retrofitting disc brake components from a more modern car; (2) by installing a disc brake conversion kit; (3) by switching to a late-model front suspension. Where it applies, the first approach has lots of benefits. Parts are often available at low

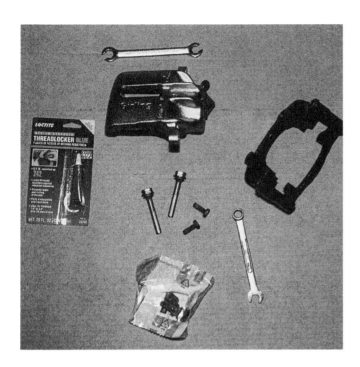

If the piston bores in the calipers are rusted, new or rebuilt calipers will be required. Loctite should be used on bolts attaching the caliper assembly.

FACTORY VS. AFTERMARKET DISC BRAKE KITS

Once you've decided to upgrade to disc brakes, you're forced with two basic approaches: the use of factory-style parts, or aftermarket parts, such as those originally manufactured for racing purposes.

Both have their pros and cons.

A downside to factory-style parts is that they aren't always as "sexy" as aftermarket racing components. Of course, this utilitarian look does tend to contribute to their often cheaper price—as does the fact that zillions are made. The vast numbers made also works to your favor when it comes time to service the systems, because parts are generally available from any dealership of that make or local auto parts stores. Auto parts stores can also help out with the parts' sex appeal, in the form of special high-temperature finishes just for brake components.

Aftermarket parts, on the other hand, are often designed for the rigors of racing service and may be more easily serviceable—but the service parts may only be available from the component manufacturer or limited other sources. And they tend to look incredible, right out of the box. But their limited production quantities and factory-applied special finishes often result in a significant price premium over factory-type parts.

cost from a salvage yard, you're using the manufacturer's engineering, and you're keeping the car stock in the sense that you're using the manufacturer's parts. The downside to this approach is that it only works when there's enough basic engineering similarity between your car's drum brake front suspension and a later model disc brake front end for the parts to swap. The second approach has the convenience of all needed parts being likely to be included in the kit. It's likely, also, that the disc brake conversion kit manufacturer will have redesigned some of the suspension components, adding engineered improvements and strength to these critical parts. The downside here is the price of the kits, necessitated by tooling and engineering costs being distributed over a fairly small product run. While the third approach may have appeal to owners of straight-front-axle cars and light trucks, this conversion is by far the most complicated and is needlessly destructive of originality in cars that already have independent front suspension.

With either the retrofitting or kit approach, converting from drum to front disc brakes is a relatively straightforward process. It consists mainly of installing disc rotors and dust shields in place of the brake drums, either by replacing the spindles or adding brackets to hold the disc brake calipers (sometimes also replacing the upper and lower control arms), installing the calipers and rotors, and replacing the existing master cylinder (typically a single-reservoir unit) with a dual reservoir disc brake master cylinder and proportioning valve. As in any brake system overhaul, the proximity of the front suspension invites inspecting and replacing worn steering and suspension parts such as the tie-rod ends and ball joints or king pins.

The disc brake upgrade begins by elevating and placing the car on jack stands, removing the front wheels and front brake drums, then disassembling the brake shoes and related brake hardware. Unless a conversion kit is used that mounts the disc calipers to the drum-style backing plates, the backing plates also need to come off.

Removing the spindles requires compressing and removing the front coil springs (using a special tool called a spring compressor), then pressing the ball joints out of their locating holes at the top and bottom of each spindle. When compressing the coil springs, it's extremely important to be alert to the danger of a spring under compression. The spring should be compressed (shortened) only enough to remove it from its perch between the upper and lower control arms. If your tool inventory doesn't include a coil spring compressor, and you can't borrow one from a friend, you can rent this tool from most rent-all stores, or it can be purchased from most auto parts stores. Once the spring is removed, the compression tool should be released and removed. Usually, it is not necessary to compress the front coil springs for reinstallation.

New pads can be slipped into slots on the caliper-mounting bracket before the caliper is replaced.

On a retrofit conversion, parts such as the dust shields and spindles can come from a donor car as a cost-saving alternative to purchasing new parts from an aftermarket source or the manufacturer's dealer. (Tip: if you're using a later-model disc brake donor car as your parts source, it's a good idea also to get the disc brake master cylinder, which can be used as a core exchange on a rebuilt replacement.) If a salvage yard is your parts source, you'll probably want to degrease and sandblast the dust shields and spindles. These parts can be refinished with a spray can using the Eastwood's Chassis Black, or by adding a small amount of flattener (check the mixing proportions supplied with the product) to a gloss black automotive finish applied by a spray-painting system. As a better alternative, you may want to powder coat the more visible parts, like the spindles and dust shields. Powder coating is extremely durable, making this finish ideal for chassis components.

With the springs out of the way you can set about replacing the ball joints. Many GM products have the upper and lower ball joints riveted to the control arms. Since replacement ball joints are secured with bolts, you can tell at a glance whether or not the ball joints have been replaced by the type of fasteners. The upper ball joints can be replaced without removing the control arms simply by unthreading the bolts or drilling out the rivets. The lower ball joints have to be pressed out (either using a C-shaped ball joint press designed for this purpose or by removing the control arm and using a press). With the front suspension this far apart, it makes good sense to remove the control arms (which typically attach to the frame with U-bolts) and inspect the bushings at either end of the control-arm shaft for wear. Worn control-arm shaft bushings are a cause of steering wander. When a shim pack has been installed behind the upper control arms, be sure to note the location of each set of shims. Replacing the shim packs will restore the front suspension's caster setting. From this point the disc brake conversion should be a simple matter of reassembling the new parts.

Working on one side of the car at a time, you're now ready to install the spindle and replace the coil spring. This process consists of inserting the lower ball-joint stud into the spindle and threading on the nut, placing the spring in its pocket in the lower control arm, and compressing the spring until the upper ball-joint stud inserts into its hole at the top of the spindle. A floor jack placed under the control arm can be used to compress the spring by slowly raising the arm. As the spring compresses the upper ball-joint stud, it can be positioned into the hole in the upper yoke of the spindle. When the jack begins to lift the car, you'll know that both ball joints are firmly seated and the nuts can be tightened on the studs.

Next, the dust shields are bolted onto the spindles. It's good policy to chase the threads in the mounting holes on the spindles with a tap to remove any rust or debris and to use stainless-steel bolts (so that the dust shields can be removed, should that be needed, in the future). The rotors go on next. Disc brake rotors install just like brake drums. First, new bearing races are pressed in place, then the inner wheel bearing is packed with grease, dropped into its race, and the bearing retainer is tapped in place. Next, the outer wheel bearing is packed with grease, the rotor slipped onto the spindle, and the bearing placed into its race. As with brake drums, the retaining nut is seated, then loosened slightly to allow the rotor to turn freely—yet without free play—and cotter-pinned in position.

With the rotors installed, you're ready to mount new pads on the disc calipers and bolt the calipers onto the spindles. Some disc brake conversion kits use brackets attached to the drum brake backing plates to hold the calipers. One of the advantages of disc brakes is the ease with which new pads are installed—a much easier job than

The front disc brake assembly shown here has been installed in place of original drum brakes using all factory parts. In this installation, disc brake spindles from a vehicle a few years newer fit into the ball joints, making the conversion as easy as bolting on the disc brake parts.

For cars that will be driven, a dual master cylinder and a power brake booster are safety upgrades to consider, along with front disc brakes.

replacing drum brake shoes. The final step in this location (aside from bleeding the hydraulic system and remounting the front wheels) is connecting the calipers to the hydraulic system with new flex hoses.

With the upgrade work completed at the front wheels, the action now moves to underneath the hood. Here you'll replace the drum brake master cylinder with a unit designed for disc brakes (and possibly convert to a safer dual-braking system in the process), and add a proportioning valve to the system, and a vacuum booster, if power brakes are desired. Disc brakes require a different master cylinder than an all-drum-brake system, because the disc brake master cylinder has a significantly larger front fluid chamber. On a dual-reservoir drum brake master cylinder, both chambers are basically the same size. The greater

stopping power of the front discs and amount of fluid needed to move the disc brake caliper piston are the reasons for the larger front chamber.

The proportioning valve is a new item added to the system. Its purpose is to increase the stopping force at the front wheels. When the brakes are applied, and the car begins to decelerate, weight shifts forward. If an equal amount of pressure is applied to both the front and rear wheels, the weight shift toward the front would cause the rear brakes to lock up and the wheels to slide on the pavement, while the front brakes would exert only a small amount of braking effort. Stopping such a vehicle at speed would be almost impossible. To correct this imbalance, the proportioning valve supplies more pressure to the front brakes and less to the rear, preventing rear wheel lockup and boosting braking action at the front, where the forward weight shift increases traction.

Upgrading to disc brakes also invites adding a power brake booster (a process described separately), so rather than simply replacing the master cylinder, you may also be installing both the disc brake master cylinder and a power assist unit.

Brake Fluid

Whenever you're overhauling or rebuilding your brake system, you have the perfect opportunity to drain the old brake fluid and replace it with fresh fluid. But with so many fluids available—DOT 3, DOT 4, and DOT 5, being the most common—you have to determine which fluid makes the most sense to use.

Most cars left the factory with polyglycol brake fluid, designated DOT 3, in their lines; however, for years, many racers and enthusiasts have chosen to use silicone brake fluid, designated DOT 5, claiming it offers certain performance advantages.

Before you can choose which fluid is right for you, you need to understand what happens to fluid and how problems develop—and how to prevent them.

According to Carmen Anastasiof, of Master Power Brakes, initially, a properly installed brake system—whether filled with DOT 3, 4, or 5 fluid—will have no moisture in it. But that quickly changes. As you drive the car and use the brakes, some of the heat generated as you stop is transferred to the fluid, causing it to heat up. When you're done with your drive and park the car, as the fluid cools, condensation will form within the brake lines.

That moisture is what starts to cause problems.

Obviously, any moisture within the brake system can lead to corrosion and rust, which will affect the system. But other problems will occur—which problems depends on which fluid you run.

With DOT 3 fluid, the moisture can be absorbed into the fluid. At first thought, this sounds like a bad thing—and it's certainly not ideal. But it does allow the fluid to be distributed throughout the system, which allows it to get away from the heat source—the caliper on disc brakes systems, or the shoes on drum systems.

DOT 4 fluid is similar to DOT 3, but features anticorrosive additives, and is therefore preferred over DOT 3 fluid.

Silicone-based DOT 5 fluid, on the other hand, does not absorb moisture—at all. What this means is that as the calipers (or shoes) heat up, any condensation that forms within them will *stay* within them, since it cannot be absorbed by the fluid. The moisture forces brake fluid out

of the caliper or away from the wheel cylinders, eventually leaving only water within them. The first problem the moisture begins to cause is the formation of rust and corrosion. The second, worse problem is that the next time the calipers (or wheel cylinders) begin to heat up, they quickly reach the boiling point of the water within them, causing it to turn to steam, which releases air into the system resulting in a loss of hydraulic pressure as the air compresses rather than transmitting the pedal pressure to the shoes.

Naturally, that steam will recondense back into water eventually—still within the caliper or wheel cylinder. The fact that the moisture doesn't leave the caliper or wheel cylinder can cause at least one additional problem in cold weather: it freezes, potentially causing a complete brake system failure.

DOT 5 fluid also causes another problem: it eats away at rubber seals in the master cylinder, calipers, wheel cylinders, combination valves and hydraulic switches causing leaks, which allow the introduction of air, which results in diminished hydraulic pressure.

DOT 5 fluid isn't without its advantages—it does often have a higher boiling point than DOT 3 fluid, for one. But the boiling point has almost no effect on the formation of moisture that can form during normal, day-to-day driving. A second advantage is that silicone fluid won't destroy paint on contact, as will DOT 3 fluid, if spilled.

Because of the inevitability of moisture forming within your brake system, Anastasiof recommends routinely changing your brake fluid, at least every two years, but preferably every year. Circle track, road racers, and autocrossers should change their fluid after every race. Drag racers should change their fluid at the start of the season, and mid-way through it.

If you're at all in doubt of whether you can keep up with such a maintenance regimen—and be honest, because this is an extreme safety concern—then you should use DOT 4 fluid.

Bleeding the Brakes

When a hydraulic brake system is refilled with fluid, air becomes trapped in the brake lines. If you're working alone, you'll need a special suction tool to bleed the air from the brake lines. If you have the help of an assistant, the suction tool isn't needed. Either way, the process is quite simple. With the suction bleeder, after filling the reservoir(s) on the master cylinder, you'll attach the hose from the device to each bleeder screw (on the wheel cylinders or disc calipers), and suck out the air. With an assistant, the first step is to gravity-bleed the system. This

New brake lines and flex hoses, shown at the front of this restored chassis assembly, are safety musts. Stainless-steel brake lines, cut to correct lengths with proper bends, are available for many 1950s and 1960s cars.
Mike Cavey

is done by attaching a short section of plastic tubing to the nipple of the bleeder screw at the wheel cylinder or disc caliper farthest from the master cylinder (you'll want to drop the open end of the tubing into a small can or jar to catch the small amount of fluid that will drain out with the air) and opening the bleeder screw a "crack." While the fluid is displacing entrapped air, there's a risk that the master cylinder fluid reservoirs may drain empty. If the reservoir empties, air will be drawn into the lines—just what you're trying to eliminate—so you'll want to station your assistant near the master cylinder during this step to keep the reservoirs topped with fresh fluid. When you see a steady stream of fluid running through the tubing, you can close the bleeder screw.

Since air may still be trapped in the hydraulic system, you and your assistant will now pressure-bleed the brakes. Step 1, make sure the fluid reservoirs in the master cylinder are topped off and replace the reservoir cap. Step 2, have your assistant pump the brake pedal until a hard pedal is achieved. Step 3, tell your assistant to hold pressure on the brake pedal, and not to release the pedal until instructed to do so. Step 4, position yourself at the bleeder screw farthest from the master cylinder and open the screw. Likely, air will bubble out with the fluid. When fluid stops running, close the bleeder screw and tell your assistant to again pump up the brake pedal. Step 5, refill the master cylinder reservoir. Repeat this procedure until the fluid runs clear of air at this and each of the other wheel cylinders or brake calipers.

Before operating the car on the highway, carefully inspect all brake line connections for leaks. Any leaking connections should be tightened, the brakes applied several times, and the connections reinspected. It may also be necessary to rebleed the brakes.

ADDING POWER BRAKES

Where power brakes were a factory option, installing a booster unit is a simple, straightforward procedure. Where power brakes were not on the dealer's wish list, a power booster can still be added, but with a little more finagling.

New booster units are available from specialty suppliers and can often be purchased at swap meets and salvage yards. With the latter sources, a Hollander's Interchange Manual helps in matching up years, makes, and models of vehicles sharing the same booster unit.

Once the needed parts have been gathered, assembly consists of installing a T fitting in the vacuum port to the intake manifold, mounting the booster and master cylinder assembly on the firewall and connecting it to the foot pedal, then reconnecting the brake lines. At this stage, just a couple hookup steps remain: reattaching the warning light wire to the proportioning valve and installing a vacuum hose between the T fitting on the manifold and the vacuum inlet on the booster unit.

By multiplying the pressure you can exert on the brake pedal, power brakes not only add a margin of safety, but they give the brakes a surer feel.

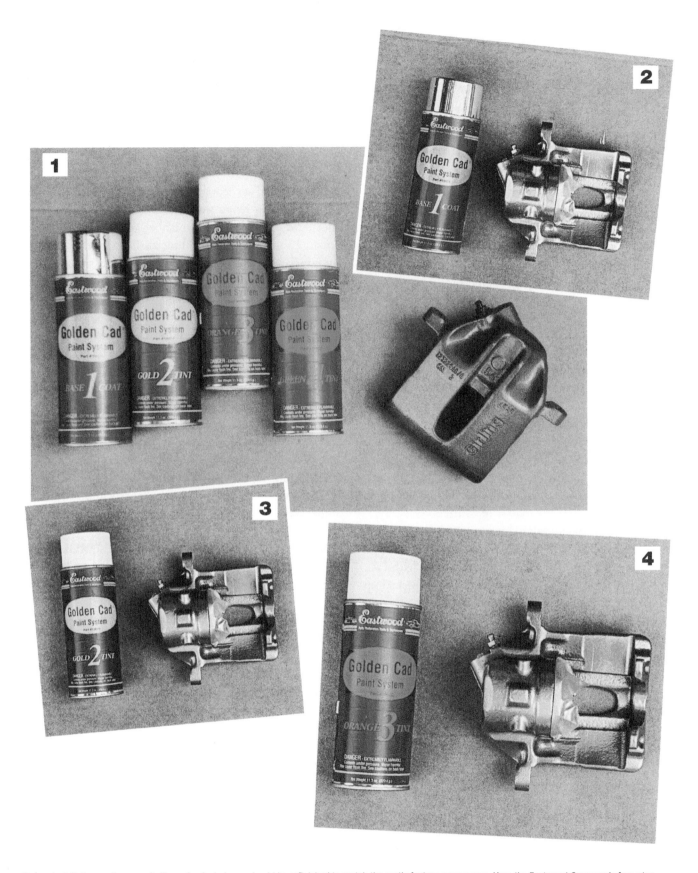

Before installation on the car, rebuilt mechanical pieces should be refinished to match the part's factory appearance. Here the Eastwood Company's four-step Golden Cad coating system is applied to a disc brake caliper to give the appearance of cadmium plating.

Chapter 15
Restoring Mechanical Assemblies

A car is a complex aggregate of mechanical assemblies: steering, suspension, engine, transmission and driveline, and brakes. On a collector car, all are likely to need attention, so the questions at hand are (1) which mechanical assemblies need attention, (2) to what degree do they need it, and (3) how much of the work do you feel capable of doing yourself? Let's look at the possibilities.

Unless the car has extremely low mileage, has been impeccably maintained, or major mechanical assemblies have been recently overhauled by former owners, you can plan on all major mechanical components needing some attention. To help you determine where mechanical attention is needed, I have provided a list of diagnostic strategies for each major mechanical assembly (excluding brakes, which were covered in the previous chapter). These will show what needs to be repaired and whether minor or major overhaul is needed. Remember, in a show car restoration, all mechanical assemblies will likely be rebuilt to factory-new condition as a matter of course.

To answer the big question, how much of the work you feel capable of doing yourself, you're likely to draw on past experience, the degree to which you've worked with cars. If you have some mechanical training or have picked up the basics by maintaining daily drivers and helping friends, you may feel competent to tackle most mechanical work short of rebuilding the engine and transmission. (Some restorers will feel competent there, too.) If your experience under the hood of a car has largely been to change the oil, you may decide this is the time to learn what makes a car tick. It's possible to become quite mechanically adept learning while doing, but to do so, and to be sure the repairs you make are done correctly and are safe, you'll need to ask lots of questions, read shop and service manuals, watch instructional videotapes, and have mechanically savvy friends look in from time to time at your work.

It's also possible that you don't know what happens when you turn the key in the ignition—and don't want to know. If "mechanically challenged" best describes your adroitness with a wrench, you'll need to find someone capable and competent to do the work for you. Unlike a new car that can be serviced at the manufacturer's dealer or any number of independent repair shops, collector cars require a technician who, first of all, remembers the old technologies (many of today's service technicians have never even seen an ignition system with contact points and a condenser), is willing to tie up his shop waiting for parts, and does not fear angering you, the customer, when he explains that his initial repair estimate only covers a fraction of the total cost. Service technicians with this combination of knowledge, patience, and trust are becoming increasingly rare.

Whether you do the work yourself or hire it out to a professional, the first step in mechanical restoration is to assess the condition of the major mechanical assemblies. As discussed in Chapter 3 on the subject of selecting a restorable car, a car's mechanical condition is a lot easier to assess if it runs. The first diagnostic list makes this assumption. Later we'll run through a list of static diagnostics that aren't dependent on the car's ability to move under its own power.

DIAGNOSING MECHANICAL ASSEMBLIES

To check the condition of the mechanical assemblies, we'll take the car on a short test drive. It's best if we can take the car out on the highway.

It's a good idea to carry a notebook and write down all perceived problems. These can be checked out later with static (stationary) tests.

Interpreting the Diagnostics

Let's look at the notes. How did you describe the steering? Did it feel loose, not especially responsive in turns, and requiring nearly constant correction on straight stretches of highway?

Steering

On most collector cars, steering is a rather primitive design consisting of a series of levers driven by a steering box that's likewise a high-friction device and prone to wear. Watch a scene from an old movie showing someone driving a car. The steering wheel is being played back and forth

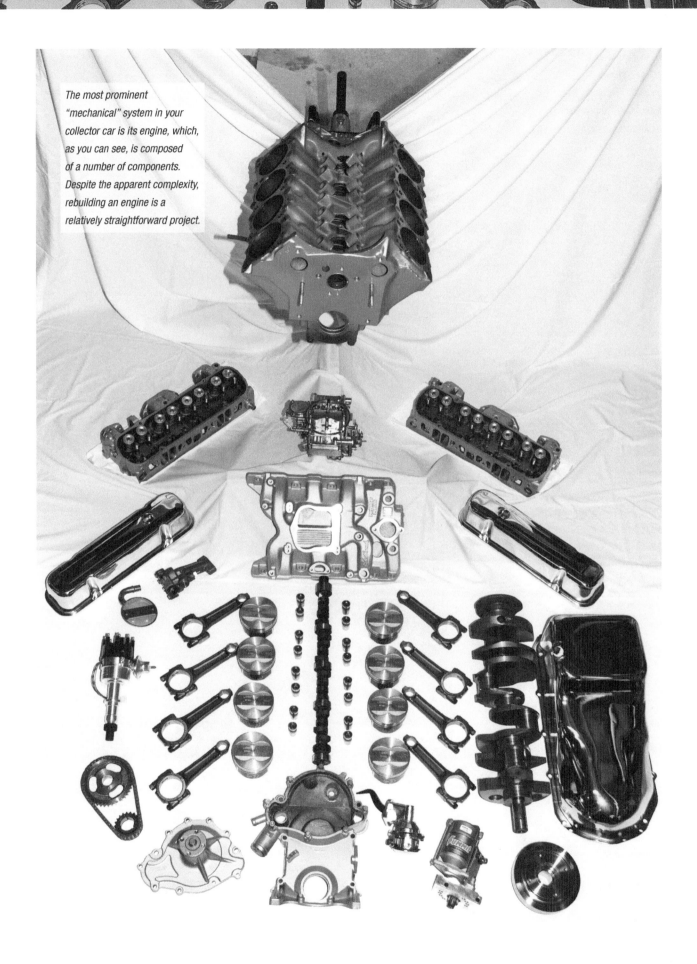

The most prominent "mechanical" system in your collector car is its engine, which, as you can see, is composed of a number of components. Despite the apparent complexity, rebuilding an engine is a relatively straightforward project.

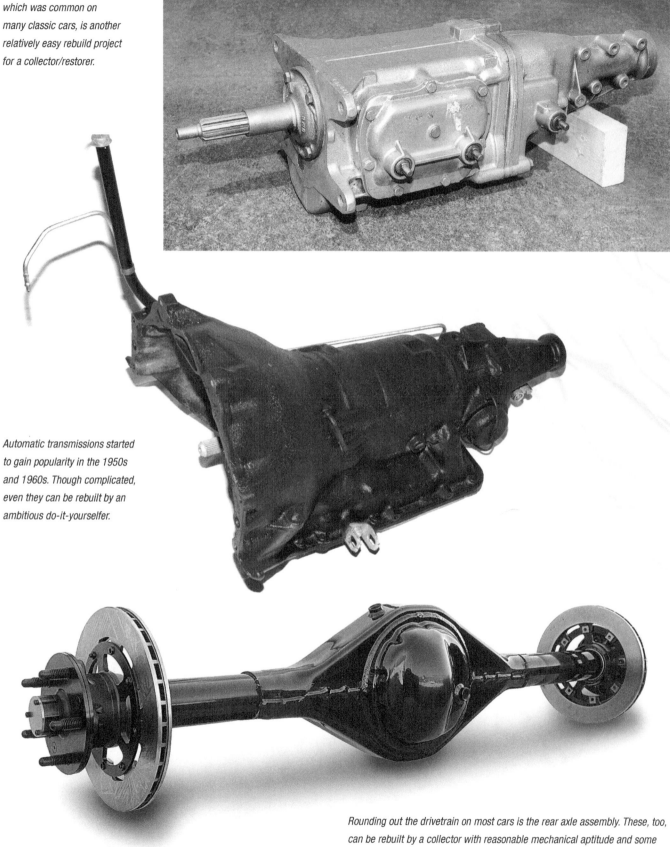

A manual transmission, which was common on many classic cars, is another relatively easy rebuild project for a collector/restorer.

Automatic transmissions started to gain popularity in the 1950s and 1960s. Though complicated, even they can be rebuilt by an ambitious do-it-yourselfer.

Rounding out the drivetrain on most cars is the rear axle assembly. These, too, can be rebuilt by a collector with reasonable mechanical aptitude and some patience. AFCO photo

Steering, brakes, and suspension are the three largest remaining mechanical systems that need to be reconditioned when restoring your collector car.

To prepare an engine block for a rebuild, it needs to be reconditioned by a machine shop. Minimal work should be degreasing and checking it for cracks. Optional work includes boring and honing the cylinders, milling the cylinder decks (to ensure flatness), and honing the main bearing saddles. Here, we've mounted the block to an engine stand so that the engine is at a comfortable work height and can be rotated easily, and we're cleaning the already machined block prior to rebuilding, to make sure no metal shavings remain in the engine.

Before your crankshaft gets reinstalled, it, too, should be machined, which should include cleaning, crack inspection, and "turning" the main and rod journals to remove any scratches. Balancing is a good idea, but can be skipped if the engine won't be run much and especially if it won't be run at high rpm.

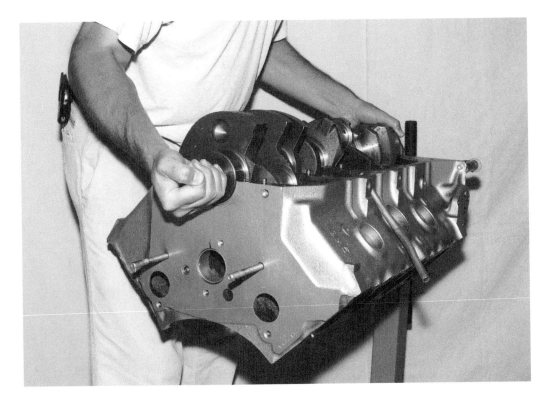

Replacing the camshaft is a great opportunity to improve power and drivability. Flat-tappet camshafts, which were used in nearly all cars until into the 1980s, are not compatible with most modern oils, so if you're running a flat-tappet cam, be sure to add a ZDDP oil additive to prevent premature lobe wear.

like the balance wheel in a mechanical clock. Of course, the car in the movie is often a set piece on a sound stage and the driver is only pretending. But the see-sawing steering motion isn't exaggerated; that's the way older cars are driven. Still, there's a difference between steering that's tight (as the manufacturer intended) and steering that's worn and loose, which makes the car unsafe to drive. A few simple tests performed with the car sitting in your driveway will quickly show the difference.

Static Steering Tests

1. With the car parked, engine off, reach through the driver's window and rotate the steering wheel. How far does the steering wheel turn before you see the front tire begin to turn? This distance, called play, indicates the degree of looseness throughout the steering assembly. Properly set up, the steering has no play.

2. Jack up the car so that both front tires are free of the pavement. With the car's weight supported on jack stands,

Modern bearing shells often feature antiwear coatings and special construction that helps them minimize friction, yet maximize durability.

When replacing pistons, you may find that you have a number of decisions to make, from the material from which they're made, to the compression ratio they'll provide (given a certain combustion chamber size), to whether they'll feature any kind of friction-fighting component. Cast-aluminum pistons are what most nonperformance engines came with. Forged aluminum pistons were used in performance engines. A modern alternative is a hypereutectic piston, which is sort of a hybrid that blends the benefits of the cast and forged pistons.

grip one front tire at the 3 and 9 o'clock positions. Now jiggle the tire back and forth. Does the entire steering linkage and opposing wheel move as you jiggle the tire or does the tire feel like it's connected to the steering by rubber bands? Naturally, everything should move as an assembly.

3. With the tires still off the pavement, grip the tire at the 12 and 6 o'clock positions. Again attempt to jiggle the tire. Movement from this position indicates worn king pins or ball joints (pieces that allow the front wheels to turn) and possibly loose or worn wheel bearings.

Note the responses to these tests in the notebook. After assessing the other mechanical assemblies, we'll look at the steps for restoring the steering to like-new operation.

Suspension

Suspension wear can make driving both uncomfortable and dangerous. On the road test you were using comfort as your guide to suspension wear. As you perform the static tests you may discover suspension wear that makes the car unsafe to drive.

Most vintage engines use a timing chain with iron sprockets to turn the camshaft. Over time the chain stretches, which allows the cam timing to vary erratically. Every rebuild should feature a new timing set.

171

A new oil pump will ensure that your rebuilt engine has adequate circulation of life-saving oil through its various oil galleys and passages. Pumps are often available in standard, high-volume, or high-pressure. Unless your car is going to be raced, a standard volume pump is usually sufficient.

Static Suspension Tests

1. With the car parked on a level surface, does one corner of the car appear to sit lower than another? If you're sure the car is parked level, you can check for sag with a yardstick. Sag at one corner indicates a weakened or broken spring at that location. If the car sits abnormally low at one end (unweighted), both springs at that end may be weak or broken.

2. Standing at a corner of the car, push down on the fender or bumper. Does the car return to position and then stop, or does it continue to bounce, indicating worn shock absorbers?

3. Crawling underneath the car, look for damage or severe wear to the suspension mounts. On unit-bodied cars, rear spring hangers sometimes tear enlarged holes in the sheetmetal frame structure. Also on unit-bodied cars with detachable front engine and suspension cradles, the entire suspension and engine support structure can loosen at the body mountings.

Engine

Engine performance, though an excellent indicator, doesn't tell the whole story. Several observations made as you drove the car were intended to give clues as to the engine's internal condition. Low oil pressure, for example, is a sure sign of internal wear, especially the main crankcase bearings, and the engine may need an overhaul. Likewise, blue smoke from the exhaust or smoke from the road draft tube (the long section of pipe running out from the breather cap) on engines built before 1967 (when the federal government mandated a closed crankcase ventilation system) are signs of cylinder wall and piston ring wear.

Gray smoke from the exhaust on a fresh start-up indicates water vapor in the exhaust. If this goes away as the engine warms up, the condition is normal. If gray smoke is still seen after the engine has been driven for a few miles, it may indicate coolant seeping into the combustion chamber.

Cylinder heads should be rebuilt before being reinstalled. Again, cleaning and crack inspection are requirements. Mill their mating surface to ensure flatness, plus a performance valve job. Yours may also need new valve guides, and you should consider having screw-in studs installed to replace pressed-in studs, which can literally fall out, over time.

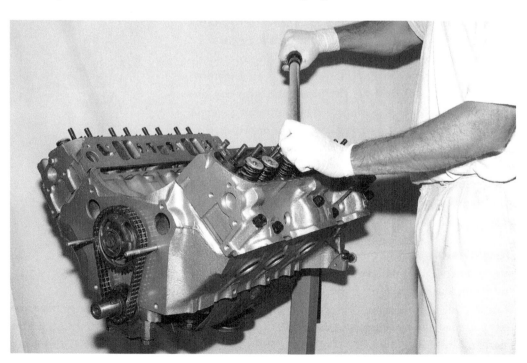

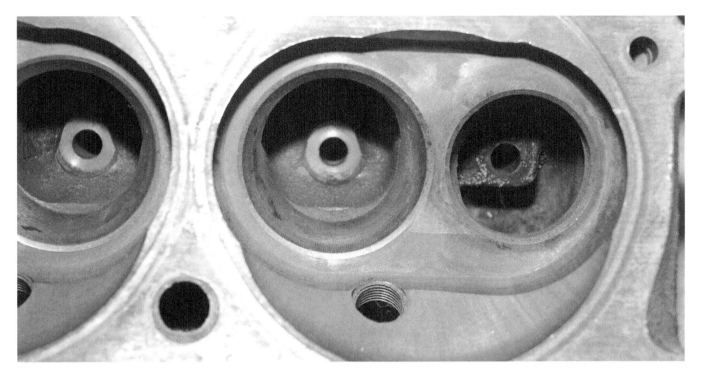

If you plan on driving your collector car much, you should consider having hardened valve seats installed, or possibly replacing your original heads with later heads that came from the factory with hardened valve seats. The need for hardened seats came about when lead was removed from gasoline in the early 1970s; the lead had helped lubricate the valve seats, preventing wear. This head has a factory-hardened seat, which you can identify from the blueing of the cast iron around the valve seat. The factory very briefly applied intense heat to harden the seats; most aftermarket hardened seats are inserts of a harder metal alloy that resist wear.

Your heads may also need new valve guides, which are the "tubes" (at the top of the photo) into which valves are inserted. They wear over time, increasing oil consumption and friction. You should consider having screw-in rocker studs installed to replace pressed-in studs, which over time can literally be pulled out of the head. Screw-in studs are especially recommended if you've replaced your camshaft with a performance cam with mechanical (i.e., "solid") valve lifters.

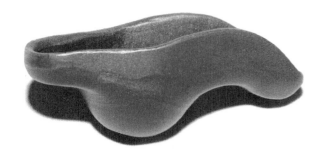

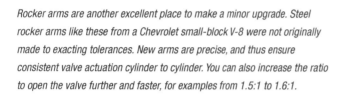

Rocker arms are another excellent place to make a minor upgrade. Steel rocker arms like these from a Chevrolet small-block V-8 were not originally made to exacting tolerances. New arms are precise, and thus ensure consistent valve actuation cylinder to cylinder. You can also increase the ratio to open the valve further and faster, for examples from 1.5:1 to 1.6:1.

An even better suggestion for upgrading rocker arms is to replace stock, stamped steel arms with roller rockers. Models are available with a roller tip, or with a roller tip and a roller fulcrum. Both minimize friction and improve accuracy.

Intake manifolds can also be improved or replaced during a rebuild. You can either port your stock intake for a modest flow improvement, or replace your stock intake with an aftermarket model, most of which are made of aluminum to run cooler and reduce weight. For a "stealth" look, even aluminum intakes can be painted to resemble a stock model.

Prompt starting means the engine's electrical and fuel systems are in good form, and the engine stopping abruptly when the key is turned off indicates strong compression in the cylinders. Still, a few more tests can be made that don't require operating the car.

Static Engine Tests

1. If known, what is the engine's true mileage? Engines in older cars typically need rebuilding after 60,000–70,000 miles.

2. Is anything known about the car's maintenance? How often did former owners change the oil? Religiously changing the oil and filter at 3,000-mile intervals is the single most important factor in extending an engine's life. What's the condition of the oil currently in the engine? Black oil suggests poor maintenance.

3. With the engine idling, listen to the exhaust. A sucking sound indicates a burned valve.

4. With a compression tester (this relatively inexpensive tool is available from auto parts stores, Sears, and other

Most vintage cars utilize a carburetor to mix fuel and air, though some models featured fuel injection, even back into the 1950s. You can rebuild the carb or F.I. system yourself, or you can send it off to companies like Holley's Custom Shop, which can rebuild almost any carb for a reasonable fee.

If you really want to improve drivability, you may want to consider replacing your car's carburetor with a modern, electronically controlled fuel injection system. Holley's Commander system was among the first on the market, though others now exist that more closely resemble a carburetor, to retain a classic look.

CONDITION OF MECHANICAL ASSEMBLIES CHECKLIST

Steering

Does the car wander excessively? (Keep in mind that older cars require more steering effort and attention than newer vehicles.)

Does the car pull either left or right?

Are noises audible from any of the wheels when the car turns a sharp corner?

Suspension

Does the car handle small pavement irregularities smoothly without deflecting the steering or setting up a jouncing motion?

Does the car lean excessively on corners or nose-dive excessively when braking?

Does the suspension bottom out (make a loud clunk) on more severe bumps or hard acceleration?

Engine

Does the engine fire up quickly and idle smoothly, or did the starter crank what seemed an excessive interval and the engine idle roughly?

Does the engine run smoothly?

Does the engine make odd noises, a clattering sound when idling (indication of a worn or loose valvetrain) or a deep clunking, knocking sound (indicating worn bearings)?

If the car has an oil pressure gauge (as opposed to simply a warning light), does the oil pressure reading drop to 0 when the engine is idling?

Does the oil pressure needle register at least in the middle of the gauge when the engine is operating at highway speed?

If the car has a temperature gauge, does the needle register in the middle range as the car is operating?

Is blue smoke noticeable in the exhaust after the engine idles for a short time?

Does smoke blow out of the road draft tube and/or crankcase breather during or after driving at highway speed?

Does the engine stop virtually immediately after turning off the key or does it seem to turn one or more revolutions before stopping?

Driveline

Does the driveline clunk when the car is shifted into reverse?

Does the clutch work smoothly?

Does the transmission (manual or automatic) shift smoothly?

Does an automatic transmission appear to slip in any of the gears?

Does the transmission and/or rear end make excessive noise?

If equipped with an overdrive transmission, does the overdrive work?

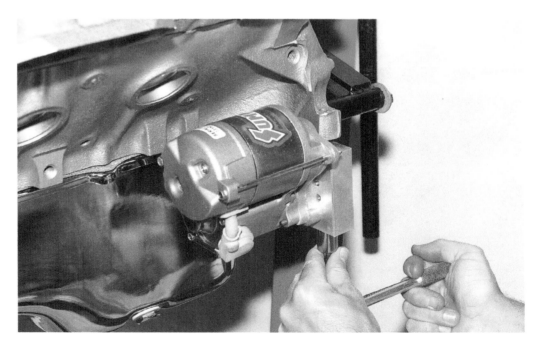

While a vintage starter can be rebuilt, modern gear-reduction starters, like this inexpensive model from Summit Racing Equipment, will turn over your engine faster, yielding faster starts. Some simple spray paint may be all that's needed to camouflage them so that they don't stick out under your hood.

Crankshafts should be stored on end to prevent bending.

tool outlets), check the compression of each cylinder. Compare the readings to normal compression shown in the service manual. Low compression readings are a signal that an overhaul is needed.

A compression test is done by removing a spark plug and placing the compression tester in the spark plug hole. With the coil wire removed from the distributor (so the engine won't start and run), have a friend crank over the engine with the starter while holding the compression tester in the spark plug hole. The compression reading will show on the instrument's dial. Repeat this procedure for each cylinder.

Transmission and Driveline

Transmission and driveline wear usually makes itself known through noise and degraded operation (a clunking sound as reverse is engaged, a slipping clutch, difficulty shifting, or the transmission slipping out of gear), yet a few under-the-car checks will add important details to the picture.

Static Transmission and Driveline Tests

1. Does either the transmission or rear end appear to be leaking fluid? If so, seals likely need to be replaced, and if these components are operated low on fluid, internal damage is likely.

2. With an automatic transmission, pull the dipstick and check the color of the fluid. Healthy automatic transmission fluid is bright red. Brown, burnt-smelling fluids are a sure sign of severe wear calling for a complete rebuild.

3. On cars with open driveshafts (exposed universal joints), grip the driveshaft at either end and check for play, indicating worn universal joints.

OVERHAULING MECHANICAL ASSEMBLIES

In a complete factory-new restoration, all mechanical assemblies will be removed from the car, cleaned, rebuilt, painted, and reassembled. In no case is a mechanical assembly's condition left to chance. In this setting, the driving and static tests described thus far would guide the overhaul, but even seemingly sound assemblies will be disassembled, inspected, and rebuilt to eliminate any trace of wear.

On a nearly new or partial restoration, the engine is likely to be removed to give access to the engine bay for cleaning and painting. If needed, the engine will either be

177

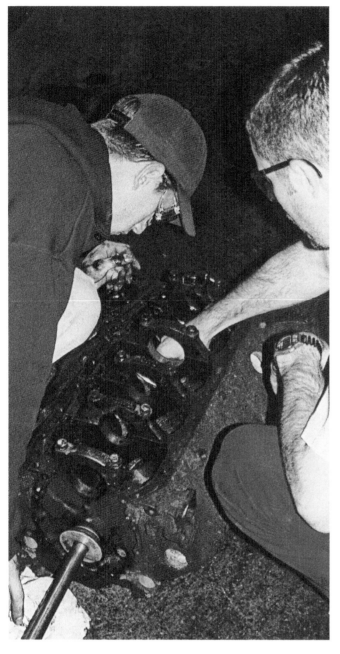

As part of the engine rebuilding process, the camshaft bushings will be pressed out and replaced.

freshened or sent out for overhaul. The steering, front suspension, and brakes would likely be rebuilt at this time; on manual transmission cars, the clutch would be inspected and replaced if needed while it is readily accessible. All components appearing to be functioning normally would be cleaned and painted, but otherwise left undisturbed. Although this approach is attractive from the standpoint of time and money, it leaves the car prone to mechanical failure, for there's no way short of a tear-down and rebuild to truly assess the condition of a mechanical assembly.

The assumption with the overhaul guidelines that follow is that you would use a service manual and other instructional resources (like videotapes) for the step-by-step repair sequences. The discussion that follows is general in nature and intended as an orientation (rather than how-to) to overhaul procedures for the mechanical assemblies.

In restoring mechanical assemblies, nuts and bolts typically need to be replated. The original cadmium plating is no longer available. Bright zinc makes an effective substitute and can be applied by most commercial platers. For the plater's convenience, you will have nuts, bolts, and related hardware plated in bulk lots, so you'll need to photograph or note which bolts go where.

Steering Overhaul

By the nature of its rather primitive design, the steering on most collector cars is easily within most hobbyists' mechanical ability to rebuild. Essentially what's required is replacing any loose tie-rod ends on the steering linkage as well as loose king pins or ball joints (depending on which steering/front suspension design the car has) and possibly rebuilding the steering box. Loose tie-rod ends and king pins/ball joints would have been detected during both the road test and static tests. You can also detect loose tie-rods by grasping and shaking the steering linkage at its connecting points.

To replace a loose tie-rod end, the linkage is first disconnected using a special tie-rod puller or a so-called "pickle fork" (both tools are available from most auto parts stores, Sears, and other automotive tool outlets). Then the tie-rod end is unscrewed from the linkage section. Before unthreading, however, a clamp has to be loosened. Also, before turning out the tie-rod end, count and record the number of exposed threads. The new part will be threaded into the linkage to this same point. Now, holding the linkage with a pipe wrench, unscrew the tie-rod end with another pipe wrench, unless the threads are so rust-frozen that the tie-rod end won't turn. When this happens, the threads should be soaked overnight with penetrating oil and the unscrewing attempted again. If the threads are still locked, the linkage end will need to be heated with an oxyacetylene torch to loosen the rust's grip. The new tie-rod end is threaded into the linkage, stopping with the same number of threads exposed and the clamp tightened. Before the car is made operational, you'll have the steering checked at an alignment shop, but for now you'll use the old specifications.

King pins and ball joints are typically replaced in conjunction with overhauling the front brakes, since the brake assembly at the front wheels needs to be disassembled to

A small but important detail: while the engine is apart for rebuilding, the freeze plugs should be removed and replaced.

Restorers may want to improve their engine's performance by polishing the combustion chamber and intake ports. The Eastwood Company

Although hidden underneath the hood, a restored engine is one of the car's crowning features. Shutterstock

access these parts. Replacing king pins requires two special tools: a bushing driver and a king pin reamer. In lieu of purchasing the tools, the bushings can be pressed in place and reamed by a machine shop to fit the new king pins. The process for replacing either king pins or ball joints is best followed from the shop manual for your car.

Although rather simple in design, the steering box can be challenging to overhaul. Designs other than GM's recirculating ball have such high internal friction that severe wear is likely on any car except a low-mileage one. If play is traceable to the steering box (detected by disconnecting the steering linkage from the pitman arm—the lever attached to the steering box—and having one person hold the pitman arm while another attempts to turn the steering wheel), then the steering box should be removed and

rebuilt. Likely, you'll send the steering box to a rebuilding service or purchase a new or rebuilt replacement. The problem here is that often the steering box and steering column are one assembly and to get this unit out of the car, you have to remove the steering wheel.

The steering wheel is supposed to come off easily with a puller, but on older cars the wheel is often rusted to the shaft so that the puller is likely to have little effect except to damage the steering wheel hub. John Twist of University Motors Ltd. says he has a sure-fire method for removing stuck steering wheels. With Twist's method, you pop off the horn cover and loosen the steering wheel nut until it passes the end of the shaft. Next, soak penetrating oil around the end of the shaft. Now one person sits in the car and grips the wheel at the 3 and 9 o'clock positions. As

On overhead-valve engines, the intake valve (left) is much larger than the exhaust valve. Whether or not the entire engine needs to be rebuilt, often the heads are pulled and the valves removed. On engines built before about 1969, this procedure is important to install hardened valve seats, necessary when using unleaded gasoline.

This head has been hot tanked to remove not only external grime but also sediment from the water passages and deposits from the combustion chamber and intake and exhaust passages. The next step will be to replace the valves and springs.

Before reusing the old valves it's important to check for wear on the valve stems using a micrometer. Wear beyond certain tolerances can cause a poor seal on an engine that burns oil.

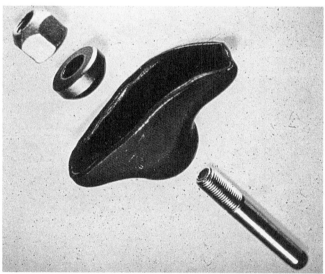

Rocker arms on Chevrolet and Ford small-block engines, and other, newer V-8 engines, mount on studs that are press-fit into the head.

the person in the car pulls the steering wheel toward him, a helper places a large hammer over the nut and raps the head of the hammer a sharp blow with another large hammer. It may take a few raps, but it works.

When reinstalling the rebuilt or new steering box, be sure the box is bolted tightly to the frame. Likewise, make sure all tie-rod ends are properly tightened and cotter keyed. Finally, lube all fittings.

Suspension Overhaul

Both the driving test and visual inspection looked for springs that had lost their tension, loose mountings, and worn shock absorbers. If the vehicle sits lower than normal, the springs should be removed and either re-arched or replaced. (Factory photos showing proper stance, comparing the car with a restored example, or a sagging corner are giveaways of spring sag.) The typical arrangement on U.S.-built cars from the early 1950s is coil springs in front and leaf springs in the rear, although Chrysler Corporation used torsion bars instead of coil springs in the 1950s and 1960s, and Buick, Chevrolet, and a few others used coil springs all around during the same decades. Both coil and leaf springs are relatively easy to replace, though coil springs require a special tool to compress the spring for removal. While new coil springs are being fitted, bushings for the independent front suspension—as well as the king pins or ball joints—and shock absorbers will also be replaced. This work is typically done in conjunction with rebuilding the front brakes, since the brake assembly must be removed to access the front suspension and steering parts.

If the car is sagging at one of the rear corners, there's a good likelihood that the rear spring for that side is broken. Often, one or more of the shorter leaves in the spring set will break, still allowing the car to be driven, but causing the car to sit lower at that corner. If the main (longest) leaf breaks, the car is unsafe to drive, since leaf springs also serve as location arms for the rear axle. If the car is a high-performance model and has been driven aggressively, damage may also have been done to the spring mounts and other traction and/or stabilizing arms that may be on the car.

Although leaf springs can be rearched, new springs that have not been subjected to metal fatigue are preferred.

Engine Overhaul

Although most hobbyist restorers have the mechanical ability to remove the engine, rebuilding an engine requires a higher set of skills and equipment and is best left to a professional. If the engine is original to the car (the engine's originality can be determined by coding on the engine showing build date, as discussed in Chapter 4 regarding research, or the engine number is used on the car's title), it's important that the engine be rebuilt, not replaced. On a show car restoration, it may also be important that the engine's accessories, including such items as the intake and exhaust manifolds, carburetor, generator, water pump, and various mounting brackets, be original to the car. Where these have been replaced during earlier

Flexplates and flywheels may need machine work or replacement, depending on their condition. On many engines, the flywheel has teeth around its circumference, which the starter engages to crank the engine. If teeth are broken or missing, you may need to replace your flywheel to prevent starting problems.

Automatic transmissions can benefit from the installation of an aluminum oil pan, which will help keep the transmission fluid cooler, improving transmission life.

You should also replace your universal joints, to ensure proper, smooth operation. Bad U-joints can not only cause clunking sounds but can also cause troubling driveline vibrations. An out-of-balance driveshaft can also cause vibrations, so it's wise to have your driveshaft dynamically balanced.

When rebuilding your rear axle assembly, you should inspect the ring gear (here, attached to a differential carrier) and the pinion gear for signs of damage. This would also be the time to consider changing your assembly's gear ratio, to either improve performance or maybe to improve fuel economy.

repairs, original-type parts may need to be located, as discussed in the research chapter.

When removing the engine, be sure to tag all wires (even when new wiring will be installed) and meticulously store and catalog all bolts and assorted hardware. When rebuilding the engine in a 1950 Studebaker pickup, I casually placed the carburetor linkage on a shelf underneath

my workbench. Enough time passed before the engine was ready for reinstallation that I completely forgot where I had stashed the linkage so that I wound up using a replacement linkage located at a salvage yard. Of course, as soon as I brought home the replacement, I found the original.

To remove the engine you'll need a portable hoist, commonly called a cherry picker. This tool can be rented at

On many collector cars, the suspension pieces are worn and need to be replaced. If you're sure the car is parked level, you can check spring sag with a yardstick. Coil springs are removed quite easily using a spring compressor to shorten the spring length. The Eastwood Company

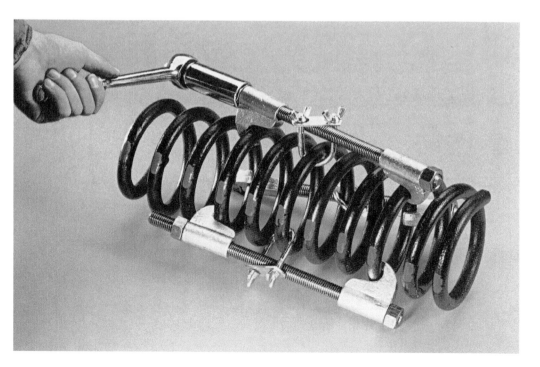

most tool rental stores. The steps for removing the engine will be listed in the service manual. Be sure to save all grounding straps and note their locations.

Before crating the engine or transporting the engine to the rebuilder, remove all accessories such as the generator and starter. These you can rebuild yourself following the steps in the service manual. Alternatively, you can send them to a rebuilding service or purchase rebuilt replacements. On pre-1970 engines that were designed for leaded gasoline, it's advisable to request that the rebuilder install hardened valve seats to allow the engine to be operated on today's unleaded gas. Using unleaded gasoline in engines designed for leaded fuel can cause rapid valve seat wear, possibly requiring replacement of this vital area in a short while. The rebuilder may suggest other upgrades, such as machining to allow insert bearings on engines originally using poured babbitt bearings, or improvements to the engine's internal lubrication system. Changes of this nature won't be visible externally and can dramatically improve the engine's operation, often making the engine quieter for highway travel and increasing its longevity. Before reinstalling the engine, you may want to replace the generator with an alternator and upgrade to solid state ignition. (The benefits of these electrical modifications are discussed in the next chapter.)

With the engine out of the car, you can turn your attention to cleaning the engine bay in preparation for painting. The radiator will need to be removed for pulling the engine and it can be sent to a radiator specialist (these shops should be available in your locale) to have the core boiled out and rodded to remove obstructing sediment. A badly deteriorated core will need to be replaced. If the

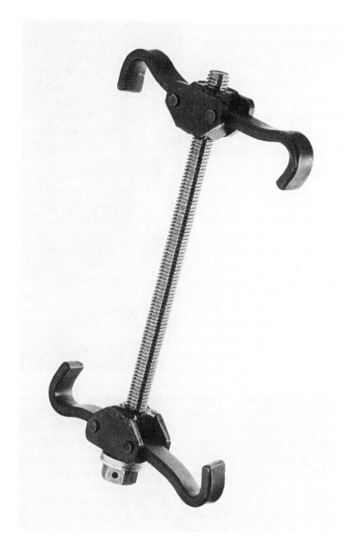

Don't try to use some sort of cobbled-together clamping arrangement for compressing coil springs. The tools could slip off, likely causing injury and damage. Instead use the correct tool. The Eastwood Company

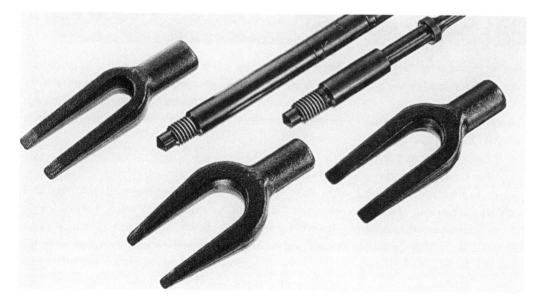

Steering linkage can be forced apart using a pry bar and a large hammer, but the proper tools lessen the risk of damage and injury. Called pickle forks, these separators squeeze between connectors in suspension and steering linkage pieces. The Eastwood Company

You can often improve the steering feel of an older vehicle by either upgrading to whatever "fast ratio" (lower number) steering box was available when new, or sometimes to a newer steering box with an even faster ratio. Many such swaps are simple bolt-in swaps.

Whether you're replacing your steering box or not, you should install a new "rag joint" or steering coupler. An old coupler can result in sloppy steering.

New suspension bushings will really make a difference in an old car. Original bushings were usually rubber, which deteriorates over time, causing slop. You may have the option of replacing rubber bushings with polyurethane bushings or even solid aluminum models. But beware that harder bushings will create a harsher ride.

radiator is seen prominently at the front of the engine compartment (as is the case with MGT series sports cars), you may want to enhance the radiator's appearance by polishing the copper tank that's soldered to the top of the core. Just ask the radiator specialist to give you the tank after it's been separated from the core. You can smooth any dents using the straightening techniques discussed in Chapter 11 (however, without filler), then polish the copper to a high gloss using the buffing techniques described in Chapter 7.

Driveline Overhaul

On cars with manual transmissions, if the engine is removed for service, at a minimum you'll want to inspect the condition of the clutch. Unless the clutch, pressure plate, and related hardware show only minimal wear, this is the opportune time to replace the clutch and other parts of the clutch assembly. If the manual transmission shifts

Replacement shocks are another must of a restoration. They're not just a comfort or handling issue, they're also a safety issue.

Wheels can be restored or replaced. These are 15x7-inch Pontiac Rally II wheels on a car that was originally available with Rally IIs, but only in 14x6 size. The increased diameter allows for the use of lower-profile tires, which minimize sidewall flex, and thereby improve handling responsiveness.

Your collector car's cooling system prevents the engine from overheating and resulting in damage. Unfortunately, older radiators can become clogged, or just lose their cooling fins, minimizing their efficiency. A local radiator shop can power-flush your radiator and pressure check it. If need be, they can usually replace the core or repair the end tanks to ensure your radiator is in proper working condition.

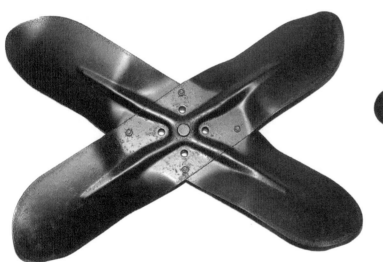

Older classic cars came with fixed-pitch cooling fans to draw air through the radiator when the vehicle is stopped. Such fans are heavy and inefficient, especially at high vehicle speeds, when they aren't needed at all.

A Flex-A-Lite variable-pitch fan flattens out at higher engine rpm, to produce less drag. Additional fan blades may further increase flow and efficiency.

smoothly and gives no indication of excessive wear (no growling in gear or other internal noises), the transmission should be drained and refilled with fresh gearbox oil.

If the car has an automatic transmission, shifting as noted in the driving test and the color of the fluid are indications that overhaul is needed. If the transmission appears sound and you're only repairing those mechanical

assemblies that show clear signs of trouble, then preventive maintenance consists of draining the fluid and changing the filter (located inside the pan on the bottom of the transmission). If the transmission is leaking fluid, the defective seal should be replaced.

On cars with overdrive transmission, if the overdrive doesn't work, the problem is likely electrical. Using the

No matter what fan you use, you should consider installing a fan shroud, which helps direct the air flow by creating a venturi effect (just like in your carburetor) to draw more air through the radiator. If a full shroud like this one wasn't available on your model, universal shrouds are available (from hot rod supply shops) that can be camouflaged to blend in with almost any engine compartment.

overdrive troubleshooting guide from the service manual, along with the unit's electrical schematic, you should be able to isolate the problem component. You'll find guidelines for tracing and troubleshooting electrical circuits in the next chapter.

If the universal joints at the transmission and differential ends of the driveshaft show signs of play or looseness, they should be replaced. With open drivelines, this is a simple process that's clearly described in most service manuals. On closed (also called torque tube) drive, the universal joints are enclosed and may not be accessible until the engine and transmission or entire driveline and rear end are removed from the car.

Gear and bearing noises are not the only reason for overhauling or replacing the rear end. If the car's final drive gear ratio causes the engine to turn at what you feel to be an excessively high rpm, you may want to replace the rear end with a "higher" (lower numeric ratio) unit or have a lower-ratio gear set installed in your car's rear end. For a quick and easy way, find out the car's rear-end (presuming open drive) ratio, jack up one rear wheel (remember to use a jack stand), then with the car in neutral (wheels blocked), rotate the tire; count the number of turns the driveshaft makes for each revolution of the rear tire. This ratio of driveshaft turns to rear tire turn is the car's final drive gearing. An example might be 4.11:1, in which case the driveshaft would turn slightly more than four times to the tire's single revolution.

An alternative to an engine-driven fan is an electric one, like this AFCO model. It can be mounted to the front of the radiator to push air through the radiator, or behind it to pull air through. Again, use of a shroud is recommended. AFCO photo

An engine oil cooler can really help protect your engine and/or transmission better by cooling the oil so that it doesn't thin out or break down.

With mechanical repair, you'll probably find your appetite for the more complex jobs whetted by successful completion of the simpler tasks. Still, whenever you move into unfamiliar ground, be sure to follow closely the repair sequences in the service manual and talk to fellow restorers or seasoned mechanics about your project. Work done incorrectly can be expensive to correct and you'll have the double disappointment that your failed effort is likely to be discovered when you believed your restoration project to be finished—not a good time psychologically for a big letdown.

Chapter 16
Renewing the Car's Wiring

If you're wondering whether or not your car's wiring needs replacing, the simplest way to make that decision is to take a close look at its condition. If the insulation is cracked or maybe even missing in places, or new wiring has been spliced in and old wires wrapped with electrical tape, a new harness is definitely in order. Failure to replace deteriorated wiring invites problems on the road, burned-out electrical equipment, or an electrical fire that can destroy the car as well as the building in which it is stored. If you have any doubt about your car's wiring, replace it. On a frame-up restoration, you will install a new wiring harness as a matter of course. As you will discover, the procedure is not difficult and does not require expertise with electricity.

TOOLS AND SUPPLIES

To install the new wiring harness you will need a shop manual with the car's wiring diagram, pliers, wire strippers, butt connectors, assorted screwdrivers (regular and Phillips), a socket set, locking pliers, and test light, or preferably a multimeter.

You should place your order for a new harness two to three months ahead of when you plan to install the new wiring. Order the harness only from a reputable supplier for your collector car or a harness manufacturer. You won't save any money buying a bargain wiring harness. With its inaccurate color coding, wrong wire size, incorrect wire lengths, and incompatible connectors, the bargain harness will either have to be remade to fit the car or discarded and replaced with a quality wiring harness from a manufacturer such as Rhode Island Wiring Service. With a quality wiring harness you'll get not just the correct color coding and correct gauge wire, but also the right connectors. Without correct color coding, the harness will be almost impossible to install; wire gauge is especially important for those cars with 6-volt electrical systems, and the original-type connectors are essential if you're going "plug and play." To be authentic, wiring harnesses in cars built prior to the mid-1950s should have fabric-covered wiring.

Along with the harness it's a good idea to buy a supply of rubber grommets, used to plug holes where the wiring

Compared to modern systems, collector car electrical systems are . . . well . . . antiquated. This fuse panel from a late-1960s Chevy contains only a few glass-tube fuses and has been crudely patched with jumper wires to power add-on accessories.

passes through the firewall and other locations in the sheet metal. These grommets should be available from the harness source, if not from a parts supplier for your car.

HOOKING UP AND ROUTING THE NEW HARNESS

With a quality harness you should receive an instruction sheet showing hookup connections. For a frame-up restoration, the wiring is removed when the car is disassembled. This means that you will need to refer to photos you took of your car before assembly as a guide to where to route the harness. If you forgot to take the photos or the wiring was already out of the car, you can take photos or make diagrams showing the location of the wiring in other original or correctly restored cars. As a double check against the instruction sheet, you should also have a service manual with a wiring diagram for your year and model car to refer

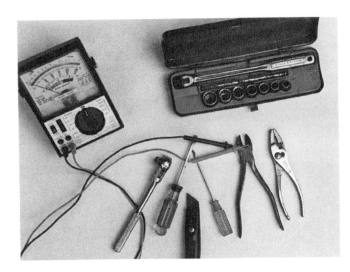

To install a new wiring harness you will need assorted screwdrivers, a socket set, pliers, and a multimeter.

able to read the wiring diagram will be a great help if you become confused, as you are installing the harness, about which wire attaches to which terminal on a component. Usually the answer will be apparent in the wiring diagram. Seeing circuits traced by the insulation color on the wires will also show why it is so important to have a correctly color-coded harness.

Wiring diagrams for cars built before the 1950s won't show signal lights because prior to this time signal lights were an aftermarket add-on, installed either by the dealer or owner. Since signal lights are important for safety in today's traffic in which other drivers will probably mistake hand signals as gestures, it's important to add this feature on cars not so equipped. Often the harness will be sold with a signal light option. It may still be necessary to convert the parking and taillights to double filament bulbs and add a signal light switch (if your car doesn't already have one), but having the signal light wiring in the harness avoids botching up the new wiring by splicing in extra strands to work the turn signals.

Besides signal lights, you should look at other options the harness may offer. Some harness makers give a choice of fabric- or plastic-covered wiring. If your car had fabric-covered wiring originally, and your intent is originality, then fabric wrapping it is. But if you are restoring or refurbishing your car to drive, plastic-coated wire is a better choice because it will be more durable. If your car has an overdrive transmission, that accessory will also require a separate harness.

to as you install the harness. (Wiring diagrams can also be purchased separately from a service manual.)

The wiring diagram will help you understand your car's electrical system and may be needed later to troubleshoot any problem circuits. Before replacing the wiring, it's a good idea to spend enough time studying the wiring diagram so that you can trace a circuit and follow the color coding scheme. The wiring diagram shows the circuits by labeling each wire with its color (and sometimes its gauge as well). As you study the wiring diagram you will be able to trace various color wires from a component (the taillight for example) to its power source or ground. Being

Sometimes you'll salvage connectors and other components from a donor car. Jessica Kibbey

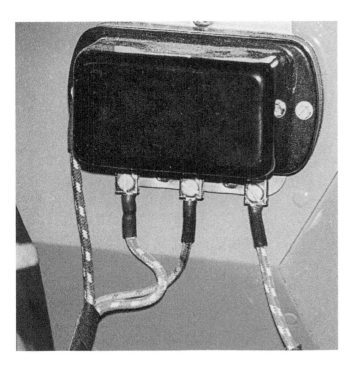

It's important to buy a quality harness from a reputable supplier. A quality harness will be manufactured from correct gauge wire with original-type wrapping, and the individual wires will be correctly color-coded to match your car's wiring diagram. Instructions with the new wiring harness should tell which color wire attaches to which connector on a component, such as the voltage regulator shown here.

It's important to make sure that grommets are installed in holes where the wiring harness passes through body panels. Otherwise, the wiring will chafe against the metal and cause a short, which could destroy the vehicle.

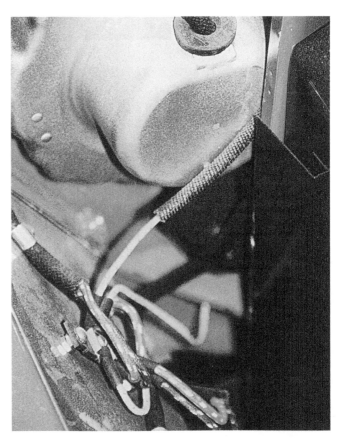

Be sure all connections are tight. Sometimes it may be necessary to pinch a connector to make good contact on a terminal.

Headlight wiring will typically join the main harness at a junction block, as shown here.

A multimeter can be used to test for internal shorts in electrical components, as is being done here to check the armature and field coils on a starter.

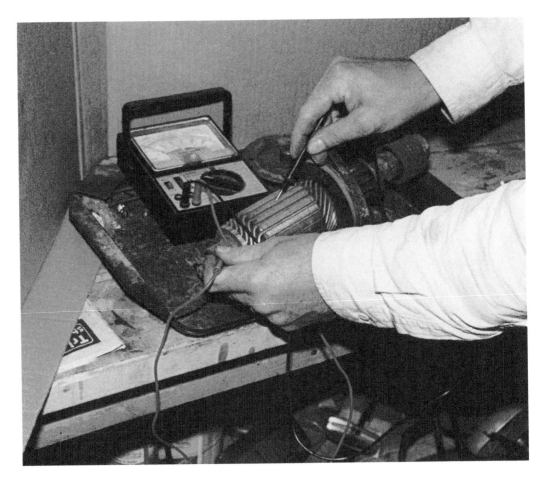

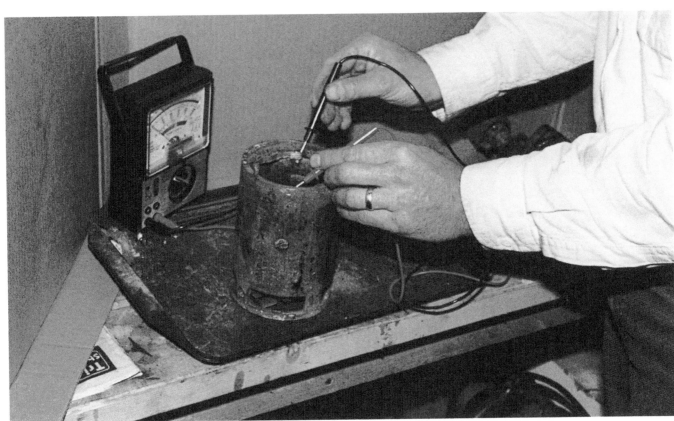

Installing a harness isn't just a process of matching the wires to their connections. It is also important to be sure that the contacts are clean and that every circuit, especially the lights, which are grounded through the body sheet metal, have a good ground connection. Electrical systems in most older cars used the body metal and frame for ground. This ground path is easily broken by rust, or on restored cars by heavy coatings of paint. To ensure a good ground, it may be necessary to scrape the paint from the place where an electrical component touches or mounts onto the body or frame. To help ensure a good ground connection, new or replated bolts should be used to mount electrical components, never-painted bolts, or rusted fasteners.

INSTALLING THE HARNESS

Where you begin installing the new harness is arbitrary. You can start at either end (at the headlights or taillights), or in the middle (at the instruments). If the old harness is still in place, the portion of the harness that goes to the lights and connects to electrical components under the hood can easily be installed by disconnecting the old wires and replacing them with new wires, one terminal at a time. As you pull away the old harness you can fit the new wiring in its path. If the old wiring has been removed, you will have to follow the wiring diagram and the color connection instruction sheet that came with the harness.

The most difficult connections are under the instrument panel, where a congestion of wires occupies a small space and where you almost have to be a contortionist to get yourself into a position to see the terminals you're trying to attach the wires to. Removing the seat cushions or sliding the seat all the way back gains a little space, but you're still working upside down in a very cramped space. Frustration may mount as you try to fix a light source in the right spot to see the terminals. You'll ease your stress by concentrating on one connection at a time. Having an assistant read the color coding from the instruction sheet as you make the connections will help speed the process.

You may find that the main wiring harness does not run all the way to the lights. It's common for the headlights and parking lights to use a separate harness. This may also be the case with the taillights. These additional link-up harnesses may be included with the main wiring harness, or sold separately.

To replace the headlamp wiring you'll need to remove the retaining ring and headlight. On older cars, the insides of the fenders are open, which allows the tires to throw mud and road salt against the headlight buckets. Where this type of fender construction is used, you may be

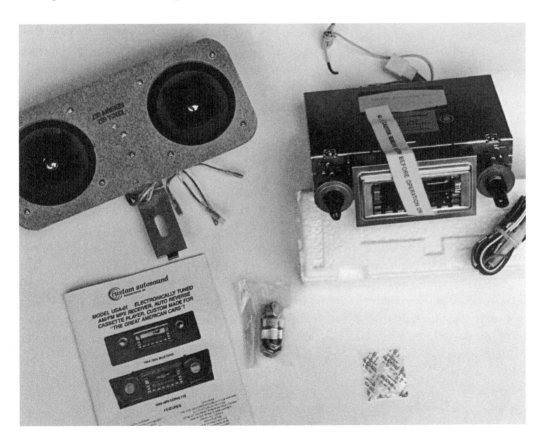

On older tube-type radios, radio restoration services can replace the original electronics with solid state, adding FM and tape-playing features if desired. The alternative for more reliable and higher-quality sound is a replacement radio designed to fit the original location in the car's dash.

ELECTRICAL SHUTOFF

Replacing frayed and decayed wiring certainly gives great peace of mind, but even so it's wise to disconnect the car's battery from the electrical system during storage, even if the car will only sit for a few days. If your car has an original electric clock, it is imperative to disconnect the battery, because the clock will run down the battery in a relatively short period of time and burn itself out in the process. Even on cars without clocks it's wise to disconnect the battery because of the possibility of an unnoticed trickle discharge somewhere in the system that will not only discharge the battery but could start a fire.

Rather than loosen and remove a battery terminal each time you park the car, the easier method is to install a quick disconnect switch on the battery terminal. If you plan to enter your car in shows, this switch can easily be removed at show time.

With the switch in place, it's just a matter of getting into the habit of turning the disconnect switch when you park your car. You will also find that the switch provides a small measure of anti-theft protection, since would-be thieves may not notice the switch or want to take time to bypass it.

A battery quick-disconnect, like this one from the Eastwood Company, can give you peace of mind when storing your car. It's a simple, no-mess way to disconnect your battery, preventing it from being drained by a short, and can even help prevent a fire while your car is in storage.

shocked by the condition of the headlight buckets. If the bucket assembly has just surface rust, it can be sandblasted and repainted, but if portions of the headlight bucket have rusted through, the metal will have to be repaired or replaced. This isn't the kind of surprise you want to encounter when you think you've finished with metal repair, so it's best to inspect the condition of the headlight assemblies before replacing the wiring.

After connecting the wiring to the headlights on both sides, you can turn your attention to the parking lights. Here, too, you will need to remove the lenses. If you convert the parking lights to function as turn signals, you may need to modify the light sockets to accept double-filament bulbs. If the parking light lens gaskets have deteriorated, they should be replaced.

From the engine compartment, the next stop is the dimmer switch. This is a simple hookup, unless the dimmer switch has been replaced with an aftermarket item. If it has, the wiring connections may not match the harness instructions or the wiring diagram. If the switch is an aftermarket part, you may want to replace it with a quality reproduction switch from one of the vintage car parts suppliers.

The brake light switch is another simple connection. If this switch shows signs of corrosion, it should be replaced. On cars with brake and clutch pedals that depress toward the floor, as opposed to swinging toward the firewall, the brake light switch is likely to be hydraulically operated and

mounted on the rear of the master cylinder. Replacing this switch is a simple matter of screwing out the old switch and screwing in the new. You won't lose any brake fluid and will not have to bleed the brake system in the process.

From the brake light switch to the taillights, the harness typically runs along the driver-side frame rail and attaches to the frame on the inside with clips. New clips may be included with the harness. If not, and if the clips from your car are missing, you'll need to order replacements from your parts supplier.

The taillights connect similarly to the parking lights. However, it is not necessary to change the sockets and bulbs for signal lights because the taillights already contain double-filament bulbs. The signal lights will use the brighter stop light filament.

If you have made the signal light conversion, you'll need to install a turn signal switch. Vintage-looking turn signal switches that attach to your car's steering column and are color-coded to the wiring harness are available from restoration parts suppliers. Among the remaining details are hooking up the horn and interior lights. The horn wire runs up the inside of the steering column to a single wire connection at the horn button. Usually the horn button comes loose by pushing down evenly on the button and turning it counterclockwise. The new horn wire is pulled up through the steering column by tying it to the old wire. If the upholstery is not being replaced, wiring that runs inside the doorpost covering and headliner to a dome light can be similarly snaked behind the upholstery by the old wire. Otherwise, interior wiring is run before the upholstery is replaced.

Installing a wiring harness is much easier than it appears when you first lay out the new harness. By the time you finish, you'll wonder why some wizard hasn't color-coded all of life's complexities.

HOW TO TROUBLESHOOT ELECTRICAL PROBLEMS

All-new wiring doesn't necessarily mean every electrical component and accessory will work. Why not? Several reasons. The harness connections may not have been firmly seated for good contact; the connectors on the component or accessory may be corroded; or the component itself may not work, either because it is burned out, has an internal short, or fails to make a good ground connection. To understand what may be causing an electrical component not to work and to be able to troubleshoot and repair the problem, it's necessary to understand that electricity flows in a closed loop called a circuit.

An automobile's electrical system consists of numerous circuits, originating and returning to the battery. The battery itself is a storage device for chemical energy. It does not contain a completed circuit. A warning: Never attempt to complete this circuit by placing a wire directly across the battery poles. A circuit should always contain a resistance,

It's no fun to slide behind the steering wheel of your collector car, push the starter button, and have nothing happen. The main reason for a low or dead battery is insufficient recharging by the generator. Installing an alternator will keep the battery charged with limited driving. A 6-volt alternator for pre-1954–1956 cars is shown here.

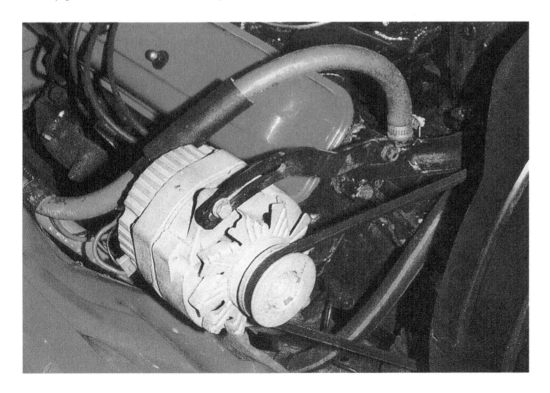

The alternator mounts in place of the generator as this collector has done on his 1956 Studebaker.

BRIGHTER BULBS

When you're overhauling your collector car's electrical system, it's the perfect time to make certain upgrades to improve its lighting performance.

If your car uses standard sealed beam headlamps, you can generally upgrade them to halogen headlamps by simply swapping the bulbs. Halogen headlamps provide a noticeably brighter light than sealed beam units, which makes driving at night both easier and safer.

A step beyond halogens are High Intensity Discharge (HID) or Xenon-gas headlamp assemblies. Unlike sealed beam and halogen bulbs, HID and Xenon systems use a miniature "cartridge"-style bulb that is inserted into a housing. Hella manufactures composite housings that are direct replacements for sealed beam and halogen bulbs, but receive their HID bulbs and some Xenon-gas bulbs, though you may need to modify your wiring harness (or come up with an adapter) to make them work. You may also need to install a power relay to ensure a sufficient supply of current to the upgraded lamps without risk of burning up your headlamp, dimmer switch, or old, questionable wiring.

Other bulbs, such as turn signals, taillamps, or marker lamps can be upgraded with easy-to-swap Light Emitting Diode (LED) bulbs that simply plug into your existing light sockets, instead of a standard bulb. LEDs illuminate more quickly than standard incandescent bulbs, are brighter, last longer and use less electricity. They're even available in several colors—white, yellow/amber, or red—depending on your needs.

Alternatively, some custom LED logic boards are available that can be installed into your collector car's light housings. In contrast to the simple LED bulbs, the LED logic boards often provide more even lighting, which is especially important for wide or tall light units. However, installation of LED logic boards may require some modifications of your original housings, making it a less desirable path for many owners.

such as a light bulb, matching the car's voltage to control the current flow. If the current is allowed to flow freely with no resistance, the circuit (in this case the wire and the battery) will heat up very quickly, possibly causing the battery to explode! Resistance acts like a valve to control current flow. When a circuit breaks and allows current to flow to the battery without passing through a resistance, a short circuit results. If the short circuit contains no resistance besides that created by the wiring, it will rapidly heat the wiring (possibly burning out the wiring harness) and drain the battery. Short circuits are the most common cause of automotive fires.

Since in most cases the car's body, frame, and engine are made from steel and iron (metals that are good conductors of electricity), it's common, especially on older cars, for the wiring to run one way: out from the battery to the electrical components and accessories. A combination of the body, frame, and engine typically completes the circuit. This works fine until corrosion (rust) or paint buildup breaks the circuit. Then the components along the wire's path won't function. Let's look at a few examples and see how to troubleshoot the cause of the electrical problems and then how the problems can be corrected.

If you've got the new wiring installed and all hooked up and, say, the lights, horn, heater, or some other electrical accessory won't work, the malfunction can be traced to three possible causes:

1. Current is not reaching the component. (There's a break in the circuit ahead of the component.)

2. Current is not completing its loop to the battery. (There's a break in the circuit after the component.)

3. The component itself has failed.

Applying these three possible causes to a nonfunctioning taillight, we can apply troubleshooting logic to solve the problem. For the example, let's assume that when the headlight switch is turned on, only one taillight illuminates. If the car still had its original wiring, we might suspect a break in the wiring leading to the taillight. If a new harness has been installed we can assume that the wiring is intact, but that connection to the taillight may not have been properly made, or that the wiring inside the taillight itself may have shorted. A circuit can break ahead of the failed component due to:

1. an incorrect or poor connection;

2. a break in the wiring leading to the component or, in the case of a taillight, inside the component; or

3. a short (the circuit is grounding ahead of the component).

A circuit will also fail to conduct electricity if it is open, meaning that it does not make a complete loop and current cannot return to the battery via ground. With a nonfunctioning taillight it is also possible (and indeed likely) that the taillight bulb is burned out.

The first step in electrical troubleshooting is knowing that the problem has a logical cause. Seasoned technicians will tell you always to look for the simplest cause first. In our example, this would mean removing the taillight lens and inspecting the bulb. Frequently, a bulb's failure is visible by a broken filament (the tiny wire inside the bulb). But a failed bulb isn't necessarily the problem and replacing a bad bulb won't necessarily fix the problem. If this is the case, it's time to begin the troubleshooting process.

When you replace your car's battery, a modern model, such as this one from Optima Batteries, can provide significantly more cranking power (rated in Cold Cranking Amps, or CCA), which makes them also helpful when you're just trying to power your car's audio system while you relax at a show.

BETTER BATTERIES

Battery technology has advanced considerably since the pre-war era of weak, six-volt systems—and even since the 12-volt systems of the muscle car era.

Today's batteries—though still 12 volts (technically, 12.6, since each "cell" contains 2.1 volts)—produce substantially more Cold Cranking Amps (CCA), which is the power available at zero degrees Farenheit for 30 seconds. Today's batteries are also typically sealed, maintenance-free models, making them a no-muss, no-fuss solution.

If you're concerned about originality, there are some specialty firms that allow you to encase modern battery guts in a vintage battery case, so you can have the best of both worlds.

We'll start by determining whether or not current is getting to the bulb. Two devices can be used to check current flow. One is a simple test light that you can buy for a few dollars in the automotive section of a discount mart or an automotive parts store, or make yourself from an automotive electrical socket and two short sections of wire (one serves as a current pickup and the other completes the test lamp circuit to ground). The other testing device is a multimeter. A multimeter is superior to the test light because it shows the amount of current the circuit is receiving, not just whether or not current is reaching the component. These meters are available from discount marts and electronics stores usually for only a few more dollars than the test light.

Whether you are using a test light or multimeter, the connections are the same. The hot lead (the red lead on the meter or commercial test light) goes on the point where current should be entering the component. In the case of the taillight, the contact point is the button in the bottom of the light socket. The other lead (which will be black on a commercial product) goes to ground, in this case against the side of the socket. Now turn the headlight switch on. If the test light illuminates, or the meter needle swings into the appropriate current range on its dial, you know that current is reaching the bulb. But current may be flowing to the light socket and not triggering the test device. This could be the case if the component (the taillight, in our example) isn't making a good ground (thereby completing the circuit).

If the test device doesn't show current flow, the red wire should be kept on the contact point and the black wire touched against some location on the body or chassis where it's certain to make a good ground, preferably an unpainted surface such as a spot of clean, bare metal or a plated bolt. If the test light or meter now shows current flow, the problem is with the ground. A poor ground can often be corrected by cleaning the contact area between the component and the body or chassis metal it mounts to. If the light socket is dirty or corroded, you will also clean the socket using mild steel wool or emery cloth. Test the circuit again. This time touching the black ground wire to the socket will show if the grounding problem has been corrected.

Sometimes a good ground is hard to make through sheet metal. When this occurs, an easy fix is to run a ground wire from the component to a grounding point on the chassis. This fix should not be taken on a show restoration because the extra wire will be nonoriginal and will cause judges to deduct points. But on a car that is being restored primarily so that it can be enjoyed and driven, the ground wire ensures a functioning circuit. Otherwise, you'll need to make sure all contact surfaces between the component and the body and the body and frame are clean so that the grounding path can function as it did when the car left the factory.

If the test device doesn't show current flow with a good ground, the circuit is broken somewhere ahead of the component. Now you need to find the location of the break. This is done by tracing back along the circuit's path, following the wiring harness and then referring to a wiring diagram, until you come to a switch, connection, or some

A cheap, easy, effective upgrade for your electrical system involves replacing your incandescent bulbs with LED (Light Emitting Diode) bulbs, like the one on the right, from Year One. LEDs illuminate more quickly, are brighter, yet use less power than incandescent bulbs.

component powered by the same circuit. Here you'll again test the circuit for continuity (current flow). With a taillight, tracing back along the harness would take you to the light switch on the dash panel (or brake light switch if only the brake lights wouldn't illuminate). In this instance, you would check to see if the circuit is live to the switch. To do this the red lead of the test light or multimeter would be placed on the hot lead to the switch (the wiring diagram will show which lead supplies power to the switch). If current is flowing to the switch, the faulty taillight may be caused by (1) a corroded connection, (2) the wrong wire attached to the switch, (3) a faulty switch, or (4) a break in the wire between the switch and the taillight.

A poor connection is corrected by removing the wire going to the portion of the circuit that is dead (the taillight wire in this case) and cleaning the end of this wire, plus its contact, with a piece of emery cloth. After replacing the wire, the switch is turned on to check the circuit. If the component works, the problem is solved. If it doesn't, the wires may be reversed in their connections to the switch. You can double-check the wiring diagram and harness color coding to see if the wires have been reversed, or simply reverse the wires and try the switch. Again, if the light works, the problem is solved. It's also possible that the problem is with the switch. The test for a defective switch is simply to bypass the switch. This is done by removing the wire to the component (the taillight in this case) and pressing it against the hot lead to the switch. If the component works, the switch is the culprit and will need to be replaced. The last scenario is a break in the wire itself. This condition is often the case with older wiring, where the insulation has

frayed, allowing the wiring to corrode or come in contact with the frame or body metal. An open (broken) or shorted wire simply needs to be replaced.

Following this logical step-by-step troubleshooting process, you can solve any electrical problem. When you come across nonfunctioning electrical accessories like the horn, clock, heater motor, fuel sending unit, or radio, for which replacements may be difficult to find, look for repair services specializing in rebuilding these older electrical accessories. These are often located in the classified ad section of hobby magazines.

RE-ENERGIZING YOUR CAR'S ELECTRICAL SYSTEM

It's no fun to slide behind the steering wheel of your collector car, push the starter button, and have nothing happen. Nuts, dead battery! If your garage is on a hill, maybe you can roll the car out the door and let it kick itself to life as it rolls down the grade. Otherwise, you'll have to wait for the battery to charge, haul out the jumper cables, or bring over another battery and do a jump start. It sure is a lot easier just to have the starter to spin the engine to life.

The main reason for the low or dead battery plague is that most of us don't run our cars often enough or long enough for the generator to fully recharge the battery. The blame really doesn't lie as much with the pampered use we give our cars as it does with the inefficiency of the generator that is the heart of our car's electrical system.

Generators do a good job of keeping a vehicle's battery charged during high-speed, long-distance highway driving. They do a poor job in short, low-speed runs (the pattern of much of our hobby driving). So what's to be done? How about a weekly hundred-mile cruise at posted speeds? Not practical? Then the other option is to hook up the battery charger every 10 days or so. Sounds tedious and we'll probably forget the charger routine. Wait, there's another solution. How about replacing that lazy old generator with a spunky, high-output alternator? Since an alternator produces as much electrical energy at low speeds as a generator does at high speeds, using an alternator to energize your car's electrical system will keep the battery at full charge just from occasional around-town runs.

Wiring the alternator into the existing electrical system is simple. Chances are the biggest challenge will be engineering a new mounting bracket. You'll begin by removing the generator. First disconnect the wiring to the generator, then loosen the bracket that adjusts belt tension and slip off the belt. Next, remove the mounting bolt. The generator can now be lifted free.

Similarly, for many cars, you can upgrade your original sealed beam headlamps with either halogen bulbs or High Intensity Discharge (HID) models like this Hella model, from Year One. Available for cars with two round or four round headlamps, the lens assembly is a direct-fit replacement for the original headlamp, though you may need to make some minor, easy modifications to the headlight electrical connectors—including installing a power relay—to make them function. But it's worth it! HIDs are brighter and far safer than even halogens.

Mounting an Alternator

Step 1. If the alternator will require a different mounting bracket, fit this bracket in place next.

Step 2. Mount the alternator. Make sure that the alternator pulley aligns with other pulleys driven by the same belt.

Step 3. If the alternator's mounting position causes the belt to run at an angle from the other pulleys, adjust or refit the mounting bracket until the belt runs on an even plane.

Step 4. After making any necessary adjustments, pull back on the alternator until the belt is tight, and reattach the belt tension bracket. Now all that's left is the wiring.

Wiring the Alternator

Step 1. Disconnect the "Batt" wire from the voltage regulator and attach it to the back of the alternator.

Step 2. Run another wire from the alternator's white wire to the "hot" side of the ignition switch or "Batt" side of the coil.

Step 3. Remove the old voltage regulator, and the job is done—unless your car's electrical system is positive ground. Alternators are negative ground, so you'll need to reverse the electrical system's polarity.

Reversing Polarity

Step 1. Turn the battery around in its box so that you can attach the positive post to the starter cable and the negative post to ground.

Here's a tip: You'll get better starter response if you connect the ground cable to a starter bolt and not the frame.

Step 2. Reverse the wires on the coil and the amp gauge.

Your car is now negative ground and its electrical energy source is a high-output alternator that'll keep the battery fully charged, even on short hops. Just make sure the battery cables are clamped tightly to the battery posts before you head down the road. Should a clamp work loose, you'll probably burn out the diodes in the alternator (big money repair). If you make a practice of loosening a battery cable when your car is sitting for a period of time, buy a battery switch and install it. That way you won't risk a cable coming loose on the road.

Converting to an alternator-energized electrical system won't cost a lot of money and you'll save yourself that dead battery disappointment, plus all the hassle of keeping the battery online for those times a friend stops by and you say, "Want to go for a ride in my old car?"

Another possible upgrade is to convert existing manual, crank-style windows to power windows, using a power window regulator like this one, available from a number of aftermarket companies.

Chapter 17
Restoring Your Collector Car's Interior

Thanks to the availability of kits to re-cover worn and tattered seats, hide or repair a cracked vinyl dashboard, replace sagging and soiled headliners as well as ratty door and interior panels, you can renew your collector car's interior yourself and in so doing not only save a professional trimmer's fee, but also experience the satisfaction of transforming your car's appearance literally from the inside out. Renewing the interior is done after painting, so the work has to be done very carefully to avoid nicking or marring a fresh finish.

Typically, the interior will have been removed from the car for bodywork and painting. This being the case, the seats could be recovered at the point when they were removed, then sealed in plastic and put away for later installation. Completing a relatively small project like this at an early stage in the car's restoration can give a sense of accomplishment that will make the final goal seem a bit closer, perhaps buoying your spirits at a time when parts and pieces strewn about your garage and the achingly slow progress of bodywork makes the finish line seem lifetimes away.

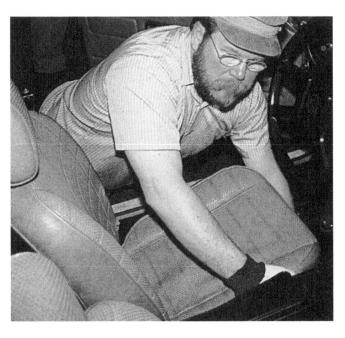

Bucket seats can be removed from the car by one person. When re-covering bucket seats, do one seat at a time. That way you can use the other as a guide.

RE-COVERING SEATS

Bucket seats can be removed from the car and re-covered by one person, but a bench seat requires an extra set of hands. If you're re-covering bucket seats, do one seat at a time. That way you can use the other as a guide, if needed, for fitting the cover and reassembling the bottom and back rest. With bench seats, do one cushion at a time.

After removing the seats, set up a work area to disassemble the seats and install the new upholstery. A workbench provides the best arrangement because it places the seat at a comfortable height, but you can use the corner of a garage or basement floor as well. To keep the upholstery kit clean while it is installed, cover the work surface with cardboard, old sheets, or towels.

You will begin by taking the seat apart (on rear seats, the cushions removed separately and no further disassembly is needed), typically removing the folding side supports that attach the seatback to the bottom cushion. Turning the bottom cushion over, you can now remove the seat supports and slide rails. Place all screws, springs, and assorted bolts, nuts, and washers in a coffee can or other container as they are removed so that the fasteners will be readily available when you're ready to put the seat back together.

If the upper cushion uses a stiff back panel, remove this panel next. If no screws are visible, pry gently on the panel to note the location of clips, which can then be pried out to remove the panel. This done, you can prepare to strip off the old seat covering by cutting the hog rings that attach the cover to the seat frame and slitting the cover at the corners with a utility knife. Cutting the cover not only saves time, but also reduces the risk of damaging the cushion as you peel off the old covering.

On older cars, the seat springs will be made up of rows of coils attached to a light steel framework. On more modern cars, the seat springs will consist of wires laid out in a flat, waffle-weave pattern. With bucket seats you may find a rubber mat supporting the foam padding. Coil and wire (or rubber) springs are re-covered differently, so the procedures are described separately.

Re-Covering Newer-Style Wire or Rubber Spring Seats

On bucket seats, the cover may use a retaining wire (technically called a listing wire) to draw it into a recess formed into the seat cushion. To remove the cover it will be necessary to locate the tie-downs attaching the listing wire. Often these are hidden in the cushion.

If a listing wire is used, you'll want to retrieve it from the old cover. The kit may not include a replacement. If the wire is rusted, as is sometimes the case, a new wire can be fabricated from a coat hanger or welding rod. Before using a replacement wire with a new cover, be sure to curl the ends to keep the wire from puncturing the fabric.

With the seat disassembled, you can inspect its condition. A frame with broken or sagging wire springs will need to be replaced. If the seat uses a rubber spring mat, and the rubber is torn or stretched, you'll want to replace it with a new mat. A rusty frame should be cleaned to fresh metal and repainted. If the seat covering has been torn, exposing the cushion, pieces of foam may have been worn away or the foam may have begun to disintegrate. If the cushion is badly deteriorated, it should be replaced. Sometimes new foam cushions are supplied with the kit, or may be available from the kit supplier. If not, a better-condition foam cushion will need to be located, perhaps from another seat. If the damage is minor, it can be repaired by cutting new pieces of foam and attaching them to the damaged area using trim adhesive.

When any necessary repairs have been made to the frame and cushions, the next step is to install the new cover. Along with the hog rings, the kit manufacturer may have supplied new listing wires and clips. These should be spread out in the working area. You'll also need the hog ring pliers. Make sure you have the correct cover for the cushion, then:

1. Fold the cover inside out.
2. If the cover has an insert for a listing wire, slide the wire into the seam. Feed the wire slowly, guiding it through any bends to make sure the wire doesn't puncture the seat covering.
3. Position the cover by laying it over the cushion. If a listing wire is used, fit the wire into the groove in the cushion.
4. Attach clips or hog rings—whatever the kit uses—to the listing wire so that the wire is pulled into position in the groove.

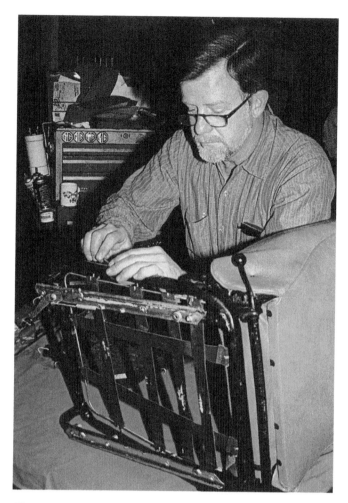

After removing the seat, set up a work area to disassemble the seat cushions and install the new upholstery. A workbench provides the best arrangement, because it places the seat at a comfortable height.

Note: Where the listing wire sits too deeply in the cushion to be fastened with hog rings, and clips are not supplied and the originals cannot be reused, you may want to tie down the listing wire using a sail maker's curved needle and thread.

5. If the seat has a pleated center section, as found in early Mustangs, or a waffle-weave imprint, as on early Corvettes (similar designs were used on many 1960s era cars), check to see whether the insert is aligned squarely on the cushion.
6. Now pull the cover over the cushion. This would seem to be easy, but often presents somewhat of a challenge because while the cover is being stretched over the foam cushion, it also has to be turned right side out. To avoid tearing the seams, work from corner to corner, gripping both sides of the corners as you work the cover over the cushion. Keep progress consistent by pulling the cover only partway over a corner, then moving to the next.

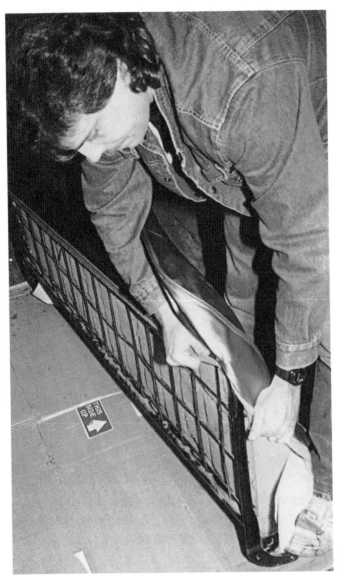

With larger bench-style seats, the shop floor sometimes makes a convenient work area. To keep the new covering clean while it is being installed, cover the work surface with cardboard, old sheets, or towels.

7. Make sure the listing wire is still tightly fastened, pulling the cover's center section into the cushion. If the cover is too loose, adjust or replace the clips holding the listing wire in place.

8. Slipping one hand underneath the cover to manipulate the cushion, make sure the piping sewn into the seam along the edge of the cover aligns with the outline of the cushion.

9. When the piping makes an even border around the cushion, pull the flaps taut over the sides of the cushion and attach the fabric to the seat frame with hog rings. Note: Some covers have seams sewn into the ends of the flaps to hold a wire (to keep the fabric from tearing away from the hog ring). If the original wires are not reusable, replacements can be made from a coat hanger or welding rod.

10. Turn the cover over frequently to check it for wrinkles and alignment on the cushion. Keep pulling the cover taut and attaching the fabric to the seat frame with hog rings.

A few small wrinkles or creases may remain, even with the most painstaking installation. Heating the wrinkle or crease briefly with a hair dryer will allow the cover to stretch so that the wrinkle can be pulled out. Placing the cover in warm sun for a short time has the same effect. However, be careful not to pull the cover so tight that there's no give. The cover has to flex with the cushion when the seat is used; otherwise, the seams are likely to tear.

This sequence is repeated four times to re-cover a set of bucket seats. When the new upholstery has been fitted to all the cushions, and the panel inserts (if used) have been replaced on the seatbacks, the seats are reassembled by reattaching the side supports and slide mechanism, then they are replaced in the car. Upholstery kits are not difficult to install and require only one special tool: the hog ring pliers.

Re-Covering Older-Style, Coil Spring Seats

With the seats stripped bare, you can inspect the spring sets for cracks or tears in the seat frame as well as broken or badly sagging coils. If the spring sets are severely damaged, you have two alternatives: find a better set, or rebuild the ones you have. On newer cars, sound, re-coverable spring sets may still be located at scrap yards or swap meets, or in want ads placed in a club newsletter or posted on the Internet. Where replacements aren't available, the original spring sets will need to be rebuilt by welding to repair damage to the frame and replacing broken or sagging coils. Rusted metal can be cleaned by sandblasting or a combination of Rusteco gel and scouring with a wire brush, then treated with a protective coating of rust-resistant paint.

With the spring set ready to be re-covered, it will first be wrapped with the burlap covering supplied with the kit. The burlap attaches to the seat and backrest frames with hog rings that are also supplied with the kit. The purpose of the burlap covering is to keep the padding from settling into the coils. Hog rings are just what the name implies: split rings intended for use on an animal. If the supply with the kit runs short, you can buy more at a farm supply store. Although hog rings can be crimped closed with ordinary pliers, special hog ring pliers, available from the Eastwood Company and other specialty tool suppliers, work best. Hog ring pliers have grooves in

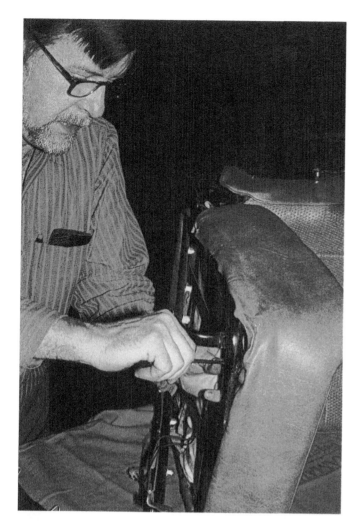

To take a bucket-style seat apart, you'll typically remove the folding side supports that attach the seat back to the bottom cushion, then the cushions from the seat supports. Be sure to save all fasteners.

With newer bucket seats you may find a rubber mat supporting the foam padding. If the rubber has lost its resiliency, this spring substitute will have to be replaced.

the jaws to hold the rings, enabling the person using the tool to locate and crimp the ring with one hand, leaving the other hand free to maintain a snug fit on the covering. Attempting to crimp hog rings with regular pliers requires both hands to hold and crimp the rings.

With the burlap in place, a layer of cotton padding may be supplied to cover the top and sides of the springs. You should assume that the kit maker has given you the exact quantity of padding (and other coverings) needed. If you lay the padding over the springs and there seems to be too much, make sure you have the right padding for the spring set—maybe you've used padding for the seat bottom on the seatback, or vice versa. Don't cut any excess until you are sure everything is installed right. If the kit includes foam rubber padding, this layer goes on top of the cotton. If the kit does not include foam padding, you will probably want to purchase a sheet of inch-thick foam

rubber to place over the cotton padding. Otherwise, as the car is driven, the cotton will compress, lowering the cushion height and giving the seat a less comfortable feel. Foam rubber is resilient so it will preserve the seat's cushiony feel and maintain the right cushion height for many years. The padding and foam are held in place by the cover, which will be fitted over the cushions next.

As you pull the cover over the padded spring set, you have three goals: (1) to align the cover seam with the edge of the cushion, (2) to work out all wrinkles in the covering and pull the fabric tightly enough so that it won't sag when you sit on the cushion, and (3) to avoid pulling the covering so tight that the cushion loses its resiliency. If the old cover used a listing wire to help it fit the cushion's contours, you will need to insert the wire salvaged from the old cover into the seam sewn into the underside of the new cover. Once you have worked the cover onto springs, so that the seam conforms with the outline of the cushion, and once you have worked out the wrinkles, you can turn the cushion over, pull the fabric tight, and begin to attach the covering to the spring frame with the hog rings.

The sequence for attaching the seat covering begins at the front. Here you will clip the covering to the seat frame

AUTHENTIC INTERIORS AVAILABLE FOR MOPAR MUSCLE CARS

More than just big-inch Wedge and Hemi V-8s set Chrysler Corporation's muscle cars apart from the pack. No other car interiors had the glitz of the Mopar interiors. Open the door to a Satellite GTX, a Challenger, or a Road Runner and you'll see what I mean. Garish interior color schemes like gold and black or scarlet and white are likely to strike your eye. Flashy as the colors are, what makes the interiors in these cars especially attractive are the special weaves and grains stamped into the vinyl.

Duplicating the weaves and patterns Chrysler used in its 1960s performance cars is the specialty of Legendary Interiors, a supplier of authentic interiors for Mopar muscle cars and all letter-series Chrysler 300s. Along with interior coverings, Legendary Interiors also supplies correctly shaped foam padding for front bucket seats. The replacement foam padding is especially helpful to convertible owners whose original seat paddings have often crumbled and disintegrated from exposure to the sun. The detailed, step-by-step instructions that come packed into a Legendary Interiors kit make re-covering seats and door panels a do-it-yourself job. About the only guideline not mentioned is to do the job on a warm day or in a heated area. Vinyl becomes very stiff when cold and to fit the new seat covering without wrinkles, the temperature should be at least 65 degrees Fahrenheit.

Above: *For convertible owners and others with cars in which the original foam padding has decayed or disintegrated, Legendary Interiors makes replacement cushions.*

Left: *The interiors in 1960s-vintage Chrysler muscle cars were the flashiest on the market. This front bucket seat is upholstered in a striking red and white. Note the silver Forward Look medallion in the center insert. This seat-covering kit from Legendary Interiors is a bull's-eye match for the original.*

with a few hog rings along the front edge. Next you will pull the fabric snug and attach a few hog rings at the rear. The rings have sharp ends and easily penetrate the covering. If the covering has too much give, or not enough, you can remove the rings at the rear of the frame and allow a little more slack or pull the covering tighter. By adjusting the tension from the back of the seat, any holes left from refitting the hog rings won't be noticed. When the covering has the desired snugness, it should be pulled slightly tighter to allow for future stretching, then secured to the frame with hog rings spaced about 2 to 3 inches apart.

Repeating this process on the other spring set (cushion or backrest) finishes the seat upholstering job. Re-covering a car's seat cushions is easy enough so that after one set

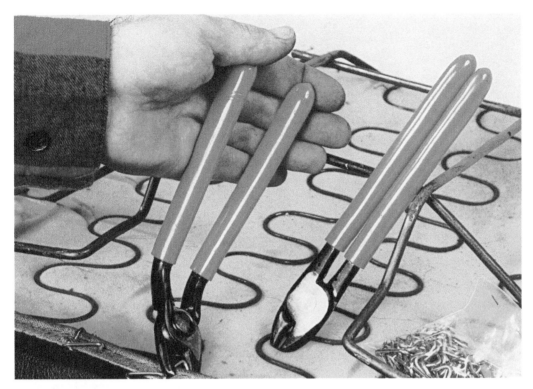

On more modern cars, the seat springs will consist of wires laid out in a flat, waffle-weave pattern. The tool shown here, called a hog ring pliers, is used to crimp the metal rings used to attach the new covering to the seat frame. The Eastwood Company

Prying loose the rubber mat's retainers isn't half as difficult as reinstalling the retainers with a new mat. You'll need a helper to hold the seat frame while you force the retainers back in place.

you'll feel like a pro and can give advice or assistance to friends who are restoring their cars.

INSTALLING INTERIOR COVERINGS

Besides seats, a car's interior coverings include carpet, door panels, footwell and rear seat liners, headliner, package shelf, dash covering, and sun visors. In many cases, these items are also available for do-it-yourself installation. Although the interior coverings would be purchased during the car's mechanical and body restoration, their installation would wait until after the car returns from the paint shop with its gleaming fresh finish. This means that great care will need to be taken to avoid marring or scratching the finish (which includes the doorjambs and painted interior

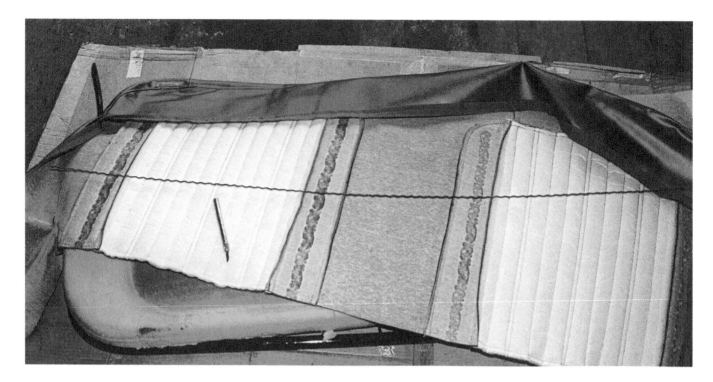

A retaining wire (technically called a listing wire) is often inserted into the seam at the bottom of the cover to prevent the cover from tearing loose from the seat frame. It's important to remove these wires from the old cover for reuse.

surfaces) as you move in and out of the car to fit the new interior. One important word of caution: never carry tools in your pocket as you work around a fresh finish. It is too easy to lean against the car with a screwdriver dangling out of a side pocket, or sit in a freshly re-covered seat with a screwdriver poking from a rear pocket. Damage that occurs in only a split second may take weeks to undo.

Carpet

The first interior covering to be replaced will be the carpet. In order for the carpet to lie flat against the transmission hump, it either needs to be molded to the floor of the car or to consist of multiple pieces, each cut to fit a specific part of the floor's contour. Where both types are available, the multiple piece (cut pile) carpet is likely to have been used by the manufacturer. A molded, one-piece carpet is easier to install. Besides originality, the multiple-piece has another advantage. If only one portion of carpet shows sufficient wear to warrant replacement, it may be possible to purchase only that section. However, there's little likelihood of a good color match, because of both differences in dye and fading of the original. Still, it may be possible to replace just the front carpet and keep an original rear set, the color difference not being easily visible.

When purchasing new carpet, avoid buying a universal carpet kit. What you'll receive will be a strip of carpet,

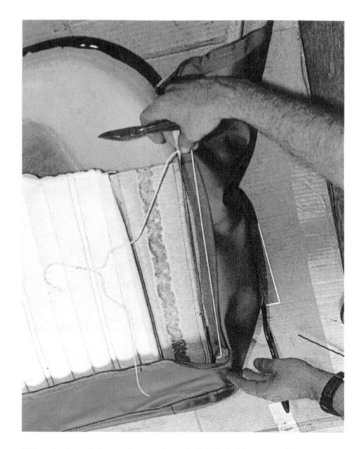

If the wire is rusted, a replacement can be fabricated from a coat hanger or welding rod.

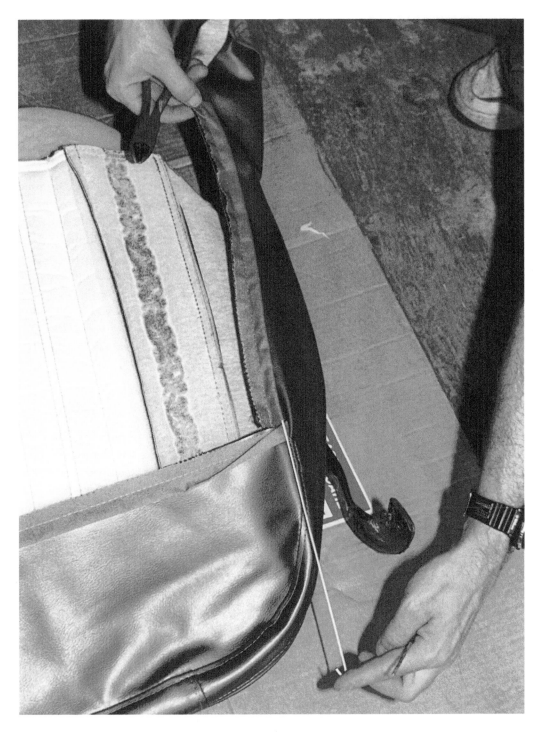

Before inserting the rod into the cover flap, be sure to curl the ends to keep the wire from puncturing the fabric.

roughly the dimensions of the car's interior often in a neutral color—probably black. What you won't get is carpet that fits the floor's contours or has openings sewn into it for the accelerator pedal, headlight dimmer switch, seat belts, and other floor-mounted items. In short order you'll find a universal carpet to be a waste of money.

For some applications, the carpet will glue into place. For others it will be held by sill plates, seat supports, seat belt anchors, and the bottom edge of various interior panels. As you removed the original carpet, you may have seen a layer of fiber matting and below that perhaps a layer of rubber for sound deadening and insulation. The replacement carpet will likely lack these underlying layers. You can duplicate at least the function of the cushion material installed by the factory by laying down a thin sheeting of ceramic cloth, which will act both as heat barrier and sound deadener. This sheeting, which is available from Corvette Central (see Resources) and other suppliers, may

If the seat covering has been torn, exposing the cushion, pieces of foam may have been worn away. If the damage is minor, repair can be made with a swatch of cotton or a small piece of foam either glued in place or covered and secured with duct tape.

be precut for your car's interior, or sold in a universal-fit roll and cut to fit. The carpet, molded or in pieces, would be placed over this underlayment. A properly made carpet kit is not difficult to install and has a transforming effect on the car's interior.

Seat Belts

With new carpet in place, you may wish to replace or renew the car's seat belts, or add seat belts if your car pre-dates this safety feature (many cars from the 1960s had front seat belts, but none in the rear). In renewing seat belts you have a couple of options. You can send the old belts to a reconditioning service like Ssnake-Oyl Products (see Resources) or boil the old belts on the stove in a pan of black (or appropriate colored) dye. If the car was not origi-nally equipped with seat belts, you may wish to add this safety feature using belts salvaged from a later model car. In doing so, be sure to establish strong anchor points for the mounting brackets; don't just drill holes in the sheet-metal floor pan. Plates of ⅛-inch or thicker steel welded to the underside of the floor pan will provide mounting points that won't pull loose in the event of an accident.

Another option to consider is the availability of more effective, retractable three-point seat belts, similar to those used in modern cars. Several restoration parts supply companies sell kits that allow you to retrofit modern-style belts into your collector car, thereby greatly improving your safety and that of any passengers you might have. Be advised, however, that these kits may require some modifications of your interior panels and even to the body structure to securely anchor the belts.

Door Panels

After removing the armrest, window crank, door handle, door lock knob, and any other hardware, pop loose the clips holding the door panels using a U-shaped clip-lifter tool (available from the Eastwood Company as well as most auto parts stores). Often the door panel has a lip that fits over the window opening, so you'll need to lift the panel slightly to pull it free. With the panel removed, you'll have access to the door's interior to lubricate the window mechanism and door lock, and make repairs to either or both of these items. Both mechanisms can be removed—though before attempting to do so you'll probably want to refer to instructions and illustrations in a body service manual. Removing and replacing the window mechanism is a lot like working a Chinese puzzle. While you have access to the door's interior, you should treat the metal with a rust inhibitor. Only recently have the manufactur-ers applied any coating to car door interiors. Consequently, if you haven't yet looked inside the doors, you may be surprised to see an ugly-looking coating of surface rust—which probably can also be seen by looking into the door through the window opening. Options for a rust inhibi-tor include a paint-over-rust primer followed by a wax or petroleum-based rustproofing (available in aerosol cans), or a coating of old engine oil. Used oil, saved after an oil change, contains acids that make it an ideal rust inhibi-tor not only for door interiors, but also for pouring into rocker panels—any interior cavity not directly covered by

In some cases the cover may be held in place by spring clips. These are quite easy to install. Just pull the cover tight over the frame and push the clip in place.

To snug the cushion all the way up under the cover, you'll need to reach one hand under the cover and nudge the cushion into place.

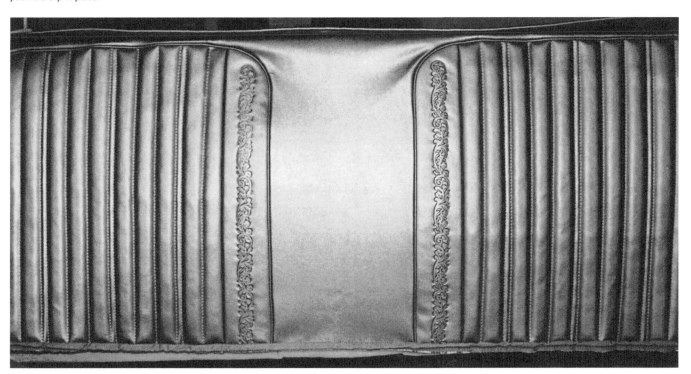

The last step is working out the wrinkles. Pulling the cover tight over the cushion will remove most of the wrinkles. A stubborn wrinkle or crease can be warmed with a hair dryer, allowing more slack in the cover.

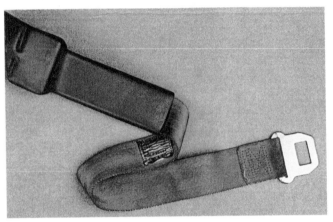

When renewing the interior, chances are the seat belts also need reconditioning. These belts not only show soil, but the spring in the retractor mechanism has broken, so the belts will be sent away to a reconditioning service for new webbing and a rebuilt mechanism. If the buckles needed replating, this would be done also.

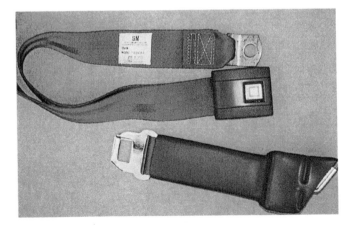

The soiled seat belt assembly had been sent away to Ssnake-Oyl, the seat belt refurbisher, for new webbing and repair to the retractor mechanism. The restoration work was A++ quality, with new webbing color matched exactly to original, the retractor mechanism repaired, and the original GM tag cleaned and resewn in its original position.

upholstery. The acid in oil will eat into the surface rust while the oil film will protect the metal from rerusting.

Assuming you're replacing the old door panels with new ones from an interior supplier, the next step is to seal the openings in the inner door panel with a sheet of visquine (thin plastic). A slip-over garment wrap from the dry cleaners or garbage bags work well. The function of the plastic is to keep moisture that seeps into the door through the window opening from soaking into the door panel's cardboard backing, possibly warping the cardboard and staining the panel's cover or causing mildew and water spots. The plastic attaches easily by laying a bead of silicone caulk around the outer edge of the door's inner surface and laying the plastic against the caulk. The silicone will hold the plastic in place while you attach the new door panel and make a weather-tight seal. Door panels install in reverse fashion from which they were removed, typically slipping the upper lip over and into the window opening, then seating the clips, replacing screws that often hold the panel at the bottom, reconnecting the armrest, window and door release handles, door lock knob, and any other hardware.

Footwell and Rear-Seat Liners

When you renew one set of interior panels—the doors for example—you'll likely feel compelled to do the rest. Differences in color, vinyl pattern, or fabric weave are certain to be noticeable between new door panels and the adjoining footwell and rear-seat liners. If the other interior linings are available for your car, you'll want to order the entire set. An exception would be later model cars where the rear-seat liners are molded plastic. Here it may be desirable to clean or paint the liners to restore their original appearance. (Painting to restore an older vinyl interior is described below.)

Unlike door panels that are usually held by clips, footwell and rear-seat liners are generally positioned by chrome-plated sheetmetal screws. At the bottom, these interior coverings help secure the carpet, and at the top they offer support for the headliner. Interior liners in the vicinity of the door openings also help secure the windlace (a tube-shaped seal covered by upholstery fabric or vinyl) that surrounds the door opening.

If the interior liners are predrilled for the mounting screws, installing them is a simple matter of making sure the liner is properly aligned and then screwing it in place. If the screw holes are missing, as is common since the actual screw locations vary, then you've got to probe for the holes, which can be tricky. The tool to use for probing the holes

To remove door panels it's first necessary to dismount and remove all hardware and accessories, namely the door handle, window crank, and armrest.

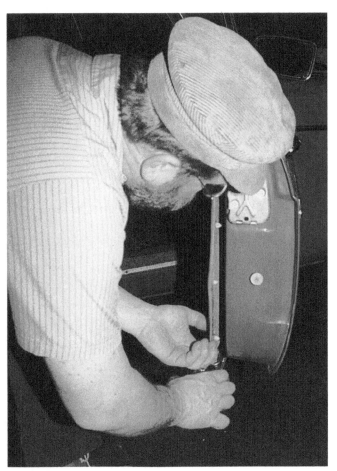

Door panels typically pop loose by prying out the clips holding the panel to the inner door assembly. Don't try to pop the clips loose with a screwdriver.

is an awl (a sharp, pointed pick). But you'll want to be sure you're as close to the hole as possible before puncturing the liner's covering. Taking careful measurements of the screw hole locations, transferring the measurements to a template, then testing the hole locations with the template mounted in the liner's place is the best way to avoid puncturing the liner in the wrong locations.

Headliner

Manufacturers have used two very different methods to suspend car headliners. The traditional method, used through the 1960s, attached the headliner to bows (initially wooden and later metal) that mounted to the car roof. This type of headliner is immediately recognizable by the seams where the headliner attaches to the bows. A newer method glues the headliner to a molded panel that itself attaches to the car roof. (On today's cars the molded panel is given a color-harmonized finish to eliminate the headliner.)

With either method, you'll begin attaching the headliner in the center of the roof and work outward, an equal distance forward and back, then repeating to make sure the liner is correctly centered. On the bow design, making the cutout for a dome light can be a tricky step. It's essential that the headliner be positioned correctly before making this cut. On the molded roof panel design, the headliner is attached with glue. Here it's important to remove all traces of the old glue before attempting to attach the new headliner. If even traces of old glue or fragments of headliner fabric and glue remain, the new liner won't make a good bond. Again you'll begin gluing the new liner at the center and working outward. When installing a vinyl headliner, if spray adhesive won't hold, you can use contact cement. Before doing so beware that since contact cement is applied to both surfaces—the molded roof panel and the back side of the vinyl—and bonds on contact, you may only get one chance to lay up the liner wrinkle-free. The answer is to glue a small section at a time.

A special tool, called a door panel clip lifter, shown here, is used to pry the clips away from the door frame.

While you've got access to the door latch and window mechanism, be sure to lubricate all moving parts.

Before replacing the door panel, cover the window opening with visquine or other thin plastic. This plastic sheeting can be glued or taped into place.

Vinyl Dash Cover

On cars built since about the mid-1960s, it's common for the dashboard to be overlaid by a vinyl covering. Often the vinyl's function is to cover a layer of high-impact padding that helps protect occupants from injury in the event of a crash. As it is subjected to extremes of heat and cold, and as the sun bakes out resins that keep the vinyl pliable, the cover cracks, exposing the padding and giving the dash a wounded look. When that happens, it's time to renew the cover, a job that can be accomplished several ways.

On a show car restoration the cover will be replaced. This requires removing the metal dash cap, which can be as simple as loosening a few screws or as complicated as disassembling the entire dash—gauge cluster included. A body manual for the car will show the required procedure. Because of the very tight bends, especially around the ends, it's extremely difficult—bordering on impossible—to cut and glue a new cover yourself. Instead what is needed is a custom-molded piece of vinyl that will slip into place

Authentic-style reproduction door panels are available for most popular 1930s to 1970s cars from a number of suppliers. Hampton Coach makes this combination mohair and vinyl door panel for an early 1950s vintage Chevrolet.

215

With later model cars, the rear seat liners are molded plastic. Rather than replace these pieces, it may be more desirable to clean, or clean and paint, the liners to restore their original appearance.

over the padding or new padding and cover. (Sources for replacement dash covers are listed in the Resources.)

Much easier than removing the dash to install a new cover is repairing the damage with an overlay. These cover-up covers are molded to be an exact match for the damaged vinyl they're purchased to hide. Before installing an overlay, you'll cut back the vinyl that has curled up at the break and fill in the crack in the foam padding. Next,

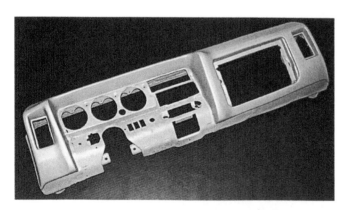

On cars built since about the mid-1960s, it's common for the dashboard to be overlaid with vinyl padding. Because of the contours in the dash, it is very difficult—if not impossible—to apply a new cover yourself. Instead, you'll probably order a replacement cover from Just Dashes, the largest supplier of dash board covers for collector cars. The first step in replacing the cover will be to remove the dash and strip off the vinyl overlay. Jim McGowan

you'll fit the new cover in place. (Typically the overlay will extend from the base of the windshield to the lip along the front of the dash and wrap over that lip.) If the dash has defroster vents, the overlay will have openings for those vents. Properly installed, a cover overlay is virtually invisible. Still, you wouldn't want to use this repair on a show car. It's meant for use where the main concern is an effective cosmetic repair. The overlay glues in place following the manufacturer's instructions.

A third approach seeks to hide the damage with a patch. The trick here is to locate a piece of matching color vinyl (kits are sold containing several vinyl swatches and a graining tool). The patch is cut to fit, grained to match the cover, and glued into place. Unless the crack is very small and located nearly out of sight, a patch is going to be noticeable, maybe not at first glance, but certainly under scrutiny. Its purpose is a quick fix.

Sun Visors

The use of vinyl for interior coverings also extends to sun visors. Here the likely deterioration isn't cracking as much as fading or the thread either rotted or missing from the seam bias. The seams are difficult to restitch due to the cardboard inserts used as stiffeners. Purchasing reproduction replacements or finding better condition originals are the best options.

A re-covered dash, installed in a 1972 Pontiac GTO, shows the factory fit of the Just Dashes cover. Jim McGowan

Refreshing an Original Interior

If your collector car has led a pampered life, shows low mileage on the odometer, and only needs some refreshing, you're not likely to gut and replace the interior. Indeed, you shouldn't. Though reproduction suppliers go to great effort to duplicate original materials and color schemes (as evidenced in the description of seat covering kits for Mopar muscle cars from Legendary Interiors), you're likely to spot some subtle differences in the factory original.

Besides a thorough cleaning, steps to refreshing an original interior often include removing the bottom-cushion seat covers and repadding the springs or replacing the foam cushion, using vinyl dye or paint to recolor vinyl-covered seats (leather can also be redyed), repairing small tears or cracks in vinyl coverings with a patching kit, and reweaving or patching small holes or tears in fabric.

The steps to repadding springs or replacing foam cushions are the same as listed in the previous re-covering seats section, except you'll use the old cover. Be careful when removing the hog rings so that you don't tear the fabric or vinyl. Any needed repair work can be done with the cover removed. One winter, squirrels nested in a roadster I had stored in a neighbor's barn. Their damage could have been worse; the car suffered only a small hole eaten in a side of the front seat cushion. We were able to cut a piece of original fabric from a hidden area of the seat and sew it in place of the damaged fabric, not just hiding, but entirely replacing the damaged section.

Fabric paint works very effectively to renew faded vinyl seat and other interior coverings. You'll want to practice first on a seat from a parts car or some scraps of material. You don't want your car's interior to look like it's had a

217

The color of vinyl and plastic interior pieces can be changed or renewed using aerosol spray products. The Eastwood Company

Where original trim items like this convertible top well cover are going to be rejuvenated and reused, the first step is a thorough cleaning using a household detergent.

Spraying the discolored vinyl with a color spray restores the liner to like-new condition.

"paint job." The vinyl patch kit mentioned above is also described as a method for repairing dash covers. A small hole in fabric, such as a cigarette burn, can be rewoven using threads from a patch of the original cloth cut from an unseen area. The actual reweaving is done something like the process my grandmother used to use when darning my grandfather's socks, and is best done by a fabric repairer, possibly located through a dry-cleaning service. Repairs, while never invisible, are at least less noticeable.

What is highly noticeable is the condition of the car's interior. All new or refreshed, the interior completes the last major step in the car's restoration. With the exception of replacing a convertible top, the remaining steps—gluing on the weather stripping and some final reassembly—are well past the light-at-the-end-of-the-tunnel stage. You've probably reached the stage where the car is ready for that first drive!

Chapter 18
Replacing a Convertible Top and Renewing Weatherstripping

My friend Phil, whose 1964 Ford Galaxie is featured in this chapter, purchased his car from the original elderly owner. Although the car has low mileage (64,000 miles accumulated over some 35 years; that's less than 2,000 miles a year!) and has spent much of its life in storage, the top proved once again Isaac Newton's second law of thermodynamics: everything in the universe is moving in the direction of entropy—decay, winding down. Most noticeable were the broken rear window, victim of a toy truck handily stored by one of Phil's sons in the top well, and chunks of fabric missing from the rear corners. Less noticeable were a dried-out front bow weather seal, with some resulting rust damage to the front bow and decay of the top pads in the vicinity of the missing covering.

Phil was well aware of the visible decay, which had limited the car's use. Corrosion of the top bow caused by the dried-out weather seal caught him by surprise. This story has a lesson: like a leaking roof on a building, a convertible top that allows moisture into a car will cause damage, noticeable or not. Lesson corollary: a convertible top isn't a cosmetic covering; it's a functional part of the vehicle that needs to be kept in good condition.

If you're installing a convertible top as part of a restoration, there's a strong likelihood that the old top has been removed and you're working with the bare bows. The process is much easier if you're starting with the old top in place. If you removed the old top to repair and paint the bows, hopefully you took photos or a videotape of how the top

My friend Phil's 1964 Galaxie convertible still had its original top. The glass back window had broken when it encountered a toy truck one of Phil's son's had placed in the top well, and the fabric had torn away from the rear bow on the passenger side. A tear in a convertible top is like a leak in a roof: it lets water into the car, with potentially disastrous results.

The instructions call for removing the old top starting at the header bow. The first step, then, is to lower the top.

looked when you started and the steps of its removal. You may also want to photograph the convertible top on similar cars—with shots taken from the inside as well as out. If you're replacing the top because of decay and deterioration (as in Phil's case) or to upgrade your car's appearance, you have the old top as a guide. Remember the rule: whenever possible, take apart or remove only one side at a time. That way you have the other side as a guide.

Years ago, when every community larger than a crossroads hamlet had a convertible top shop, getting a new top installed typically meant a new vinyl or canvas covering and keeping the pads and back window. In a restoration, these companion pieces are usually replaced and need to be ordered with the top (pads may be included in the top package, but not the rear window), along with the front bow weather seal, as well as side window weather seal that fastens to the top frame.

Step one, then, is to locate a convertible top supplier and purchase a new top and related pieces (the rear curtain or glass, windshield header and side window weather seal, top boot, and well liner). Although several suppliers of

restoration parts for mid-1960s Ford Galaxies list convertible tops in their inventory, Phil chose a top from Hydro-E-Lectric (see Resources) for two important reasons: (1) this company is a leading convertible top supplier, providing tops and related items for all U.S.-built convertibles between 1955 and the present; and (2) the company has a reputation for quality. The supplier's inventory is important because it's convenient to order all needed items from the same source. At the point where Phil placed his order for the top and rear window, he wasn't aware that the windshield header weather seal needed replacing. A call to Hydro-E-Lectric's 1-800 number had all weather seal items packed and shipped the same day. Quality is essential if you want a long-lasting, good-looking top. The top that Hydro-E-Lectric supplied Phil for his Galaxie matched the car's original factory top in all details. As with other restoration products, your best bet is to buy only from reputable suppliers. This is especially important with a convertible top, which can't be returned for a refund once you've begun to install it on the car.

For hobbyists like ourselves, Hydro-E-Lectric offers a videotape showing a convertible top installation from

Phil uses his cordless screwdriver to remove the screws securing the header bow weather seal. With the weather seal out of the way, the staples that hold the top fabric to the header bow are removed.

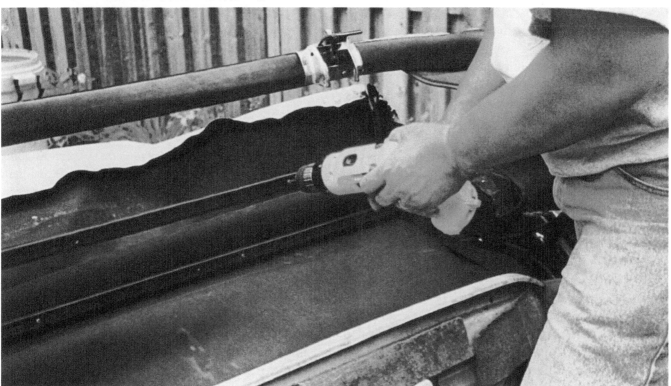

With the top free of the header bow, Phil removes the retaining strips that secure the top to the second and third bows.

At the rear bow, Phil pries up the cover strip that covers the staples that tack the fabric to the bow.

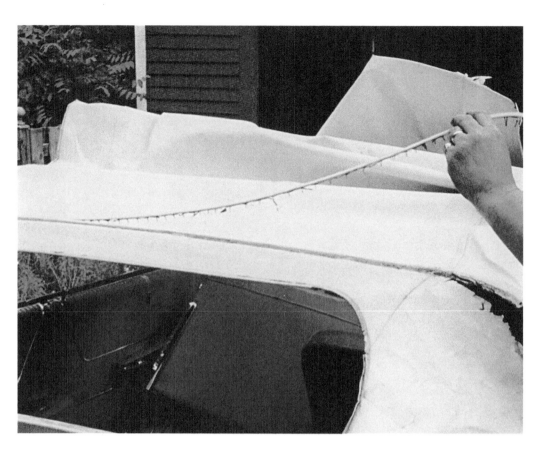

start to finish. This videotape can be purchased or rented. Phil and I rented the tape and watched it a couple of times before beginning the installation; then we watched selected sequences when we had questions during installation. The video shows a new top being fitted to a late 1960s Ford Fairlane, a midsize model but otherwise similar to Phil's Galaxie. Although enjoyable to watch and overall very helpful, this instructional video omits three steps we'd like to have seen: (1) removing the well cover; (2) installing the rear window; and (3) replacing the top pads. Phil spent nearly a morning in the trunk of his car trying to remove the well liner. In desperation, he gave the fabric a tug, and the liner collapsed on his face. Turns out that the liner on his car just clips in place. Since the rear window and pads on the car in the video were in good condition, they weren't replaced. Phil's rear glass was broken and new pads came with the top, so we needed some tips on replacing both.

Along with the videotape we also had Hydro-E-Lectric's instruction sheet and a couple of other convertible top installation sequences. In the middle of the job, we had a visit and helpful comments from a hobbyist friend who'd just put a top on his Mustang. Before starting this project, it's a good idea to ask around your circle of collector car enthusiasts for those who've had experience replacing a

REPLACING VENT WINDOW GLASS

Cars built prior to the 1970s typically had vent panes in the front windows to deflect air into the driving compartment. This glass is often discolored, sometimes cracked. The accompanying photo sequence shows how to replace this glass.

convertible top. You're likely to get some good tips, possibly also a helpful hand with the project. If you're installing a convertible top for the first time, you'll need an assistant. What better choice than someone who has experience.

GATHERING EQUIPMENT AND MAKING PREPARATIONS

Although the mechanic's tool set and restoration supplies you have gathered will provide nearly all the items you'll require to replace a convertible top, other tools and supplies you'll definitely need include:
- A socket wrench set matching your car's nut and bolt dimensions (U.S. or metric); an air-powered wrench for use with the socket set is strongly recommended
- Assorted screwdrivers (flat blade and Phillips); also pliers

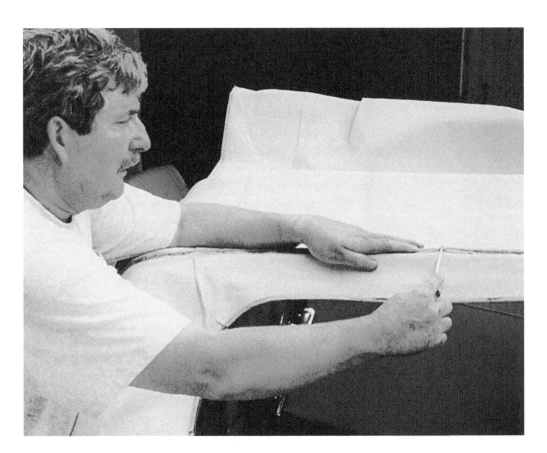

Phil found a pick to be the most efficient tool for prying out the staples.

The top fabric also fastens to the side rails leading up to the rear bow. The top mechanism has to be raised in order to free the fabric.

Cap nuts hold the weather seal that lines the underside of the top frame. If this weather seal is still intact and resilient, it can be left in place. If it has deteriorated, it will need to be replaced.

- Sharp scissors and a supply of single-edge razor blades or a utility knife with fresh blade(s)
- A pick (pointed tool with a screwdriver-type handle), also diagonal cutters (wire cutter) for removing staples
- Tape measure and chalk (white)
- Staple gun and supply of ¼-inch and ⅜-inch staples
- Upholstery glue—one aerosol can
- Plastic sandwich bags and marker to hold assorted screws and fasteners
- A coat hanger to snake retaining cables through channels sewn into the new top

As soon as the new top arrives, open the box. (Note: Never cut into a cardboard box containing upholstery or any type of soft contents with a utility knife; the risk of slicing into the product is too great). Remove the top and lay it out in a clean area so that the packing creases can begin to smooth out. Phil laid his new top over the old top on his car. Also take inventory of the contents. If the top doesn't include new pads, and these appear to be worn on your car, you'll need to order a pad set. Likewise the back window and windshield header, as well as side window weather seal. If the well liner is deteriorated or discolored, now is the time to order this item; the same goes for the top boot.

You'll want to pick a warm (sunny) day for the top installation project or have a warm, well-lighted shop to work in. Below about 75 degrees F a vinyl top will be stiff and hard to stretch. Although an experienced top installer can remove and replace a convertible top in a working day, hobbyists should set aside a couple of days, perhaps a weekend. You're less likely to become frustrated and make mistakes, or worse, be injured if you're not working against a clock.

Removing the Old Top

The old top can't just be ripped off; it needs to be removed with care. The starting point is at the front bow, so you'll need to unlatch the top from the windshield header and raise the mechanism so that you have convenient working access to the underside of the front bow. The sequence proceeds from front to rear as follows:

1. Remove the header bow weather seal. (Save the screws in a sandwich bag; remember to label the bag with a marker.)

The brackets attaching the top to the car are hidden underneath the well cover, which is secured by screws to a bulkhead behind the rear seat.

2. Carefully pry out the staples holding the top fabric to the tacking strip. The tacking strip can stay in place and be reused if you avoid tearing it up.

3. With all the staples removed, peel the top fabric away from the header bow (it may still be held in place by upholstery glue). With the top partially raised, the covering will flop down toward the second bow.

   The top is held to the second and third bows by retaining strips that slip into flaps sewn to the underside of the fabric. It is also still somewhat connected to the header bow by cables that run through flaps sewn along the sides of the top. The cables (which may be wire or elastic) are attached to the top frame at the header area and behind the third bow.

4. Unfasten (remove screws) from second and third bow retaining strips. Slip strips out of flap and set aside for reuse.

5. Remove the fasteners that hold the weather seal to the frame in front of the rear bow (both sides). The top fabric will be glued to the frame underneath this weather

Lacking clear directions, Phil had a great deal of difficulty finding the clips that released the well liner along the trunk side. He spent about a half-hour in this position pulling and tugging. Finally, the liner popped free.

The motor operating the top mechanism hides behind the rear seat. The bottom cushion simply lifts out. The seatback is held by a retaining bracket.

seal. Pull the top flap loose from the frame on both sides. Doing so will expose the fastener or clip holding the side cable to the frame.

6. Now raise the top to allow slack in the side cables. Slip the cables loose from the rear clip or unscrew them. Cables can be left attached at their front mounting.

The covering is stapled along the top of the rear bow and to the retaining brackets inside the top well. To access the bolts holding the brackets, you'll need to remove the well liner. Usually this fabric piece is held in place by clips. You may be able to reach the clips for the well liner from the trunk, but you'll need to remove the rear seatback to access the bolts to the retaining brackets.

Typically, you'll find three sets of brackets: a long center bracket holding the rear window and curved brackets (or bracket sets) on the sides securing mainly the rear corner sections of the top, but also the outer portion of the rear window. If you are replacing the rear window, remove all these brackets. If you're not replacing the rear window, remove

only the side brackets. You'll need a long socket extension to reach the bolts. An air wrench speeds an otherwise tedious bolt-removing process. You'll find the top fabric and pads stapled to tack stripping in the brackets. If you're keeping the old pads, remove only the staples holding the top fabric.

VINYL TOP REPLACEMENT

Sometime during the 1960s, vinyl tops became quite popular because of the upscale image that they provided. On some cars—most notably the 1970 Plymouth Superbird—vinyl tops were standard equipment to hide imperfect bodywork beneath. Unlike the Road Runners on which they were based, Superbirds featured a flush-mounted rear window. However, Chrysler determined that it would be cost-prohibitive to properly smooth the seams of the welded-in window plug. The solution was to install a vinyl top, which completely hid the imperfect seams beneath.

Unfortunately, original tops often absorbed moisture as they aged, or as they developed cracks or cuts allowed moisture to seep through, leading to rust development on the roof sheet metal. So, after you peel off your existing vinyl top, don't be surprised if you find that the roof needs attention—and possibly some replacement sheet metal.

Vinyl tops are glued to the roof of the car, and the edges are covered with bright trim moldings. This simple installation method makes them relatively easy to replace, assuming your roof isn't in need of any work. Some kits are in multiple pieces, which can make installation a bit tricky, but only in that you have to be careful when matching one piece against another.

The first step in the replacement process is to warm the vinyl thoroughly by setting it in the hot sun for a few hours so that it's flexible.

While the vinyl is warming, clean and degrease the roof (to remove any wax) so that the glue will adhere properly.

Then, when the vinyl is thoroughly warm and pliable, lay it on the roof dry and get it positioned properly. Then fold the front half back over the rear half and apply vinyl top adhesive to both the underside of the front half of the vinyl and to the roof itself. Then, with a friend's help, carefully roll the front half back into place making sure you get it properly positioned. Obviously, it won't be easy to move around on the glue, so take care to get it as close as possible and watch for ripples in the material that need to be smoothed out.

When the front half is down, fold the rear half back over the front and repeat the process. Don't be surprised if the rear half is more difficult because of the portions that extend down the C-panels. It's often easiest to leave them as steps three and four, and treat them as you did the front and back halves—fold them up onto the roof to apply adhesive, then unfold them and position them.

After the top is fully glued, carefully trim excess material and reinstall your bright trim to secure the edges of the vinyl.

Phil removed the rear seat cushions to vacuum years of dirt and debris and to inspect the condition of the top motor and wiring.

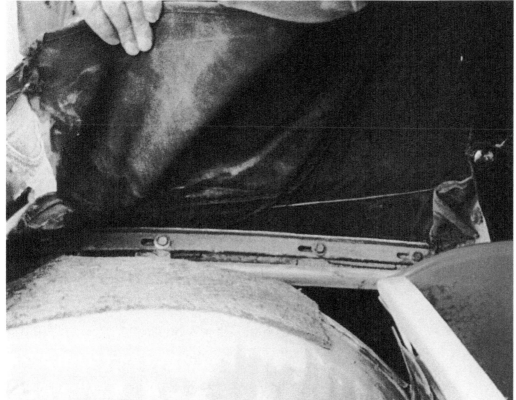

At the rear, the top is secured by brackets that bolt along the edges of the top opening. If you're not replacing the rear window, you'll only remove the side brackets. Otherwise, you'll remove all three brackets.

Note that on some cars the top pads come in two pieces, a long strip from the header bow to the rear bow and a wider rear section under the rear corners of the top. If the new top includes new pads, they may be only for the front section. Where this is the case, and the rear section can be reused, don't remove this underlying piece from the brackets. If the rear sections are deteriorated, as was the case on Phil's car, they'll need to be removed and replaced. Since these sections were not included with the Hydro-E-Lectric top, we had new pieces cut from heavy canvas (matching

227

You'll find the top fabric and pads stapled to tacking strip imbedded in the brackets. If you're keeping the old pads, you'll remove only the staples holding the top fabric, as Phil is doing here.

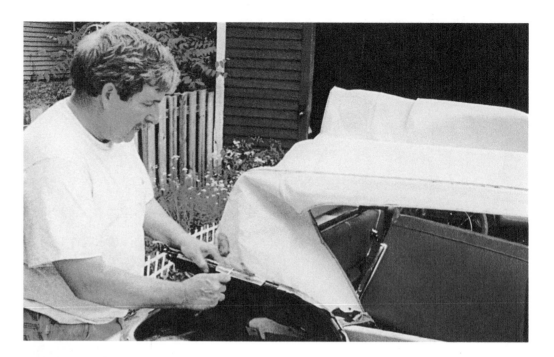

If the brackets are rusty, they should be cleaned with a wire brush, sandblasting, or chemical derusting and repainted in preparation for reuse.

the original) and sewn by a local shoe repair shop.

Now you're ready for the last sequence, removing the top from the rear bow. Here, too, you'll work through several layers.

7. Remove the screws holding the triangular stainless covers at the ends of the cover welting along the top bow.

8. Pry open the seam in the welting and pry out the staples holding the welting to the tack stripping. When free, remove the welding.

9. Now you'll see the staples holding the top fabric to the rear bow. Carefully remove these staples. The top will now lift free; however, the rear window will still be attached to the rear bow and (unless you removed it earlier) to the bracket inside the top well.

If the rear window is being replaced, its staples can now be removed from the rear bow. In some cases the upper portion of the rear window may be held to the bow with a retaining strip, which is also accessible once the top has been removed.

Installing the New Top

If you plan to replace the rear window, this comes first. Essentially, you're reversing the steps you just went through to remove the top (and rear window). This means you're starting at the rear of the car.

Replacing the Rear Window

1. Center the rear window on the long bracket that bolts to the body inside the top well. It's a good idea to lay the old window over the new as a location guide. Notches need to be cut in the window fabric for the bracket bolts. The old window will show where to cut these notches. Centering the window is very important if you want the new top to look right.

2. Staple the rear window to the tacking strip in the long bracket. Place the first staples in the center and then alternate on either side. Pull the fabric to stretch it as

With the top removed, you can inspect the condition of the pads. Some top kits include new pads.

tight as you can as you shoot the staples. If the fabric isn't tight, you'll see wrinkles in the fabric and waves in the plexiglass after you've tightened the bolts on the bracket. If this happens, remove the bracket, pull out enough staples to stretch the window tighter, restaple, and reattach the bracket.

3. With the rear window satisfactorily wrinkle-free, pull the front of the window tight to the rear bow (with the top frame clamped to the windshield header) and attach the window to the bow.

Replacing the Pads

If new pads were included with the top, these are installed next. If the old pads are still on the frame, replace only one side at a time. Removing both pads before installing the new ones will allow the third bow, especially, to shift position. If this happens, the flap for the retaining strip won't line up with the bow when you have the new top installed.

1. Remove the staples holding the pad to the frame. Remove the pad.

2. Lay the new pad in the same location and staple to the bows.

3. Repeat on the other side.

Replacing the Top

Lay the new top over the frame. (Looks good, doesn't it!) At the rear corners the fabric should have markings for holes that need to be cut to allow the bolts to slip through the brackets. These hole markers also show where the top fabric aligns on the brackets.

1. Cut out the holes indicated by the markings at the bottom of the rear corners. Place the brackets under the top fabric and slip bolts through the holes. This will correctly position the top on the brackets.

2. Staple the rear corners to the brackets. As with the rear window, it is very important to stretch the fabric as much as possible as you staple the top to the tack stripping on the bracket. If the top isn't stretched tight enough, you'll see wrinkles in the rear corners after the

Using the old window as a pattern, Phil cuts notches in the new window fabric for the bracket bolts.

brackets are bolted in place. The only fix is to remove the brackets and staples and restretch, and staple the top. Warm temperatures make the top more pliable and easier to stretch.

3. Bolt the brackets in place inside the top well. If you see wrinkles in the rear corners, you can fix the problem later. Leave the rear of the top as it is and proceed to the front of the car.

4. Raise the top a half-foot or so above the windshield so that the fabric stretches easily over the header bow. Pull the fabric tight and mark the location of the front of the bow on the fabric with chalk.

5. Now note the location of the flaps for the retaining strips on the second and third bows. If the flaps are not in line with the bows (it's likely they're not), measure the distance the top needs to be pulled forward to align the flaps with the bows and make a second chalk mark this distance behind the first mark above the header bow.

6. Raise the top a little higher so that you can easily reach the underside of the front bow. Spray the underside of

After Phil aligns the bracket with the bolt cutouts he's made in the window curtain, he'll staple the curtain to the bracket.

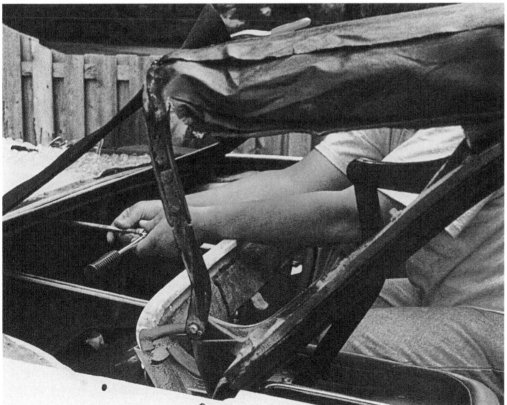

Now the center bracket holding the rear window can be bolted onto the car. On this Galaxie, the rear window is very fragile glass, so it must be handled with great care.

the bow from the lip to the tacking strip with upholstery adhesive. Likewise, spray a coating of adhesive along a strip several inches wide on the underside of the top fabric. Let the adhesive dry for the interval recommended on the label (5 minutes).

7. When the adhesive becomes tacky, pull the top over the header bow until the second chalk mark aligns with the front of the bow and press the fabric to the bow so that the adhesive makes a good bond. The adhesive will hold the fabric in place. Make sure the top fabric is evenly centered on the header.

8. Lower the top to the windshield and recheck the positioning and alignment of the retaining strip flaps with the second and third bows. Also check the location of the seam over the rear bow. If these critical alignments all match up, you're ready to staple the top to the tacking strip on the underside of the header bow.

9. Raise the top so that you can easily reach the underside of the header bow with the staple gun. Working from the center, staple the top to the header bow.

10. On some cars a beading, made by rolling over a strip of top fabric, is inserted to help prevent moisture from seeping between the weather seal and top. If the top contains a strip of fabric for this purpose, roll a bead, spray upholstery adhesive along the inside of the fabric, and press the mating surfaces together.

11. Glue and staple this bead to the top fabric on the underside of the header bow.

12. Now you can install the new header bow weather seal using the screws saved when you removed the old weather seal. Here's a tip. If some of the adhesive oversprayed onto the top's vinyl covering, you can loosen and easily remove it with WD-40. Simply wet a clean rag with WD-40 and wipe.

13. With the top attached to the header bow at the front and to the body via the tack strip brackets at the rear, the steps you still need to do are (1) securing the anti-flap cables; (2) attaching retaining strips to the second and third bows; (3) stapling the top to the rear bow; and (4) attaching the top to the frame below the rear bow and replacing the frame weather seal. Although these sequences are relatively straightforward, each needs to be done with care.

Cables designed to keep the sides of the top from flapping while driving down the road thread through slots sewn into the outer edges of the top. Whether you're reusing the old cables or using a new set that came with the top, the procedure for pulling the cables through the slots is the same.

14. Straighten a coat hanger and bend a hook in one end.

15. Insert the coat hanger through the slot sewn into the side of the top, catch one end of the cable, and pull it through the slot. Attach both ends of the cable to the frame (using whatever method is provided, screws or clips).

Retaining strips for the second and third bow slip through flaps sewn into the top and screw into the bow. The strips are easily aligned by first replacing the screws at the ends of the strip.

The seam across the rear bow must align with the tacking strip along the top side of the bow. The top must center on the rear bow. Both the alignment and centering are critical if the top is to look right. When the top is correctly positioned, begin stapling along the seam, starting in the center and alternating from side to side.

16. With the top stapled to the rear bow, align the cover strip so that it sits on top of the tack strip and covers the seam and staples. Pull the cover strip tight so that it is straight, and starting in the center, staple the cover strip in place.

17. With the cover strip stapled, roll the seam closed, and screw the stainless-steel covers over the ends of the strip.

The final installation steps consist of attaching the top flaps to the frame channels (just ahead of the rear corners) using upholstery adhesive and replacing the weather seal that attaches to the top frame and seals along the tops of the windows. The rear section of this weather seal (along the rear edge of the side windows) helps hold the top flaps in place.

If the rear corners are wrinkled sufficiently to justify removing the rear brackets and restapling the top to the tacking strips, you'll want to make sure you stretch the fabric as tight as possible while you insert the staples. You're likely to have better success if a helper holds the brackets and stretches the fabric while you concentrate on the stapling. Small wrinkles will often smooth out by themselves as the car sits in the sun.

When you're satisfied with your new top, you can replace the well liner (reattaching the clips to the brackets). To keep your convertible's top looking new, you'll want to wash it periodically with mild soap and treat the vinyl with a cleaner/preservative. These and other care and preservation steps are discussed in the next chapter. You'll also prolong the life and appearance of the top if you follow a thoughtful lowering procedure. Rather than just unlatching the header bow and whirring the top out of sight with the electric mechanism, prepare to lower the top by unzipping the

Seeing the rear window in place gave us encouragement for the steps to come.

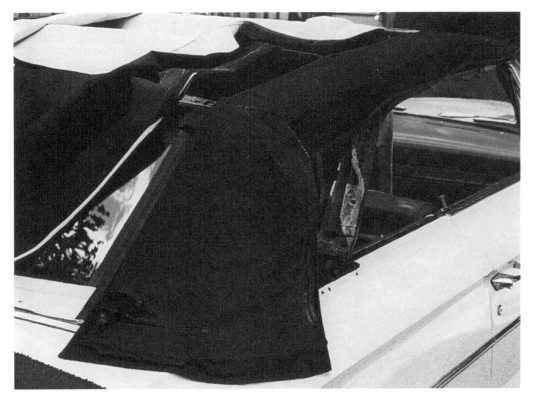

Sometimes the top pads are one piece; sometimes the rear corners are separate. On Phil's Galaxie the pads are in two pieces, and the leaking top had rotted the rear corners.

rear window. If the window is glass, the chance of breakage is as high as 80 percent if the top is lowered with the glass window still zipped in place. After unzipping the window, place it gently and evenly on the well liner. Now raise the top. As the top lowers into the well, make sure the rear corners are loose from the top frame so they won't be pinched by the frame and bows. Likewise, check that fabric and pads fold evenly between the bows. These steps will ensure that the top folds without creasing and nestles into the well so that the top boot will fit in place without stretching or pulling against the top frame.

Although convertibles look great with their tops down, their glory is a glistening top that fits as jauntily as a tailor-made suit.

Replacing Rubber Weatherstripping

If you're doing a ground-up restoration in which all the rubber items will be removed, the need to replace these items will quickly become obvious, because most will be destroyed as you take the vehicle apart. Rubber parts sometimes get neglected in the rebuilding approach. Here, deteriorated window rubber or door weather seal may not be noticed until after the car is painted. If this happens, the best time to remove and replace these rubber items is missed. The smarter approach is to take inventory of the car's rubber parts and begin ordering replacements early on in the restoration or rebuilding process. In most cases, your shopping list will soon grow to a respectable order.

Although the top kit from Hydro-E-Lectric included new pads along the bows, it didn't have the rear corners, so Phil had replacements sewn from a piece of canvas.

Signs That Rubber Parts Need Replacing

Dryness, cracking, and chunks of missing rubber are not the only reasons for replacing a car's rubber parts. As door and trunk weather seal ages, it loses its elasticity, allowing air to whistle into the car's passenger compartment and

The main pads from the header to the rear bow were also shabby and would be replaced with the new pads from the kit. When replacing the top pads, be careful to remove only one side at a time, as the pads locate the center bows.

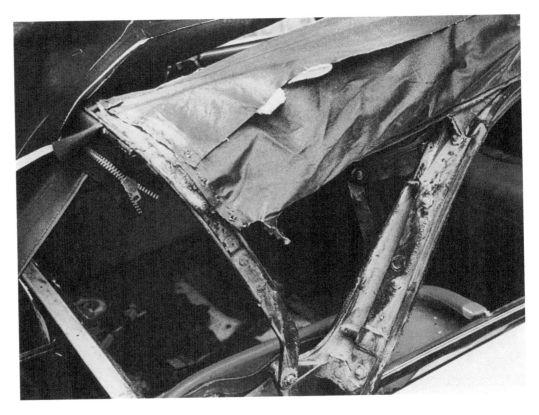

The Hydro-E-Lectric top kit includes all material for the main pads.

water to leak into the trunk. Windshield rubber deteriorates by drying out and cracking, causing water to seep into crevices, rotting the metal around the windshield opening, possibly even dripping onto the dashboard. If you are disassembling your car for a major restoration, you will want to replace all the rubber parts possible so that everything will have a consistent, like-new appearance. Even where a full-scale restoration isn't planned, you will still have plenty of reasons to replace door weather seal and many other rubber items.

Cars that have been partially or completely disassembled, or have received an amateur restoration, often lack some of the original rubber items. The problem here is figuring out what's missing. One way to determine what rubber items belong on the car, and their locations, is to order a restoration supplier's catalog or buy a copy of the factory assembly manual and compare the rubber items shown in the catalog or assembly sequences with those on the car. Likely to be missing on cars built prior to the mid-1950s are draft seals for the clutch, brake, and accelerator pedals. Floorshift cars may be missing grommets for the

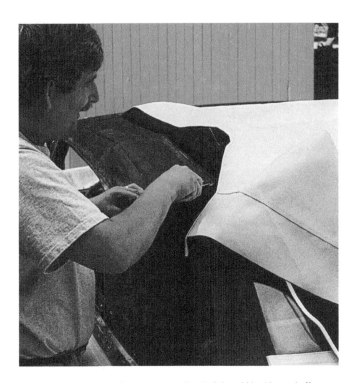

After stapling to the rear bow, excess pad material could be trimmed off.

Now the corner pad can be pulled snug and stapled to the rear bow.

gear shift, and all cars may be missing grommets for the wiring harness and other miscellaneous parts.

Installing Replacement Rubber

Rubber parts are typically installed as part of a larger process (like replacing the windshield) or as a detailing step after repainting the exterior or refinishing the interior. Usually the only difficulty in installing rubber parts is making sure they're not forgotten, and in some cases recalling exactly where they go. If your car is still intact (awaiting a

mechanical and cosmetic upgrade or thorough restoration) be sure to take photos and make notes on the locations of rubber parts before taking the car apart. If the car is already apart, take photos and note the locations of rubber parts on other original or restored cars you may find at car shows and club events, or even in scrap yards.

An example of the importance of the original rubber part's location occurs during the replacement of door weather seal. Not only is it easy to be confused about the correct placement of the rubber (does it glue to the door

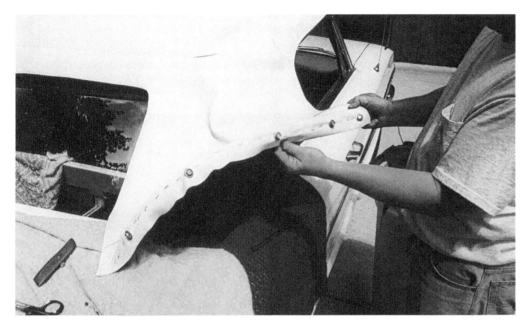

To attach the top fabric, the corner brace has to be removed again from the car. Outlines for the bolt holes help in positioning the fabric on the brace.

It's very important to stretch the fabric as much as possible while stapling to the bracket. If the fabric isn't stretched tightly enough, you'll see wrinkles in the rear corners. To get rid of the wrinkles, you'll have to remove the brackets once more and restaple the fabric, this time stretching it even tighter.

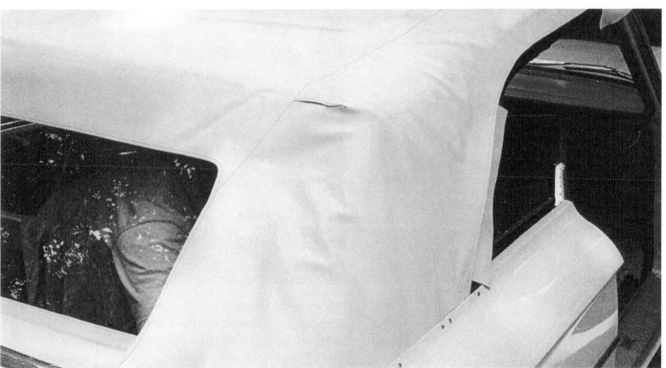

or the body?), but also about the proper location of the seam. The seam location is important on a car that will be entered in show competition, but even if competition is not your goal, it makes sense to attach the door seal in the original, rather than a haphazard, location.

In almost every instance, rubber parts are installed after painting. This is the sequence in which they were originally attached, with the result that rubber items leave the factory unpainted. On cars that use welting between the body and fender, the welting will be replaced as part of an assembly step. You'll discover that great care is required to avoid nicking or scratching the paint in the process of bolting the fenders in place. Most mid-1950s and later cars do not use fender welting.

Door weather seal attaches with special glue. This process is relatively simple, but does involve several steps. At some point, the old rubber has to be removed. Usually this is done in preparation for rust repair and repainting. Although the old weather seal can often be pulled loose by hand, usually some of the rubber and glue sticks to

REPLACING VENT WINDOW GLASS

Cars built prior to the 1970s typically had vent panes in the front windows to deflect air into the driving compartment. This glass is often discolored, sometimes cracked. The accompanying photo sequence shows how to replace this glass.

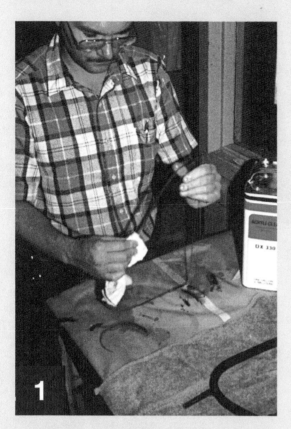

Prepare the glass by cleaning it with prep solvent.

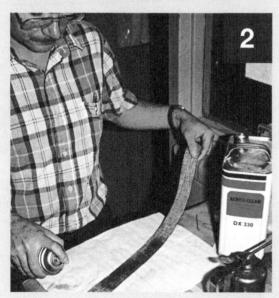

Spray the channel liner used to hold the vent glass in its frame with light oil.

Wrap the channel liner over the edge of the glass that will fit into the vent frame. The oil-soaked liner will want to slide off the glass. The liner can be held in place by pinching it against the glass at either end.

4

Carefully fit the glass into the vent frame. The glass should not slide all the way into the channel. If it does, the vent channel should be pinched slightly tighter. A press-fit is needed to hold the glass in place.

5

If the glass needs a little more nudging, tap the frame gently with a rubber mallet.

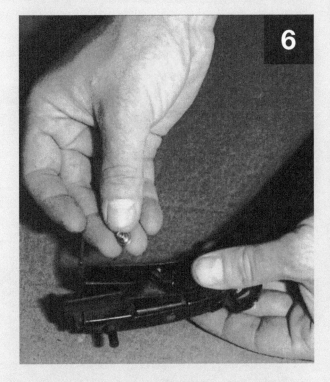

6

The vent window now needs to be fitted into its frame by installing a new hinge rivet.

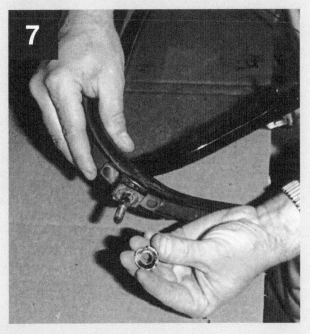

7

The vent window typically bolts into the door frame.

In preparation for aligning the top on the header bow, the underside of the bow is sprayed with upholstery adhesive.

the metal and has to be scraped clean. If you just want to replace the rubber and aren't planning on repainting, you will need to scrape very cautiously to avoid scratching the paint. Prep solvent, used to remove wax and tar from a finish, can be used to soften the old glue and should be used to clean the surface before gluing new weather seal in place. The glue can also be softened by applying heat (from a propane torch) to the underside of the metal, if this can be reached. Be careful not to apply too much heat and blister or burn the paint!

The metal around the old weather seal may look solid, but you're likely to find rust scale behind hardened or decayed rubber. If so, it's essential to clean away the rust before proceeding. When metal work isn't planned, you can clean surface rust with a wire brush or spot sandblaster, then prepare the metal with Naval Jelly, a dilute phosphoric acid gel available in hardware stores, or Rusteco gel, or simply cover the rust with a POR (paint-over-rust) product (see the discussion of derusting products in Chapter 8). The cleaned metal can then be primed and touch-up painted. If refinishing is planned, the weather seal channel should be sandblasted and any rust damage repaired.

Weather seal cement is available at auto parts stores. This glue comes in two types. One is applied to the metal and the rubber is pressed in place before the glue sets. With the other, a bead of glue is applied to both the metal and rubber. With this type, you wait until the glue becomes tacky before pressing the weather seal in place. With either

With the top properly aligned, the fabric is stapled to the tacking strip on the header bow.

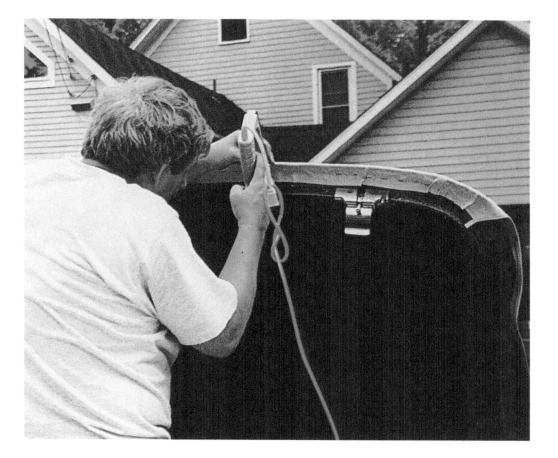

Even if the old weather seal looks good, chances are it has lost its resiliency and should be replaced. Phil installed new weather seal purchased from the top supplier, Hydro-E-Lectric.

With work completed at the header bow, the top can be latched to the windshield. Remaining steps consist of attaching the top to the center and rear bows.

After the top fabric has been stapled across the rear bow, a cover strip is attached over the staples. Bending in the sides of the strip makes a covering for the staples.

The ends of the cover strip are secured with stainless-steel covers, in this case also supplied with the kit.

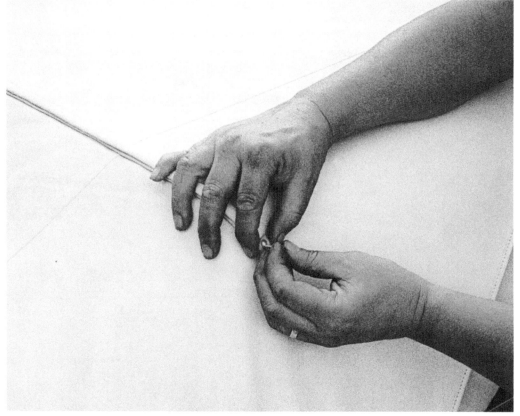

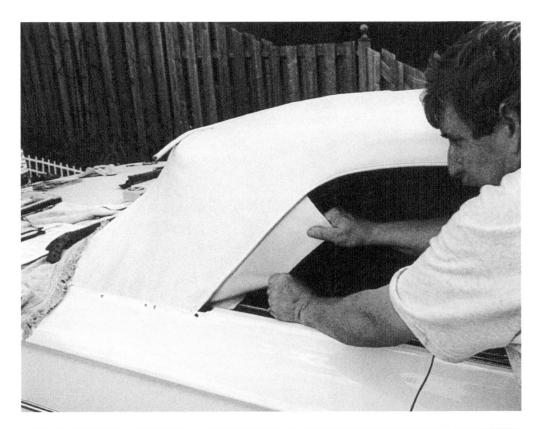

With the top fastened to all the bows, the flaps ahead of the rear corners are attached to the frame channels.

Phil was a little overaggressive with the spray adhesive, some landing on rear portions of the top. Even when dry, the adhesive softened and cleaned off easily using a clean rag moistened with WD-40.

Phil prepares the channel for the new rubber, brushing out any dust.

When replacing rubber weather seal it is very important to use quality items from a reputable supplier like Metro Molded Rubber.

type, you should be careful not to dab the glue on painted areas outside the weather seal channel. Any extra glue can be cleaned up with prep solvent, but doesn't come off easily. If necessary, the rubber can be held in place on curves and the bottom of the door openings with strips of masking tape while the glue sets. Normally the glue is sticky enough to hold the rubber snugly in place without the tape. Be sure to give the glue time to set before closing the doors.

On most cars, window channel simply press-fits into the U-shaped channel on the door frame. On some, however, it glues into place against blocks or is held by screws. If you removed the old channel, then the attaching method should be clear. If you didn't, when you buy the replacement channel, ask the vendor which attaching method applies to your car. To install new window channel, first measure the channel distance (sides and upper window frame area), then cut and bend the channel to fit the contour of the window frame.

Installing door glass sweepers (a.k.a. "window felts") is somewhat trickier. On older cars, the sweeper strips are held in place with clips. On newer models, the sweepers are

secured with staples, but clips can be used if holes are drilled for them. When installing the sweeper, make sure the glass is rolled down as far as it will go. If you need even more glass clearance, you can detach the glass frame from the roll-up mechanism and let it rest against the bottom of the door. The sweeper has to be installed after the glass is in the door, and the problem here is the risk of breaking the glass while squeezing the clips to secure the sweeper. If the window is made of nontempered automotive glass (as found on older cars and commonly used as replacement for side windows and flat windshields), it will crack very easily.

Window channel and glass sweeper material are commonly supplied in 8-foot strips. These items can be purchased by mail order from vendors such as Restoration Specialties and Supply or directly from the vendor at large swap meets. It's advantageous to buy these long items at swap meets, because they may have to be cut or folded to meet postal or UPS shipping regulations.

New rubber window seal is installed when the windshield and rear window glass are replaced after painting. Unless you have experience working with the large glass

Next he lays a bead of glue in the channel. He will also apply a bead of glue to the rubber.

When the glue has become tacky, the new weather seal is pressed into place. Before doing this, make sure you have figured out which way the seal faces in the channel.

pieces that make up a windshield and side window, it's best to leave this job to professionals. Besides making glass installation look easy, the professionals will also make sure that the rubber is sealed to the window channel to prevent future seepage. Replacing ventilator pane weather strip (on cars with vent pane windows) requires that the window glass and frame be removed.

Don't forget to replace your door, hood, and trunk rubber bumpers that help prevent body or paint damage and keep the car quiet as you drive down the road. In some cases, such as with many hood bumpers, the bumpers can be adjusted to help align the panels for a proper fit.

Preserving Rubber Parts

Rubber deteriorates (dulls, hardens, and cracks) when exposed to sunlight, so to keep rubber parts soft and pliable, and to preserve their freshly installed glossy look,

This weather seal glues along the channel at the end of the door. At the bottom, prongs attached to the rubber insert into holes in the door frame, helping hold the rubber in place.

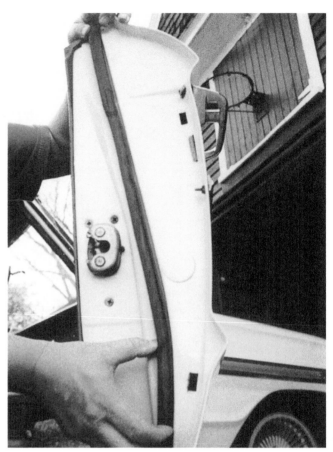

Door weather seal follows a contour stamped into the door panel. Notice that the door weather seal for this Ford Galaxie has a screw-eye at the top to help secure the rubber to the door. An inferior weather seal product might lack this important fastener.

it's a good idea to treat the rubber each time you wash your car. Meguiar's makes a rubber cleaner and conditioner that helps protect and preserve the rubber's appearance and resiliency.

New rubber and other weather seal items change a car's appearance more than you'll realize until you see the new parts in place. They give a restored or upgraded car that finished look while making the car more comfortable to drive by sealing the cab against drafts and water leakage.

Sources of Replacement Rubber

Avoid purchasing replacement rubber from discount sources. In recent years, subquality rubber items have appeared on the market, often vended at swap meets, at prices too good to be true. Remember the adage, "If it's too good to be true, it generally is."

The best sources of quality rubber parts are reputable restoration suppliers for your make and model car, or the well-known specialty suppliers Steele Rubber Products and Metro Molded Parts (see Resources for information).

For some 1960s and later cars, new rubber may still be available from the dealership's parts department. Often these "old" parts aren't shown in the parts inventory computer, but the part number (found in a parts book) may still be good, meaning it is active on the computer. If the parts department still has the old parts books, and the clerk will take the time to look the numbers up for you (be patient; find a time when the clerk isn't busy), OEM (items from the original manufacturer) rubber may still be available to you. Even the restoration suppliers will admit, you can't beat the manufacturer's parts for your car.

Chapter 19
Care and Preservation of Your Collector Car

Cars were meant to be driven. Driving them keeps bearings, cylinder walls, and other parts lubricated; it keeps gaskets and seals moistened, and air rushing around and through the car keeps it dry.

But because collector cars spend most of their time sitting still, parked, or in storage, much of the care and preservation regimen has to do with the car's lack of activity. For a car, inactivity can be as deteriorating as it is for human beings. Damage of nearly every sort can occur from the car just sitting. Rubber can rot, upholstery can mildew, metal can rust, precision-fit internal engine parts can seize, wiring can short-circuit, paint can blister, fiberglass can crack, chrome can pit, brakes can lock up, and batteries can go dead. Many collectors have set out in high spirits to retrieve his long-stored prized car, only to find a dismayingly pathetic carcass. One spring I opened the door of

One of the most common ways of caring for your collector car is keeping it clean. Washing it regularly with a quality automotive car wash detergent to remove dust, mud, bird droppings, pitch, or other contaminants can help keep your paint looking its best. Follow it up with a proper wax job to seal and protect the paint.

There are a variety of cleaning products on the market, including washing liquids, mitts, and brushes that allow you to get into hard-to-reach spots. Never use dish detergent to wash your car, unless you plan to wax it right away, because the grease-cutting formula of the dish detergent will strip the wax from your car, leaving the paint unprotected.

Vacuuming is another obvious essential, yet many people put it off or overlook it. Removing sand from the carpet is essential to preserving the carpet's appearance, as any sand in the carpet acts like sand-paper against the fibers, fraying them and making them look shabby. A powerful shop vacuum is your best bet; take your time and do a thorough job.

Protecting plastic, rubber, vinyl, and leather surfaces with appropriate protectants will keep them moisturized and looking good for years to come.

my Model A Ford roadster to discover that squirrels had nested in the seats. Not a pretty sight. A friend who stored his 1950 Packard in an earthen-floor shed came back to find a car so faded, tarnished, and decayed that he thought his car had been hauled off and another put in its place. Storage is rarely beneficial. It's seldom even benign. Often it's outright destructive. So what to do?

PUTTING YOUR CAR TO SLEEP IN A CARJACKET

Whatever your storage conditions, whether a primitive earthen-floored shed or a luxurious temperature-controlled garage, it's possible to send your car into long-term slumber embalmed like an Egyptian mummy (and we know how well they have lasted). The embalming shell is called a Car-Jacket, a specially made 7.0 mil, nonbreathable, rip-stop sheet of polyethylene outlined with a zipper on three sides. To prepare the car for storage, the CarJacket is opened fully and spread on the floor where the car will be parked. (The CarJacket can be used on an earthen floor if the surface is free of sharp stones or other objects that might puncture the bag; it's better to place sheets of plywood or OSB on the ground and lay the bag on that.) The car is driven onto the base of the jacket with the remaining material spread over the top of the car and zipped shut. Before sealing off the car, a measured amount of desiccant (provided with the CarJacket) is placed inside with the car. With the CarJacket sealed, the desiccant sucks the moisture out of the air inside the bag. Soon the car is slumbering in a dark, hermetically sealed environment—the perfect resting place.

Glass cleaner is typically sufficient to clean your windshield and windows, but occasionally you should try cleaning your windows with bronze wool (which is extremely soft and won't scratch the glass, unlike steel wool) to remove a stubborn film that accumulates over the years.

You may wonder what is different from simply storing the car under a cover. First, the Sahara-like conditions inside the CarJacket absolutely eliminate all possibilities of corrosion. Cars emerge from long-term CarJacket storage with the bare steel on brake discs still shining, electrical connections corrosion-free, chrome glistening, and aluminum untarnished. Snap off a car cover and what you see depends on the climate in which the car has been stored.

It's been said there's no ideal climate for a collector car. From the Northeast to the Midwest and along the Pacific Northwest, humidity is the enemy; on the Southern coast it's salt air; in the dry Southwest it's sunlight. Over time,

Whatever your storage conditions, whether a barn with bats nesting above, as is this collector's predicament, or a controlled-environment garage, it's possible to send your car into long-term slumber embalmed like an Egyptian mummy by putting the car into a CarJacket.

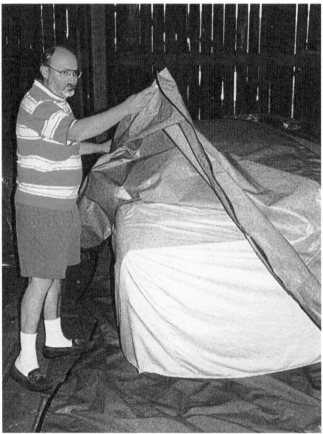

Since the CarJacket seals with a zipper, a car is easily placed into or removed from the bag. Along with the bag you receive packets of desiccant, which are used to absorb moisture once the car is enclosed in the bag.

bright sunshine dries out rubber and fades paint. Treating rubber parts like the windshield molding and door weather seal with a protectorate and keeping the finish waxed will help protect against damage from the sun's rays while the car is in use, whereas the CarJacket eliminates sunlight altogether during storage.

CarJackets provide another advantage over ordinary storage since they have proved effective in warding off rodents. It's not clear what keeps mice or squirrels from nibbling their way into the bag (which they could easily do if so inclined), but apparently what they can't smell doesn't interest them and not only does the bag's plastic aroma seem unappetizing to a rodent's nostrils, but the chewy smell of upholstery and wiring insulation that's concealed inside the bag doesn't seep through the plastic barrier.

Like rodents, thieves aren't attracted to what they can't see, so storing your valuable collector vehicle in a CarJacket makes it less susceptible to vandalism and theft. The CarJacket isn't a substitute for proper security (locks on the door, precautions of this sort), but a big gray bag doesn't attract as much attention as shining chrome or bright red paint.

As the CarJacket's supplier is quick to point out, the Jacket is not a substitute for a garage or other type of covered storage. It's not to be used for covering a car out of doors where wind can whip the bag, scuffing the car's paint or tearing holes that could quickly turn hermetically dry storage into nonhermetically wet! But any indoor setting will do, meaning you don't have to build that climate-controlled storage building after all. With care, the CarJacket can be reused year after year (small tears can be mended with duct tape) and the desiccant is recycled by baking it in a kitchen oven. There just may be another CarJacket benefit: solving the garaging problem may be all the incentive needed to buy another collector car. CarJackets are purchased directly from the manufacturer: Pine Ridge Enterprise, 13165 Center Rd., Bath, MI 48808, 1(800) 5-CARBAG. http://www.carbag.com

Preparing for Long-Term Storage

Whenever a car won't be driven for an extended period (several months or more), a series of preparations need to be taken—in addition to encapsulation in a CarJacket—to help forestall other kinds of deterioration that can occur even in a dry environment. Top on the list is changing the oil. Even if the oil in the engine looks fresh on the dipstick, before putting the car away in storage, run the engine to operating temperature and drain the crankcase and refill with fresh oil. If the engine has an oil filter, replace this also. A by-product of combustion is acid that collects in the oil. Although the oil ceases to circulate through the engine during storage, vital parts such as bearings remain covered with a thin oil film. If the oil is contaminated with acid, this film also contains traces of acid that can eat into bearing surfaces and other fine-tolerance parts. The way to prevent possible internal engine damage is simply to change the oil.

Likewise, antifreeze also develops an acidic pH over time. The long-standing recommendation has been to flush and refill a car's antifreeze every three years, regardless of whether the car is driven or in storage. There's also been a lively debate among collector car owners over whether or not to drain the cooling system for storage. Advocates say a dry cooling system won't corrode. They're right if the car is stored in a CarJacket. Otherwise condensation from ambient humidity will corrode engine water passages as much or more than slightly acidic antifreeze.

If flushing and refilling the cooling system every three years is too much of a hassle, then the answer is Evans Coolant, a non-glycol-based product that is not mixed with water. Besides solving the cooling system corrosion problem, Evans Coolant has a boiling point of 370 degrees—that's 110 degrees higher than a modern pressurized cooling system with a 50/50 antifreeze mixture! Here's a product with a dual advantage; no corrosion during storage and no overheating from boiling coolant, even under extreme temperatures.

There's a similar wet or dry debate over gasoline. Although modern gasoline breaks down much more

John Schoepke, who manufactures and distributes the CarJacket, shows how well the bag's dry storage has preserved the alloy wheels on his Alfa Romeo. Though not visible in this photo, the brake rotors are still shiny metal, just like the day the car rolled into the bag.

rapidly, there has always been a problem with gasoline turning into a thick tarry goo in cars left long uncared for. Drain the gasoline and you leave the fuel tank empty for moisture condensation. Store the car with the tank full and there'll be no condensation, but risk of gooey gasoline. Those advocating keeping the tank filled during storage say that the gasoline can be kept from breaking down by adding fuel preservative (available from auto supply stores and discount marts). The drain-the-fuel crowd isn't convinced. Fortunately, their problem—the risk of condensation in the fuel tank—has a simple solution already described: the CarJacket.

Not to be overlooked in any form of long-term storage, the battery should be disconnected and removed from the car. Leaving the battery connected risks more than just a dead battery. A small discharge that might go unnoticed in normal operation can lead to a short that could cause a fire. Then there's the battery itself, which can better be preserved and maintained outside the car. Steps to extending battery life are discussed later in this chapter.

Other precautions: be sure the hand brake is released. Parking the car for an extended period with the hand brake set can cause the emergency brake shoes to seize to the drums or the cables—an awkward condition to have to repair before taking your car out of storage. Although not required in the dry environment of a CarJacket, other parts of the car benefit from attention if it's going to sit for an extended period protected only by a car cover, old blanket, or maybe just stashed in one corner of the garage. You'll do yourself a favor to spend a few minutes sealing the carburetor with a bread bag (or large food preservation bag) and the tailpipe with duct tape. Closing off the engine's entry and exit openings not only helps keep moisture from entering the engine, but also seals entry into the exhaust system for rodents. Mice have been known to nest not only in the muffler, but also in the engine itself.

Now's the time to protect any metal parts that might rust or corrode by applying protective finishes. Metal parts like hood springs, aluminum intake manifolds, various underhood fasteners, master cylinders, and hood latches will need to be either treated to a clear paint of the proper sheen, zinc coating, an appropriate shade of paint, or possibly a light coating of oil like WD-40. But consider yourself warned about the oil method: it attracts dirt and dust, so it is likely to contribute to staining later.

Never put a car away dirty. Always clean the finish and apply a protective wax. A complete cleaning with quality products like Meguiar's Car Wash Shampoo & Conditioner followed by Gold Class Car Wax not only removes dirt and grime, but also other contaminants like road tar, tree sap, bugs, and industrial pollutants that have become embedded in the finish. Along with washing, it's also important to treat the chrome and other brightmetal as well as rubber window moldings, weather seal, and tires with protective coatings. Here, too, specialized car care products are recommended over the discount mart variety. The catch to washing your car is that you want it *completely* dry before tucking it away. The best way to dry it off is to actually drive it around town for an hour or so, to ensure that any water in the frame rails, hidden body cavities, or elsewhere has a chance to dry up or blow away. Then you want to park it and let it thoroughly cool down before enclosing it in a CarJacket.

Inside the car, the carpets and seats should be thoroughly vacuumed. Leather needs to be cleaned and treated with special leather care products (Meguiar's makes a high-quality Leather Cleaner & Conditioner; Lexol products

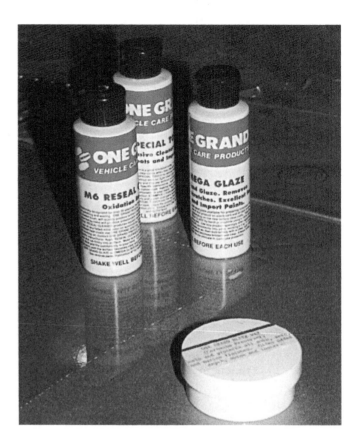

Never put a car away dirty. Always clean the finish and apply a protective wax, using quality car-care products such as the One Grand cleaners and wax shown here or comparable finish products from Meguiar's.

are also excellent). Vinyl interior coverings require their own cleaner and conditioner. Although Armorall is widely used, it is not recommended because it lacks ingredients for cleaning the vinyl and will definitely promote the growth of mold and mildew.

Some enthusiasts prefer to support their car on jack stands while it's in storage. However, cars weren't designed to be on jack stands for extended periods of time, so you're actually better off leaving the car on its wheels. For those folks who are concerned about flat-spotting their expensive reproduction tires, the best suggestion is to either move the car slightly each week (to prevent flat spotting) or just purchase a cheap set of wheels and tires to use just for storage. That also allows you to bring your correct wheels and tires inside, where they will remain better preserved.

Maintaining Insurance

Absolutely not to be overlooked during storage is insurance coverage for the full amount of the car's value. While road coverage, liability, and collision is not necessary during storage, comprehensive coverage with its protection against loss by fire and other risks needs to be maintained.

A fitted car cover should be used during short-term storage to protect the finish from airborne contaminants and to prevent sunlight from discoloring interior coverings and eroding rubber. A car cover is also helpful for protecting the finish while a car is stored inside a CarJacket.

Equally important is making sure the insurance carrier not only has the car listed for its true value, but that you have provided the insurer with an appraiser's statement of value. Asking your friend who's "into old cars" to write you a letter that lists a value figure won't do. You need to locate a certified collector car appraiser (ask members of your local car club for referrals). The certified appraiser will inspect the car with the thoroughness of a concours judge, checking the condition, authenticity, and other features of each of the car's major areas (interior, trim, mechanical, body). From the checklist, the appraiser will compile a composite score on which the value can be based. The careful appraiser's close examination of each of the car's features can prove extremely valuable, should damage occur to the car and the insurance company contest the car's insured value.

While most auto insurance agents will sell you a policy for your collector car, you can save substantially on premiums by insuring with a company underwriting only collector cars. By tying their insurance coverage to the driving restrictions of special classification "Historic" or "Antique"

vehicle license plates, collector car insurers like J. C. Taylor Antique Auto Insurance and Condon & Skelly limit their risk and set their premiums accordingly. Besides annual mileage limits and restrictions on use (the car may not be used for commuting to and from work or other commercial purposes, for example), the reduced-rate insurance may have other stipulations, like an original, unmodified engine. If you meet these qualifications and have an unblemished driving record, then the application process is a simple matter of filling out the questionnaire/application form printed in *Hemmings Motor News* and other collector car enthusiast publications. You won't be contacted by an agent. Typically you'll simply receive the policy and a billing statement in the mail. Through the impersonal nature of the application process you might get the impression that these companies would be just as impersonal in the event of a claim. Their nearly universally satisfied customers report the opposite. Typically an adjuster, familiar with collector cars, calls within hours, and the claim is often processed in just a few days.

Incidentally, it's *extremely* important that you verify that the VIN number on your insurance policy declaration page is the same as on your car, and on your registration. I've heard horror stories of insurance companies denying claims when a car was damaged, because the VIN on the policy differed from the vehicle, due to a typographical error. It only takes a minute, so do it now . . . before you need to make a claim.

Putting the Car in Short-Term Storage

Needless to say, the full regimen of preparations isn't needed for short-term storage. However, a few precautions are advisable, and cleaning should still be considered a must. The precautions consist of disconnecting the battery and covering the car with soft fabric (optimally a professionally made car cover, but alternatively one or two full-size blankets) to protect the paint from airborne chemicals and the rubber, glass, and interior from sunlight. While the battery can be quite easily disconnected by removing the ground terminal, it's more convenient to install a shut-off switch, either on the ground post of the battery or in the wiring harness. Disconnecting the battery is advisable for several reasons: it prevents fire due to faulty wiring, it can prevent accessories like old-style electric clocks from discharging the battery, and it helps ensure that the car will start when you flip back the cover for a drive.

Periodic cleaning is best done without water, for the simple reason that when a car is washed (or driven in the rain), some water seeps past the window weather seal and drops down inside the doors. Also, moisture combined with dust that has settled on the finish penetrates into body seams (as where fenders bolt onto the body) creating an ideal festering spot for rust. So even though you wipe the finish dry with a Turkish towel or chamois, some moisture remains in hidden spots to help germinate the destructive seeds of rust. And if you cleaned your car with a pressure spray at a coin-op car wash, then you've really blasted moisture into the body seams and other rust-prone areas. Dry washing is a better way.

Assuming the car is only dusty, it can be dry-cleaned by lightly wiping the finish with a moplike product (such as a California Car Duster, available from several suppliers including California Car Cover Co.; see Resources for address). Usually it's not advisable to wipe anything across a dry, dusty finish because the dust particles, which are really tiny grains of grit, will scratch the paint like sandpaper. The reason the mop can be used to clean a dry finish is that its 100 percent cotton strands are treated with a special paraffin wax that lifts the dust rather than brushing it off. The duster can be used over and over by simply shaking the mop strands before and after use.

If the finish is really dirty, it can still be dry washed using a product called Dri-Wash 'n Guard, which actually cleans the finish without water. Emulsifiers lift dirt and grime from the finish, making it possible to wipe off the film without scratching the paint. Dri-Wash 'n Guard leaves behind a protective sealant and wax coating that gives a deep shine. This product is sold through independent distributors.

For those living in arid areas, or who are simply environmentally conscious, both dry wash products mentioned have another benefit—cleaning your car without using precious water.

Extending Battery Life

Batteries in collector vehicles that are stored more than they are driven typically have very short lives. This isn't necessary. You'll get many years of life and service out of your vehicle's battery if you follow these three simple steps:

1. Keep the case clean and dry.
2. Keep the electrolyte level above the plates.
3. Keep the battery fully charged.

Dirt and grease on the case create an electrical circuit that can cause the battery to discharge in a relatively short time. When you place your collector car in storage and remove the battery, wash the case with a cloth soaked in ammonia or a baking soda and water solution. When washing the case, be very careful that none of the solution gets into the cells, as it will neutralize the electrolyte. Before storing the battery, be sure the case is wiped dry. Don't place the battery in a location (like a concrete floor) where it will pick up condensation.

Some electrolyte (the fluid in the cells) is lost each time the battery is charged. Make sure the electrolyte never falls below the top of the plates. If the plates are exposed to air, permanent damage to the battery will result. Distilled water should be used to fill the battery. On most batteries, the correct electrolyte level is indicated by a ring (¼ to ½ inch above the plates) under the cell cap. Batteries discharge when they're not used, so they need to be charged on fairly frequent intervals. This is best done with a constant charger (such as the product called Battery Tender), a slow charger that monitors the battery's voltage and cuts out automatically when the battery reaches full charge. The advantage of the Battery Tender over a regular charger is that the Battery Tender can be left hooked onto the battery and plugged into an electrical outlet. It will begin charging automatically when the battery voltage drops to a certain level and shut off when the battery regains full charge. However, as mentioned earlier, the electrolyte level should be monitored periodically, even though the Battery Tender's slow charging rate minimizes electrolyte loss.

Batteries maintain their charge better in cool conditions than in warm, so store the battery in as cool a location as possible. Never bring the battery inside or place it near the furnace. Assuming the battery is fully charged, it will survive subzero temperatures without freezing.

Before replacing the battery in the car, wipe a light coating of grease (petroleum jelly is recommended) on the terminals. The grease won't disrupt the electrical contact and will prevent corrosion, which does break the electrical flow.

Taking the Car out of Storage

If you see a puddle of automatic transmission fluid or engine oil on the bottom of the CarJacket when your car first comes out of storage, don't be alarmed. Seals and gaskets often shrink during long-term storage, causing the car to leak oil or drip fluids; they will reseal when the car has been driven enough for them to swell. However, until this happens you may want to place sheets of cardboard or absorbent mats under the car's engine and driveline when it's parked in your driveway or garage. Because of the likely fluid loss, you'll want to check all fluid levels, brake master cylinder, engine oil and coolant, transmission fluid or gear oil, differential gear oil, and power steering fluid before driving the car an extended distance, and recheck frequently until the leakage stabilizes.

If the storage has been for a substantial period of time, you may find that the car's air conditioning doesn't work. Here again, leaking seals are the likely culprit—in this case the compressor seal. Since most collector car air conditioning systems are charged with R-12 (Freon), if the car's air conditioning system wasn't converted to 134-A during restoration, this would be the time to do so. On later model cars, the conversion is relatively simple and inexpensive (requiring that the old refrigerant be evacuated and the oil removed, then new oil compatible with the new refrigerant be added and the system recharged with the more environmentally hospitable 134-A coolant). An older air conditioning system may require an overhaul (to replace a badly leaking compressor seal) and replacement of contaminated or noncompatible components (a new dryer, for example).

If you haven't used a CarJacket and your collector car has disc brakes, the rotors may be rusted and braking action erratic. You'll want to drive short distances at low speeds, making lots of stops, and avoiding traffic until the brakes perform normally. As soon as possible, run through a tank of gasoline so you can top up with fresh fuel.

The battery can be kept at full charge while the car is in storage by hooking up a constant charger like a Battery Tender. This fully automatic charger can be left plugged in without risk of overcharging and boiling the electrolyte out of the battery.

PREPARING FOR THE SEASON'S FIRST TOUR

Before making that first distance outing, a pretravel check is in order. In addition to the inspections already described, the checklist should include:
• tire air pressure, including spare
• location of jack, tire iron, and hubcap tool
• condition of belts and hoses (these rubber items can dry rot in storage)
• operation of all lights, including signals
• condition of the carburetor air filter
• a new and spare in-line fuel filter
• any erratic performance (brakes, engine), with repair if necessary

On the road, drive at moderate speeds and monitor the car's mechanical systems until you're sure everything is performing normally. When a car comes out of storage, it has to be awakened gently.

Chapter 20
Showing and Enjoying Your Collector Car

Buy a new car and you can enjoy that special factory-fresh smell for a couple of months until the aroma fades away. Restore a collector car and you can enjoy meeting new friends and experiencing interesting activities for as long as you own the car. Although there are lots of ways to meet and make new friends, joining a club puts you in contact with others of like interests and lays out a year-round roster of activities—which can include technical demonstrations (helpful in various stages of the restoration process), tours, shows, and parts swaps.

Many clubs run their tours to or through scenic locations. Often the tour may span several days, making it a distinctive and memorable vacation. At shows you can be a bystander, viewing the spectrum of cars on display while mingling comfortably with friends, or a participant, entering your car into the fray of competition. Within the collector car hobby, competition has many different expressions. Some groups make competition a game, holding "slow races" in which the vehicle taking the longest time to cross a certain distance wins the prize (though some driving skill is involved, usually the winners are the cars with the most engine cylinders and the lowest gearing) and other driving events. Others award prizes for longest distance traveled, "people's choice," and other criteria that only superficially pits one car against another. But there are also groups for whom competition is a serious matter, holding cars to high standards of restoration and authenticity. Although show competition at this level isn't for everyone, it does reward the restorer for his skills and effort and bestows a kind of pedigree on the car that warrants a premium price, should the owner decide to offer the car for sale. Preparing a car for competition at this level requires more than careful restoration; there's a whole gamut of details to be attended to that begin the day the restoration is finished.

PREPARING FOR COMPETITION

The first consideration with competition is selecting the level at which you intend to compete. If your goal is national competition, this decision needs to be made at the very beginning of a restoration to ensure that the completed car will match the standards against which it will be judged. Some of these standards were mentioned in the research chapter with the discussion of details such as matching engine and chassis numbers, parts numbers on engine components, and similar markings of authenticity that can be used to differentiate two identical-appearing cars. Where the competition is among same-make cars, the level of scrutiny over detail can be fierce, with restorers going so far as to duplicate factory flaws or errors. But if your goal is to own the best of your make, model, and year of car—a 1958 Corvette, say, or a 1967 Mustang convertible—then entering your car in its marque's national competition is the ultimate test.

If the detail scrutiny at same-make competition seems too petty or picayune, you may decide to compete with a broader mix through regional and national Antique Automobile Club of America (AACA) events. Here the competition is still rigorous and authenticity standards are high, but you're not as likely to be faulted if the water pump casting code, for example, doesn't match the engine's assembly date. AACA judging evaluates a car in four categories: exterior, interior, chassis, and engine. Within each category, individual components are graded according to an itemized point system that tallies to a maximum of 400 for a perfect score. According to AACA rules, a minimum of 365 points is necessary for a first prize award. This point base has been established to ensure that cars entered in AACA judging are evaluated against the standards set forth on the form and not against each other. A consistent judging standard as well as mandatory training for judges ensures that awards given at all regional AACA shows carry the same prestige.

Displaying your car at local or national shows is a favorite pastime of car collectors. It's an ego-stroker for the car owner, and helpful to onlookers who may be looking for help and ideas on how to restore their own collector car.

Another favorite activity is racing, which isn't as harmful to your car as you might at first think. Drag racing, autocrossing, road racing, and rallies all have classes for original, restored cars and most have rules that strictly discourage (or even outlaw) contact between vehicles and encourage gentlemanly participation. Obviously, accidents do happen, but seldomly so.

The AACA judging form works on the principle of deductions. No bonus points are added for accessories; extra items mounted on the car are judged along with anything else, and can detract from the car's overall score if deemed inauthentic to the car's period. Major penalties fall to items carrying mandatory deductions, such as sealed-beam headlights installed on cars built before 1940 or an electric fuel pump on cars originally fitted with mechanical pumps. As judges inspect the exterior, they are instructed to deduct points for wavy metal, dents, paint chips, or a poor finish. Inside the car, judges check for inauthentic upholstery material, stains, or wear and tear, among other things. Point loss in any major category can be compounded by multiple infractions. As would be expected, the engine compartment is scrutinized for grease and grime. Also on the inspection list are new-style hose clamps and other inauthentic equipment or accessories.

By AACA standards, permissible accessories, whether mechanical or dress-up, had to be authorized by the factory. In a dispute, burden of proof that an accessory carried factory authorization lies with the owner, with the judges holding final authority on accessories an owner is unable to document. Here's an example: An overdrive transmission was a factory accessory on many U.S.-built cars from the late 1930s to the early 1960s. Toward the end of this period, overdrive became an increasingly rare item. Let's say you've entered an overdrive-equipped 1962 Chevrolet Bel Air hardtop in AACA competition and the judges dispute the authenticity of the overdrive option. There are several ways you can prove the auxiliary transmission to be a factory installation, provided you have the appropriate documentation. One would be to show the chief judge (only one member of the judging team, the chief judge, is authorized to speak with the car's owner) a copy of the car's build sheet, which is the factory specification list for the car. Another would be to offer a copy of a salesman's data book, showing the overdrive option. Still another would be to point out the overdrive feature in factory sales literature. Such documentation is needed when a point of authenticity is in dispute.

AACA competition progresses through a series of steps, each serving as a steppingstone to the next. To pass the first

The first consideration in competition is selecting the level at which you wish to compete. These enthusiasts are preparing their cars for a rather low-key club-sponsored event.

THIS VEHICLE HAS A U/L APPROVED FIRE EXTINGUISHER. ☐

MEET _____ OWNER _____ MAKE _____

ENTRY NO _____ CITY _____ STATE _____ YEAR _____ CLASS _____

TOP LINE TO BE FILLED IN BY VEHICLE OWNER.

ANTIQUE AUTOMOBILE CLUB OF AMERICA

"Information on this form or a copy of the completed form is NOT available to vehicle owners."

JF010 EXTERIOR	MAX	DED	JF011 INTERIOR	MAX	DED	JF012 CHASSIS	MAX	DED	JF013 ENGINE	MAX	DED
Beading/Welting	3		Dashboard	1		Axles Front	5		Air Cond (Comp)	10	
Body Door	5 ea		Door Panel	3 ea		Rear	5		Battery	3	
Fender	5 ea		Door Sills	3 ea		Brakes	3		Belt/s	2 ea	
Hood	5 ea		Floor Cover (Mat)	5		Hyd Brakes (if added)	(10)		Block	15	
Top(Hard)	5		Foot Rest	3		Body Bolts	1"		Carburetor	5	
Panel/Trunk	5 ea		Glass	3 ea		Bumpers	5 ea		Coil/Horn	3	
Trim/Striping	10		Headliner	5		Guards/Stone Deflectors	3 ea		Crankcase	5	
Color	(10)		Instruments	3 ea		Exhaust System	5		Distributor/Mag	5	
NON-AUTHENTIC	(40)		Pedal/Lever	2 ea		Frame	5		Filter/Fan	3	
Door Handle	2 ea		Seat Cushion/Back	5 ea		Gas Tank	3		Fire Wall	3	
Gas Gen/Tank	3		Side Panel	3 ea		Hub Caps	3 ea		Fuel Supply	5	
Horn	3 ea		Steering Wheel	3		Lock Rings	1 ea		(if added)	(10)	
Light Head'	5 ea		Tonneau Wind	5		Lube Fittings	1"		Generator/Alternator	5	
Side/Parking	3 ea		Top (soft) Down	(10)		Excess Lube	1		Gauge/Control	3	
Tail	3 ea		Missing (Ironed)	(20)		Overdrive (if added)	(10)		Head/s	5 ea	
Driving	3 ea		Condition	10		Rims	2 ea		Hose	2 ea	
Sealed Beam	(10)		Material	5		Snubber/Shocks	3		Clamps	1"	
(Prior to 1940)			(Incorrect)	(10)		Spring Covers	2 ea		Manifold	5	
Material"	(40)		Trim (Top)	1		Springs	3 ea		Ov'hd Valves (if added)	(10)	
(Non-Auth Body Comp')			Fasteners	1"		Steering Assembly	5		Power Assists Steering	5	
Mirror	3		Top Iron/Bow	5		Tire Carrier/Cover	3		Brakes	5	
Radiator Shell	5		Com'l Back Window	5		Tires	3 ea		(if added)	(10)	
Grill	5		(NON-AUTHENTIC)	(10)		Trans Drive/Line	5		Priming Cups	1"	
Ornament	3		Side Curtains	2		Valve Stem	1 ea		Radiator Cap	3	
Running Board	5 ea		(if missing)	(10)		Cap·Cover	1 ea		Radiator Core	5	
Splash Apron	5		Trim (Interior)	1		Wheels	3 ea		(incorrect)	(10)	
Windshield Frame	3		Trunk Interior	5		Other			Spark Plugs	1"	
Windshield Wiper	3 ea		Upholstery	5					Splash Pans	3	
Other			(Incorrect material)	(10)					Starter	5	
			Window Frame	1 ea					(if added)	(10)	
			Other						Tape/Tubing	1"	
									Terminals	1"	
									Volt Reg	3	
									Water Pump	5	
									Wiring	3	
									Other		
TOTAL DEDUCTION			**TOTAL DEDUCTION**			**TOTAL DEDUCTION**			**TOTAL DEDUCTION**		

SUMMARY

ENTRIES IN THIS AREA TO BE IN INK

1st   2nd   3rd   Junior

Multiple Award

Visually Judged

DEDUCTIONS

Exterior ____
Interior ____
Chassis ____
Engine ____
TOTAL ____

SCORE

Perfect Score — 400
Total Deductions ____
NET SCORE ____

REQUIRED MINIMUM POINTS
1st. - 365, 2nd. - 330, 3rd. - 295
Multiple awards for scores within 10 points of highest scoring car in each class.

APPROVED

TEAM CAPTAIN

DEPUTY CHIEF JUDGE

DEPUTY CHIEF JUDGE

JF01/92

"'Max deduction 120 points per vehicle **JUNIOR CARS ONLY**

(10) Mandatory deduction

'Max deduction 10 points per vehicle

AACA Judging Standards (in Judging book). Antique Automobile Club of America

level, a car must win first prize in the Junior category (the prize is referred to as First Junior). Competition at this level is with other cars entering AACA judging competition. It's possible to enter a car in competition for a First Junior award multiple times at different AACA national events in hopes of attaining this award. (Presumably, improvements would be made to the car between each competition entry; otherwise it would be futile to re-enter. Recall that AACA judging measures a car against an objective standard, not against the other cars that happen to be entered in its class.) Once a car has received its First Junior award, it is considered a Senior vehicle and eligible to compete in the Senior category for a Senior trophy, commonly called the Duryea trophy. To achieve this award, a vehicle must receive a minimum of 375 points and be within 10 points of the highest-scoring vehicle in its class. For many, this is the stopping point; the owner basks in his or her glory and retires the car from competition knowing that it can justifiably be called the best among the best. AACA First Junior winners receive a National First Prize plaque, which must be attached to the car. Upon winning a Senior award, a Senior Tab is attached behind the National First Prize plaque. These badges serve as certifications of excellence, much like the International Standards Organization (ISO) banners that fly outside manufacturing companies that have met the Standards Organization's exacting quality standards.

Beyond the Senior award, the AACA offers two more levels of distinction. (The AACA's multiple strata of awards help keep cars that have been restored to high levels active in competition.) Senior vehicles scoring 350 points or more at a National Meet receive a Preservation award. Finally, Preservation cars receive Participation awards when entered for judging at an AACA National Meet. Throughout AACA competition, contestants are never told the exact points their vehicles score, but be assured that a Senior Award winner is about as perfect as it's humanly possible to come.

HOW TO WIN

To compete successfully in arenas such as the AACA or other well-established national clubs and events requires careful research into the competition (and judging) standards and advice from others who have competed successfully at national levels. Some organizations, like the AACA, have published their judging standards to help restorers aiming at competition within that organization's framework to prepare their cars to national competition standards. Where possible, it's very helpful to obtain a copy of the judging sheet (included in the AACA's Official Judging Manual), thereby gaining a sense of the criteria by which your car will be evaluated, the relative weight or importance assigned to the various criteria, and the point system or scale on which judging is based. Not all organizations follow the AACA model. Some use variations of a system devised by the Classic Car Club of America (CCCA) that establishes 100 as a perfect score and divides the evaluation criteria into two categories: mechanical condition and physical appearance. Unlike the AACA, which deducts points for inauthentic items, in Classic Car Club judging, breaches of authenticity can result in automatic disqualification.

Often you'll pick up helpful tips by talking to those who have been successful in the competition arena you're considering entering. One AACA winner says that he received a tip just before entering his vehicle in Junior competition that may have made the difference between his first place win and an honorable (but disqualifying for Senior competition) second place. When his vehicle rolled out of its enclosed trailer, the tires had plastic covers on the air valves. A fellow competitor spotted the new-style caps and warned about their consequence in lost points. The restorer says he scoured the swap meet around the show field and found the correct metal caps just before the judges arrived at his car; no points lost that day for incorrect equipment. (According to the AACA Official Judging Manual, plastic valve caps cost one point per cap if installed on any vehicle built before 1951.)

Serious contenders won't be driven, except onto and off the show grounds and into and out of an enclosed van or trailer. As they sit waiting for the judges' inspection, the cars must be spotless, under the hood and throughout the undercarriage as well as on all visible surfaces. Even the inside of the tailpipe should be clean and free of rust. The care lavished on a national contender may seem extreme, but no detail is unimportant. For example, if the door latch was painted rather than plated, a cloth may be laid over the striker before the door is closed to prevent the latching mechanism from chipping the paint. Likewise, cloths will be placed over the carpeting to prevent the risk of grass stains or soiling of the carpet when the car has to be driven into the show lineup. Serious competitors will arrive early and spend the hours prior to judging fastidiously cleaning every visible or reachable surface. Friends and family members are often enlisted to help. Naturally, you'll want to deliver the car with all the supplies needed for the final cleaning, polishing, and preparation routines.

When a car carries accessories the judges might question, you can fend off point deductions by preparing a display

While swap meets provide a source of parts during restoration, many collectors enjoy browsing swap vendors' stalls after the restoration is completed. Some use swap meets as an opportunity to sell extra parts collected in the restoration process.

showing factory authorization for the accessories. The display might contain sales brochures showing the accessory, letters from the manufacturer identifying the accessory and perhaps urging its promotion, factory photos showing cars fitted with the accessory, or other such documentation. The display should be placed so that it answers anticipated questions, both by the judges and discriminating admirers. An example might be a factory-authorized spare tire mounted on the outside of the trunk, Continental style. In this case, the display showing would be placed at the rear of the car where it and the Continental spare could be seen simultaneously. Many restorers also create displays to document restoration steps, highlight unusual features (such as a manual transmission on cars of which nearly all production models had automatics), or a special history or pedigree (like a racing heritage or famous earlier owners).

It's important to stay with the car until the judges have completed their evaluations, both to answer any questions and also to perform any actions the judges may require (such as opening the hood and trunk). A friend or family member should stay with the car the entire time it is on display. While crowds at national shows are generally respectful and careful of the cars, fingerprints do tarnish and too close contact can scratch the paint. At local car shows or parades, crowd control can be more of a problem. One thoroughly disgusted restorer tells of a thoughtless admirer flicking the ash from his cigarette, which landed inside the car, instantly burning a hole in the seat covering.

Most show car competitors speak of those inevitable setbacks and disappointments. They also offer two statements of advice for surmounting the obstacles you're likely to encounter. First, they urge if the goal is worth pursuing,

There's lots of camaraderie to be enjoyed from owning a collector car.

don't let setbacks and disappointments get you sidetracked. One hobbyist restorer with the full gamut of AACA awards to his credit tells of a baseball hit by neighborhood kids playing in an adjacent field landing smack in the middle of his car's freshly painted hood, days before the show where his car was to win its First Junior award. The setback was significant because he'd calculated just enough time to finish assembling the car and make preparations for the show. Now he also had to smooth an ugly dent in the hood and repaint, hoping for a perfect color match. Working later each evening and bringing in friends to help, he was able to complete the car on time.

Their second counsel is to learn as much as you can from others. In AACA competition you won't be shown a completed judging sheet on your car. You can, however, ask the judges for a critique. Their comments may be somewhat general, but by thoughtful analysis you may be able to determine the specific problems that are leading to the point deductions. You can also learn from other competitors. A helpful tip saved our friend whose car had suffered the baseball-damaged hood from a likely deduction for incorrect spark plugs. It seems that spark plugs from his car's vintage had painted bases, whereas he had installed modern spark plugs with plated bases. Quick action to paint the spark plug bases black avoided a point docking that might have meant the difference between first and second place. Assuming you've done everything you can to bring the car to the highest standards possible, you certainly don't want to miss your goal due to an oversight to which you've become blind.

At regional and local shows, standards are much slacker. Here the frustration may be that prizes are awarded on the basis of popularity rather than the quality of restoration. Judging categories at local shows are also likely to be confusing, pitting your car against others that are really in a very different league. The best advice in this arena is to realize that winning or losing may amount to little more than a toss of a coin and to allow yourself to enjoy the event.

ACTIVITIES AFTER COMPETITION

When a car has passed the ranks of judging at the national level, it's often retired from the scrutiny of competition and enjoyed on tours and other casual outings. Highly pedigreed or unusual cars may be invited to special showings such as those at Pebble Beach or Meadowbrook. Others may appear in movies or in TV shows, or in ads. Movie and TV appearances are usually arranged through brokers; advertising agencies often contact the owner directly, usually making the contact through a club directory. Companies consigning cars for movie and TV appearances will have contracts for owners to sign, specifying the conditions under which the cars will be used, stored, and returned to the owner. The advertising agencies are likely to be a lot looser, providing only oral assurances. Keep in mind that anything can happen to your car once it's out of your control. A restorer whose cars have appeared in Chrysler Corporation ads insisted that the advertising agency transport the cars to be photographed in enclosed carriers. The cars were picked up in enclosed vans as promised. However, they were returned on open flatbeds after a several-hundred-mile transport on interstate highways, where stones and debris thrown by passing vehicles could have chipped the paint and done other cosmetic damage. The owner's recourse: refusing permission to use his cars again.

Many restorers enjoy showing their cars in parades. Here's a chance to share your car with the public and bask in a little of the limelight yourself. But parades also offer challenges, namely driving slowly enough to keep pace with the marching bands and the equestrians, and to keep the car from stalling or overheating in the process. Slow driving requires a well-tuned engine and an efficient cooling system. Lacking either or both, you'll want to pick your parades on days when the temperature is moderate. Since the engine may be idling for a substantial period, both while the parade entries are lining up as well as during the parade itself, make sure there's plenty of gasoline in the tank. If the parade has an announcer, noting something about the car on the card that's handed to him or her to read will help the reader say something informative to the crowd.

After a restoration you're likely to have lots of parts left over that you're never likely to use—especially if you picked up a parts car or two. While you could warehouse the surplus, another option is to become a swap meet vendor and recycle your leftover parts back into the hobby.

You need a way to get the parts to the swap meet, so the second qualification for vending (having inventory is the first) is owning a van, SUV, or pickup, or partnering with a friend who does. Most swap meets require that you reserve a space in advance, either by calling in a reservation or filling out a form and paying a fee (the third qualification). Swap meet spaces at localized events normally sell for a nominal figure, sometimes as low as $10 or $15. The selling climate at these smaller shows can often be as brisk as at some regional or even national events. In some states the fourth qualification may be a tax ID, or filling out and sending in a declaration of sales with your Social Security number for income tax records (the profit then being declared as additional income on both your state and federal income tax). Finally, you'll hope for good weather. A few hardy enthusiasts may wander through a swap meet that's been turned into a mud hole by a steady downpour of rain, but they won't buy anything. Regardless of your sales success, vending is a great way to meet others of like interests. If you've brought a friend along to "watch the store," it gives you the possibility of finding items you've been wanting from the other vendors.

PASSING A GREAT HOBBY ON TO THE NEXT GENERATION

In recent years, the collector car hobby has come under attack from environmentalists and zoning enforcers, among others, over a variety of concerns including our cars' older technology not meeting today's clean-air standards and unsightly or environmentally hazardous storage of parts and salvage vehicles. The result has been scrappage-ordinance proposals aimed at eliminating older vehicles from the highways and more stringent zoning enforcement aimed at eliminating the old-fashioned junkyard. Philosophically, most collector car owners are not at odds with environmentalists nor those concerned about the safety and well-being of their communities. However, a significant communication gap often exists between collector car enthusiasts and their "opponents" that is in everyone's best interest to close. Car collectors can tune in to the concern of both environmental and zoning interests by joining one of the collector car advocacy groups (see Resources) or making sure their car club (local or national) participates in such a group.

The vortex of concern into which collector car enthusiasts are drawn is much wider than the United States or even North America. European collector car enthusiasts and the clubs that represent them are struggling to make their voices heard in legislation being drafted for the

European Union regarding the operation, preservation, and restoration of collector cars and trucks. In the discussion, the collector car hobby has much to say: it represents a major historical legacy of the twentieth century—and perhaps the most positive; its business dealings total in the billions of dollars annually; it's a therapeutic pastime; and it captures the imagination and interest of the young. But these benefits have to be seen and heard, which won't happen if car collectors ignore the misrepresentations of their hobby and the misguided efforts to restrict it.

Equally important is passing the hobby on to the next generation. We don't see the younger generation huddled around cars admiring what's under the hood, but that doesn't mean the right spark won't light a "fire in the belly" for appreciating, maybe even owning and restoring, a collector car or truck. What's the likely spark? It's seeing us enjoying our collector cars, which might translate into inviting kids from the neighborhood into our shop to see what we're doing, or inviting them, and maybe their parents, along for a ride.

Each spring, my wife goes into elementary schools in our community and gives presentations. Her themes vary from Japanese culture (she wears the kimono given her by our son's mother-in-law) to hermit crabs (she brings boxes the children use as their own hermit crab shells). Certainly, some of us would find the same welcome were we to offer a presentation on collector cars—and maybe thrill the kids with a ride. After all, in many of our communities, what makes a richer link to history?

The younger generation will own collector cars: they'll inherit ours! The question is will they enjoy our cars with the same enthusiasm, and will they perpetuate our hobby? The seeds we plant today will become the inspiration and enthusiasm of tomorrow.

Appendix 1
Restoration Training

Besides reading about how to restore our collector cars, we often want someone to show us specific techniques. What are the possibilities for such training? As described in the convertible top chapter, one option is viewing videotapes or DVDs describing a variety of technical options. My friend Phil and I watched the video showing how to install a convertible top several times before actually tackling the project on his 1964 Ford Galaxie convertible. While not everything we saw in the video applied to Phil's car, we at least had a sense of the sequence, knew the tools we would need, and had been cautioned about steps where a mistake could ruin the job. DVDs demonstrating a wide range of restoration techniques are available from MBI Publishing Company, this book's publisher. Visit www.motorbooks.com.

Clubs often sponsor restoration workshops where participants may be able to practice the techniques hands-on. Many times these workshops are held during winter months when members are working on their cars. Some clubs present such workshops at their national or regional meets. In these settings, the restoration workshops are often conducted by tool or equipment vendors—largely as advertising for their products, but the demonstrations are instructional, nonetheless.

Courses in welding, auto body repair painting, and various mechanical topics, offered as continuing education by skill centers or technical colleges, give the most thorough training, both in theory and in practice. Often these courses are offered at night, to avoid disrupting the participants' work schedules. Sometimes the instructor lets students work on their own projects, in which case the course tuition not only pays for the instruction, but also provides a comfortable, well-equipped shop.

Maybe you've thought that you would like to watch skills-restoration technicians for a few days in their shops. This opportunity, plus hands-on work yourself, is available through technical seminars offered by John Twist and the staff at University Motors Ltd., a Grand Rapids, Michigan, restoration shop specializing in MGs, on a variety of topics, from rebuilding carburetors to overhauling transmissions, as well as a comprehensive three-day restoration

Seeing a process demonstrated and then doing it yourself is one of the best ways to learn. Here participants in a restoration workshop learn how to polish bightmetal car parts.

workshop that takes participants through all the major restoration steps and processes.

Twist opens the restoration workshop with a discussion of safety—the starting point for any restoration activity—and proceeds to tools: the essentials for disassembly and basic repair, tools needed for common restoration processes, tools that make jobs like rust repair go easier, and again, lots of tips. Hands-on demonstrations that follow include buffing a dull aluminum part to a bright chrome-like finish, cutting away rust damage in preparation for metal repair, welding techniques (gas, arc, both stick and wire feed, and spot welding), and how to disassemble parts where the fasteners have become rust-frozen together.

As the seminar progresses, its agenda ranges from cleaning, stripping, and rust-removal techniques—with hands-on in the media-blasting cabinet—to painting and refinishing. A rust repair project continues with repair panels being welded in place, demonstrating various seam techniques (butt welding, panel overlap, and duplicating original spot welds). Additional hands-on discussions teach how to re-cover seats and install interior kits as well as repair and restore brightmetal parts. The last series of demonstrations illustrate detailing techniques both underhood and along the exterior of the vehicle.

University Motors' technical seminars are offered only in February, the specific topics and dates being set after the first of the year. (See Resources for contact information.)

Appendix 2
RESOURCES

CHAPTER 3
HOW TO SELECT A COLLECTOR CAR
Publishers
Amos Automotive Publishing
911 Vandemark Rd
Sidney, OH 45365 USA
(800) 448-3611
www.amosautomotive.com

CarTech Books
39966 Grand Avenue
North Branch, MN 55056 USA
(800) 551-4754—US (toll free)
(651) 277-1200—International
www.cartechbooks.com

Dupont Registry
3051 Tech Drive
St. Petersburg, FL 33716 USA
(800) 233-1731
www.dupontregistry.com

Hemmings Motor News
P.O. Box 100
Bennington, VT 05201 USA
(800) 227-4373
www.hemmings.com

Krause Publications
700 E. State St.
Iola, WI 54990
(800) 258-0929

Motorbooks
400 First Avenue North
Suite 300
Minneapolis, MN 55401
www.motorbooks.com

Robert Bentley, Inc.
Automotive Publishers
1734 Massachusetts Ave.
Cambridge, MA 02138-1804
(800) 423-4595 or (617) 547-4170
www.bentleypublishers.com

Source Interlink Media
6420 Wilshire Blvd., 10th Floor
Los Angeles, CA 90048 USA
(323) 782-2000
www.sourceinterlinkmedia.com

CHAPTER 4
RESEARCH: UNCOVERING A CAR'S "LIFE STORY"
Factory Invoices & Broadcast Sheets
PHS Automotive Services
(formerly Pontiac Historic Services)
P.O. Box 884
Sterling Heights, MI 48311-0884
www.phs-online.com

Mopar Fender Tag Decoding
Galen's Tag Service (GTS)
PO Box 516
Prairie Du Chien, WI 53821-0516
(608) 326.6346
www.gvgovier.com

Research Archives and Libraries
AACA Headquarters Library
501 W. Governor Rd.
P.O. Box 417
Hershey, PA 17033
(717) 534-1910

Detroit Public Library
5200 Woodward Ave.
Detroit, MI 48202
(313) 833-1000
www.detroit.lib.mi.us

Henry Ford Museum Archives
P.O. Box 1970
20900 Oakwood
Dearborn, MI 48121-1970
(313) 982-6001
www.hfmgv.org

National Automobile Collection
10 Lake St. S.
Reno, NV 89501
(775) 333-9300
http://automuseum.org/

CHAPTER 5
SETTING UP SHOP AND WORKING SAFELY
Basic and Advanced Tools
Lowe's/Kobalt Tools
Visit or call your local Lowe's Home Improvement store
www.kobalttools.com

Mac Tools
505 N. Cleveland Ave.
Suite 200
Westerville, OH 43082
(800) 622-8665
www.mactools.com

Sears/Craftsman
Visit or call your local Sears store
www.craftsman.com

Snap-On Tools
P.O. Box 1410
Kenosha, WI 53141-1410 USA
(877) 762-7664
www.snapon.com

Specialty Tools
The Eastwood Company
Box 3014
Malvern, PA 19355-0714
(800) 345-1178
www.eastwoodco.com

CHAPTER 7
RESTORING THE CAR'S BRIGHTMETAL TRIM
"Home" Plating Kits:
The Eastwood Company.
www.eastwoodco.com
(see address above)

Caswell Electroplating
4336 Route 31
Palmyra, NY 14522-9719
(315) 597-5140
www.caswellplating.com

Plastic Chrome Pplating:
Mr. G's Rechromed Plastic
5613 Elliott Reeder Rd.
Ft. Worth, TX 76117
(817) 831-3501

Electroplating on Plastic
Custom Coating Corp.
4794-C Woodlane Circle
Tallahassee, FL 32303
Phone/fax (850) 562-0538

CHAPTER 8
CLEANING, STRIPPING, AND DERUSTING
Cleaners & Cleaning Equipment
The Eastwood Company
www.eastwoodco.com
(see address above)

Environmentally Safe Degreasing, Derusting Products
GreaseMaster and Rusteco
Ecoclean
100 N. Meadows Road
Medfield, MA 02052
(888) 399-2600

Parts Washers and Pressure Washing Equipment
Harbor Freight Tools
3491 Mission Oaks Blvd.
Camarillo, CA 93011
(805) 388-3000
www.harborfreight.com

Northern Tool & Equipment
2800 Southcross Drive West
Burnsville, Minnesota 55306
(800) 221-0516
www.northerntool.com

Sears/Craftsman
Visit or call your local Sears store
www.craftsman.com

TP Tools and Equipment
7075 Rt. 448
P.O. Box 649
Canfield, OH 44406
(800) 321-9260
www.tptools.com

CHAPTER 9
ABRASIVE BLASTING
Abrasive Blasting Equipment and Supplies
The Eastwood Company
www.eastwoodco.com
(see address above)

Harbor Freight Tools
3491 Mission Oaks Blvd.
Camarillo, CA 93011
(805) 388-3000
www.harborfreight.com

Northern Tool & Equipment
2800 Southcross Drive West
Burnsville, Minnesota 55306
(800) 221-0516
www.northerntool.com

TP Tools and Equipment
7075 Rt. 448
P.O. Box 649
Canfield, OH 44406
(800) 321-9260
www.tptools.com

CHAPTER 11
SMOOTHING DENTS AND REPAIRING METAL
Leading Tools and Supplies
The Eastwood Company
www.eastwoodco.com
(see address above)

Sears/Craftsman
Visit or call your local Sears store
www.craftsman.com

CHAPTER 12
APPLYING THE PRIMER COATINGS
POR (paint over rust) coatings
POR-15, Inc.
P.O. Box 1235
Morristown, NJ 07962-1235
(800) 457-6715; fax (973) 887-8007
www.por15.com

The Eastwood Company
www.eastwood.com
(see address above)

HVLP paint spraying systems
The Eastwood Company
(see address above)

TP Tools and Equipment
www.tptools.com
(see address above)

CHAPTER 13
APPLYING THE FINISH COAT
Eastwood Automotive Paints, HotCoat™ Powder Coating System and Various Finishing Products
The Eastwood Company
www.eastwoodco.com
(see address above)

Automotive Paints and Refinishing Supplies
The Eastwood Company
www.eastwoodco.com

3M Automotive Finishes
www.3m.com

DuPont Automotive
www.dupont.com

R-M Paint
www.rmpaint.net

Powder Coating Systems & Supplies
The Eastwood Company
www.eastwoodco.com

CHAPTER 16
RENEWING THE CAR'S WIRING
Alternators for Generator-Equipped 6- and 12-Volt Electrical System Cars
Fifth Avenue Antique Auto Parts
415 Court St., Clay Center, KS 67432
(913) 632-3450; fax (913) 632-6154
e-mail: fifthave@kansas.net

MSD Ignition (Autotronic Controls Corp.)
1350 Pullman Drive, Dock #14
El Paso, Texas 79936 USA
(915) 857-5200
www.msdignition.com

Powermaster
7501 Strawberry Plains Pike
Knoxville, TN 37924 USA
(865) 688-5953
www.powermastermotorsports.com

Wiring Harnesses
Lectric Limited
6750 W. 74th Street - Suite A
Bedford Park, IL 60638 U.S.A.
(708) 563-0400
www.lectriclimited.com

Painless Wiring
2501 Ludelle St
Fort Worth, TX 76105
(817) 244-6212
www.painlessperformance.com

Wire Wrap Tape
The Eastwood Company
www.eastwoodco.com
(See address above)

CHAPTER 17
RESTORING YOUR COLLECTOR CAR'S INTERIOR
Seat Belt Reconditioning
Ssnake-Oyl Products
Rt. 2, Box 296-6
Hawkins, TX 75765
(903) 769-4555; (800) 284-7777
www.ssnake-oyl.com

Carpet Sound-Deadening Underlayment
Corvette Central
P.O. Box 16
Sawyer, MI 49125
(800) 345-4122; (616) 426-3342
Fax (800) 635-4108; (616) 426-4108
e-mail: mail@corvettecentral.com
www.corvettecentral.com

Dodge, Chrysler, Plymouth Interior Kits
Legendary Auto Interiors Ltd.
121 West Shore Blvd.
Newark, NY 14513
(800) 363-8804; fax (800)-SEAT-UPH
www.legendaryautointeriors.com

Ford, Mercury Interior Kits
LeBaron Bonney Co.
P.O. Box 6
6 Chestnut St.
Amesbury, MA 01912
(800) 221-5408
www.lebaronbonney.com

Chevrolet, Buick Interior Kits
Hampton Coach
P.O. Box 6
6 Chestnut St.
Amesbury, MA 01913
(888) 388-8726
www.hamptoncoach.com

Mid America Motorworks
P.O. Box 1368
Effingham, IL 62401
(800) 500-1500
www.mamotorworks.com

National Parts Depot
900 S.W. 38th Ave
Ocala, FL 34474 USA
(800) 874-7595
www.npdlink.com

Original Parts Group
1770 Saturn Way
Seal Beach, CA 90740 USA
(800) 243-8355
www.opgi.com

The Paddock
P.O. Box 30
Knightstown, IN 46148 USA
(800) 428-4319
www.paddockparts.com

Year One
P.O. Box 521
Braselton, GA 30517 USA
(800) 932-7663
www.yearone.com

Vinyl Parts Restoration
Just Dashes
5491 Lemona Ave.
Van Nuys, CA 91411
(800) 247-3274
www.justdashes.com

CHAPTER 18
REPLACING A CONVERTIBLE TOP AND RENEWING WEATHERSTRIPPING
Convertible Tops for All U.S. Cars 1955–1998
Hydro-E-Lectric
48 Appleton
Auburn, MA 01501
(800) 343-4261; fax (508) 832-7929
www.hydroe.com

Rubber Weatherseal
Metro Moulded Parts, Inc.
11610 Jay St.
Box 48130
Minneapolis, MN 55448
(800) 878-2237
www.metrommp.com

Steele Rubber Products
6180 Hwy. 150 East
Denver, NC 28037
(800) 447-8049
www.steelerubber.com

CHAPTER 19
CARE AND PRESERVATION OF YOUR COLLECTOR CAR
Evans Coolant (not water based)
Evans Cooling Systems
496 Fricks Lock Road
Pottstown, PA 19465
(888) 990-2665
www.evanscooling.com

Car Care and Storage
AirChamber US
Dallas, TX USA
(214) 520-3430
www.airchamber.us

California Car Cover Co.
9525 DeSoto Ave.
Chatsworth, CA 91311
Toll free (800) 423-5525
www.calcarcover.com

CarJacket
Pine Ridge Enterprise
13165 Center Road, Bath, MI 48808
(800) 5-CARBAG
www.carbag.com

Covercraft
100 Enterprise Blvd.
Pauls Valley, OK 73075 USA
(800) 426-8377
www.covercraft.com

ShelterLogic
(860) 94-LOGIC
www.shelterlogic.com

Car Care Products
Meguiar's Inc.
17991 Mitchell South
Irvine, CA 92714
(800) 347-5700
www.meguiars.com

Mothers Polish
5456 Industrial Drive
Huntington Beach, CA 92649-1519 USA
(714) 891-3364
www.mothers.com

CHAPTER 20
SHOWING AND ENJOYING YOUR COLLECTOR CAR
Club Listings
Old Cars Weekly annual car club issue:
www.oldcarsweekly.com
Hemmings Vintage Almanac
www.hemmings.com

Judging Standards
Antique Automobile Club of America
501 W. Governor Rd.
P.O. Box 417
Hershey, PA 17033
(717) 534-1910
www.aaca.org

Car Collector Advocacy Organizations
COVA/CVAG
Box 2136
West Paterson, NJ 07424-3311
(800) CARS-166
www.covacvag.com

APPENDICES
Training
University Motors Technical Seminars
6490 East Fulton
Ada, MI 49301
(616) 682-0800
www.universitymotorsltd.com

Index

CPSIA information can be obtained at www.ICGtesting.com
Printed in the USA
LVOW02s2056260315

431828LV00007BA/7/P